My Winter Under
the Cabo Sun

My Winter Under the Cabo Sun

An American's Experience Close Up

T. D. Lake

Stormy River Publishing

Cover Art: © KarinaUrmantseva / iStockPhoto.com

ISBN: 978-1548465124

ACKNOWLEDGMENTS

There are many I'd like to thank for their camaraderie and support during my three months in Cabo San Lucas, Mexico, including my friends at Cabo Cantina: Andres, Jorge, Ismael, Ray, Guillermo, Gabriel, Martin, Roberto, Leo, Totito, Oliver, Fabian, Efrien, Elio, Edgar, Julio, Rita, Ceci, and the rest of the crew. Also, special thanks to Pedro Lopez and Facundo Lopez the owners of Guadalupana, Hector and Saul at Esteban's, Gabriel at Gardenias, my neighbors Mario and Lupita, Ramon and Rodrigo at Esquina, Reuben in the marina, and Fernando, the tire expert. You all enriched my life in ways beyond description. I have tried to present my feelings for you in this book and am grateful for all your understanding and help.

Some of the names of the characters in this book are fictional. So are a few of the characters, though their profiles were inspired to varying degrees by real people. Some of the scenes in this book are not intended to be factual accounts of the events described, but there are similarities, of course.

CONTENTS

Introduction

I lead a pretty adventurous life that includes a lot of travel around the world and multiple residences. My travels often extend for many months at a time. In November of 2016, I made the decision to spend the first three months of 2017 in Mexico with two objectives in mind. First, I wanted to write a book in the same journalistic style as my last one, *A Baguette a Day*. I chose the month to month format to give structure to my experience and provide an on-going context for my adventures. Rather than going to numerous cities in that period of time, I chose Cabo San Lucas for all three months so I could get a good feeling for the town and, more importantly, get to know the local people. Second, I've always wanted to learn Spanish. Immersing myself for three months in the culture with a dedication to learning the language could give me a good start toward my goal of fluency.

Yes, someday I will be fluent in Spanish. I will always remember where my first lessons in the language took place. I will never forget my friends in Cabo who made my experience memorable and fulfilling. I am grateful for their unbounded help. I left Cabo a better person. I left with better listening skills, more empathy for my fellow man, and a commitment to being less judgmental of others. Oh, and by the way, I can have a conversation in Spanish if I keep it simple and go slow. It's a good start.

PROLOGUE

So, suddenly you decide to take a break in your life. Maybe take some serious time off, like three months. Go someplace different, someplace far away. Maybe do something you've always wanted to do, but didn't have the time. Maybe do nothing, see what doing nothing feels like. Maybe escape your present life and fulfill a dream. All kinds of opportunities are out there for you. Do stuff like fish for Marlin, learn a foreign language, take cooking lessons in your favorite cuisine, be a beach bum, globe-trot, explore the land of your forefathers, climb a mountain, raft a great river, become a health nut. Stuff like that. If you're nodding your head to any of those thoughts, this book is for you. Read on and live vicariously while you learn about Cabo San Lucas, Mexico.

I closed on a townhouse I bought in Durango, Colorado in December of 2016 just two weeks before I flew to Cabo San Lucas in Mexico to launch myself into the new year with a three-month adventure. I needed a break from the usual. I booked my trip to Mexico long before I even thought there was a chance I'd be living in Durango, so you see, it wasn't the prospect of facing a cold winter that sent me south. At the time of my booking, I was on the tail end of a visit of six months in Asheville, North Carolina with no place to go in mind. I moved to Asheville in June thinking it might be a fun place to spend the summer and fall. If I liked it, maybe I'd commit to a life there. It was a fun place for the six months I was there but it turned out that it was not a place I wanted to live.

I will say I had a lot of fun in Asheville in 2016. That was easy. I was there during the prime months of good weather which for me, meant a pleasant summer in the mountains followed by a colorful fall. Asheville is a funky, arty town tucked away in the blue ridge mountains of western North Carolina, two hours west of

Charlotte and two hours east of Knoxville, Tennessee. This part of the world is as pretty as any place in America. The beauty of the mountains would never change, but the city of Asheville was in the throes of change. And I didn't want to live there because of that.

When I moved into my rented condo on the edge of the downtown, I could see that Asheville was clearly in the middle of a big transition. It is a transition taking the town in the wrong direction in my opinion. Over the summer, it was easy enough to see the town as it had once been, a small college town of down-to-earth people of all ages and backgrounds, doing a lot of outdoorsy, fun things. Indoorsy, it is high density in artsy-craftsy and craft breweries and fantastic restaurants representing every international cuisine a foodie could desire. The local population of blue and white-collar people is liberally sprinkled with hippies, the homeless, heavily tattooed women, and hillbilly musicians, along with an ever-increasing population of well-educated retirees. Asheville culture is hugely colorful, fun, and happening with a wonderful mix of activities that gave it a special vibe for years, unlike almost anything else in America, but it is changing. High rise condos are being built right in the middle of town. These towers of concrete and brick would eventually overwhelm the charm, grace, and authenticity of a beautifully aging old southern town. The shadows of these towers shift all day to cover much of the town in shade, putting an end to sunny outdoor cafes and sunlit street life. That direction did not interest me, so I left in November to regroup.

I left Asheville for the drive to Scottsdale, Arizona on Thanksgiving Day. Scottsdale is a very upscale community where I lived a long time ago but I didn't want to live there again. I knew the town well, so it would be a good place to think things over and, maybe, identify a town where I could live. Asheville wasn't that place. Nor was Scottsdale. Having given up on Asheville in early November, I didn't have a clue where I wanted to live so at that time I booked three months in Cabo San Lucas, Mexico for something different. I always wanted to learn Spanish so I made that my goal for Cabo.

To my surprise, I bought a house in Durango, Colorado the first week of December, before I even got to Scottsdale. I signed the deal a month before my plane left for Cabo. It all happened pretty fast. En route to Arizona from Asheville, I made a slight detour north to visit Durango. My twin sister was the one who suggested that I look into it. She thought it was a town I'd like. And, it was close enough to her home in Sedona, Arizona that we could easily visit each other. Within a week, it all made sense to me. I like four seasons. I like towns that aren't too big or too small or sandwiched between other towns. I like towns with character and history. I like towns with a lot of nice people. And I always wanted to live on a trout stream. Durango delivered on all counts.

On the first day of December, my offer was accepted on a three thousand square foot townhouse that I could lock up for months at a time and not worry. That concept and timing fit nicely with my plans to go to Mexico. I closed quickly on the property, just before Christmas, celebrated the holidays in my new home, which was furnished with nothing except an air mattress and a chair. I left for Cabo four days after New Year's Day to begin a new adventure. I was looking forward to a happy new year. It was off to a great start and no telling what was in store for me for the next three months.

Three months later, I returned to the U.S. with a good start on speaking Spanish at the conversational level. I also came back with a book in journal format about my adventures in Cabo San Lucas. I changed a few names to protect the innocent. And the guilty.

CHAPTER ONE

Week 1

<u>Waiting at the gate - Thursday, January 5</u>

I've been sitting in the Phoenix airport for the past hour organizing my thoughts around my trip to Mexico. In two hours, my plane takes off for Los Cabos International Airport, or SJD, for you airport-code freaks. I don't know what SJD stands for, San Jose something, maybe, likely. Sometimes the letters make sense, like AVL for Asheville and JFK for Kennedy airport in New York. And, of course PHX for Phoenix, very logical. By the way, I think Phoenix has the best airport name of all, Sky Harbor. What a perfect name, says it all! Of course, most flyers don't know that name; they simply call the airport Phoenix or, maybe refer to it by its PHX code as easily as they call Los Angeles' airport LAX.

But not all symbols coincide with the airport location or logic. Many don't really have a connection at all to the airport location, like ORD for Chicago. Some cities got a bad roll of the dice, like SUX which is Iowa's Sioux City airport. I don't know if the code OMG can be considered good or bad for an airline but it exists; it's the code for Omega Airport in Namibia, Africa. I know stuff like that because I have travelled a lot over the years. A lot!

While I sit here at my assigned gate, surrounded by passengers waiting for the flight before mine. I'm a little tired so I try to close my eyes and get my thoughts organized about my impending visit to Mexico. Despite my fatigue, from the stress of having to arrive hours in advance of my flight, I feel good. This is because I always build in time for screw-ups like a flat tire en route. Nothing like that happened this time, thankfully. I'm focused on the adventure ahead of me. It's exciting. I am really looking forward to spending time in Cabo San Lucas, a tiny town sitting on an intersection of the Gulf of California and the Pacific Ocean.

Cabo San Lucas was once a small fishing village and now it is a significantly larger place. It's a Tequila Tourist destination. Its history goes farther back than that. It was launched into the tourist world's conscious, like many off the beaten path tourist destinations, by some visits by celebrities long ago. In this case, Richard Burton, Liz Taylor, and John Wayne. It is located at the bottom of Mexico's Baja California Peninsula, an easy flight south of the border for anyone living in California or Arizona. A not so easy drive, about twenty-one hours from San Diego.

In a way, Cabo can be described as the gateway to the Gulf of California, a sea which is a remarkable body of water that balloons northward for about nine hundred miles. It is so rich in aquatic life and indescribably beautiful under its surface that Jacques Cousteau once called it the world's aquarium. Not surprisingly, that makes it a sportsman's paradise for big game fishing. It became that place for fisherman shortly after World War II when word got out that four hundred and fifty-pound Marlins were being caught there. That's a big fish. I don't think anyone catches fish that size any more. The big ones are mostly gone.

Fishing is not the only draw in Cabo. For the rest of the tourist population Cabo is a lot of sun, a lot of fun, and a lot of tequila. And a pretty cheap place to visit. And, of course it is Mexico, which is a marvelous country. Cartels are a nasty fly in Mexico's salsa. They are the dark side of Mexico and an association that has unfairly tainted Mexico. The illicit drug trade is not something Mexicans are happy about. It makes them cringe, if not fearful. From my previous visits, all shorter than this one, I know that Mexico is country of kind and friendly people who have traditional values, not to mention a love for crazy colors way beyond the rainbow. Also, Mexicans go to lots of fiestas, which is at the core of their culture. I also have to add that Mexican food is one of the world's great cuisines, notably for its rich regional diversity but also because it outscores most of the world's other major cuisines in nutritional value. As a pescatarian, that's right up my alley, which is one of the primary reasons I picked Mexico for an adventure.

Of all the things I would like to do in the next three months, besides eating well, learning Spanish is at the top of my list. Many language experts proclaim that the best way to learn a language is through immersion. Well, that's what I'm doing, immersing myself in a wonderful culture for three months to see what happens. I've never studied Spanish before so I'm going into this cold. Of course, like you, I already know some Spanish. Who doesn't? If you think about it, just about everyone knows some Spanish words, like maybe dozens of them if you really think about it. Here are some of the words I know already as I contemplate the challenges of learning Spanish: *señorita, americano, fiesta, enchilada, baño, tequila, vino, quesadilla, macho, gringo, piñata, margarita, latino, hombre, padre, rodeo, Los Angeles, adios,* and *uno, dos, tres.* See, lots of them. Tons. Are you surprised how many of those you know? Gee, maybe I already speak Spanish, I just don't know it.

I also speak rudimentary French having lived in France for a couple of years fairly recently. I wonder to what extent my familiarity with French will help me. Since this adventure materialized, I have been constantly reminded that it is also a latin language, so the challenge shouldn't be too difficult. I'm not sure I buy into that reasoning. I am not very good with foreign languages and I am told that after the age of ten, it is not so easy to learn one. French was tough, but I learned that, so I am optimistic. Sometimes I don't even feel like I'm very good with English, especially when I write. I know, I know, my grammar needs a little work. Get over it. Writing is an adventure too, an imperfect one. As long as I remind myself that I don't have to be perfect with Spanish, I will continue to believe that I can learn a lot in three months.

<u>Boarding the plane - Thursday, January 5</u>

I've traveled a lot in the last forty years, including many flights overseas. I still get excited about my adventurous undertakings despite how much I have come to hate the ever-worsening airport experience. I don't need to get into how much worse moving through airports is these days compared to the years and decades before 9-11. I remember the days when you could be dropped off at LaGuardia curbside outside your airline ticket counters thirty minutes before your flight's scheduled take-off, walk uninterrupted through the airport right onto the airplane and then buckle up. Five minutes later the plane would take off. Don't believe me? Ask anyone over sixty if what I said could be true. My oh my, how things have changed since then!

When my afternoon American Airlines flight out of Phoenix started the boarding process, I had quite a while to wait since I was Group 3 in the queue of the different boarding groups. Only one group was behind, Group 4. You would think that Group 3 meant that there were two groups in front of me. No, that's not right. There were actually seven groups ahead of me. Seven. Group 3 had a special name, as I saw it, the chopped liver group. Yes, two numbered groups were in front of me, along with five other special groups. These are the groups of people who had seating priority over me: passengers who need extra time boarding (i.e. passengers with disabilities and those traveling with children), First Class, Top Frequent Fliers, Star Alliance Gold Elites, Silver Elite members, US Airways credit card holders, and passengers who paid extra for Choice Seats. Then, after all of those groups, Groups 1 and 2 were called before I could say Bingo! Group 4 must have been comprised of refugees, though as the last member of Group 3 to line up, I didn't see anyone behind me. Hmmm, no Group 4, which I guess means no refugees. All in all, it doesn't matter because everyone has a seat and the plane won't leave until everyone on board is seated. This time, there were no requests of the passengers to take a later flight to accommodate over-seating, a rarity. No worries. Of course, the plane was full, which didn't surprise me and I didn't care. I was on my way to Cabo San Lucas!

<u>Taking off - Thursday, January 5</u>

I was thankful I had an aisle seat for my long legs and that was enough to make me happy for the two-hour flight. I was feeling good, almost light headed with the reality of another adventure underway. The flight attendant finished up her endless monologue of rules and regulations just as the plane made a U-turn into its final runway for an on-time take-off. I made sure my phone was off, as instructed. I never understood why that rule exists but it does and airlines make a big deal of it saying that phones interfere with navigation which, of course, can't be good. But really, interfere with navigation? I have to assume that's true and that's always enough to get me to comply to the attendant's request to turn off my phone. They're pretty serious about this request.

I turned off my phone moments before going airborne. Not everyone did. The flight attendant's request was not enough to get the young adult male in the aisle seat directly across from me to turn off his. I don't know why I felt compelled to say something to him. I knew no one else would. What? Are they a bunch of chickens? Timid souls? Or, sensible, tolerant people? Am I the only one who cares about safety regulations? So what was compelling me? Maybe because he was so annoyingly loud and flaunting his resistance to the restriction, and totally oblivious to everyone's wonderment that someone was still on the phone as the plane's wheels left the tarmac. We went into our climb. Higher and higher into the sky with an acceleration that pushed us back into our seats, the usual. Way off the ground the guy was still talking and finally I couldn't hold back any longer.

Pressed back on my seat by the forty-five-degree incline, I turned to Mr. Big Mouth, who was half my age and loaded with arrogance. As politely as possible, I spoke over his conversation: "Excuse me. Phones are supposed to be off." Clearly it was a request to hang up. He stopped mid-stream in his conversation.

He turned his head to look directly at me. He replied in a voice even louder than the one he was using in his conversation and said to me rather harshly: "You think you're the fucking police?!" It was not the response I expected. Of course, I gave him a response he didn't expect either, a lie: "No, I am not the fucking police, but I am an Air Marshall." That shut him up. He ended his conversation abruptly, as my words registered, and faced forward. I think I heard some silent cheering, if there is such a thing.

That arrogant jerk and I didn't exchange another word. I enjoyed the rest of the flight reading Lee Child's latest Jack Reacher novel *Night School.* I love Jack Reacher. He and I are roughly the same size. And he's fiercely independent, like me. I felt like Jack Reacher when I shut that jerk up. I also felt like an Air Marshall, but unarmed. I even surprised myself with that comeback. Sometimes I can be one bad hombre. I rarely deliver comebacks that good. In fact, ninety-nine percent of the time, like most people, I don't even think of a good comeback until it's way too late.

The bald eagle has landed - Thursday, January 5

I got through the Cabo airport in a matter of minutes except for ten minutes in the line to get my passport stamped. Nice agents. A quick stamp. Tourist friendly. No questions about anything, just waved me through with my small backpack. They want you in as soon as possible so you can start spending money. I waited less than five minutes for my only checked bag to show up on the belt. No issues with it, so I walked into the lobby where I would decide my next step. I was now on the loose in the Baja.

Daylight was fading quickly; darkness would set in within the hour. I surveyed the scenery in front of me, which was dominated by a jumble of Mexicans yelling Taxi! Others were holding signs, none with my name. Off to my right was a large man seated at a desk just inside an open window with the words Transportation above it. He was looking right at me. Clearly, he could tell that I was in the throes of indecision and he was sending out a vibe that he could help. And he did. I went over to him. He spoke English. So did I. I decided to postpone my immersion until I actually stepped out of the confines of the building. We talked. I paid him ten bucks for a group shuttle voucher and was assigned a shuttle dock for a shuttle bound for Cabo San Lucas that would leave the airport in ten minutes.

I was told the shuttle would take an hour or so. Much later, when I was in the shuttle, I concluded that I was a little rusty as a world traveler. I knew I made a mistake at the Transportation window by not asking the ticket maestro how long the "or so" of his estimate would be. So that said, I reminded myself of a lesson I forgot. Ask a lot of questions! It didn't really matter to me. I'd get to my destination sooner or later. I wasn't in a hurry and the price was right. I could have taken a taxi, all to myself, for the forty-five-minute drive into town. That would have cost about seventy-five bucks, a lot more than the shuttle. I would have said yes to that choice but my frugal side always kicks in when I travel. I thought it was a waste of my money. Had I done my homework on airport transportation options, I would have discovered that a new bus system was in play that ran into the city every twenty minutes from the airport with a ride time of an hour. The charge was five bucks. Next time, dufus.

As it turned out, I shared the shuttle with five darling young women who flew in for the thirtieth birthday party of a girlfriend who would be meeting them in two hours at Señor Frog's on the Cabo marina. I know I'm getting old when I start referring to thirty-year-old women as darlings. Even though they were exactly that. All sweet, bubbly, and mature enough to be beyond the days of youthful drunken craziness, but still with a sheen of naivety about them. I flirted heavily, out of habit. Old habits don't die easily. But I didn't flirt at the creepy level, just at the ridiculously nice level. Probably the borderline shameless level. Whatever it was, it was a truly hopeless level driven by the age difference.

Yes, the conversation in the shuttle was in English, another postponement of my immersion plans. The darlings didn't speak Spanish, so immersion was easy to postpone once again. They were all friends from their college days at the University of Montana. I was having so much fun chatting with them and pretending that I was cool, that I didn't really notice the elderly couple, about my age, sharing the shuttle with us. I think the couple must have climbed into the wrong van, or maybe I did, because by the time we got to their drop off point in some huge condo complex well out of sight of anything, nearly two hours had passed. But no worries, I wasn't afraid of running out of stupid stuff to say to the darling girls. I lived with decades of practice doing that. It was the bathroom I was getting concerned about, or should I say lack of one. Something else that comes with age, I guess, bathroom issues. Dammit.

Thirty minutes later, shortly after the silence of fatigue kicked in for all of us, I confronted the unexpected threat of being carsick. Fortunately, the van driver pulled up to the security gate at a complex on the north edge of Cabo called Coromuel. That was me. Time to jump out. I had arrived in one piece in front of my new home for the next three months!

I gushed a goodbye to the girls (girls in their thirties) wondering if I'd bump into them again, maybe out on the town celebrating. Of course, I wouldn't see them again unless I saw them first. It only took a second for me to face the reality that they probably got their party started just after my bedtime and partied way into the early hours of the night. They would probably end their evening just about the third time I got up for the bathroom. That would be close to dawn. About right for the grandfather age group. I said goodbye to the driver too, finally using the few Spanish words I knew. *Muchas gracias señor! Adios!* I said this after I tipped him. As I said, I am generally frugal, except when I'm not, but I gave him a tip that was equal to the cost of the shuttle ride. And why not? It was only ten bucks and it was a nice chunk of *dineros* for him. He needed it a lot more than I did. Already I began to marvel over how cheap things are here in Mexico. I could be a big tipper without really being a big tipper. Immersion was underway.

<u>My Condo at Coromuel - Thursday, January 5</u>

The shuttle drove off heading for downtown Cabo as I stood facing Coromuel's security booth, complete with a live guard. He was standing and staring at me from his booth. I think he was expecting me. My condo rental is an Airbnb arrangement. The owner whose name is Alejandra but goes by the nickname of Ale, would not be meeting me. Instead, she provided me with very explicit instructions for my entry into Villa #10 inside the small complex named Villa Paloma. Fortunately, as it turns out, the guard was expecting me, clearly, so I didn't have to stumble with my Spanish other than confirming my name was Señor Lake. All he did was nod and point, so I just walked past him and veered to my next destination, the laundromat named *Ola*, a word that means wave, not to be confused with the bull-fighting exclamation Olé. I was told it would be open late, good thing, because the hour was getting late.

I walked into *Ola*, which was not much bigger than a standard hotel room. Washing machines and dryers ran along every wall, interspersed with two double sinks. In the donut hole of this laundromat was a very good looking *señora*, probably in her fifties, who I was told by Ale would give me the keys to the kingdom. She looked at me and said, *Si?* I told her my name is Señor Lake. She smiled. I was sure she too was expecting me as she took two steps to the small counter at the entrance where I was standing, grabbed a set of keys and handed them to me with a smile. I certainly was feeling the power of my name. Next time I'll use the full sentence. *Mi nombre es Señor Lake.* Good for Ale. Clearly, she had warned every one of my impending arrival. And I say thank you to that.

The first day in any foreign country comes with trepidations and mystery, the less of both the better, for every traveler. I thanked the Señora, true to my immersion, turned around and walked out, towing my roller bag over the poorly cobbled driveway in the direction of another security gate, this one for my building Villa Paloma, *sans* guard. *Sans* is French for without. I don't know the Spanish word for without. I probably could use the Spanish *no* instead of the French *sans*. Immersion requires flexibility. And improvisation. After thinking about it, I could say *no guardia*. In Spanish, the negative is easy; just put the word *no* in front of the statement. A lot easier than French.

Security for my building was in play. Another secure entrance after the guard at the entry gate was a good thing. I waved the plastic card attached to my key chain like a magic wand over the electronic plate at the gate and buzzed myself in. From there, as Ale instructed in her email to me, I walked right through the foyer tunnel into the pool courtyard and turned left before the pool. With a few more steps and another quick left, I was standing in front of Villa #10 thinking it was all too easy. The keys on the key chain were color coded and within ten minutes of passing Coromuel's gate guard, I walked into my condo, my home for the next three months, thanks to Airbnb. And Ale.

I like Airbnb - Thursday, January 5

I like Airbnb. I've used it many times, all over the world. I am rarely disappointed but almost always the places fall a bit short of their photos. I think this is what every real estate photo does to reality. My first reaction was one of concern, because my new residence was smaller than I expected and not quite as nice as I had hoped. That's from the shock of dealing with the expectation set up by the photos.

The bathroom was my first stop and right away I took a liking to the roomy walk-in shower. That counted for a lot. The entire floor in the condo was tile, which I liked. Carpets were bothersome and rarely clean so the absence of any was a good thing. This tile was a cream color with gray inch wide grout, wall to wall, which actually lightened the place up, and lightened my feelings about the place. The kitchen was an alcove off the open living room and dining area. Its narrow counters were also tile, smaller than the floor tiles and in my favorite color, aqua. The refrigerator was a nice size, more than adequate for my simple needs. There was a microwave on the countertop not far from the sink, though I didn't care about that because I never use one. A four-burner stove was next to the sink and, from Ale, I know I had all the kitchen utensils, pots, pans, dishes, and glasses I'd need. A small wooden dining table with four matching chairs was the only furniture in the dining space and the living room was spartan too, just a sofa, and a coffee table in front of it which would be just perfect for my feet, giving me a level leg. The sofa was facing the TV, waiting for me. This was all good in the name of simplicity, which is a name I am very attached to. I checked the windows for ease of opening and access to fresh air. Three of the five were louvered glass panel windows which are okay, especially for air flow but not for mosquitos unless they have screens. Fortunately, these three windows had screens, however a bit battered. Some mosquito will find its way in. The other two windows were two large vertical panels of glass with one of the panels on a slide for more of that open-air feeling if I wanted to slide it open. They didn't look very substantial to me, but I wasn't really worried. I'm not sure why that's true. I think paying attention to security is very important. Maybe the security guard at the entrance was creating a false sense of security in me. Also, the curtains for the two bedroom windows and the dining room window were inadequate. I like privacy so I knew I'd have to do something about improving them. The solution will come to me, maybe tomorrow, but it wasn't something I had to deal with on my first night.

Ten minutes after walking through the front door, which was the only door, my roller bag and back pack were unpacked. The principle contents comprised a week's worth of clothes, primarily my standard uniform: seven black t-shirts, three pairs of khaki shorts. I also had three light weight tropical short sleeve shirts for fancy nights out. They were immediately hung in the closet to drop out the wrinkles. To round out this incredibly adequate wardrobe, I was wearing a pair of skinny blue jeans, which were the only long pants I brought with me, and a long sleeved, white, button collar Brooks Brothers cotton shirt, in other words, my Juan Valdez sun shirt. The rest of the stuff in my suitcase was miscellaneous basics.

My back pack held the expensive items, like my laptop and my iPad and my iPhone. I packed my iPhone though I turned it off with no intention of using it. The pack also held all the basics I would need for surf casting except the rod. These basics didn't amount to much: a reel, extra line, weights, some lures, a set of hooks, leaders, some bait ties, and a hog nosed pliers for de-hooking. I postponed buying the rod until I got here. My boning knife for cleaning the catch was in the suit case. It was an evil looking fifteen-inch blade that I never could have carried through security. I like fishing. It would round out my triad of activities here in Cabo with learning Spanish and writing a book.

Unpacking was a snap. Took only ten minutes, if that. I like to travel light and I am thinking that a suitcase and a half is pretty light packing for three months. Clothes were never a big deal to me when traveling because there are laundromats in every town, like Chinese restaurants. Of course, I knew one wouldn't be far from Coromuel. Now it can't get any easier; I've got the *Ola* laundromat across the street, inside the Coromuel complex. It doesn't get easier than that. I've always traveled light and pack light because I know that if I really need something I can usually buy it on the go. And as a writer, I could show up at just about any party in jeans and a t-shirt because, after all, I am a "creative" person, which gives me some flexibility beyond most dress codes. That's about it. T-shirts and shorts for three months of sunny days in the 70's. I was feeling pretty good after unpacking and, suddenly, my one bedroom and one bath condo looked just fine to me. It would work nicely for my simple needs. Yep, I am happy with it, and why not!

The neighborhood at night - Thursday January 5

I was a bit tired in a physical sense, the shuttle ride from the airport really wore me out. That ride took longer than my flight from Phoenix. Besides being a bit worn, I was also a bit wired over the fact that I was in Cabo. A combo that rarely lasts. It wasn't even ten o'clock. I decided to investigate the neighborhood. As I walked out of the compound past the security guard at the front gate, that rush of adrenaline I experienced thirty minutes earlier was exactly that, a rush. It was over before I knew it. Up and down in a heartbeat. Suddenly I was only good for about fifteen more minutes, if that. I'd never make it into the downtown area.

On the sidewalk, not far from the security gate, I did a three-sixty to check my surroundings. I couldn't see anything that interested me within a few blocks in any direction. I saw only one place that might be interesting. It was an authentic looking Mexican restaurant across the street, named Guadalupana. It was closed. Ale told me the walk to the marina, which is the hub of Cabo, was only twenty minutes. I suppose I could have done it and taken a cab back but opted out. I saw it as a pointless hit and run. I was not in a hurry; after all, I would be here for three months. It was easy to see that I really was on the periphery of Cabo activity. That was all to the south. To the north, mostly desert. From googling maps, I remembered that somewhere out there, about a mile or so was a Walmart. No sidewalk leading in that direction. And I knew there was a Costco beyond that, not much farther to the north. To the west of me, I recalled a map that showed a Home Depot, which I remembered from a bout of googling. There is a sidewalk, but it's a long walk. Emptiness to the east except for a lit-up soccer field a half mile out there, beyond that somewhere in the distant darkness was the beach lined with lit up condos. I talked myself into staying on sidewalks, which meant I could go south, towards town, west toward Home Depot, east to the beach, but not north to Walmart. I walked toward town, about five blocks, as far as a Pemex gas station when I ran out of gas, but Pemex couldn't help me. I decided to call it a day. Time for bed. I was in Cabo, ready to begin my life here, but the official start would have to wait a bit, until *mañana*.

The start of a new day - Friday, January 6

I slept in. Till nine. Must have been way more tired than I thought. I had no food in the house except for a couple of Nature Valley granola bars that Ale left me in a welcome basket. That's fake food, closer to a candy bar. She also left me a bottle of a red varietal Chilean wine. Sweet of her, the wine. That combo would have been a crazy breakfast for launching my adventure down here. I passed on the wine for breakfast, of course, to be enjoyed some other time. I threw the sugar laden fake-health snack bars into a waste basket next to the fridge. I can't stand stuff like that. It's not even food, which reminded me that I had no food in the house. None. *Nada.* But I wasn't done with rummaging through the kitchen cabinets.

Wow, what a nice surprise! I found an old Osterizer blender in the kitchen cabinet under the sink, buried way back in there, easy to miss. I checked it out immediately and was elated that it worked. Before I came down here I debated for days and days whether or not I should lug my big beautiful Vitamix blender down here so I could keep up with my daily regimen of vegetable/fruit smoothies. In the end, the day before my flight, I decided it was too much to carry. Too heavy and too big. Instead, I said to myself I'll buy one in Cabo. Well, I am very happy to have made this discovery of Ale's *licuadora*, which is a Spanish word that translates directly into liquidator. I repeated it a few times. Every time I say that word, especially if I lower my voice as much as possible, I think of Arnold Schwarzenegger, the liquidator. Oh, that's right, he's the terminator, not the *licuadora*.

Of course, I don't yet know the locations of the stores I need, except Walmart. I have a feeling I will be putting a heavy reliance on Walmart, especially since it's just up the street from me, only a mile maybe two at the most. Oh, I know that sounds simple, you know, "up the street." But, that street is actually a highway right up to my street corner, the corner where it downsizes to an insanely busy boulevard. There is no sidewalk there, only a skinny shoulder beyond that corner intersection. I am perfectly aware that cars drive sixty miles an hour with *loco* drivers behind the wheel of most of them. It was easy to see that I would be risking my life getting to and from Walmart. But I had no choice, really, unless of course I took a cab. Something to think about.

Danger aside, Walmart has been in my plan all along. Before I got here I decided that I would buy a bicycle in the first few days and make it my principle mode of transportation. Buses chugged along; however cheap, not for me. Besides, I hate waiting at bus stops. Taxis were indeed the fastest way to get around town, but they are very expensive down here and not always within a whistle. Waiting for one is also a deterrent for me. Renting a car makes no sense for me. A rental car is ridiculously expensive, especially with insurance, for three months. The only real solution to my transportation needs is a bicycle. That would be a Day Three purchase. Since this was Day Two, my first full day in Cabo, I decided I'd walk to the marina, which is the heart of the tourist trade, and eat breakfast in one of the restaurants overlooking the yachts, a view that always put me in a vacation frame of mind.

The walk to the marina - Friday, January 6

The walk into town from Coromuel isn't much of a walk, about twenty minutes. It just seems like a long walk because there's so much going on, and so much traffic. It didn't take long for me to know that I couldn't see myself walking to and from the downtown every day, and certainly not twice a day, which could be necessary. Maybe three times a day if I do one morning, noon, and night. Almost unthinkable, however much I like exercise. In my original plans, I didn't envision riding a bike for every junket but I quickly decided that, indeed, I would be doing that. Ah ah! Another reason to get a bike as soon as possible! Maybe even this afternoon! Surely Walmart will have one for me. If not, I can go to Costco, join the club, and buy one there. I need to get my basic needs addressed as quickly as possible, so I can get into a daily routine, something I cherish. Sometimes structure is a good thing, especially if you are writing a book.

The walk to the marina was of course very interesting. It was my first time. A whole different culture was in front of me, behind me, and passing me on both sides. No surprise there. The sidewalk reminded me of the year that I was living dangerously in Puerto

Rico, where the sidewalks were very similar in character. And risk. What I mean by that is that sidewalks here and there are more like an obstacle course than anything we see in the States. Besides being tricky, they can be outright dangerous.

The first obstacle I ran into was a wire attached to a lamp post that ran to the top of a fence on the other side of the sidewalk. It was about seven feet off the ground. It could decapitate someone given extremely unfortunate circumstances. Someone, maybe the fence owner, ran the wire from the post to the fence to keep the fence from falling into his lot. I get that. But it was a potentially dangerous thing to do. Curiously, it is only seven feet above the sidewalk, not much higher than what it would take to decapitate a bicyclist sitting straight up in the seat. Such as me. I made a mental note and wondered if it would eventually sag a bit, thus posing a very real threat, especially because it was not easy to see. Worse at night. I made a mental note to tie a plastic bag around it at its midpoint sometime in the next few days. You know, flag it, make it easier to see. Sometimes I think I'm crazy to think of stuff like that, but nothing I can do about it. It's me.

The sidewalk from Coromuel to the marina actually turned out to be just about the craziest sidewalk I've ever encountered. And surely it wouldn't be the only crazy sidewalk in Cabo. I knew that from my previous visits to this colorful country. Sidewalk hazards on Mexican streets were not unusual, more the norm. I could see that it was important for pedestrians, as always, to stay focused one step at a time. The many possibilities for injury became evident with my progress and, I was sure, there were some pitfalls as well. First, besides my encounter with the over-hanging wire, traffic signs for the cars were sporadically posted in the middle of the sidewalk, for no identifiable reason. And I mean smack dab in the middle. Why? What planning commission does that? What construction crew does that? The nice thing about that is you can't miss them as a pedestrian, unless of course you're walking with your head down as you text away on your smart phone. Or watching for holes you could fall into. Cars could easily miss them, but pedestrians couldn't. There is another threat I encountered numerous times along my walk: all kinds of cracks and construction scars, and numerous open holes, some the size of a shoebox. Some of the holes could easily swallow a person's foot. A couple of these "holes" were underground junction boxes for city power and irrigation that had lost their lids. A couple other deep holes were just flat out holes, erosion maybe. Ankle breakers, all of them. A minefield. All easy to overlook, literally, and dangerous if a person doesn't see one. Also, the sidewalk has so many uneven grades and inexplicable speed bumps along with countless ins and outs of swerving disjointed angles along the way that one would think that the sidewalk was put together piecemeal over hundreds of years of different technologies, built mostly on moonless nights, and, yes, by blind laborers. Why? I constantly asked myself how this snakelike rollercoaster minefield of a sidewalk could possibly come into creation? I've been to Mexico before and I know there is much to like and many aspects make Mexico unique. This sidewalk fell under the unique category.

I walked to the marina without injury. The boulevard took me to within a block of the yachts. The wharf was a beehive of activity. Tons of tourists, everywhere. It was easy, too, to see that the boat basin was rimmed with tightly packed restaurants and bars. No surprise there, just what one would expect. Even though all these establishments smack of tourist traps in overdrive, I confess, the marina is a magnificent sight. I could see that right away. I like almost all boat basins but this one is particularly interesting for those of us who enjoy viewing a stunning array of yachts, charter fishing boats, and boat taxis occupying hundreds of slips, all tucked away in a harbor surrounded by Cabo's baked hillsides. A wonderful mix of eye candy for boat lovers.

The crown jewel of the harbor today is the yacht named Double Haven. It is moored at the end of one that docks that protrudes into the center of the harbor. You couldn't miss it. Its name, in foot high letters, was easy to read from a hundred yards out. I'm guessing its length is about one hundred and seventy-five feet, which is a little more than half the length of a football field. Every inch of it makes it a drop-dead gorgeous four-deck world-cruising luxury yacht. How much does that baby cost? Probably in the neighborhood of twenty million dollars. With that purchase, it comes with twin five-thousand-gallon gas tanks. This means when you pull up to the fuel pump and say fill 'er up, it will cost you about $27,000. Ouch! I say if it flies, bucks, or floats, rent it!

My first walk along the marina, end to end - Friday, January 6

Along with hundreds of other tourists, I strolled through the marina on the sidewalk that meanders between the boats and the restaurants. Nearly every restaurant is fronted by a polite and friendly Mexican inviting you into his restaurant for the best food in the marina and the promise of delicious margaritas. These "hosts" are all nice but it doesn't take long for the incessant invitations to wear on me. Still, I smiled and thanked every one of them, mindful that I would be in town for three months and will see them again. I might even get to know some of them on a first name basis. I would be walking the marina many times in the next three months, maybe even daily. I was pretty sure of that because it was the best show in town. Besides, I like to look at yachts. I think they are symbolic of adventure. And they're beautiful. Even sexy.

Walking the marina sidewalk from end to end takes about thirty minutes, longer if you stroll. It's a very interesting walk. The harbor has an irregular shape to it. It is comprised of eight straightaways that eventually encircle the marina, like a horseshoe, with the entrance to the harbor at the open end of the horseshoe, of course. Seven of the straightaways are jammed with restaurants, bars, and other businesses dedicated to tourist entertainment, including a dolphin aquarium and dozens of ticket booths for fishing charter boats, diving, and parasailing, among other activities. However, one straightaway is deadsville (love that word) because it is comprised of a vast stretch of unkempt landscape that features a massive concrete structure of a hotel abandoned in the early stages of construction. This skeleton of a building is six floors of a forlorn structure of cubicle rooms and all the other rooms that comprise a hotel, all fully exposed, absent a facade. Just countless surfaces of gray concrete, nothing else, sitting there completely neglected while the structure collects dust carried in by the Baja winds. It just sits there, looking abandoned for the ages, behind a chain link fence. It was easy to see that it had been there for a very long time. Years. A few of the palms trees in the front of the building were topless, which told me that they were victims of a hurricane. The last one that hit Cabo was Odile in 2014. It did a lot of damage. Maybe it was the one decapitated them. Maybe it was one of the hurricanes before Odile. I wish I knew the building's story. I'm sure I'll find out in the coming weeks.

It was a good walk, but hunger was gnawing at me so my stomach was now in charge. Time to eat. I liked the look of a thatched palm roof on a restaurant. I think of palm trees when I see them and when I think of palm trees I think of great tropical vacations. It's a lot of nice imagery created in my head. One of the many thatched restaurants was Solomon's Landing. I was guessing the food there was good because it was a hopping place, loaded with loaded tourists sipping margaritas and easily profiled as retirees. My crowd, I guess, dammit. I didn't mind playing tourist on my first day and why not, after all, I am a tourist too, even though I will be here longer than most tourists. I want to go local as soon as possible, which fits with my concept of immersion. It also means I probably won't be coming to Solomon's Landing again. Eating in a "tiki" restaurant packed with English speaking tourists doesn't qualify as immersion. I might have to revise the immersion concept I initially envisioned. It looks like a fun place.

Solomon's Landing for breakfast - Friday, January 6

There is a small bar towards the back of Solomon's Landing. I opted for a seat at the bar facing the marina instead of a table overlooking the marina walk. Even if I wanted a table overlooking the marina walk I couldn't have gotten it without waiting. Besides, when I eat by myself I rarely take a table, unless it's a bar stool table in the bar area. Not everyone likes to sit at a table by themselves to eat a meal. I'm one of those people. The bar is just fine and sometimes a good conversation comes up, though generally I like to be left alone. I can watch sports on the TV or, with a book in hand, I can read. It works out fine for me. In this case, there was no TV and I didn't have a book. It would be a quick meal. And why not, I had lots of things to do to get myself properly launched on this escapade. Next time I'll bring my instructional book, *Spanish for Gringos*, a workbook for people wanting to learn the language.

I had practiced a little Spanish before I came down here so I could do a few basics like greetings, order beer and, of course, find the bathroom. Beyond that, I was in new territory. The Mexican bartender swooped in and said hi. He asked me in perfect English what I'd like to drink and if I wanted a menu. In perfect English, I ordered a Pacifico and said yes to the menu. A beer? Really? At ten in the morning? I caved claiming it was my first day on vacation so why not? People around me were drinking, mostly margaritas, so why not a drink for me? I didn't think I'd make a habit of it at this hour every day, so no worries. That said, it's looking like it's harder to get into immersing myself than I thought. I am pretty sure this is probably not the kind of restaurant I should be going to, given my interest in learning Spanish.

The *nuevos rancheros* I ordered and devoured was excellent and did the trick. I could see that quality and quantity went hand in hand. This is usually true of Mexican food. This is something I've always known and one of the many reasons to love Mexico. I did not have a second Pacifico. That would have been real cause for concern even though I almost caved to this very seductive thought: why not, amigo, you're on vacation? The meal and one beer cost me eight bucks including a nice tip. Cheap for all I got. Thank you strong dollar. With my stroll around the marina completed and, now, an empty breakfast plate in front of me, I had formulated a plan to launch my new life here. I knew what the next step was. I moved up the timetable. It was time to go to Walmart!

<u>The road to Walmart - Friday, January 6</u>

The walk back to Coromuel after a late breakfast at Solomon's Landing took a half hour. Solomon's was in the heart of the marina, which added the extra time to my hike back. I stopped in my place to grab my back pack, which I would need to carry some food back to the condo, whether or not I got a bike. That took all of thirty seconds, and then I took off for the thirty-minute walk to Walmart. Coming and going at Coromuel I made a point of saying something to the guard. *Hola. Buenas tardes* and *Cómo está?* were all good choices. I tried them all. Once out the gate, I turned left, which pointed me in the right direction.

Just north of that gate, about fifty yards up the sidewalk, there was a tiny specialty restaurant. The sign above the window awning indicated that the restaurant's name is Doggy Style. Right away I sensed a bad sense of humor at work. My hunch was confirmed by the words written on the awning itself, words which clearly worked to create a unifying theme: Nice Buns! Tasty Wieners! Ah ah, it wasn't a sex shop but the owner's idea must have come from one! I quickly concluded it was a hot dog specialty shop. It was closed, in the middle of the day. Maybe it was a night time restaurant. Or simply no longer in business. Whatever it was, the overall look and the concept were so tasteless I knew I'd never walk in and order something. The food was probably tasteless as well.

Doggy Style was a hundred yards behind me. I paused on the sidewalk, to see my options for getting safely across the streets at the intersection. This was a major intersection where the highway coming into town was immediately downsized to a boulevard in a seemingly futile attempt to slow traffic and prepare it for entry into the commercial world of Cabo San Lucas. I could easily pick up the pattern of the stop and go lights, but I wasn't sure the drivers could. They were quick to jump lights and run through the yellow lights well into the red. Getting to the other side may sound easy enough, but the chaos of the drivers speeding in every direction made me a little nervous. They weren't exactly paying attention to the lights. I paid close attention to the lights with great care and timed it right to get me across six lanes. I stopped on the other side on a small island between the streets behind me and the frontage road in front of me. I wasn't completely across so I watched incoming on the frontage road to time my next move. Yep, one more lane to cross. Sounds simple enough.

As I stood on that little island, all I could see in front of me was the desert and a concrete ribbon of in-coming cars on pavement which tapered from a ribbon to string-size in the distant northern hills, bifurcating the desert as far as I could see. Cars were coming right at me as I stood on a pedestrian island supporting the stop and go signal for the lanes behind me, not for the lane in front of me. The island, my tiny island of concrete raised about eight inches above the pavement, forced the oncoming cars to take a sharp right turn before merging on to the main road that ran behind me. Their goal could be none other than to pass other cars but not be passed. All these vehicles coming in on the highway and its frontage road were blowing past me front and back at insane speeds, leaving back drafts that could invert an umbrella. No one was slowing down, really, and my presence at the heavily marked crosswalk certainly didn't slow anyone down. The yellow flashing light for my crosswalk didn't help. Like me, it was ignored. No one indicated any inclination to yield to me or assist me in any way that would make it safe for me to get across that single lane. To get to Walmart, which I knew to be about a mile to the north, just over the crest, the frontage road was the last road I had to cross. If I wasn't careful it would the last road I tried to cross.

The craziness of all the traffic around me in all directions reminded me of Demolition Derby, a TV show I watched as a kid. It was some kind of offshoot of NASCAR racing in which the driver of each car tried to be the last one running on the track. This is a victory accomplished only if all the other cars are rendered inoperable. There is no second place. The real excitement of this concept was generated on a race track that was a figure eight configuration. All around the track the drivers tried to demolish other cars without putting their own car out of action.

Most of the destruction occurred at the intersection of the figure eight's two circles. As I stood on the little concrete island, I felt like I was at the Derby's intersection. That's what I was seeing all around me. The Mexican word for this is *loco*, which means crazy.

Eventually, I made it across but I wasn't out of the woods, so to speak, though I was into the desert. It was obvious that it was very risky to walk on the shoulder of the frontage road. Only a fool would try that. Note, I'm trying it. Same with riding a bike. I might not last one minute. I could see a bit of a shoulder, erratic as it appeared, as far as I could see, which was far enough. It was my path to Walmart. Walmart was on my side of the highway. The shoulder would get me to Walmart 's driveway without having to cross another busy street. It was the only hope I had for making it to Walmart and back.

The shoulder between the frontage road and the desert would have to be my path. For much of the way, I could see that it gave me plenty of walking space to feel reasonably safe from on-coming traffic except for a one hundred yard stretch that designers of slaughter houses would probably call the death chute. In that stretch, there wasn't much of shoulder, down to twelve inches most of the way. That stretch was simply a skinny strip of gravel and dust running along the edge of the paved frontage road. The pavement was on one side of it and a long run of dense needled desert foliage ran along the other side. Metaphorically, I was walking a tightrope. There were no escape hatches in the chute. It didn't give me any leeway. Just barely enough for me to use. Like I said, for that distance it was easy to think of it as the death chute, even if I hugged the scrub brush.

The death chute required an all-out sprint in order to maximize my survival odds. The good news is that the shoulder widened considerably once I made it through the chute, if I made it through the chute. Of course, I wasn't about to take my eye off the cars coming at me, at any time. In that perilous stretch, I would have to be on constant alert with no escape plan other than to throw myself into the desert scrub to avoid any car that looked like it was going to hit me. In some places, the scrub was so thick I was not convinced I could leap into if necessary. It certainly wasn't inviting. Where my path was only a foot wide put me at highest risk, so I had to be absolutely sure I could get through that part of the chute when no cars could put me in jeopardy. This would be true for me on the return trip from Walmart as well. Nice. At the beginning of either end of the chute, I would have to wait like a jackrabbit, motionless, poised to run when I had the chance. If I couldn't make it in one uninterrupted dash, I could take it on section by section, inserted into the brush, I suppose. If necessary, repeat. Repeat. Repeat. Until I made it out of the chute. I made a mental note to never again run the chute during rush hour because I'd never make it to the other end.

A very long minute later, I made it. The intersection was a half mile behind me. The chute was right behind me. I felt as though I had left civilization behind me, too. So it seemed. Just over the rise a thousand yards ahead of me, out of my sightline, was the shopping center anchored by Walmart. To my right, all desert. Ahead, Walmart is a patch of civilization surrounded by the desert terrain, like an oasis. For me it is an oasis. I wondered if I'd be leaving it today on foot or on a brand-new bicycle.

Welcome to Walmart in Mexico - Friday, January 6

I made it through the chute my first time, unscratched, however truly scary it was. I want to say that the first time of doing anything challenging is the scariest time. I am not fit enough to sprint a hundred yards on foot without dropping dead from a heart attack, may be an age thing, so getting through it was an unknown until I actually got through it. One chute plus three quarters of a mile later, mostly on gravel and dust, I walked into Walmart with a determination to buy a bike that afternoon, my second day in Mexico. I walked in with the confidence that I would find what I was looking for. I've bought bikes at Walmart in the past. It's not that hard to find a decent bike for not much more than a hundred bucks in the States. I am sure it's about the same thing in Mexico.

The Walmart store pretty much looked like every Walmart in the States. I recall seeing an excellent selection of bicycles at Walmart stores in the States, so I was hopeful I would have a choice of a couple of nice bikes. When I walked in I quickly saw that half the customers were white folks and the other half were Hispanics. Just like the Walmart stores in the States! I found the sporting goods department in the middle of the store. It was not an impressive section. There was only one rack of adult bikes and they were all the same model, ten of them: mid-size, fat tires, kinda chunky cruisers. Painted shiny black with brick red sidewalls on the tires, a small basket in front of the handlebars, and a rear wheel flat rack. That was the entire selection, that design or none. Welcome to Walmart in Mexico, where things might be what you expect, or not.

I bought the cruiser. A hundred and fifty bucks, which is the equivalent of fifty dollars a month rental fee. Just before I leave I could give it to some lucky Mexican boy and make his day. I got a cable lock, too, off the shelf behind me. None of the tires on any of the bikes had air in them, but a very young and sweet salesgirl helped me get my bike into shape. To my surprise, she had a pneumatic air hose at the end of the rack of kiddie bikes. It took her less than five minutes to fill both tires. Clearly, she had done this before. She also got her hands on an adjustable wrench so I could get the seat up to its highest point, though it would still look like a low-rider, and she adjusted the handlebars up a couple of inches, to the max, to better suit my size. I climbed on and made a couple of runs up and down the main aisle, much to her surprise. Shocked a few customers, too, though one American cheered me on. Maybe he thought I was stealing it and trying to ride out of the store. *Hola* was a good thing to say during my test drive. It made the Walmart sales girl laugh so I guess it was okay. I liked the bike. I thanked her and told her I'd take it. Mission accomplished.

However, I was not done with Walmart. I still needed a few things, like food. I left my bike in a corner by the bakery, grabbed a shopping cart which, in Spanish, is *carrito de compras* and bought a few other things, including eggs for breakfast, some *queso*, a few small bags of frozen *vegetales*, and ingredients for several days of blender smoothies. I checked to see if my bike was still parked where I left it every two minutes. I had picked out all of the stuff I needed to cover me for a week with some variety. It made for a bulging backpack and overflow on my handy little bike basket.

For some reason, I had known for a long time that cucumber in Spanish is *pepino,* which happened to be the name of the Mexican farmhand from the reruns of an old TV show called *The Real McCoys.* Strange that I remembered that, though I didn't know the meaning of the word at the time. I thought it was just a name. No telling what other memories were buried in clusters of neurons tucked away in the recessed crannies of my aging brain. I'm not a trivia expert, but I also know that The Lone Ranger's sidekick was an American Indian named Tonto, a pejorative nickname, played by Jay Silverheels. In Spanish, *tonto* means fool. Kinda sad that the show's writers did that to him. Must have been their private (and stupid) joke.

I paid for my bike and a load of essential foods and rode out of the Walmart parking lot quite content. *Muy contento.* I was feeling good right up until I remembered that I still had to make another run through the chute, this time *with* the flow of traffic. And, with a load of groceries. The only consolation is that I'd be getting through it a lot faster because this time I was on a bike. The downside is that I would be exposed fully in the traffic lane for the full length of the chute, with no conceivable way I could leap into the scrub bushes to save my ass. Clearly, I'd have to make it a rule to wait for a nice break in the traffic whenever I went either way and pedal as if my life depended on it. Because it did. As it turned out, I made it through the chute easily enough this time. After that, I knew I could deal with the chute going both ways in the days ahead of me with little or no sweat. I made it back to Coromuel in less than fifteen minutes. I was thinking that my condo's location at the midpoint between Walmart and the downtown was going to work nicely. More happiness. A very good start.

What about fishing? - Saturday, January 7

I like to fish. Whether it's fresh water fishing for bass, walleyes or Rainbow and Brown trout, or ocean fishing for a million different species, it's all fun to me. In the past year, a dear friend of mine in Portland, Oregon introduced me to surf casting one day when I was visiting him. He and I drove to the Pacific coast in his Titan truck loaded with his fishing gear, gear which included a couple of very long fiberglass rods, each about twelve to fourteen feet long. He parked on the beach in a public park and we walked fifty yards to the surf, hands full of gear and a long rod for each of us. Ten minutes later both of us were flinging fresh squid bait a hundred yards out into the incoming waves. Within minutes, fish hit and we hauled a dozen in. The fish were hooked. So was I.

Surf casting for fish was one of my top priorities for my life in Cabo, for fun and for food, so I looked around to see how I could make that happen. It is easy to find fishing tackle shops in Cabo because Cabo is one of the great sports fishing capitals in the world. I found one in the heart of town. I parked my bike against a lamp post and locked it up before walking into Minerva's bait and tackle store. The manager, a Mexican man in his thirties named Raoul, spoke excellent English as I tried to wade through my questions with the few words I knew in his native tongue. I stumbled but he got it. He understood I was after information.

From Raoul, I was able to discern that I was up a creek, so to speak. If I wanted to fish off the beach, he said I would have to drive an hour or so over to the Pacific shoreline and cast my bait out there. He said I couldn't do it here in town on the tourist beaches encircling Cabo for two reasons. First, above all, the fishing this season was lousy. I clearly understood him when he said, "No luck from the shore, you have to go out on a boat." Second, the hotels on the shore would call the police and chase you away because they didn't want you hooking their guests. I remembered to ask if I needed a license to fish on the beach. Happily, Raoul said, no. I think that particular freedom is in place to allow the locals to fish off the beach at no cost.

I got on my bike and rode off into the sunset. Frankly, it all sounded lame to me, but talking to Raoul was a start. I decided further investigation was necessary for me about fishing off a beach here. There were fish out there, I thought to myself. C'mon, this is the Sea of Cortez! As for going to the Pacific coast, I wasn't eager to rent a car for day to go there in search of some unknown territory to fish. I also was tempted to say that Raoul was trying to talk me into going out on a charter boat. That alternative was much better for local business, of course. Since I got here I've been hopeful that I could just get on my bike with my fishing gear and ride to the beach, catch something for dinner, and then ride home for some homemade sashimi or grilled fish. Maybe that can still happen.

Fishing Charter in the Sea of Cortez? - Tuesday, January 10

Since I love fishing so much, any person I talked to about it would suggest that I charter one of the ten gazillion fishing boats for a half day on the Sea of Cortez. When I walked my bike the full length of the marina, as I did every day thus far, I must have encountered twenty Mexicans, maybe more, offering me their sport fishing services. I said, *no, gracias* to all of them. It's an invitation that is hard for many, many people to resist. After all, one of the main reasons people come here is to fish, mostly for Marlin.

The waters in this part of the world are known for the best Marlin fishing in the world. And, the waters around Cabo are known worldwide for great fishing in general, not just Marlin. Besides those big beautiful billfish, the tournament fishermen chase Wahoo, Dorado (also known as Mahi-Mahi), and Yellowfin Tuna. Lots of Snapper and Grouper to be caught as well. The fishing is so good here that it is no surprise that Cabo is the home to more big money fishing tournaments than any other place in the world. Millions of dollars are awarded as prize money every year. It's that big. I've always known that. Of course, many of the Mexicans selling charter services ask me why I said no to going out on a boat. Good question, and fair to ask. Why not? The answer is simple: I hate throwing up. That is something I almost always do when I get on a boat on big water. This tells you a lot about why I am interested in surf casting. It's my only choice down here.

A daily routine begins to take shape - Tuesday, January 10

My cruiser gives me great freedom in getting around quickly and has a lot to do with creating some structure for my day. Buying a bike was the smartest thing I could have done to enhance my living experience in Cabo. I established a routine right off the bat. While there was plenty of variation in my activities every day this first week, a pattern emerged. I was slow to get out of bed in the morning because the first thirty minutes of wakefulness would be spent reading the news from Trumpland and reviewing my book *Spanish for Gringos*. The former makes me really happy that I am here in Cabo, out of the fray. The latter really helps me get in the frame of mind for focusing on my mission. I try not to dwell on the former and don't see it as something I want to discuss with the Mexicans. Not surprisingly, when Trump's name comes up, they have nothing nice to say about him. No surprise there. More importantly, breakfast is always easy. I fry two eggs and make a blender smoothie.

The smoothie part was a habit I got into over a year ago so I had the process down pat. I stuff two big handfuls of kale or spinach into the blender container and top it off with a half a dozen chunks of frozen mango and a banana or skinned cucumber. Add a half cup of pineapple-coconut juice, a teaspoon of turmeric (I brought a spice bottle with me) and fill the container with water. Blend and bingo! I'd have a glass with my eggs and then a couple more glasses spread out through the day. Better than munching on Fritos and other crap through the day.

After breakfast, which was basically after rush hour, I rode my bike every day to Walmart for some food basics, to re-stock the inventory of kale etc. and buy whatever gadget or thing I might need. Of course, the Walmart run was also an opportunity for exercise and mingling with Spanish speaking store personnel, especially for chatting up the cashiers. This daily trip also means a couple of thrill rides through "the chute." Once back to my condo, I get into a little organization from my purchases, which takes all of three minutes, then two hours of studying Spanish. Mid-day hours are usually spent exploring the town on the cruiser and reading the signs and saying *Hola!* to people. This part of the routine always provided me with a nice bit of exercise because it's the longest ride of the day, though it certainly is not a cardio workout. Back at my place for late afternoon hours of studying Spanish and maybe some reading, and maybe some writing. More cruising at night, to see the sights and observe Cabo's nightlife.

On some days, I grab a lounge chair at the pool outside my front door, sit in the shade and read a book. Presently, I'm reading *Humans Who Went Extinct* by Clive Finlayson. The author is a leading exponent of the relationship between climate change, ecological change, and human evolution. It's a fascinating book that provides a grand hypothesis for the development of mankind over millions of years. It really makes me think, which is a good thing. I think all good writers need to read a lot and I love reading. Reading makes me a better writer. Clearly, I need to read a lot more.

By the end of the afternoon I've finished off the remainder of the blender contents, some of which contributed to my lunch along with a banana. At dusk, I jump on my bike and ride down to the marina for the stimulation of contact with other humans, the ones who haven't gone extinct. I like to engage in light conversations in Spanish wherever I can. The hawkers that lined the boat basin restaurants were always chatty with tourists so they are quick to say hi to me and, surprisingly, compliment my bike. They love my cruiser and are always surprised when I tell them I bought it at Walmart. I like to say it is a Walmart special or *especial de Walmart*. Some of the Mexicans become very interested and ask me how much I paid for it. To me, it is funny that my reply of three thousand four hundred pesos is often countered with the English retort "No, in dollars." I tell them one hundred and fifty dollars. They think that's a really good price for my bike. After an hour or two of riding past the restaurants and shops, and dodging traffic, I go home for dinner and decide how I want to spend my evening. Studying usually wins out. I think this first week was more about acclimatization than anything else, though I could see the week's evolving routine worked well for me.

Dinner almost always is steamed vegetables and lots of water followed by a couple hours of studying, writing and reading. It's funny to me that I haven't launched myself into Mexican food in this first week. Oh, I stopped in a few bars here and there and knocked down a couple of beers, along with a margarita every once in a while, to break up the routine but that even felt a little off to me because I was so committed to establishing a healthy routine. As I said, I never really liked eating a meal by myself at a restaurant, even if I was at the bar in front of some sporting event on TV. That thinking will have to change soon because it is depriving me of the fantastic cuisine that Mexico offers.

As it turned out, each day's agenda actually provided quite a bit of activity in this first week, which made for consecutive nights of some great sleep. I wasn't in a hurry to do anything. Taking my time, feeling my way around, and getting into the rhythm of life here seemed to be a good thing. I am a tourist but I am not leading the life tourists typically lead here, not the ones that are here for less than a week or two anyway. I was looking forward to eleven more weeks in Cabo.

I've got a maid - Wednesday, January 11

I didn't know maid service was part of the rental deal, but I now know I've got a weekly maid. She showed up today at my door. We figured it out together, that she would be doing my place every Wednesday. That means general clean up, dishes in whatever state they are in, new linens for the bed and fresh towels in the bath. I didn't get her name only because it was in a happy state of shock with this news. She's probably younger than me, but she looks older. Manual labor does that. It took two her hours, which is what she said she needed. Before she started, I pulled the cruiser out of the condo, out of her way, and with my empty backpack, I rode to Walmart for some odds and ends while she did her work. I got back a little before the two hours was up so I waited shirtless at poolside for her to finish up. Fifteen minutes later she walked out with all her household stuff. I jumped up and thanked her. I doubt if the standard rate for house cleaning service people is much above very low, if that. I pulled a hundred pesos out of my wallet for a little extra for her labor. That's about five bucks and enough to put a big smile on her face. Every Wednesday, how nice is that! I get a clean condo and she gets a few extra *dineros*.

My name is Tomas - Wednesday, January 11

I conclude my first week in Mexico with the commitment to introducing myself from here on as Tomas instead of using my one letter first name of T or the combination of TD. Tomas works. It is a popular name. Easy to say, of course. And, it is easy for me to think of myself here in Mexico as a Tomas because my professional artist name is Tomaso DiTomaso, a self-chosen Italian moniker I picked just because it seems like a fun name to me. And arty, because everything in Italy is arty. I created the Tomaso name twelve years ago, so it is second nature to me now. Tomas is close enough to Tomaso. It was an easy decision to switch to a traditional Mexican name. A one letter name is confusing here. No one in Mexico is known as T, which is pronounced *Tay*, or by any one letter of the alphabet. It is too unusual. It begged questions of "Why?" and requests to repeat it over and over again for clarification. Tomas works. Tomas it is.

CHAPTER TWO

Week 2

<u>Cabo crowds - Thursday, January 12</u>

I really like to ride my bike around town. I go everywhere, not just the touristy places. I can explore the streets of Cabo for hours because I have a lot of time to myself when I'm not studying or practicing Spanish and when I'm not writing. I am sticking to my plan of not rushing into things. I am going with the flow. Of course, sometimes I think that means I'm lazy. I know there's a side of me that is not quick to sign up for the things other people like to do in Cabo, like going whale watching. I know myself well enough to admit that I don't particularly like to be in crowds of people, even small crowds, especially on big-water boats (a personal nightmare). To me a group of eight or more is a crowd. I won't do really big stuff, like concerts or sports events such as big-league baseball games. I get overwhelmed quickly among hundreds of people packed together. The thought of thousands of people in one venue undoes me in a matter of seconds. Fewer than eight people can be a crowd to me if I don't really enjoy being in their company. As a writer, I like to hear stories but I don't like small talk. So in some ways I'm mingling with people and in other ways I'm avoiding them. I am especially trying to avoid tourists, but that's hard not only because they are everywhere but also because, frankly, it's nice to let up on my drive to speak Spanish once in a while. And, I love a good conversation. In any language.

Being fearless when speaking Spanish isn't easy - Friday, January 13

I am perfectly aware of my heartbeat preceding one of my attempts at striking up a Spanish conversation. The pace picks up. I wish I could say I am fearless because in a way, that's what it takes. I just pretend I'm fearless because deep inside I am nervous as hell. I don't know why that is, some childhood baggage maybe, but every time I have to tell myself "you can do this" just before I attempt a conversation with a Mexican. And then I jump into it, usually stumbling right from the start.

Yesterday I stopped in front of one of those booths on the marina manned by a Mexican trying to sell tourists a charter fishing experience. It was a slow afternoon, really slow. I never want to interrupt someone while they are working, but this guy did say hi to me first and no strolling tourists were within fifty yards. We had greeted each other several times since my arrival because I cruised the marina sidewalk on my cruiser every day, sometimes twice a day. There is some familiarity between us.

This time, unlike before, I dismounted my bike after I said. *Buenas tardes*, which means good afternoon, words that most Gringos know, I think. Before noon, you say, *Buenas días*, but after noon and until eight o'clock you say *Buenas tardes*. I got that right, but my next line didn't work so well. I meant to say, "It is a quiet day," which for me was this: *Es un día tranquilo*. I cleverly substituted the word "tranquil" into that sentence because I didn't know how to say "quiet." You see, the thought in my head was pretty good: I knew I could say it's a tranquil day. Simple enough, right? Instead, my mouth tripped and said, *Es un día tequila*, which means, "It is a tequila day." He looked at me funny and replied, *Tequila?* I wasn't aware of my word switch so I thought he was suddenly offering me tequila. And why not? Mexicans are very friendly and everyone in Cabo drinks tequila. When I replied *No gracias, no tequila* is when my tongue made me realize that I used the word tequila instead of *tranquilo*. He smiled at me and said, *Tequila es bueno*. Of course, tequila is good. Sadly, this exchange is happening in seconds and he surely thinks I am a fool. In my attempt to recover, I said *No, no señor* and hesitated long enough for him to think I was disagreeing with his observation about tequila. My head is spinning fast while my tongue is moving in slow motion. All I could do was laugh and follow up with what I meant to say along, *Es un día tranquilo. Tranquilo. No tequila.* He got my mix up and laughed too. I rode off smiling painfully, mostly because of my screw up and that fact that I couldn't even remember how to say, "see you later." Of course, I know now, as I did then but twenty seconds too late, that would be *hasta luego*. At that crucial moment, which is when I needed those words, I tripped over my tongue. Nerves did that. So much for telling myself to be fearless. I wanted to climb in a hole. I had to laugh at myself. Had to. But it took a while to do that.

Cabo is a very cool place - Friday, January 13

I've learned a lot about Cabo since my arrival. Of course, there's much more to learn, I'm sure, and there are lots of activities unique to Cabo that I haven't done yet. Even though it's one of the top five tourist destinations in Mexico, it doesn't feel overwhelmed by tourists, like many other places I've been to. It definitely does not have that Miami Beach look defined by rows and rows of high rise beach condos. Cancun is like that too. Cabo certainly isn't anything snappy like Puerto Vallerta's arty Malecón. It seems tiny. There are no tall buildings in this little harbor town. However, I have heard that there are plenty of massive time share four and five-story condominiums north of town that run up the beach from Cabo to San Jose Del Cabo, the small town thirty-five miles north of Cabo. I was at one of those huge, first class timeshares eight years ago, called Dreams, so I have some recall of what's going on in that sector. A lot more mega-units of timeshares and resorts are under development these days. It's some kind of building boom, maybe because of the strong dollar, maybe because of the gush of Baby Boomers retiring, maybe because lots of people, for different reasons, just want to get out of the United States. Maybe because it's a great place to go if you want to get out of Dodge for a getaway. It's a place that you can visit on a regular basis because it's only a couple of hours out of the southern half of the States by air. A little longer for everyone in the States who needs snow tires in the winter.

<u>Whale watching - Friday, January 13</u>

I think Cabo got its international notoriety from Marlin fishing, but over the years it's become well known for other things. In my junkets up and down and around the marina district, I see lots of promotions for whale watching charter boats. I have heard tourists rave about the experience. I am sure it is totally cool for anyone who loves big animals. Cabo is definitely a special place for whale watching on this ecological marvel called Earth. I am well aware of the potential excitement I'd experience watching whales breach the surface close up. This takes place out in the open water of course, where there's a lot of rough water. And I would feel very bad about throwing up on a whale and maybe everyone around me in the boat. Still, it is tempting to go out on a windless day and get close up to these great leviathans of the deep. I know there are drugs that could help me by diminishing the certainty of my motion sickness. But to zero? Yes, maybe, I've been told, better living on the high seas through drugs. Which I should consider. I should get something to help me so I can see the whales. Maybe a Scopolamine Transdermal Patch. A friend uses those and she's thinks they work. They work for her anyway. I hate the idea of using one and then, once on the water, discovering that they don't work. It's just too risky for me.

This is the best time of the year to see whales, all kinds of them. They have migrated great distances to come here for mating, birthing, and nursing. Lots of them! I learned just this week that Gray whales are the ones seen most often. But there are other kinds like Humpbacks, Sperm whales, and Blue Whales. One of the whale promotion people on the marina told me that sometimes Orcas are seen too, but that's a rare sighting. Is an orca a whale?

Of course, it frequently goes by another name, Killer Whale. Must be a yes answer to my question. Dolphins are out there as well. That's no surprise to me. Did you know whales and dolphins are mammals? Did you know we are mammals? Did you know that I don't have a lot of faith in our educational system? To be sure that you knew that, I had to ask.

Save the dolphins! - Friday, January 13

I think Dolphins are in all the big bodies of water on the planet, not just the Sea of Cortez. Which reminds me, there is one place here where I wish there weren't any Dolphins: the big land based aquarium right on the southwest corner of Cabo's marina. Captive dolphins are in that aquarium and that upsets me very much. Three, maybe four of them. I won't even buy a ticket to see how horrible it must be for them. I just know it is. Logic right? A big ocean animal in a swimming pool is cruelty beyond words. I am also upset by the line of people waiting to get in for the show. If they weren't there, the dolphins wouldn't be there either! I wish people knew better. I wish they were there to protest rather than support that venture, a venture which I heard brings in millions of dollars of revenue to the city, so don't hold your breath for the shutdown. I wish the sightseers knew how horrible the life of these captured, contained, restricted, and abused dolphins must be. In the back of my head, I tell myself "Free the dolphins!" every time I pass that monstrous concrete dolphin prison. I also think of that Michael Jackson song in the movie, *Will You Be There*. I'll have to figure out some way I can contribute to putting an end to that abuse. Maybe I will while I'm here. I hate to see stuff like that. But that's just me. Maybe I should donate all of the proceeds of this book to an organization the fights that kind of abuse. Maybe you should tell all your friends to buy my book. Help me save the Dolphins!

Some great beaches - Saturday, January 14

There are other fun activities here too, besides whale watching. Like exploring other aquatic life. Leatherback turtles land on the beaches to lay eggs. That can be a thrill to experience. It's easier to see seals. I like seals. I've already seen a couple around the boats in the marina. Some are regulars and have been given names. Like Scooby. They are always fun to watch. Wherever fish are being cleaned, seals are nearby, often within a few feet. Scuba diving is popular too. So is snorkeling, which I prefer over scuba. And, some of the beaches are terrific for swimming, but not all of them. I think I will be exploring most of them in the next several weeks. I like beaches, especially tropical beaches.

I confess that I was in Cabo for a long weekend twenty-five years ago. I barely remember it, but I did learn that the Pacific beach is way too dangerous for frolicking in the waves. I recall that friend of mine from San Francisco visited Cabo two weeks before I did on that long-ago junket. He stayed at a hotel on the Pacific coast, which is over the hill and south of the marina. Though "stayed" might not be the best choice of words. He didn't last a day. Five hours after he landed at Cabo International, he flew back to San Francisco. Sad. Thirty minutes after he checked in, he ran out of his room in his bathing suit, excited about a romp in the ocean, which was very reachable from the "ocean view" sliding glass door of his room. Picture this: way too enthusiastic about a swim in the Pacific, he sprinted across the beach and high stepped it into the water. He made about thirty feet off shore before a wave slammed him, rolled him a few times in the hard sand bottom and broke his arm. End of story, except to say the break was so bad he had to return to the U.S. immediately for emergency surgery.

I've always known the Pacific beaches are simply too dangerous for swimming, but there are many fine beaches around Cabo. All of them are on the Sea of Cortez, not the Pacific side, but north of the famous Arch.

Medano Beach - Saturday, January 14

Since my arrival, I've heard a lot about a really cool beach in Cabo. It is basically right in the town, a couple of blocks from the marina. The beach is *Playa el Medano*, better known as simply Medano. It's an easy find because it is adjacent to Cabo's marina entrance but hidden by the shoreline buildings. I had to go to the very end of the marina walk, close to the harbor entrance, before I could see it. I actually stumbled on it a few days ago at the end of the marina on a walk, but today was the day I thought I'd take a walk to the harbor entrance and explore the beach.

Close to the entrance to the harbor, on the north side, at the very end of the marina walk, I dismounted my bike and pushed it at my side onto the fine, white sand. It was easy for me to see that Medano Beach runs north as a vast white crescent beach for maybe two miles. It is a postcard beach. I could see a section up ahead that was heavily populated with commercial beach umbrellas and a row of restaurants lining the beach, about a quarter of a mile in front of me. Towering over and the restaurants, set farther back, were countless condos, hotels and timeshares. Upon leaving the end of the marina sidewalk, I pushed my bike through the dry white sands about fifty yards to get the the wet, firmer sand at the water's edge. Much easier for a biker that way. I had to stop and take it all in. What an eyeful!

Medano is a beautiful beach with two miles of white sand delivered by the gentle lapping of the Gulf waters. I can see jet skis lined up fifty feet off-shore, tethered on buoys and ready for rental. The beach vendors, dressed in their white pajama-like uniforms and large straw sun hats are waiting to pounce. They are congregating in pockets up and down the beach, prepping for the incoming late morning flood of tourists. The Gulf waters are sparkling under the morning sun. There are two cruise ships anchored five hundred yards off the beach in the middle of all the sparkles. One is almost hidden behind the other. I can't see its name. The one that is front and center, parallel to the beach, is the *Norwegian Jewel,* which thoroughly dominates the view from the beach. It is huge, like an elephant in one's living room, you can't miss it. Your eye goes right to it, a manmade monstrous anomaly of steel and plastic anchored in a pristine setting in the midst of the bay backed by the endless horizon of the Gulf of California. The ship is probably twelve or thirteen stories of rooms to satisfy the travel whims of thousands of its passengers. I imagine hundreds of them, maybe a thousand, will spend the afternoon on this beach, making it difficult to see the sand underfoot. It will be that crowded. I won't be here then. I like beaches best in the morning, before they become over-populated by sun worshippers, beachcombers, beach walkers, and oglers.

Once I left the wet sand, I got a good work-out pushing my bike from the water's edge through the dense dry sand in the direction of solid footing. Up ahead, I could see there was a boardwalk that would get me up on the street that fronted the beach bars. To get there, I cut through dozens of rows of sparsely populated lounge chairs and umbrella tables, the empties, like the vendors, waiting for the hordes of tourists to show up. In two hours, there won't be an open seat in the house. Even without the onslaught of tourists on the beach, it was easy to feel the electricity and appeal of this tropical beach. I wish I liked spending more time on beaches more because this would be a great one to be on all day, every day.

After seventy yards of pushing my way through the sand, away from the water, and through the furniture, I got on solid ground, a boardwalk of uneven, worn wooden planks at first, then concrete. Moving up to the top of the walkway with umbrella-land behind me, I could see that the beach bars, with their inviting entrances, looking irresistible. Cabs and cars were already pulling up to the walkway to discharge their passengers. Valet parking was already in play. Handfuls of early arrival tourists were milling around in light tropical clothing and bathing wraps, mostly under a haberdashery of straw hats, floppy and not.

Four or five iconic beach bars ran in a neat row for a hundred yards, fronting the beach. I didn't go into any of them but I made a mental note to check them out sometime in the next week or two. Or maybe tomorrow. The two that looked most interesting to me are Mango and The Office, both advertised access to the beach and held the promise of delicious margaritas. Also, both had the busiest doorways. That perfect combo of access and margaritas for a beach bar was available to everyone, day after day. For me, it was time to head home and get to work having discovered that Medano Beach was more than a beach.

Margaritas, the beverage of choice - Saturday, January 14

There is no doubt that Cabo is a great tourist destination. Two mega-big boats with the cruise line companies are anchored off Medano right now. I saw one in the first week. I am expecting to see one every week I'm here, maybe two at a time. People are having fun everywhere or looking for it. It is easy to see that there is indeed a lot of drinking going on, especially margaritas, which might be the drink most often credited with causing people to do crazy things, mostly late at night, after I've gone to bed. Dancing on table tops is among the least crazy of crazy things. Shucking clothing is a little crazier, especially if one gets down to the bare minimum and sometimes to just the bare. I know margaritas were my fuel when I've done crazy things in bars, though that was decades ago. What! Am I that old that I describe my past in terms of decades? As for getting naked in public? I won't confess to that but I suppose everyone should try it once, and hope the experience doesn't include an arrest. Funny, aren't I?

Of course, what I hear about Spring Break here in March creates an expectation that I will be a witness to, what? Let's just say "wild things" is the phrase that comes to mind. Everything in excess. As for an overview of that impending annual monthlong event, one's imagination of the craziest things possible perfectly lines up with what actually happens here in Margaritaville. I guess I'll see if that's true when March shows up. At the moment, it seems pretty far off. That's a good thing but don't think that the margaritas ever stop flowing. They don't.

Caboholics Day - Sunday, January 15

There is a weeklong annual celebration that's coming up called Cabaholics Week. This one is the sixth annual celebration. It runs the week of February 11, just two weeks out there. I see it advertised on posters and in-house chalk boards. It appears to be a tourist promotion run with the support of many small businesses. It does have a charity element to it, though what exactly it funds is not clear to me. Yet. It is defined by a week of organized partying for people who refer to themselves as Caboholics. These are people who are dealing with an incurable disease, self-diagnosed and categorized as an addiction. What exactly is the addiction? It is an addiction to Cabo and all the great things it has to offer. I'm sure I'll learn more about this event, especially since I will unavoidably be a witness to some degree. It might be a big deal, hard to tell just from a few posters.

Taking a step back from the Margaritaville of the Baja, I can say that not everyone here has a margarita in hand. Or a piña colada, which is another favorite in the marina. It seems to me that most people are reasonable about their fun here and pay attention to their limits when it comes to drinking. It's not as if everywhere you go you see people stumbling drunk. The over forty crowd is probably reasonable, which seems to be in the majority while I've been here. A good share of this age group would be the cruise ship cruisers. In the past several days I've seen three different cruise ships anchored in the bay. I haven't been here very long at all so I don't know if that's normal or just a seasonal rush. Probably seasonal.

I see lots of people walking around the marina and in and out of the nooks and crannies of the small bars and shops tucked into the streets off the marina, of all ages. There are plenty of pedestrians holding a bottle in hand or some kinda drink in a go-cup. I have heard that the police here are very tolerant about stuff like that unless there's some kind of endangerment going on. Who knows what would qualify for that? All in all, I am guessing no more drinking takes place here than any other Mexican resort town. Which may be a lot! *Ay caramba*! As I said earlier, the serious partying occurs in March. Spring Break officially starts March 1, six weeks out there. The average age of tourists for that month will drop by twenty years, and Cabo will be overwhelmed by teenagers. I expect the observations that come with that experience will be in sharp contrast to what I've been witnessing this month. Sharp contrast. Super sharp. Mega sharp.

<u>Lunch with Olivia - Monday, January 16</u>

On one of my cruiser excursions away from the marina and into the neighborhoods of Cabo, which I guess you could call the *barrios*, I worked up an appetite. For Mexican food, of course. About fifteen blocks from the yachts, I pedaled up the gradual slope away from the harbor and passed a tiny shack, almost invisible in the shadows of the trees. It was quaint and even charming, if ramshackle can be charming. A rustic piece of weathered wood siding flipped up to create a cut out for a service window. I could barely see the interior had a set up that was a kitchen in a shack as I rode past it.

Two hours had passed since the lunch hour, a meal that I skipped thus far. This might be a perfect time to make up the loss and satisfy my appetite for dinner. I decided it was. Fifty feet past the kitchen, I turned around and dismounted right in front of the hut that just as easily could have been a dilapidated children's playhouse. I could easily see a few burners on a plank on its backwall, cooking stewpots of something. Next to them, a bigger stewpot of something else. A little old Mexican lady was working all three but stopped everything to greet me. She was about five feet tall and looked at least eighty years old. Could be a hundred. Could even be sixty. She was an ageless ancient. There were three white plastic tables off to the side of the hut, almost behind it and out of view from the street. Each had two or three white plastic chairs. Everything on the lot was in the diffused light of the shadows from the trees that towered over her kitchen. No customers in sight. Just me. No surprise because it was the middle of the afternoon, dead center for lunch and dinner.

I mustered up the courage to greet her in Spanish. Getting started never comes easy. The greeting part is easy enough but what comes after that is a guess. I asked what was on the menu through of course there was no menu. It was the only way I knew to inquire about my choices. They had to be relatively limited in a tiny operation like this. When I stepped up to the window, I could more easily see the pots on a makeshift stove top built over a jumble of wires and propane tanks. I recognized rice, of course and what looked like beans in the two smaller pots. I asked what was in the big pot. Or I thought I did with my limited vocabulary, aided by on-going gesticulations. On hindsight, I think I asked what is in the best pot. Close enough. She got me. She said it was *vegetales con pollo.* That's vegetables with chicken, but she spoke so fast with only a few teeth in her mouth, she had to say it four times before I understood. Mexicans are such a patient people. I learned some patience from them. I smiled and said *si, es bueno.* which was enough of a call to action that she started heaping food onto a plate meant for me. I could see that the choice of meat was chicken. I eat chicken once in a while though rarely touch pork or beef. She ladled huge portions out of those three pots. There was so much food going onto my plate that I started scanning for take home boxes. A fruitless effort. She carried my plate out the side door and placed it on one of the plastic tables. She withdrew napkins and plasticware from one of her apron pockets and set the table for me. Exceptional service for a meal that could feed three people. I was very sure she didn't have Coke Light and very sure she did have Coke. I ordered the latter and got a can set in front of me with a straw. It was perfect. I pulled up a chair and settled in with a big smile of approval on my face.

She and I were the only ones on the property. Just the two of us. I introduced myself, then got her name, which is Olivia, and gestured for her to take a seat at my table. She smiled, seemingly happy to join me even though I spoke very little Spanish. She sat and gave me her undivided attention. I opened with my standard schtick about learning Spanish and then proceeded to ask her questions about herself. She said she grew up in Mexico City but married a man from Cabo fifty years ago. I did the math. She could be my age, sixty-five. Maybe even younger than me. It's Mexico, that happens all the time. For fifty years they lived in the small but well-kept house in the next lot, she pointed to it, and raised six kids, three boys and three girls. I think she said one of her boys died in an accident of some sort. Her husband died two years, ago, she said, and I could see tears welling up in her eyes. Maybe for her lost son or her husband, or both. I said, *Lo siento* because I was truly sorry. They must have been very happy together. After two minutes of grief in silence, she smiled at me, indicating it was my turn to talk a little about myself by asking me if I was an American.

As it turned out, Olivia was so much fun to talk to. We figured things out even though she didn't know a single word in English. Not one. We laughed many times, exchanged a few serious stories, and pantomimed quite a bit. Ninety minutes later we both ran out of gas. It is tiring for almost anyone to communicate for very long without sharing a common language. It was time for me to go. I don't remember when I finished the last bite of that huge lunch, but I wasn't surprised that there wasn't a morsel left on my plate. The food was very good and I was very hungry. *Muy deliciosa!* Mexicans have a word for a country meal, which is one that includes rice, beans, vegetables, and a protein. It's called *comida corrida,* which is slang, I guess. Here is the full translation of those two words: Some kind of traditional Mexican meal of meat, rice, and beans, served in large portions so big that they couldn't possibly be eaten in one sitting, but all of it gets eaten. Funny, aren't I? I paid her ten bucks for everything though the bill was only four bucks. The conversation was priceless. We were both very happy about the time we spent together. I promised I'd come back sometime and then rode off to somewhere else.

Mango bar on Medano beach - Tuesday, January 17

I walked into Mango today after locking my bike to a bike rack out front. I came up behind Mango yesterday from the beach and made a mental note to check it out. That's what I'm doing, checking it out. I was dressed like everyone else in the neighborhood. Nothing fancy here and Mango was no different: standard attire was shorts, t-shirt, and sunglasses. I *hola*-ed the hostess, said I'm going to the bar and didn't slow down. As my eyes adjusted to the low level of light that comes with most tiki bars. The dining area was on my left. It was empty, which is to be expected mid-afternoon on a weekday. On my right, was the kitchen. It preceded a smaller dining area, which also had a lot of open tables. Plenty of people were in Mango. All the tables along the railing were taken and people stood two-deep wherever they could to get a view of Mango beach tables ten feet below. Everybody likes a view of the beach.

All the people near the railing had a view of the beach, of course, but they weren't looking at the water. They were gawking at the entertainment. As I approached the railing I noticed that a lot of clothing had been substituted with bathing suits. And why not, it is a beach bar. I could hear, but not yet see the main event. It was audible because there is an emcee blasting on outdoor speakers. His voice is big and loud and friendly. And full of energy. Like the emcee at stripper bars, if I remember correctly from thirty years ago with clients. What exactly he was saying, I'm not sure, something about "let's do it, ladies." I guess I was about to find out what "it" was. I moved in and took a position behind a couple about my age standing at the railing, which was a good perch overlooking the scene below. I am six-three so I could easily find an unobstructed sight line. Everyone is looking at the people on a small slightly elevated stage in the center of Mango beach tables. I acquire the same view and now know what "it" meant.

It, the it of it all at Mango, is a game of Musical Chairs with six scantily clad women, which is the way it is with bikinis. The women were gyrating in a small oval circling five chairs. I'm guessing they started with more participants and more chairs. I walked in halfway through the game. You know the game but it does have a different element to it. I can see a touristy guy sitting back in a chair at one end of the oval. As each babe passes in front of him they do a little shake and a twerk or two or three for him. How he got that seat, I don't know, but clearly, he was having fun too. Maybe he gets the winner. It is definitely a younger crowd at the beach tables. Fogies upstairs, please, at the railings. Below, on the sand, the crowd is an even mix of women in bikinis and guys in bathing shorts, some with tank tops, some without. A typical beach crowd, youthful, yelling, and grooving to the entertainment. I am sure the babes on stage are tourist volunteers, drawn from the audience. And I am sure they are having fun. And I am sure they are drunk. And, I confess, I am having fun, like everyone else, watching these women cavort on stage. Can I call them babes? Yes I can, I decided, once in a while, as long as it doesn't sound creepy.

As the game goes, the emcee suddenly stops the music and the scramble for an open chair was on. That created a crazy jumble of babes and, of course, one got aced out. She was wildly cheered for her effort, took a bow, and danced off the platform stage in a way that girls I knew in college never danced. She was out of the competition. For what? Probably free bar drinks. Just what the winner would need. But that's my sarcasm at work. Oh, the music picks up again, but the women contestants remain seated. The emcee is a chatterbox. Killing time makes sense; it keeps the crowd at Mango engaged longer for more drinks. He is waving an open bottle in the air, undoubtedly tequila, while instructing the babes about something I can't exactly hear. Oh, I see. The babe sitting at end of the five remaining chairs just tilted her head back with her mouth open. The emcee is behind her and pouring tequila from the bottle into her mouth, presumably filling it up. He then works his way down the line and does the same to the other four contestants After the fifth babe got her fix, he continues the show with more chatting, more of his schtick. I'm guessing he's stalling this time to let the tequila kick in before the next round of music begins. If this is the usual practice between each round to the winner's chair, I am guessing (a lot of guesswork here) the final two babes won't even be able to find the last chair, let alone sit in it. Drinking games. Life is crazy at that age. The kids were all having fun.

I don't know whether to laugh or cry, but truth be told, it sure is funny to watch these insane babes playing this insane game only wearing tiny bikinis. In a way, I am thinking it is almost obscene, but I'm trying to remain open-minded and say it's just kids having fun. It almost makes me wish I were twenty again. Almost. At the end of the Musical Chairs game, the winner is cheered and gets some kind of wrist band for first place, which I learned from the person standing next to me is free drinks for the rest of the day, which is just what she needs. It is a youthful crowd and they're all having fun. Good for them. That's what vacations are for. I shouldn't be judgmental. If I were twenty again I'd probably be right in the middle of all that craziness. But since I am sixty-five, it was interesting to see once, as part of the Cabo experience, but now it was time to move on to other things that interest me more.

When I walked out, I left a big tip and two empty beer bottles behind me. It is not likely that I'll make a habit of coming back for the daily afternoon craziness at Mango. I'm guessing (a lot guessing, I know) that Musical Chairs is a preview of what's to come in March, but dialed up even more. That will take crazy to new heights. It might be fun to see that. My rationale is that I never did the Spring Break thing that college kids do so it's okay to see what I missed. I had to work my way through college and my boss didn't give me time off for Spring Break. In my memories, Spring Break in my college days was more like the 1960 movie *Where the Boys Are* starring George Hamilton, Yvette Mimieux, and Paula Prentiss. Pretty tame stuff in that movie compared to now.

Lights out! - Tuesday, January 17

Within minutes of walking into my condo on the day of my arrival, I was concerned about my bedroom curtains: they didn't fit the two windows very well. This meant I didn't get the level of privacy

I cherish, especially while living on the ground floor. That was almost two weeks ago. I am a privacy freak, always have been. It's not a modesty thing with me. No, it's more like a need to feel that I am completely shutting out the world from penetrating my living space. More importantly, I like a very dark bedroom for a good sleep anytime of the day. I do not want to get up with the sun.

I took a close look at the three windows, the two in my bedroom and the one in my living room. The one in the living room didn't need black out curtains but the two bedroom windows did. Did I feel like buying curtains for Ale? No. Did I feel like spending any money at all to satisfy my interests in privacy and sleep for thirty days? Not really. Well, maybe a little if that's what it took. But I had to do something. I had some ideas but I decided first to ride the cruiser to Walmart, walk up and down the non-food aisles, get some ideas, then examine my options. The solution will reveal itself when the time is right, which is one of my mantras. After thirty minutes of time spent in the product-packed aisles of Walmart, I purchased what I needed and went home satisfied that the solution did indeed reveal itself.

Just over two hours later, I finished covering my three windows to my satisfaction. I stood back and admired my work. It reflected practical, effective solutions at very little cost. The total expense for my home improvement project was just under twelve dollars for all three windows. That amount includes a big silver roll of duct tape, which is a requirement for nearly every home improvement project. No surprise there. The modest effort that went into the living room fix took up about ten minutes of my time. The two bedroom windows were each about the same, maybe a couple of minutes more. I did good.

For the living room, I purchased a plastic eight by ten foot, sky blue tarp, the kind you might tie over the back of your pick-up truck to keep things under it dry and prevent them from flying out of the truck. That kind. I kept the original half-fold in it because it fit the glass-louvered window perfectly that way, which is to say it exceeded the boundaries of the window by nearly a foot both sides and the bottom. I hung it on the curtain rod that was already in use, which meant covering up the current curtains. That part was easy because the tarp had grommeted holes running along its edges. I used five fist-sized loops of thick twine to run through the grommets and around the curtain rod. The design gave the window full coverage and it game me easy access to the handle for adjusting the louvered glass panels. An extra benefit is that when sun light hit it, it became a beautifully bright sky-blue color which created a slightly diffused blue tint into the room. It was a happy light. I was happy.

I didn't use a tarp in the two bedroom windows. I wanted total black-out for them. I got exactly that by covering each window with a couple of carefully spaced, super-sized, black plastic garbage bags. Hefty was nifty for this job. The duct tape secured the plastic bags in place on the window frame inset. Mission accomplished, and that's no George W. Bush baloney. I'm done with that household project. I might even leave all that stuff up for Ale when I leave. If she doesn't like it, and it's highly likely she won't, she can clear all three windows in less than five minutes. Of course, she'll remove that stuff, it is ugly. For me, practical overrules ugly. At least in this case. That said, maybe my handiwork will allow her to infer that her curtains aren't really adequate for privacy freaks.

More Spanish, please! - Wednesday, January 18

Every night before I turn out my bedside light to go to sleep I review two pages in *Spanish for Gringos*. Because it's the last thing I read, I think it will stick in my head more. I'm not sure of that, but maybe that helps. I've been spending a lot of time with this book. I talk to myself when I read through some of the words. I write stuff down. I go back to the beginning all the time and repeat pages. Some are getting that worn look. I jump around a lot. I try to memorize words listed on the vocabulary pages and make sense out of Spanish sentences on other pages. I take this book with me wherever I go.

I also just started an online application for learning Spanish. It's called Duolingo. This software describes itself as bite-sized lessons. And it's free. I am using that to help me learn Spanish as well. I probably spend thirty to forty minutes a day with it. I like it. It's short, easy, and non-judgmental. The Duolingo software sends me a daily reminder to do it. And as long as I keep it up I advance on the Duolingo ladder to fluency. That's helpful. I see that reminder every time I check my email. Nagging works on me.

Sometimes I sit in front of the TV watching a soap opera in Spanish. I heard this is a good way to learn Spanish too. I don't understand a single thing anybody is saying unless it's hello, thank you, and goodbye. It's almost annoying but a lot of people tell me this is a good way. The women are really hot in these soaps, so even if I don't understand what is being said, I can enjoy watching the shows. Hmmm, maybe that's how it works, kind of an accidental learning experience while ogling. My biggest problem is that everyone in the soap speaks so fast I can't even pick out one word. It's all a blur to me. I am constantly asking myself if people are serious in telling me I should do this. Today, I listened intensely to a half hour of one soap. I kept thinking that several weeks might pass before I even pick up a word or two. But that's okay I tell myself, because, like I said the women are hot and eventually I will understand some of the things being said. More to the point, I also believe that one day I will go from zero comprehension to total comprehension. Yes, I suddenly will be able to understand what everyone is saying. That will be the tipping point.

I will continue to watch TV for at least thirty minutes a day because I think it is good for my ear to hear what Spanish sounds like. You know, the cadence, the pronunciation, syllable emphasis, and those rolling r's, you know, all that stuff. I have to add that I do like the commercials however, because they use simple words and often put them on the screen so I can see them. I guess at this point, I'd rather watch an hour of commercials than an hour of soaps even though the women aren't hot in the commercials.

I think I'm off to a good start, but I know I can do better. I am not truly immersing myself in the Spanish speaking world. Not with the intensity or exclusivity I originally envisioned. However, I've also concluded that it would be impossible to do anything if I actually did it that way. It's not realistic. Case in point, sometimes English-speaking Mexicans have to explain things to me in English so I can learn the Spanish equivalent. I do everything I can to stick to Spanish, especially when interacting with a Mexican. And, of course, if the Mexican does not speak English, then there's no choice for me. In that case, Spanish is it. Maybe that's the only aspect of this adventure that I can truly call immersion - those personal moments of person to person communication in Spanish. This interaction requires so much concentration that, sometimes, I think my head is going to explode. It's complicated because there are times when I am forced to speak English. If a tourist says something to me I can't turn and run away, can I? Hmm, maybe I should do that, especially if I think my head is about to explode.

So, here's where things are at the moment. I've got my book, an online course, TV and and billboards. Newspapers, too. All this is not enough. I know what's missing. I need more interaction with the locals. I need conversations that will take me beyond hello, a beer please, and how are you. Way beyond that. I need to get into real conversations in Spanish. I'm not sure how to do that. Maybe some ideas will come to me tomorrow. The solution will reveal itself when the time is right. The solution will reveal itself when the time is right. The solution will reveal itself when the time is right. My mantra.

A list of things I've learned as a bicyclist - Wednesday, January 18

When crossing a street, always look both ways, and then do it again, especially look the wrong way on a one-way street. At night, come to a stop before crossing a street. Look extra carefully for cars because not everyone has their headlights on.

Do not assume that drivers see you. Or even care about you if they do see you.

Just because you have the right of way, don't assume a driver will give its to you. Thinking that you have the right of way is not the right way to think.

Get as far away from a bus lane as possible when a bus is coming up behind you. Some bus drivers like to play King of the Road.

Stop signs and stop lights are not something that every driver pays attention to. Stop signs are a total waste of government money; no one stops, everyone rolls, and some accelerate. Maybe stop signs are invisible to Mexican drivers, seems that way at times.

Even if you think you see all the cars around you and you feel safe to cross a street, assume that a motorcyclist will come out of nowhere, maybe just to give you a good scare. There's no explanation for this.

Don't get bothered over the fact that a metal post holding up a traffic sign is sometimes placed in the middle of the sidewalk. Just step around it, but be careful because drivers like to knock down these signs for some reason.

When the stop light turns yellow at a busy intersection, expect to see at least five cars make it through, maybe as many as ten. If there are more cars wanting to get through the intersection, assume this is true for a red light too.

Thorns aren't the only hazard on the surfaces of the roads and sidewalks. I am constantly dodging holes and cut-outs in the sidewalk pavement. Many of these were big enough to accommodate a person's foot and a few were two or three times that size. It was never obvious why they were there and, judging from the litter in them, I'm guessing that many of them had become permanent features of the walkway. The larger holes could easily damage my rim, enough to put the cruiser out of action. The primary problem with the roads, besides the traffic, was the constant presence of random debris along with some substantial obstacles, some that were big enough to annoy a bus driver but not stop him. I think they thought of me as an obstacle.

Some random observations - Wednesday, January 18

You can trust the food in local restaurants, but don't trust the water.

Never pet a Mexican street dog, even it is on a leash. Even if it has a muzzle because it can still scare the shite out of you.

Mexicans are really nice. They will always smile, especially if you smile first. It is good to smile a lot. It makes everyone feel better.

It is generally not good to leave your cell phone on a restaurant table or bar after you walk out, but in Cabo, it will still be on the table an hour later or the manager will be holding it awaiting your return.

If you are victim of a theft, the police are really nice and will treat you with respect. But be patient because you shouldn't expect them to help you unless you speak fluent Spanish and plan on staying in Mexico for at least six months. Most police do not speak English. Justice moves slowly. And even with that, do not count on the outcome you want. It is very hard for tourist-victims to get justice. No one knows this better than thieves. Fortunately, thieves in Cabo are scarce.

A lot of the food packaging looks exactly as it did when you were a kid. Advances in packaging made in the States haven't made their way down here. For example, you will need a knife or a scissors to open the chip bags. A hedge clippers would be even better.

A lot of foods, like soup, tuna, and beans come in cans with pop tops with a ring pull, just like tennis ball cans in the sixties. Only NFL players have the strength to open these. Expect to cut yourself where you least expect to in any effort to open a pop top can, especially if you are using a screw driver or hammer to assist.

If you are preparing food yourself, and you have a can of something, you must have access to a manual "turn the handle" can opener. Don't bother looking for electric can openers. For a different reason every time, the manual openers don't always work, but it sure feels good to get lucky if you can open a can with one.

Never drink water that is not bottled. Tap water is especially risky business. The best Mexican water is called Tequila. Ask for it at every meal. Best when taken in a shot glass with no ice. Be sure to drink lots of water.

Tip no less than twenty percent. It will help compensate the hard-working servers who get no tips from too many stingy tourists. I saw a table of eight American cruise ship ladies pay for a two-hour lunch. I also saw the tip they left, about a buck. The servers shook their heads in disappointment. So did I.

If you missed it above, never pet a Mexican dog. I think tourists smell funny to them, but funny good. Gringo must be a flavor to them. Maybe something like a hot dog or nice chunk of raw beef. Maybe even gringo fingers look like hot dogs to them. That would explain a lot of bites.

If you take the regularly scheduled express bus from the airport to town instead of a cab, the cost differential will pay for your airline ticket home. A shuttle van will get you to town cheaper but it's cramped and makes many stops. A local bus will get you to town even cheaper. Unfortunately, on the local it will seem to you that you can walk into town faster than the bus will get you there. It's a very long walk. It will feel like half a day, so don't walk. Take the express bus.

Ask any Mexican for help if you are lost or can't find the building you are looking for. They will always happily help you, maybe even lead you right to your destination. No one could be nicer.

Whenever you can, drop ten pesos into a beggar's cup. It's only fifty cents to you but it's a lot to them. It will make them happy. It will make you happy too.

A lot of cars down here have a security system we are all familiar with, you know, that one that causes the car's horn to start honking if the car is interfered with... by thieves? By the wind? A hard landing by a ladybug? Tremors from an earthquake in Oklahoma? They all can do that, I suppose. Well whatever it is, you recall how annoying that repetitive tin horn honking is, which is why U.S. cars are now programmed to automatically stop the honking after five honks. That's pretty honking good, and thank goodness I say to that. But, it's different here in Mexico. Here, the car is programmed to stop honking when the car battery dies. That really honks me off. Especially in the middle of the night.

CHAPTER THREE

Week 3

<u>One benefit of the Coromuel complex - Thursday, January 19</u>

Within the condo complex of Coromuel, which is relatively small, there are two laundromats close to the parking lot, inside the security gate. That's right, two! They are next to each other. Go figure. No, I don't know why. One look and it's easy to conclude different management. When I first arrived, I picked up my condo keys from the *señora* in the one named Ola. I don't know anything about the other laundromat, not even its name, though I've walked past it a dozen times. Maybe two weeks sounds like a long time not to do laundry, but in case you are wondering, I washed and rinsed most of my clothes last week in my sink. It was easy because I have very few clothes. But so what? I don't really know why I elected to do it myself with two laundromats across the parking lot. On hindsight, totally silly of me. Weirdly frugal. Or too lazy to walk across the lot and hand 'em over to the *señora*. I can't remember her name. I should know from the first night here but I was so tired I don't remember what she said. I also should know her name because she was so nice that first time I met her. I like her.

When I first laid eyes on the interior of Ola, it was easy to see that *señora* works very hard. Bags of laundry were everywhere on the floor, reminding me of some episode of Hoarders. I think her place is open all day and into the early night six days a week. It has to be, I'm sure, because that's the only way she could get all those clothes laundered.

This morning I gave s*eñora* a fresh plastic trash bag of all my clothes, the small amount I have, except two hanging shirts and the clothes on my back. She said they would be ready at the end of the day, *el final del dia*.

The day passed quickly. I picked them up at four. I had to make sure they were mine, so I pulled them out of the bag in front of the señora, and *voilà!* This is a French word I like to use to call attention to something accomplished; one of my favorite words. The Spanish counterpart might be olé. The clothes were mine. And they were clean, had a fresh scent once again, and folded beautifully. She charged me two dollars for that clean folded load. And then she surprised me, as well, by handing me eighty dollars in a mix of pesos and US dollars that she found in one of the pockets of my shorts. I often leave coins in my pockets, but not dollars. Never eighty dollars! I wouldn't have missed it, because I didn't. Very sweet of her. I asked her name. She said she goes by Juanie. I thanked Juanie profusely and slipped her an extra five dollars for her honesty. By the time I returned to my condo, I was feeling bad that I only duked her five bucks. It would be too embarrassing, probably for both of us, if I walked back and gave her some more money. Maybe I could come up with some other way to repay her honesty more appropriately.

Flowers in the laundromat - Friday, January 20

I woke up this morning fairly early, as usual. Generally, I am not a late sleeper, but it's something I'd like to try at some point. Today wasn't the day. I woke up with an answer to last night's burning question of what nice thing can I do to pay Juanie a little extra for returning eighty bucks to me. The answer I came up with in my sleep, where else, was to get her some fresh flowers, a nice little bouquet. Maybe in a nice little vase.

By ten in the morning, which is when stores open here, I found Baja Flowers. I had googled it and wrote down the address. It was the nearest florist. I took off on my bike to find the store, happy that it was somewhere in my neighborhood, in the real part of town, not the tourist part. I got a picture of its location from Google maps and pasted it into my head, so I had a pretty good idea where I was going. This was a smart thing to do. From experience, I have learned that in foreign countries finding a store or a specific address isn't always as easy as one expects. I was well into this reality twenty minutes later when I could not find the store that was only ten minutes from my condo. So much for my memory. Like I said, I had a good picture of the street location in my head, though apparently not good enough. I knew I was close. I said to myself that it couldn't possibly be farther than eight blocks. Believe it or not, I had a Plan B. Before I left my condo, I wrote that address down on a small slip of paper, which was in my pocket. Therein in lies the help I needed to find my future florist. No, I didn't have my cell phone because I am not using my cell phone in Mexico. Here, I am forced to do some things the old-fashioned way.

Having an address in hand can be a good thing. It works particularly well when street numbers are on buildings and street names are on corner signs. But, when abroad I've experienced plenty of times a building isn't marked with a street number. This is especially annoying in the States where you wouldn't expect that to be a problem. That wasn't my problem. My problem was finding the names of the streets, not the house numbers. There is huge lack of street signs in the neighborhood. Hard as it is to believe, street corners rarely had any signage. I did see a street name once in a while, painted on a building that was close to a corner of an intersection, but those instances were too far and few between. Finally, which wasn't a long time after I had been looking on my own, I asked someone on a sidewalk if they could point me in the right direction of the address I was searching for. They did. Baja Flowers is only three blocks away, on a corner of an intersection that was absent of any and all street names. Now I know. In the future, I'll get a better Google map in my head.

I walked into Baja Flowers and right away knew I was in a good store. It had a great look and gave off a good vibe. Very tasteful stuff on display, first class. The man at the service desk greeted me with my first step into his store. In English. He introduced himself as the owner. I tried my Spanish, of course, made a little headway, but I am glad he could help me along the Spanish road with his English. I ordered a bouquet of mixed flowers to go. When asked, I told him that I didn't want to spend too much. I asked him if two hundred pesos, which is ten dollars, would get me much. Oh, and I wanted them in a glass vase. I didn't think ten bucks would get me anything, not even a glass vase by itself, but that was my starting point since I didn't have a clue what kind of prices I was getting into. To my surprise, he said okay and would see what he could do. He told me to come back in twenty minutes. An invitation to come back was a good thing. I was expecting him to say, "Don't come back you cheap gringo!" I thanked him, left the store, and got on my bike to kill twenty minutes of suspense by exploring the neighborhood. While riding, I reflected with happiness how nice Mexicans are. This man was so kind, patient with my Spanish, and willing to work with me on my request.

Twenty-five minutes later I walked out of Baja Flowers with a clear glass vase full of water and, more importantly, full of a gorgeous mix of beautiful cut garden flowers in an extremely tasteful selection and arrangement. All for ten bucks. I was stunned. I was effusive in my gratitude on my way out, of course. Maybe it was charity. I can't explain it. In the States, the arrangement would cost at least a hundred bucks, maybe more. Juanie will be really surprised and, I imagine girlishly happy over my gesture. I called that right, *amigo*. Fifteen minutes later, she was.

The Arch is Cabo's icon - Saturday, January 21

The Arch is the most famous rock of a giant peninsula of rocks spun out of the mini-mountains that shelter the harbor. It is known worldwide as the icon of Cabo San Lucas. I know of its popularity because I see more tourists pose with The Arch in the background than with any other background scenery. It's on posters too, of course, and a zillion postcards. No surprise there. The string of baked brown hills leading to the Arch are recognizable in their own right, like a series of milk chocolate kisses. That's how I see them. People don't seem to care that The Arch is not visible from downtown Cabo. Everyone knows it's there, hidden a bit. The Arch and The Arch rocks are synonymous with Cabo San Lucas and beyond that, no one really needs to know anything else. Most don't want to. Most don't know that the Spanish name is El Arco, which sounds an awful lot like Spanglish to me. For all its fame and Cabo glory, three weeks have almost passed and I have yet to see it close up. I should, but when?

I shouldn't delay this adventure so I can put an end to the comment laced with disbelief, "What? You haven't been to The Arch yet?" Vendors on the wharf are starting to say this to me too, not just tourists I chat with here and there. Hey, I've been told that it doesn't take much to see it. I just jump in a water taxi for ten bucks, with or without a glass bottom, and take a spin out there. Ten bucks roundtrip. It is one of those natural wonders that people don't forget. Ever. This is also one of those natural wonders that people don't forget. The arch is so imprinted with Cabo imagery that a photograph of almost any other arch in the world will trigger the response, "Is that Cabo San Lucas." I think some Americans think the *Arc de Triomphe* is El Arco. It wouldn't surprise me. Geography is not a strong suit for ninety-nine percent of American high school graduates. I think that number is rising, but that's irrelevant.

The Arch, a towering brown arid craggy rock with a quadruple barn-size hole in it, is the geological divide for the Pacific Ocean and the Sea of Cortez, the latter also known as The Gulf of California. By the way, both names for this body of water appeared on sixteenth century Spanish maps, so they're acceptably interchangeable. There's a crazy side of me that says that The Arch is the divide between two possibilities. One, there is a very high possibility, almost guaranteed, that I will throw up on a boat on the Pacific side. Two, I'll probably throw up on a boat on the Gulf side. Sunset cruises around the point into the Pacific are popular promotions around the marina. That doesn't interest me at all. If I go to The Arch, and I will at some point, I think I'll take a water taxi for a glance at it and then ask to be dropped on a beach out there first chance I get, get onto the sand, get my land legs back, and hang out at the beach for an hour maybe three before taking another taxi back into the marina. The taxis go straight to The Arch beaches and back without lingering in big water. For the most part, I can see from shore that the ride is smooth because the open water is fairly sheltered by the milk chocolate kisses that lead out to The Arch.

The two beaches at The Arch - Saturday, January 21

I know from promotion materials that there are two beaches worth visiting at The Arch: Lover's Beach, which is *Playa del Amour* in Spanish, and Divorce Beach, which is *Playa Divorcio*. Maybe that's Spanglish, I don't know for sure. Someone must have given a lot of thought to naming these two beaches. Absolutely suitable names, I am told. I hear, mostly from marina vendors, that Lovers' Beach is nicer than Divorce Beach. Everyone prefers the former to the latter. I could have guessed that. Love is always preferable to divorce. First comes love then comes divorce, is how it usually goes. Eventually.

Lover's Beach is on the gulf side, so its waters are calmer. You can go into the water there, swim and snorkel all you want, which is what I learned in snippets of Spanish from the vendors. Divorce Beach, not surprisingly, is a rocky, cold, unforgiving beach, that can be dangerous, even treacherous. Yes, treacherous! It is perfectly named. It is on the Pacific side. That means it's ocean water, ocean waves, and ocean currents. Leaping into those waters could mean death. Signs are posted everywhere telling people to stay out of the water, so I am told. I am also told that you can easily walk from one to the other. First Lover's, then Divorce, then Lover's again. Sounds about right. I'll get around to trying it, maybe just Lover's. Divorce doesn't sound like it has much to offer me.

Guadalupana - Sunday, January 22

A few doors north of the Fairfield Inn is the restaurant Guadalupana. It is pretty close to being across the street from my complex. Since it is the closest bar to me, I was hoping it could be a convenient place for me for a night cap once in a while, if turns out to be that kind of place. Or a convenient place to grab a meal, if it turns out to be that kind of place. So far, I'm feeling neither opportunity is likely. But I haven't been inside, yet.

Guadalupana is between an office building of financial services, a.k.a. loan sharks and a slow-going, heavy duty, concrete construction site. Not a good place to be. It gets lost in the shuffle. It is a fairly nondescript restaurant in a fairly nondescript building. The exterior walls are a rusty terra cotta color which supports some lime green shutters for the two windows flanking the double door. The shutters are always closed, maybe not even shuttering real windows. Two big green rectangles on a rust brown wall. It's lost as a baloney lettuce sandwich between two slices of brown bread. Worse for the owner, it is a location that is easy to miss. And it has an entrance on a sidewalk that is absent of any pedestrian traffic. North of it is a no man's land of mostly highway and desert. The Fairfield Inn, an outer edge hotel, is a hundred yards to the south, towards town. Even on my cruiser riding up the sidewalk, when approaching Guadalupana from town, it is easy to not see it. This must be a truly local restaurant whose survival is dependent on Mexican customers, not gringos.

Overall, it has the hidey-hole look to it. It has an arched double door entrance. These two doors are always open for business in the late afternoon until early evening, which is how I know it's a restaurant. I can see right in when the cruiser goes by on my way home at night. The inside is lit up like a gymnasium. The open doors expose a very big open room with a high ceiling and filled with furniture, maybe five rows of tables running about six deep. I don't recall ever seeing more than two tables occupied. On my rides, I occasionally get a glimpse of one or two men inside, always on their feet, usually at the bar. They must work there, same two guys every time I go by. I think. One is always behind the bar. The bartender, of course.

Let's just say, the restaurant is not compelling. It makes me think it is a restaurant that has seen better days. But it must be in play, the doors are open and it's lit up every night. Too bad it's not more lively. I was hoping it turned out to be one of those hidden gems that a tourist, such as me, stumbles into and, in doing so, makes a great discovery. I can't really imagine tourists stumbling into this place, they are nowhere to be seen on the block, though plenty of them stumble around town. It must be a choice of the locals, which to me, means it might be real good food. It might be one of those secrets intentionally kept from gringos so it doesn't lose its authenticity. Maybe that! Still, where are the customers? I'll investigate later in the week. Or next week. Or never. But not tonight.

Cabo Cantina - Sunday, January 22

It's Sunday, well into my third week here, and another perfect day of blue skies, sunshine, and the promise of warm temperatures throughout the day. A promise always kept. Besides being a beautiful Sunday, it's an important Sunday, to me. Today the Green Bay Packers, the team I've rooted for forever, is playing in the NFL conference championship game against the Atlanta Falcons. The Falcons are a slight favorite but the Pack has had some great wins this year as the underdog. Aaron Rogers is always a threat when his receivers are healthy. They are. It should be a good game. I don't know anything about the Falcons, but their reputation says they're really good this year as a well-balanced team.

I'm cruising up the main street that runs north and bisects the heart of the marina. It's fifteen minutes before game time and I need a bar with a big TV screen. And a bar stool. The former is easy to find in the marina district. It's that latter that will be tough at this critical time period.

The street is one block off the marine sidewalk so it has a lot of businesses running along both sides but a thinner game crowd than the bars located right on the marina. Fine by me. I don't particularly like crowds, especially noisy, drunk crowds. Besides, better odds for a bar stool for me in town than on the marina. I am returning from my daily ride to the mouth of the harbor, coming around the bend when I spot an open-air tiki bar on my right. It's not a real big place, not nearly as big as the tiki bars on the marina. I see the screens right away and an especially big one inside the confines of the bar for bar stool viewing. It is a chummy, warm, inviting bar and, I can quickly see it hosts a mix of fans for both teams. Lots of team jerseys and caps, even a foam rubber cheese hat on one Packer crazed customer. A cheesehead from Wisconsin, of course, and diehard Packer fan. That makes two for sure.

I might be in luck. I spy two open bar stools in front of the big screen, both with empty glasses. Recently vacated, no doubt, very recently. It is the perfect seat in a place that will be particularly lively all afternoon. I hastily dismount, yank the cruiser up the curb, kick the kickstand, ignore locking it up, and dash for one of those two open bar stools. I'm a running back now, zig-zagging my way past tables of impeding fans to get to one of those bar stools before someone else does. I need a touchdown to win the game. A few more feet. Touchdown! I claim one of the stools with my Seattle Seahawks cap that someone gave me last week and order a Pacifico before returning to my bike to secure it to the nearest lamp post. I got lucky, really lucky. I am off to a good start as far as plans go. I like the place from the get-go.

The tiki bar is the Cabo Cantina. I am very happy with my spot at the bar. As I reclaim my chosen seat, I have a quick exchange with the very engaging bartender, name of Jorge. He is a tall, muscular Mexican, close to my height, a lot younger than me, and, unlike me, a little chunky. I can see in a minute that he is out-going and clearly good-natured, speedy, and a master at what he does. I like him right away. It will be a fun way to spend an afternoon.

Moments later, the empty bar stool next to me is claimed by an American man. He's about my age, maybe a little younger. After he orders a Tecate, I introduce myself to him. Camaraderie at the bar is infectious, even feverish for the game. His name is KT. He says like the name of his beer Tecate. I didn't get that at first. As I understood it, his name should be TK, like the order of consonants in Tecate. I ask him to clarify my confusion. He enlightens me. The back half of the beer's name is pronounced kah-tay, close enough to how Mexican pronounce the two letters of his name KT. That explains it, but the only way I'll remember it now is to remember his initials are in alphabetical order, because the Tecate thing doesn't work for me. Maybe because my Spanish isn't quite there.

KT and I are into the game. We're both Packer fans. It's a good game but not looking great for the Pack. KT and I swap some background at commercial breaks. He is a full time real estate guy in Cabo, works with his wife, who is also an agent. He has been here for twenty years and, clearly, he knows his stuff, though not at all fluent in Spanish. He's easygoing and a smart guy. He lives ten miles north of town on a beach property that looks down the shore toward downtown Cabo. He shows me the view of Cabo on his iPhone and it is spectacular. From his living room window, his view also includes the Arch, which is unseeable from downtown Cabo. Too bad for downtown residents, he says. KT parks his car in some lot nearby and then gets on his motorized skate board to get around town. How cool is that! I saw him place it under his feet when he took a seat at the bar stool. It's funny, my reaction was this is a big kid for skateboarding. Anyway, for all kinds of reasons he is an interesting guy, not just because he's the oldest skateboarder in the world. We swap cards and agree to stay in touch. I'd like that. I don't have to speak Spanish all the time. I'm a semi-immersionist.

I'm into my third Pacifico. It's not looking good for the Packers. Not good at all. Right now, it's more fun to watch Jorge. He is a whirlwind of service and is talking to everyone and no one at the same time. Even so, he allowed me the time to say I'm learning Spanish and he found time of his own to swap a few Spanish words with me. I know I will come back to Cabo Cantina again, when it isn't so busy, for a Pacifico and to say hi to Jorge. Maybe talk a bit with him if the place isn't too busy. His English is really good and that can work in my favor as a Spanish student.

After the game, I ride back to my condo, disappointed that the Packers had their ass handed to them. They were never in the game. They lost 44-21 to a powerful, well-balanced team. The Falcons were unstoppable. They deserved to win. I'm guessing they will be this season's Super Bowl champions. I don't see how anyone can stop them. Maybe Tom Brady can, but that would take a miracle after witnessing the Packers go down like kittens under a steamroller. Nice visual.

What! No, not the police! - Monday, January 23

This is about my first encounter with Mexican police. Two marina cops. They cornered me in the marina this afternoon. I have been riding up and down the marina sidewalk for over two weeks, every day, very carefully, and considerately of pedestrian tourists, of course. If I can't ride pretty much without a zig or a zag, that means too many tourists are in the way. In that case, I walk the cruiser. I am always polite. This is not my country; politeness is important. And then it happened, very suddenly.

I mildly protest, to no avail because the two cops who were suddenly standing in front of me don't speak English. My protest is the only word that comes to mind in this moment of stress: *Hola*. They came out of nowhere, something cops are very good at, and confronted me when I was fiddling with my lock in the process of wrapping the lock's cable around a lamp post outside a bar called Griceldas. One of them, the quiet one, moved in and then stood threateningly with his hand on the cruiser's seat. The other was talking to me very rapidly, in Spanish, of course. Much too fast to give me a clue about what he was saying. I don't think he is asking me if I like Cabo. I don't hear the word *drogas*, which is Spanish for drugs. And I don't have any drugs on me because I never do. Oh, suddenly I got the theme of his words, maybe. He is gesturing over my bike.

I asked myself, Why now? I decide to play dumb and pretend I don't know Spanish. That is easy. I am very convincing with that ploy. I don't really understand anything that is being said to me. Looking dumb and confused is my strategy for the moment. It is so easy. The talker seems to be tapering off and then gets to what sounds like a two-word summary: *No bicicleta!* That, I understand perfectly well. The rest was fluff, I suppose, to establish the gravity of my offense. I also understand the trigger finger at the end of an outstretched arm. It is pointing me in a direction that would get me off the marina. I didn't understand what the cop with his hand on my bicycle seat said to me. Maybe something like, "Go, or else we will kill you" but my Spanish isn't good enough to be sure. Maybe that's just my imagination at work. I am not happy about this development. Seriously, "Why now?" is a good question. But, it is also a stupid one because I know there is no answer to it even if I knew how to ask it. If I did know how to ask it, I'd still have a problem understanding the answer. Best to shut up and go. I have no choice but to leave the marina sidewalk, but not on two wheels. I'm not about to argue with the *policía*. I need to be polite with the police. I am a guest of their country.

I found a different lamp post for my bike in one of the parking lots behind the marina bars. As I lock it up, I am feeling angry that my joy in riding my cruiser past all the boats and bars had just been taken away from me, for no apparent reason. This is the first time since I got here that I did not experience the joy that comes with vacations. Dernit.

I am learning Spanish - Monday, January 23

Of course, I tell myself every day that I am learning Spanish. I have an opening line with every single Mexican I need to talk to or want to talk to, except for the police the other day. On the heels of every friendly greeting, such as *Buenas días,* I follow up with the sentence, *Estoy aprendiendo español.* It is a terrific sentence to know because the other person knows right away what's happening, or won't be, with communication. When I say in Spanish that "I am learning Spanish" nearly every Mexican smiles and is glad to hear that and is patient with me and wants to help me and thinks I'm terrific and encourages me and on and on and on and that's all good. That's how powerful those words are.

If you have ever been to Paris without using a single word of French then you have surely discovered how rude Parisians can be. The French don't particularly like it when someone comes up to them and just starts speaking English, even though almost all educated Parisians, especially those in the tourist business, are perfectly fluent in it. If an American just said, *Bonjour* and only *Bonjour* to a French person, the French heart opens up a little bit. More with more words in French. More than *bonjour* is better than nothing of course. None at all is a big mistake. Once a person gets past that first speed bump in the language barrier, they get to see the warm, friendly side of every French person. I think this is a universal scenario. It certainly seems to me that this is true in Mexico, too.

Beyond saying I am learning Spanish, I try to make it clear that the principal reason I am here for three months is to learn Spanish. I stumble through that mouthful of course. Whenever I make up long sentences I am quickly reminded how mouthy Spanish is and how often the rolling r comes into play. I make a mental note to practice rolling my r's. I learned how to do it in French so it is not at all daunting in Spanish, but it is a different roll. The trick is to remember to do it. My inadequacies are quickly evident, but they are way more likely to elicit sympathy and understanding from the listener than disdain. And, often, I get a smile back along with these three words of infinite wisdom: *poco a poco*. Little by little.

<u>Lourdes at Esteban's - Monday, January 23</u>

Esteban's is across the street from my complex and then about three blocks down the street, which makes it that much closer to the marina. It is not the last stop for a drink on my way home from the marina. It could be the second last, except for the fact that I never stop there for a drink. The last stop could be a restaurant a block up the street, Guadalupana, a place I haven't yet visited either. The Fairfield Inn sits between these two restaurants. With this configuration, all Fairfield Inn guests walking into town must pass Esteban's coming and going. This is the clientele that probably keeps Esteban's afloat. It is clearly for tourists, though I rarely see more than a smattering of customers at the tables in the covered outdoor sidewalk patio, has to be tourists. And when I do, I wonder who those few souls are and why they picked Esteban's. My best guess is that they are staying at the Fairfield Inn. Esteban's is convenient for them, very.

Are the customers on Esteban's patio so hungry that they can't go the short distance into town to pick from an impressive smorgasbord of restaurants, many on the water with a vista of some fantastic yachts? Are they so tired that it's too much exercise to walk fifteen blocks to the marina? Too much time and expense to call a taxi? Or, maybe they don't care about food and they pick Esteban's for the convenience to their hotel? Or, maybe they are the only ones that know that Esteban's has a killer meal special all day long? I am guessing the correct answer is the last option: the meal special. From what I've seen on my daily rides past the restaurant, only a handful of people know about the special. Too bad for the rest of the world. The special posted on the sidewalk sandwich board in front of Esteban's is killer. The sandwich chalk board says "Chicken, rice, beans, salsa and chips, a beer and a shot of tequila for only ten bucks!" It may not be three-star Michelin food, but, really, how can chicken, rice and beans not taste great in Mexico? C'mon, it's Mexican food, probably the greatest cuisine in the world, in my humble opinion. Ten bucks is cheap. That's how much a cocktail in the marina will cost.

The hostess graciously hawking at the front door most of the evenings is a very beautiful woman. She is probably in her early fifties sporting a bit of the Sophia Loren look. Her name is

Lourdes, a real mouthful of lip movement, three syllables. She likes to wear dark blazers with tailored slacks.

Two nights ago, just after dusk, I briefly stopped the cruiser on the sidewalk at Esteban's front door on my way home to say hi to her. See what's up. I got her name then. I told her mine. Tomas. She could speak a little English, what I call restaurant English, so we chatted for a minute. I speak a little Spanish, what I call no Spanish, so that's why we chatted only a minute. The conversation hit the wall too quickly. I would like to have spoken to her a little longer because she is so beautiful and because I could get some really good practice stumbling over my Spanish while I looked into her beautiful brown eyes. It was a perfect opportunity for me to learn from really stupid mistakes. If I had stayed any longer, I would have learned a lot.

Perfect weather - Tuesday, January 24

I am well into my third week here. Since my arrival on January fifth, the weather has been perfect every day. Sunny and blue skies, day after day, with an average high temperature of 75 degrees F. I looked at average lows too and saw 54 degrees F but I'm having trouble believing that because it occurs at four in the morning when I am sound asleep in a warm bed. When I go out at night, it has been without a sweater or a jacket. It's been that warm. The warm air sticks around in the early part of the evening. Perfect for t-shirts in the evenings. That's right, I am not Mr. Fancy. Not Beau Brummell. I'm not even sure who he was other than some ancient Frenchman known for his style in clothes, probably foppish at that.

As it turns out, I happen to have a very well-developed sense of style in clothes. My look is very contemporary, practical and *faux couture* (which is French, look it up). I am very consistent in my garb, that being black t-shirts with khaki shorts, sometimes cargo shorts. Preferably cargo shorts, actually. Sometimes referred to as trailer shorts. That may be, but as I traveler I happen to like the extra set of flapped pockets under the primary side pockets.

Great for transporting sandwiches long distances. Preferably in baggies.

As I was saying the weather is delicious here. I saw a wisp of a cloud the other day but it did not have a deleterious effect on the steady perfection of the weather. I have heard that summers are unbearably hot here, but I won't be here then so summer temperatures are simply not an issue for me. Like many people, especially those here to escape the winter cold far to the north of Cabo, dining *al fresco* is very appealing. It's a shame I don't have a dinner partner while I'm here. *Al fresco* has a nice romantic element to it. You know, dinner under the stars. I just cannot comfortably sit at a dining table by myself. I can sit at a bar by myself, but not a table. Maybe I should add *novia* to my list of Cabo objectives. *Novia,* you may know, is Spanish for girlfriend. It's possible. Yes, a *novia* for *al fresco* dining *sous les étoiles*. There, I did it: English, Spanish, Italian, and French in one sentence. In case you are wondering, s*ous les étoiles* is French for "under the stars." It's easy to mix up languages. I do it all the time.

The cruiser's first flat tire - Tuesday, January 24

A flat tire was inevitable. I knew it would happen sooner or later. Probably sooner because there's a lot of crap on the streets. Big crap and little crap. And some really little crap, tiny crap, tons of it, like nails, tacks, and bits of glass that are often difficult to see.

I woke up at my usual time in the morning, which is whenever I feel like waking up. Today, eight. Sun's well up but my black out "curtains" keep the daylight at bay. They work well and, except for a few flecks of light at the edges of the garbage can liners, I can't tell if it's day or night outside. The tell is usually the gardener who likes to hose down the tropical plants right outside my poolside bedroom window. He squirts my windows every day. He must think I am not sleeping. That noise tells me it's around eight. Sometimes he throws a loogie into the garden, which disgusts my deep tranquil inner self. People started exiting the building about that time too, yakking in Spanish. There are English speaking tourists occasionally renting a weekend condo here, but they usually sleep in, well past eight. I never hear English spoken outside my window in the mornings. When I walked into the kitchen I glanced at my bike just inside the door. Dammit. It was easy to see that the front tire was flat. A walker. Dammit. The time had come. I went over to it, knelt on the floor and within twenty seconds found a nail head where the rubber meets the road. I wasn't about to remove it. I'd leave it in as evidence of the crime.

After my breakfast out of a blender, I dressed for success, sure that I could find someone to fix my flat tire. From my daily excursions in and out of the real streets of Cabo, I could recall seeing several open-air tire shops, all looking like tiny one-man operations dedicated exclusively to car and motorcycle tires. Maybe I'd get lucky and find one of close by, one that could fix a bicycle flat. Moments before I left my place, I googled "flat tire" in Spanish. *Neumático desinflado* came up. I'd have to say it aloud many times on my safari to get a fix, however obvious it would be to anyone working the shop. If I panic into locked lips, I can just point to the tire and pick at the nail head. I pushed the cruiser out the door to begin the walking safari.

Five blocks down the boulevard, toward town, I was even with the Pemex gas station. Aha! It occurred to me that I could inflate the deflated and have an easier time searching for a tire shop while riding instead of pushing. Every pump is manned by someone in a gray uniform. I picked the only chick, smiled, did my Spanish greeting thing, and then forgot how to say flat tire. By the time I got through the greeting, she was already kneeling and removing the valve cap. Efficient. She was very friendly, which was no surprise because I have now concluded friendliness is built into the Mexican culture. She said no charge. I said *gracias* and then surprised her by plopping a ten-peso coin into her hand. Fifty cents. The tire rode well and I rode out of the station to find my guy.

After zigging and zagging for seven or eight blocks through the locals' turf, I found a shop that might be able to help me. A small, very brown and wrinkled man was working on a tire propped up on a wooden crate. I rode my bike up his short driveway and almost into his arms as he was already alert to my arrival. I did the greeting thing, including the Spanish for flat tire. My memory worked sometimes. The man was smiling with a display of a very white set of teeth. I dismounted. He took my bike from me, overturned it, and had the wheel off and the inner tube out of the tire in less than two minutes. Very impressive speed, like the pit crews at the Indy 500. This was a man who knew what he was doing. And I was a man who was relieved because I would have my cruiser back on the roads of Cabo in less than fifteen minutes at that rate. He finished up with the air compressor and returned the bike to me, with flat as good as new. When I asked how much, *Cuánto cuesta?* He said, *Gratis, señor*, which I quickly understood to mean free as in "no charge." I think he decided to give me a freebie because I gave him my standard introduction, that I am a gringo trying to learn Spanish. He clearly appreciated my effort. We spent the next ten minutes talking about his business and the racks of tires on his driveway. And, yes, we talked about his family too. And, my twin sister. In short, we hit it off. He introduced himself as Fernando. He is an extremely likable guy. I decided he would be my friend, if he was open to that. I think he decided that too. I insisted he take some money. I made him take a hundred pesos, gushed *mucho gracias*, and rode off with two good tires once again.

Mariachis - Tuesday, January 24

When the marina restaurants are full to the gills with tourists engaged in drinking and dinner, it is impossible to walk the length of the marina sidewalk without hearing a mariachi band. They often play at lunch, too. Or wander around in the middle of the afternoon trying to pick off tourists wherever they can find them. But it's at the busiest times, like dinner, that the mariachis have their best audiences. The mariachi groups usually consist of four or five musicians but I've seen two and three work the tables for the thin crowd in the afternoons. Sometimes this abridged version is simply dressed in street clothes, which is not the traditional garb of the mariachis. In the evenings, the musicians go full bore with their traditional *charro* suits. This is an elaborate outfit, often with silver decorations, tight trousers, ruffled shirt, short jacket, and a very fancy *sombrero*. The larger versions of roving mariachi musicians usually consist of four or five men, though the traditional groups size can be much bigger, close to a dozen for catered events, but that many musicians won't work in the crowded marina. Typically, I've seen a quartet comprised of some combination of violins and guitars or an accordion. There is almost always one type of guitar called the *vihuela*, which is a high-pitched, round-backed guitar that provides rhythm, and a second guitar which is a bass guitar called a *guitarrón*, which also provides rhythm. These are the two mainstays of mariachi music. Trumpets are great for accents and are part of a traditional mariachi band but they are too intrusive for the intimacy of a small band walking between clusters of tables in busy restaurants. Accordions are fairly common.

The mariachi musicians always encourage the *turistas* to sing along. And the tourists find it hard to resist. It doesn't take much encouragement. I know that's true because I have been seated next to a table courted by mariachi singers many times. Sometimes I pretend they are playing for me so I can better feel the Cabo experience. When I do that, I contribute to the tip money, of course. The best part of the performance is always when the tourists sing. You know then that everyone is having fun and everyone has probably had too many margaritas.

For five bucks, the mariachi band will play any Mexican song you request. Not surprisingly tourists almost always request one of two songs: *Guantanamera* or *La Bamba*. Few people know the lyrics but that doesn't stop the singalong. For the former, I usually chime in with my own words that go something like this: *one-ton-of-tomatoes, I want one ton of tomatoes, oh yeah, one ton of tomatoes.* Yeah, something like that. A couple of margaritas help. Ritchie Valens put *La Bamba* on the top of the charts and here in Cabo it's number one in our hearts. I hear both songs all the time on weekends. Sometimes the music carries across the yacht basin, in which case everyone in the marina gets to enjoy the mariachis.

My second visit with Fernando same day - Tuesday, January 24

After Fernando fixed my tire in the morning, the day passed slowly, which is what it usually does in Cabo. Something was gnawing at me all day long and I knew exactly what it was: I should have paid Fernando a lot more. Good grief! I gave him a hundred pesos. That's only five bucks. That's pathetic. Fixing a flat in the States would cost forty bucks. The afternoon was almost over, but it was still in play. I got on my bike and raced to Fernando's shop, wanting to beat the day's timeclock. He was working alongside the crate again, with a tire on top of it, just as he was when I when I saw him for the first time. I hailed him and rode right up to him and his surprised face. He looked at me and said, *Otra vez?* Again?

I told him right away that I was sorry and felt bad that I hadn't paid him more, but not in those exact words. I couldn't say exactly that in Spanish to save my life. But he understood my explanation as to why I was back. I thanked him for being a "professional" and "very kind" which are words I know how to say in Spanish. He graciously accepted my offer of ten more bucks, bringing the total to fifteen, which still seems so cheap to me. It was enough and maybe a lot of money for him, especially since he originally said *gratis* to me. I will remember to be generous next time, at least as generous. And there will be a next time, unfortunately for me, fortunately for Fernando.

Total immersion is not possible - Tuesday, January 24

I've had to modify my concept of immersion. I actually began my adventure here with a commitment to speak only Spanish, at all times. Only! I must not have thought that through very thoroughly. It is not possible, of course. I need English to get me over the speed bumps and to deal with necessities that my limited Spanish cannot deal with. I also need to speak English in dealing with important, official, or legal aspects that require absolutely clear communication. All this puts an end to my desire to immerse myself fully. I'm probably the only one surprised by this revelation. Still, I am committed to speaking Spanish when it is a sensible learning opportunity. I continue to surround myself with Spanish publications and my trusty workbook *Spanish for Gringos*, along with my online studies with Duolingo. And some TV. So, I may not qualify for total immersion, but I think I can say I am waist deep into it. That makes me partially immersed, something I can live with. I guess I won't be drowning in it.

<u>Dinner at Esteban's - Tuesday, January 24</u>

Several days after I met Lourdes I stopped by in the afternoon for an early dinner. I had skipped lunch so hunger was kicking my stomach. I wanted to try the ten-buck special. It was late in the afternoon, about four. I asked the waiter, Hector, what time Lourdes comes in. He said five. That means I had less than an hour to eat and run. I wasn't ready to see Lourdes again, not that day. I need to learn some more Spanish so I could have a little better conversation with her next time we talked.

Hector hung close to my table. Fine by me. The more Spanish, the better. Hector's English was good enough for a bit of chatter with him. He said Lourdes works six nights a week, which struck me as being a lot. Hector said he also works six nights a week. So does Saul, who is the other waiter. I thought about this and it reinforced my initial impressions of Mexicans: they are really hard workers. I respect them a lot for that. Hector and I kind of hit it off. Since I was the only customer on the patio, maybe the only one in the restaurant he gave me his undivided attention. From him, I learned that Lourdes is not married. Hector also said she doesn't have a boyfriend. I think that's what I understood him to say. He got into some word territory that was new to me.

The menu special was great. I knew it would be. I loved it. I passed on the tequila and I still think ten bucks was a real deal, even without the tequila. I describe the food as delicious, basic

Mexican cuisine. The kind every American knows and loves. Plus, unlimited chips and salsa. I like chips and salsa, especially chips with spicy hot salsa, the kind of heat that makes my forehead sweat. Hector brought a bottle of fire, really hot stuff, some brand of habanero sauce, to the table at my request, which means he understood my gestures indicating really hot. I paid the ten plus a generous tip, fifty percent. I thanked him and made my getaway on the cruiser before Lourdes showed up. As I rode away, I thought of Lourdes. She really is pretty. A sharp dresser. After about fifteen seconds of that I knew it was never going to go anywhere beyond me stumbling over sentences at the front door with her. But it was fun to think of more than that. Remember, I like spicy hot. That's Lourdes.

My neighbor Martina - Wednesday, January 25

Today, I met the middle-aged woman that lives on the fourth floor of my building, which is the top floor. I suppose one could say it's the penthouse floor but since all the condos are identical in this building, you can't say it's a penthouse. Her name is Martina. She is not Spanish but she speaks Spanish. She is not American, but she speaks English. She is Dutch, which means she speaks the most difficult language in the world. Maybe it isn't, but when I lived in France with Dutch friends and neighbors nearby, I thought it was pretty difficult. A lot of uchhhs and occhhhhs and throaty stuff that only a true Holland native can deal with. In a way, it makes me think of Spanish because Spanish is a very mouthy language, too, loaded with rolling double r tongue challenges. When I practice Spanish by reading aloud, my mouth wears out after about five minutes. *Mucha boca.*

Martina introduced herself to me at the bottom of the stairs, just outside my door, after coming down four flights breathless and in a hurry. But she did stop for half a minute to say hi, which is nice of her. Besides the rapid exchange of our names she wanted to know if I was interested in renting her place for the summer. I said no. She parried with a request of me to find someone who will. I said I'd do the best I could to find that person. Then she ran off, in a hurry to go someplace.

Me, I'd never rent Martina's place in the summer. Or the fall, winter or spring. I can't imagine going up and down those stairs all day long, especially at least twice a day with the cruiser. Torture if it's a hot summer day. The cruiser is a very heavy bike. It might even be dangerous to try lugging it up or down because the stairwell does not have a railing. She must have a time of it going up with an armful of groceries. I'll have to be on the lookout to give her a hand when needed.

Martina is an attractive, sturdy woman, with long, flowing, wavy auburn hair. When face to face, I now think she's probably only a few years younger than me and packs a lot of energy from what little I've seen of her. That has to be true, because without an elevator in the building she must get a good work out going up and down the stairs several times a day. When I see her in the future, I'll stick to English. She'll be a good break from Spanish. Especially smart of me to avoid Spanish coming at me a hundred miles an hour with a Dutch accent. I might not get more than a minute of her time, ever. She's moves fast, which is too say she seems to be on the run every time I see her. I'm glad she's nice. That's a real plus. I hate having cranky neighbors.

My first time in Guadalupana - Wednesday, January 25

I don't stay out very late on most Wednesdays or any day for that matter. Hardly ever and not here yet. Maybe it's because I'm single and over sixty, and not into whatever I used to do in the evenings when I was younger. I didn't have a big night of partying tonight. I didn't even have a small night. At about seventy-thirty the sun had called it quits. I called it quits, too, for the evening after downing two bottles of Pacifico at The Tiki Bar in the marina. Doesn't sound like much, but since I only had a blender breakfast for the entire day, I was actually a little buzzed. I turned on my cruiser flashers, the red one under my seat facing traffic coming up on my back and the white one on my handle bars for on-coming traffic.

Buzzed or not, riding on the streets of Cabo is always a little risky. It's the other guy I worry about. The drunk driver or the one texting. I worry about those *loco* local white buses, too. Some have drivers that like to scare me intentionally. I am sure of that. I usually try to take the sidewalk all the way back to Coromuel. Except for a few tight spots like the skinny sidewalk that runs past McDonald's and sporadic clusters of pedestrians, I can make it home without riding on the street.

I passed a place called Esteban's shortly after McDonald's and made a mental note to look into it. It had a nice patio, under a big awning, off the sidewalk. I didn't see any customers so I made a a mental note to drop in some time when it looked a little busier. Besides, I was ready to conclude my evening with the usual commitment to silence until the next day. But noooo, just up ahead, I saw light pouring out of the open double doors at Guadalupana. I have been curious about that place from the start. I took it as a sign to go in, see what's there. Go for the light! That's what a moth once told me. A couple of beers led the way. I rode right up to the open doors, one tire in and one tire out, saw that the place was empty except for the two men I had seen in there at other times in passing. But I couldn't back out. It was too late for that. I waved since the cruiser's front wheel was already inside the restaurant. The man at the bar railing at the far end from me, was a dark haired, portly Mexican, about my age. He gestured for me to come in, apparently with my bike. He was talking to a stocky gray-haired Mexican behind the bar, presumably the bartender. I dismounted and pushed my bike through the double doors, looked around, and paused. I gestured to a spacious corner, just right of the door, as a place to park the cruiser. Got a nod of approval. I preferred having it indoors rather than leaving it on the sidewalk. I guess they understood the same. I thumped the kickstand, then killed the flashers, turned and walked toward the two men.

As I approached I could see the one at the bar railing had a half inch stripe of white hair running up from his forehead hairline through the dark ones in the center of scalp. Of course, it reminded me of a skunk. Beers at work. Mostly, as I approached, in my head I asked myself "What are you doing?" I couldn't answer the question and believed I'd figure something out when I got up to them. And I did. Words came to me. I used my trusty opening line. I began with good evening, which is *Buenas noches,* and then *Estoy aprendiendo español.* Besides saying "I am learning Spanish," I stated my name and asked them theirs. They greeted me warmly. We were off to a good start. That's how I met my next two best friends in Mexico: Pedro, the waiter, and Facundo, the bartender. They are the Lopez brothers, the owners.

Pedro and Facundo did not speak a lick of English. That was not a problem. They were so open to me and me to them that we communicated remarkably well. I said I was hungry, though I wasn't. I meant to say I am thirsty, which is *Tengo sed* but I said, *Tengo hambre,* which means I am hungry. Literally, I have hunger. I felt committed so I happily took a menu when Pedro handed one to me. He seated me at one of the tables by the bar. I ordered dinner, which was a surprise to me. That wasn't part of the plan. I guess I wanted to keep the conversation alive. We three were having lots of fun so why not continue over dinner. That's what I say. Facundo took my drink order, a *Cuba Libre,* rum with a Coca-Cola Light and a slice of lime. Yep, a *Cuba Libre.* Not what I needed, but that's what popped into my head and out of my mouth, which was interesting because I hadn't had one of those in years. He put it on the bar for Pedro to deliver it. Pedro did and took my order to the kitchen, directly to the head chef, which he said was his wife. Fish tacos, rice, beans, chips, and salsa. Perfect. When my order arrived, I invited Pedro to join me at my table. There were no other customers. He was very hospitable, so why not? I got a full explanation on what everything was and how to eat it, specifically, how to construct a taco using the rice and beans and half a dozen condiments presented to me in a tray alongside my plate. For over an hour, Pedro sat across from me at my table and Facundo stood at the bar a mere eight feet from us. He barely moved except once, to fix me another drink. We three got along just fine, every word spoken was Spanish. They were excellent teachers. Patient and understanding. Also, they both were perfect in timing with correcting and aiding me in my struggle to speak Spanish. Not too much, not to little, just the right amount of porridge.

When the time came to end the evening, I was actually sorry to ride out of Guadalupana, but it was time to say goodnight. They were minutes away from closing time. Nine. Always nine. We three *amigos* had a lot of fun. I was glad the place was empty the entire time because I got to be with Pedro and Facundo. I had a delicious, authentic Mexican meal and a non-stop conversation peppered with charades and pantomime. And laughter. I promised I'd come back tomorrow or the next day. There was every reason for me to believe that Guadalupana would be a great place for a nightcap, my last stop before bed. This would not be the last time. However, I don't think dinner will be on the docket again. I didn't need all that food, especially late in the evening. One Cuba Libra was fine, too. Two was one too many. I'll have to draw the line at three.

When I rode into the restaurant two hours ago, I was wary of everything about Guadalupana; it seemed cold, drab, and doomed. When I left, it was bright, warm, authentic, a great place and, best of all, run by two great guys. How perfect! What a day! All week long, I recognized the need for some real conversations in Spanish to enhance my learning experience, but didn't know how to make that happen. Tonight, I pushed the cruiser out the double doors and rode off into the darkness, flashers flashing, homeward bound, feeling indescribably happy because I now have three new friends: Pedro, Facundo, and my flat fixing friend Fernando.

<u>I'm not fluent in Spanish yet, but working on it! - Wednesday, January 25</u>

Wow. I'm just ending my third week in Cabo. I think my Spanish is improving. I'm sure of it. I know more words. I've not really jumped into conjugating verbs yet, though I am using some verbs already in small sentences. Duolingo has me flirting with verbs. Thankfully only the present tense at the moment. Since I can go at any pace on Duo that I want, I suppose I could move more quickly into verbs. Right now, I'm comfortable with learning more words every day and some grammar basics. If I don't know the words I won't have a clue what people are saying. I have to do more than just build my *vocabulario*, of course. There is much to learn to with regard to grammar. For example, Spanish words have a gender attached to them, and it sometimes changes depending on the usage. French assigns gender to words too, so the gender thing isn't a new concept to me. Like French, I just have to learn which words are male and which are female. And like French there are basic guidelines for that, but lots of exceptions, of course. Exceptions are par for the course in any language. And, like French, there is no logic to it.

Speaking of French, my familiarity with that language contributes to my comprehension of Spanish. It also contributes to my confusion. I can see the similarities, of course, because French and Spanish are Latin-based languages. English is a German based language but it is influenced considerably by Latin. Consequently, I trip over my words which means that sometimes I will put English, French, and Spanish words into a single sentence. Believe it or not, when I do that the other person usually understands me. That reminds me of the importance of just throwing words out there. Very often the listener can figure out what the speaker is saying just from a few key words. Which is wonderful because, sometimes as the speaker, I don't even know what I'm saying.

I constantly brush off my own frustration in my attempts to speak Spanish. But it is not an easy brush. I flounder in even the simplest single sentence of communication. Sometimes I forget a word ten seconds after I repeated it to myself over and over. I mix up words with similar sounding words all the time. I often have to pause mid-phrase as I search for the next word because my mind blanked. Sometimes I am so far off the mark on pronunciation that even an English-speaking Mexican can't figure out what I'm trying to say. Thankfully, people usually figure out what I am saying.

I could give myself a real beat down if I reprimand myself for all the mistakes I make. I try not to be hard on myself. But sometimes I am. Also, I try to relax and remember the soothing words that I hear more than any other: *poco a poco*.

CHAPTER FOUR

Week 4

<u>Endless perfect weather - Thursday, January 26</u>

I grew up in Wisconsin. That was sixty years ago but I easily remember what it means to live through four different seasons. My memories of the cycle of seasons were all refreshed recently because I lived in the south of France for the past four years, another place where four seasons are well defined. As I begin my fourth week in Cabo, the weather has not been an issue. A t-shirt and shorts are just fine for day and night. It is so perfectly comfortable every day with exactly the same sunny, pure blue sky overhead all day long. After the sun sets, comfortably cool nights take over under a clear starlit sky. With no variation from day to day or night to night, it's easy to forget that there is such a thing as weather. It's so perfect that the perfection goes unnoticed, if you know what I mean. The highest temperatures of the day have been the mid-seventies. The early evening temperatures are very pleasant too. Later, after midnight, the temperature slowly drops about twenty degrees, dipping into the mid-fifties, but it doesn't get there until close to dawn. Perfect for fun in the day, perfect for dining al fresco in the evening, and perfect for sleeping through the night. That pretty much sums it up. I have been told that the weather I have experienced in my first month here will run well into March. Then, in the back half of March, the temperatures begin a slow climb in their march to a nearly intolerable hot summer. Of course, I won't be here then, so January, February, and March are all I care about. Good timing. Lucky me.

No parking on the marina! - Thursday, January 26

The marina police have their eye on me. I'm not easy to miss because I am the only bicyclist on the marina, riding or pushing a bike. I've never seen another bicyclist. Maybe a little Mexican kid once, with training wheels, not sure that counts as a clear and present danger to pedestrians, like me. Of course, I am no longer riding, but they still watch me closely as if, any second, I'm going to jump on and ride heater skelter into a crowd of tourists. Of course, I am thinking of doing that all the time, to spite them. Not a good attitude, I know. I need to be friends with these guys. I live here now, in their town. My activity on the marina sidewalk comes down to only two events: pushing my bike past the tourist traps or sitting in a bar nursing a Pacifico as an observer of life on the marina.

It's almost the weekend and not much time has passed since the police scolded me for riding my bike and telling me to park it a block off the marina. I didn't like that offsite parking one bit. Yes, I would stop riding but I didn't see any reason not to park it on the marina sidewalk as long as it was out of the way. I ignored last week's request to park it away from the marina. I pushed the cruiser to the edge of the walk and leaned it against a fence, well out of way of pedestrian traffic. Before I could even lock it up, a police officer came up behind me - was I being stalked? - and said I couldn't park there or anywhere on the marina. It was a different guy than any of the guys that confronted me last week. They must have printed a WANTED poster on me. That really ticked me off, but I had no choice apparently. I was no longer in the mood to suck a beer in one of the tiki bars. So instead of finding a parking spot farther in town and returning to a marina tiki bar I decided to leave the marina completely. Right on! Ride on!

Hector and Lourdes - Friday, January 27

Whenever I ride past Esteban's, which is every day at least once, regardless of what side of the street I am on, I look for Hector hanging out near the front door, filling in as Lourdes' back up hawker. I also look for Lourdes, but, frankly, I would rather see Hector. I am more comfortable seeing him and chatting with him anytime. When we talk, it's in Spanish, of course, but his English is good enough to explain a few words in Spanish to me. Also, he's an ally regarding Lourdes, and we get along on that count. He wants me to go out with her. Of course, that's beyond my imagination. He and I laugh a lot about that. I know what to do with Hector: chat, a ride-by wave, or even, from across the street, a whistle. It's not the same with Lourdes.

I do not know what to do with Lourdes. Waving of any kind seems inappropriate in any manner of enthusiasm. Well, okay, maybe a small, discreet sort of wave might be okay, like a flick of the hand, but only from across the street, nothing like the big *Holaaaaa* wave I give to Hector. Whistling to Lourdes from across the street doesn't seem appropriate either, though Hector and I whistle at each other. I am pretty sure chatting with her doesn't work either, I know all this from experience. This doesn't leave much in the way of other things to do. I also know that when confronted with an encounter with Lourdes I experience different levels of paralysis, especially in the mouth area. Why is it so hard to talk to her? Can't say for sure. Part of the problem in communicating with her is her prolonged silence after I say something, making me feel like what I said made no sense. Of course, what I said probably did not make any sense at all, but she doesn't have to rub it in with the silent treatment. When we are face to face, which has only happened a few times, she stares at me with her big brown eyes. It's too much. I have a propensity to choke on even the most basic words when she does that. Of course, I don't mean literally choke, as in Heimlich maneuver choke, I mean my mind goes blank. When that happens, I have a tendency to stand still, return her stare, and wish to god I could appreciate sharing the silence with her, but that's not what happens. This leaves me with no choice but to blurt *buenas noches* and ride away. Hector leaves us alone when Lourdes and I converse. Or I should say, attempt to converse. I know he is watching, because I see him standing across the patio. He is staring at me, too. A different kind of stare. The "you can do it" stare. I know he is rooting for me.

The screaming at night - Friday, January 27

I woke up last night from a dreamy sleep in the middle of the night to the screams of a woman under assault. That was my first interpretation. I thought the screams were coming from the swimming pool courtyard at first. Not far from me at all. A second later, my ears in focus, I re-located the source of the screams as coming through the bedroom window, not the one that was poolside, but the one open to the building next to me, into a breezeway. That seemed to be right. I needed to know for my instinctual determination to be of assistance if it came to mobilizing myself out of my condo and moving into the public realm. In other words, coming to the rescue. As my consciousness rose out of my dream state, up and up, through different layers of somnolence and then surfacing to wakefulness, I re-interpreted the scream as that of a woman not in distress but in the throes of hugely pleasurable sex. Almost fully awake, I was able to listen with a focused intensity. I have stayed in hundreds of hotel rooms in my lifetime so I had heard of great pleasure expressed in this manner many times over the years and, of course, my interpretation is also based on my own personal experience, many, many times before. Many. That said, don't believe everything you read. Anyway, I was relieved I wouldn't have to dash outside to rescue a damsel in distress.

The persistence of the screaming was impressive. I was sure it would be over in a few moments, hopefully allowing me to recapture whatever dream I was having. A few more soulful screams penetrated the silence of Villa Paloma. And a few more. I was now really impressed by such incredible drive, presumably by both parties. And what a party! I began wondering if I could ever attain that sort of delivery as well.

The screaming continued for an eternity, which is about twenty minutes after my renewed attempt to fall asleep. I didn't know if I could fall asleep at that point. With the pure, unadulterated demonstration of stamina underway outside my building, I began to doubt my assessment of the source. I turned on the light, got up, walked to the window and listened intently for additional input. A half minute later, the unabated screaming shifted into an altered state. With the shift, my brain once again gave me a re-interpretation of the scream. I concluded that it was not a woman in the throes of passion, rather, it was an alley cat getting nailed. Either by a tomcat who won't quit or, possibly, by a gang of tomcats. I don't know enough about cats to go beyond that kind of guesswork. I climbed under the covers again and lights out, literally and figuratively. That's all I remember.

Mexicans and Coca-Cola - Friday, January 27

Thirty years ago, I worked for The Coca-Cola Company, specifically for the USA and Mexico brands of Coca-Cola. The flagship brand. The aircraft carrier of soft drinks. This is a ship that had more consumer research in its files than any consumer could imagine. Of course, I saw a lot of it, the summation numbers anyway, and it is easy for me to recall the staggering consumption rates of Coke on a per capita basis in Mexico. When I worked on that business in the early eighties, Mexicans were drinking a lot more Coke than water, a phenomenon which happened in the States with soft drinks in general about the same time. I doubt if there is a worse beverage for one's health. Now thirty years later, I don't want to think of the price Mexicans have paid for consuming hundreds of thousands of gallons of sugar in that period courtesy of The Coca-Cola Company. It has been steep. Very costly, beyond measure and imagination.

This week I stumbled on an article in a Mexican publication about the consumption of Coca-Cola in Mexico. Thanks to Google Translator I was able to get a clear understanding of the article's content. The first thing I learned is that Mexico is still the country in the world that has the highest per capita consumption of Coke. That hasn't changed in over thirty years. I didn't really need to read that to believe it. I can feel that it's true, just from my observations in these past four weeks.

Anecdotally, I see Coke everywhere, not much of Diet Coke, which is called Coke Light in Mexico, and almost no Coke Zero. When I say everywhere, what I really mean is in everyone's shopping cart and in the hands of so many people on sidewalks. I can venture a guess that Coke is the national drink of Mexico. Construction workers and manual laborers carry a 2-liter bottle of the sugared poison in one hand, a lunch box in the other. It is not hard to find a teenager out and about with a 2-liter bottle in hand as well. Mexican moms walk out of Walmart with a case or even two cases of Coke or several 2-liter bottles of Coke. I think it is the item that is found more often in shopping carts in Mexico than any other item. If you spend any time here observing shopping carts, it is hard to doubt that.

The article provided the numbers that supported Mexico's domination over other countries in 2015 when it comes to guzzling Coke. Here's what it said in comparing the average annual per capita consumption of Coca-Cola among the top three countries. Mexico leads the pack at 728 eight-ounce servings per person per year. That's an average of two Cokes a day per person. America is in second place but with a much lower consumption rate of 403 servings per person per year. The numbers drop significantly after that, with the number three spot going to Canada, with 259. The big guns at the company must be salivating thinking of the growth opportunity for Coke in China and India, which have numbers of only 38 and 12 servings per person per year, respectively.

But there is some good news. In the same article, the Director General of Health Promotion said that Mexico is on the right track to reverse this consumption problem. The consumption of sweetened beverages, not just Coke, fell by nearly ten percent in the last two years in the country and bottled water consumption increased a little more than two percent, according to the results of a study conducted by the National Institute of Public Health (INSP) and the University of North Carolina. Taxation of sugar drinks with other actions, such as the elimination of advertising of foods with high calorie content in children's schedules, guidelines in schools, food counseling, primary care and promotion of physical activity, will contribute to solving the obesity problem in Mexico. Maybe the US could dial up a bit on that program as well. Both countries have a long way to go to become healthier. Giving up Coke and all other soft drinks would make a profound impact on diminishing obesity in both these countries. Fat chance. One can hope. I say tax the hell out of these poisonous bottles of sugar. That's what happened to cigarettes in the States. It worked. Now only fifteen percent of adults smoke cigarettes; that's a big drop from when the numbers were above seventy percent.

Drugs, rock n roll, and blow to go - Saturday, January 28

I don't know much about pharmacies in Mexico or what drugs that are regulated and which are not. I do know a couple that are highly illegal here, in the States and everywhere. Never a good idea to mess with those down here, unless you want to see the worst prisons in North America from the inside. This warning, which I take very seriously, is in contrast to what I hear on the streets and on the beaches. More than a few Mexicans selling cigars in public areas whispered to me that they could get me some weed and, sometimes, I get a whispered offer for some blow. Slang for cocaine. Yes, that's right, for sale through your friendly cigar vendor.

Mexico's restrictions on medically prescribed drugs are different from ours. Prescriptions aren't necessary for a lot of them that require prescriptions in the States. I see a lot of medications offered in the marina as over-the-counter purchases, medications that you couldn't possibly get in the States without a prescription. Regardless of what tourists know when they come here, it doesn't take them long to see what medications are easily available. There are pharmacies all over town and they are advertising a lot of stuff in big bold letters on their front step sandwich board signage and on posters in the windows.

Following is a list of the medications that are readily available without a prescription, in case you are flirting with the idea of flying here immediately for a little pain relief. My first choice of pain relief is the over-the-counter margarita. You don't need a prescription for that, just proof of age. The cost varies but some places offer a fix for as little as three dollars a glass. You could feel a lot better, I am told, if you take three margaritas twice a day, like at lunch and then again at dinner. Some people here say breakfast is a good time too.

Here are your advertised options to use for various maladies: Cipro, Z-Pack, Reflex, Retin-A, Tramadol, Amoxicillin, Penicillin, Bactrim, Flexeril, Valtrex, Ampicillin, Celebrex, Cortizone, Testosteroviagrane, Sleeping Pills, Diet Pills, Pain Pills, and Viagra. In the same aisle, you can also purchase cold drinks, sun block, and souvenirs.

The Tiki Bar of tiki bars - Saturday, January 28

Another beautiful sunny blue-sky afternoon in Cabo. Ain't it great, day after day. One more pearl on the string of pearls. Seventy-five degrees. Not a cloud in the sky. Not a ripple on the water. I rode the cruiser to the backdoor of Solomon's Landing in the marina. The back door was deep inside a large building of big hallways and arches and expansive tile floors. Hacienda style. No shops in this interior. It is poorly lit, comprised mostly of solid windowless walls with a few doors to the unknown and a lot of small openings in the ceiling for a good view of blue skies. I mention this because I like riding inside this complex of buildings, through the inner courtyards, and up and down the hallways. Makes me feel sneaky good. It's a very open area so access is easy and with a plethora of handicap ramps it is particularly inviting for daring bikers on cruisers. And we know how many of them there are. That would be me and me only. A few pedestrians cut through the network of courtyards but none of them give me a second look. That's a good thing. I was on the lookout for marina cops. I didn't see any inside the complex, though plenty outside. That's a good thing, too. That comes with being sneaky. It was fun to ride on very smooth and clean tiles in and out of the shadows. It really brought the kid out of me. Sneaky me.

Time to get as close to the marina sidewalk as I can on two wheels. I found a narrow alley out of the hacienda's maze leading to the marina walkway. It was just wide enough for my cruiser's handle bars to clear on both sides. Almost a knuckle scraper, but not if I rode straight and true. On the cruiser, it is easy to ride straight and true because the rider is straight and his heart is true. And he's a little crazy in a good way, probably from being so sneaky. The alley opened onto the front corner of Solomon's Landing, ten feet from its front door on my left and fifty feet from a marina cop on my right. I dismounted with great haste and pushed the bike past Solomon's Landing and kept pushing.

I liked Solomon's Landing from the start and I mean the start: that's where I had breakfast my first day in Cabo. This time, I decided to pick another place when I got even with the front door. Impulsive I was, had nothing to do with the cop. I pushed the cruiser past the entrance and moved on in search of something new. There was no shortage of choices. I was in the mood for a tiki bar, which is what I call any place that's open-air with palm fronds woven into a thatched ceiling. Most of the bars had chairs running up and down the length of the front railing for customers to people-watch the tourists on the marina walkway. Those were also good seats for a view into boat land. Up ahead, about a hundred yards, were three tiki bars in a row. I knew the names of the first two but don't recall seeing a name anywhere for the third one. I'd pick the one that gave off the best vibes. Which is to say the one with the best-looking women in it. Hey, you can get your kicks from Route 66. I get mine from a mix and a-mingle in the jingling feet, that's the jingle bell rock. How stupid is that! I'm keeping it in, even if my editor screams. He won't, because I am the editor.

The first of the Tiki bars is Griceldas Smokehouse, a name that I don't understand, but it's the largest of the three and it's true to tiki form. It's loud and loaded with big screen TVs too, and full of guys watching college basketball. Not a great vibe, if you know what I mean. The second tiki bar is the Baja Cantina. I haven't been out much at night but this is a bar with a reputation for a lot of late night action. Action sounds pretty good to me, but I'm never in it. Late night doesn't work for me. I prefer dreamland late at night. Still, it's got that classic tiki look with varnished wood furniture and overhead beams held together by thick intertwined barge rope loaded with sailor's knots. It also had a lot of TVs, something I never noticed before in this bar. Alas, it did not have the vibe I was looking for either. By the time I made my mind to nix it I was rolling up to the entrance or the third tiki bar, the one with no signage. One look inside this open-air bar and I could feel the vibe. It was good.

I locked my bike to a post way out of the sidewalk mainstream, one that was against the front facade of this bar of an unknown name to me. I stopped a tourist at the bottom of the stairs, on his way out. I intercepted him and politely asked:

"What is the name of this tiki bar?"

"The Tiki Bar."

"Yeah, this one," I replied, "I can see that, but I can't see a sign with a name anywhere."

"No," he laughed, "It's the Tiki Bar."

I looked at him, quizzically, not really understanding his reply, until he said:

"This is the Tiki Bar. Its name is The Tiki Bar."

"Really?" I countered in disbelief, suddenly feeling like English had become my second language. Who is on first. What is on second. Now this.

Abbot: What is this tiki bar?

Costello: Tiki Bar.

Abbot: Yes. This one.

Costello: The Tiki Bar.

Abbot: Yes! What is this called?

Costello: I just told you.

Abbot: No, you didn't. Say it again.

Costello: The Tiki Bar.

Abbot: Yeah, The Tiki Bar.

Costello: That's what it is.

Abbot: I know. But what is the name?

Costello: Really, The Tiki Bar.

Abbot: Really!

Costello: The name of this tiki bar is The Tiki Bar.

Abbot: Oh. I get it.

"Yep, really." He laughed. "It's a great bar, locals like it."

I said "Thanks" as he walked away and I walked in. How perfect. I wanted a tiki bar and I got The Tiki Bar of tiki bars. Now I'm ready for a beer in The Tiki Bar. I am not making this up.

As I said, the place had good vibes. I took the three steps up and in and immediately said hi to two blonde vibes sitting at the railing next to the entrance steps. They said hi back and smiled at me and, when I asked, they confirmed that this place is The Tiki Bar.

I had a nice cold Pacifico and a nice warm conversation with the two women. For openers, I asked them if this was their favorite place (Yes) and to tell me about some of their other favorite places before swapping a little background information. They've been living in Cabo for ten years. Both divorced. Both not much younger than me (my guess). Both attractive. Both fun. And then the deal breaker for me: neither of them spoke Spanish. *Nada* after ten years. Our conversation was all in English and I wanted

Spanish. Somehow, I lost sight of my original goal for the afternoon. I probably lost sight of my senses too, because I was feeling some very good vibes. I ordered a beer and we three continued our chatter. After I drained the bottle, I gave them each one of my business cards, featuring my work as the artist Tomaso DiTomaso. It had my email address on it, which was enough. I signaled for *la cuenta*. We chatted for a minute about my artwork and the samples printed on my cards before my bill came. They promised to google my art just as the waiter handed showed up.

I tried my Spanish on the waiter, a young Mexican who must be into weight lifting in his spare time. He appreciated my attempt at Spanish, I think. Clearly, I was in an all-American, English only bar. His name is Lucio. He said he works six days a week. I said I hoped to see him again for a little more Spanish. He smiled and said something I didn't understand. He was busy, so I didn't take up any more of his time. I made a mental note that Lucio was friendly and helpful with my effort. I said bye to the vibes and moved on not expecting to hear from them. This time, I wanted a different bar, not one on the marina, one where I could speak Spanish. I needed something with a different kind of vibe if I was going to be true to my commitment to learn Spanish. Three minutes later I walked into Cabo Cantina, one block off the marina.

Cabo Cantina again - Saturday, January 28

I locked the cruiser to the lamppost in front of the casino next door to Cabo Cantina. I walked twenty yards up the sidewalk to the Cabo Cantina's open sidewalk layout. I liked its openness. The sidewalk tables were very inviting in the afternoon sunshine, but I wanted a seat indoors, in the shade. Being on a busy street added a little local energy to the place that didn't exist on the touristy marina walkway. The place just had a good feeling to it, so that's why I picked it.

The overall look of Cabo Cantina is appealing with a layout that offered many seating options including bar stools, sidewalk tables, bar tables, and regular tables for four, six or eight. I like that. There was even a back room for private parties. The servers seemed friendly and greeted me with a nod or a smile as I entered. Once past the few bar tables on the sidewalk, a step up to a red tiled floor will get you formally into the place by being under its thatched roof. When I walked in, it wasn't easy to miss me as a customer calling. At six-three with worn topsiders, khaki tacky cargo shorts and a black t-shirt, all under a floppy sun hat, I profiled perfectly as an American tourist.

Ten steps in I was greeted by a short, jovial, robust, round-faced Mexican man about my age, maybe a few years older. Right away I can expect I'll get excellent service because this afternoon there's only one other customer, at the bar. I say *hola* to Jorge, who I had met the first time I was in for a beer. He is the bartender who took care of me during the Packer's defeat on Sunday. I reintroduced myself again, but it wasn't necessary because he remembered me and called me by my name. Pretty impressive memory. I shouldn't be surprised, of course, because I already know that Jorge is that kind of bartender who remembers every customer who ever bought a drink from him. And I think customers remember Jorge. He is out-going, convivial, and couldn't possibly be nicer. He is also a physical force. Besides being over six feet tall, he moves around the bar faster than a gecko on the run and does the work of three when it comes to mixing drinks when the place is packed. He clearly knows what he is doing, which was my take on him the first time I saw him.

For whatever reason, this time I opt out of a bar stool this time and slide into a high chair at a bar table for four. It's close enough to the bar that Jorge and I can throw some chatter at each other, so I don't feel it was an unfriendly move on part. I just wanted some more elbow room so I can comfortably overlook the entire restaurant area instead of right into the bar inventory. Also, the seat gave me plenty of room, not just for my open *Spanish for Gringos* workbook on the table top, but with plenty of room left over for a Pacifico and a food order. Today, a late lunch was on the docket.

Within thirty seconds of parking my body at the bar table and opening my book, a tall, sturdy Mexican waiter comes up to me with a menu and service. I like him right away. He has a great smile of bright white teeth. He has shiny dark eyes. He speaks English fairly well. I waste no time in telling him that I am learning Spanish. That I've been here in Cabo only four weeks. That I will be here until April. And that I prefer not to speak any English at all. His name is Andres. I introduce myself as Tomas, of course. He really warms up to my commitment to Spanish. Mexican servers are really appreciative of customers who try to speak Spanish. Frankly, they don't get that out of gringos very often. I think it's actually a surprise for them when they run into it because so many of the bars in the marina have only American and Canadian customers who do not even attempt Spanish.

When I walked in business was slow. An hour later and with a vegetarian burrito and two beers in my stomach business is still slow. This pace turned out to be a good thing for me. Andres hung at my table. Perhaps he was happy to have someone to kill the time with him. Perhaps it was simply in his good nature to gravitate to customers. Or he is simply drawn to friendly people. That would be me. Perhaps he just felt good about helping me with Spanish. Or all four reasons. I really enjoyed his presence at my table; he had an indefinable and very likable presence about himself. We laughed a lot. He has the right kind of banter and pacing that created a very comfortable learning experience. He was enthusiastic from the start in helping me along with my Spanish. It was a good learning experience for me, of course, because Andres was able to explain so much to me. And, it was a good learning experience for him because I was able to help him a bit with his English. Clearly, it was a win-win situation we both enjoyed. I left a big tip for him and the promise to return tomorrow. He seemed to be happy with that, on both counts. I was happy too because I felt I suddenly might have two new friends, Jorge and Andres.

We are all Americans - Sunday, January 29

It's funny what topics come up in my random conversations with Mexicans around town. I now stop to chat with just about any Mexican that looks open to exchanging a few words with a gringo. It is easier for me to muster the courage to do this because I know that a lot of them, notably the ones in the tourist business, want to speak English as much as I want to speak Spanish. We can help each other, so sometimes conversations really take off, especially in the marina. Of course, I really don't care what the topic is, I'm just happy to try out my Spanish. I'll chat about anything. Except Artificial Intelligence, black holes in space, and String Theory. I don't understand every word spoken to me, of course. Sometimes I don't understand any of them. Comprehension comes and goes with this way of learning. But I'm learning more words every day, so this experience gets better and better with time. I listen very carefully, almost strenuously at times, to understand what the topic is in the conversation. I'm happy if I just get that much out of a conversation. Lack of comprehension doesn't stop me from smiling and nodding as if I am comprehending everything being said. I don't mind asking someone to repeat whatever they said. It comes with immersion.

I had an interesting conversation in Spanish this morning. Actually, they are all interesting to me at this stage in my learning, but this one was particularly interesting because I was listening to a point of view that I had heard long ago, but had forgotten. The Mexican I was talking to this morning is a vendor acquaintance named Ruben. He is jovial and always smiling. I like him. He has one of the nicest tourist activity booths on the marina walkway. Ruben is one of the friendliest vendors. He talks to every tourist that is coming towards his booth. He can do this easily because his English is pretty good. For me, he's always good for a one-minute conversation in Spanish, maybe two if I'm lucky, before he has to get back to his job of hawking the sidewalk tourists in English. The marina is the best place for me to find Mexicans like Ruben, interested in a minute or two of chit chat with gringos during a lull in business, which occurs whenever strolling tourists are scarce. For many of them, it's a good chance to get an English lesson from a gringo, so we help each other with learning the other's native language. Business was in a lull with Ruben.

On the marina, I think all the vendors have seen me many times over the past few weeks, so I am no longer a stranger to most and, obviously not a typical weekend getaway tourist. Almost all of them say hi or at least nod. A few greet me by name. Some call out compliments to the cruiser. My bike is a good conversation starter, for sure. I probably know half a dozen vendors by name and chat with them sporadically, depending on whether they are busy or not just because the bike is something easy to talk about. They are all aware of my interest in learning Spanish, of course, which greases the skids for these impromptu conversations.

Anyway, back to my conversation with Ruben. I guess we moved far enough into our burgeoning friendship for Ruben to express a disappointment about the use of a particular moniker: American. That's the word that bugs Ruben. He explained to me, in Spanish, of course, which I requested, of course, that I am an American and he, too, is an American. All Mexicans are Americans too. This is true, he lectured, by virtue of their shared residency in North America. He pointed out that all the people in Central American are Americans as well. We took turns naming the countries south of Mexico. I added that we might as well call everyone in South America an American, too. We started naming countries in South America, too. Listening carefully to each other's pronunciation. He smiled and quickly agreed. Ruben and I saw eye to eye on this. Easy enough. I didn't argue, he has a point. He and I are Americans. North Americans.

However, self, I guess citizens of the United States are "the" Americans because that's what US citizens called themselves with the founding of our democracy. Citizens of the U.S. weren't even the first to call themselves Americans. The name was an offshoot of Amerigo Vespucci, an Italian explorer and map maker who explored the Atlantic coast of South America, but never North America. Never. The "America" identity appeared on some of his maps, but, like I said, not for North America. About that time on maps, North America was identified as Terra Nova meaning New Land. I suppose we should be Terranovians, instead of Americans. I think our forefathers claimed the name America by virtue of being the loudest voice in declaring it so. I got Ruben's point. I was very agreeable and moved on happy with another shot at speaking Spanish, over any topic.

Coincidentally, as I rode away, the light bulb in head clicked on. I recalled perusing the Huffington Post online this morning. In the Mexican edition, I kept coming across the word *estadosunidenses* in articles about the U.S. Of course! That's who we are specifically to the Mexicans. That's their name for people of the United States. Less and less is it *americanos*. If you know that *Estados Unidos* is the name of our country in Spanish, you will get it too. U.S. citizens are Americans, of course, but Ruben can say he too is an American, per his definition. Citizens of the U.S. are also *estadosunidenses*. Ruben can't say he is that too, by any definition.

My Tommy Bahama shirts - Monday, January 30

Now that Juanie at Ola has done my laundry a few times I am very much aware of what I am wearing. And what I am not wearing. I've not been wearing any of my three short-sleeve primo Tommy Bahama button shirts. They are pretty snazzy, but not so snazzy just hanging in the closet. Gee, I could have come down here with fewer pieces of clothing, an appealing thought to me. But since I have those shirts, I probably should up my game. But when? I wonder what it will take for me to do that, for me to swap out one of my black t-shirts for a few hours of the Tommy Bahama look. What exactly is that look down here? Who wears that brand? Can't say for sure, but in the States, I think it is the brand name for middle-aged guys who have done pretty well in life. Guys with a tropical bent. Guys that have a lot of money because these shirts cost over a hundred dollars each. Unless you get them at a secondhand shop, like I did. I don't know if I can easily give up my t-shirt uniform to convey that tropical look even though I am in the tropics. Sub-tropics, more accurately. It will take a special event for that to happen and I don't see any on the horizon. I'm not a special event kind of guy.

The daily circuit through town - Monday, January 30

As with almost every day, after riding to Walmart, I rode the cruiser into the downtown area. Sometimes I do this twice a day. I'm walking the marina sidewalk less and less after going there almost every day for the first few weeks. I need the exercise my bike gives me and since the marina cops don't like me to ride on the marina sidewalk, I haven't been going there as much. I'm still in an exploration mode with aimless junkets into the streets well out of the tourist sections. Nonetheless, almost every day, the core of my ride includes a circuit that takes me into the thick of the tourists.

From Coromel, I take the cruiser down the Lazaro Cardenas Boulevard with the flow of traffic going into *el centro*. Once in the heart of town, I ride past six or seven blocks of the shopping district's stores, all crammed with the merchandise I expected to see in a tourist district. I hate all that cramming and all that junk. I call it crippy crap. I can't believe that stuff sells. Maybe it doesn't. After that I turn left onto Paseo de la Marina Boulevard. A right turn would take me up a very long and steep road that runs up the hill to the tony Pedregal neighborhood. I take the marina boulevard to its end, which is the mouth of the harbor, just past the coast guard station. I like to stop and dismount at the jetty that defines that side of the entrance to the harbor. It is easy to sit there for ten minutes observing the boat life on the bay and absorbing the beautiful view out over the water as far as the eye can see. It's a great view of Medano beach. It's fun to watch the boat traffic moving in and out of the harbor, all dedicated to the tourist trade. It really gives me a sense of how busy this place is. On most days, one of the big cruise ships, like a Princess, is anchored in the bay. I've already seen several this week. They are big boats, stunning in size actually. Each is a floating city that floods Cabo with thousands of tourists after the anchor is dropped.

My return ride is a slightly different route because of the traffic flow created by one-way streets. For my return trip, I start out on the Paseo de la Marina Blvd. which is the road I came in on. It quickly loses its boulevard status and becomes a big one-way street that takes me through the heart of the tourist district, the opposite direction from when I rode into town. En route, well after the coast guard station, I go right past the dolphin tank. I can't pass that massive concrete swimming pool without experiencing a pang of sadness for those captured, impounded lovely sea creatures. A few blocks past the dolphin prison is Cabo Cantina. It's on my right. I like the guys there. I'm getting to know them, almost all of them. I'll drop in again. When I've been doing my little circuit this week, I usually stop at the curb in front of Cabo Cantina when it feels right, which means one of the servers is on the sidewalk by the restaurant's outdoor tables. It means a chance to try some Spanish. If no one is on the sidewalk, I just yell and wave as I go by, maybe calling out, *Hasta luego!* like a deranged gringo. This time, I yelled. A minute later the one-way street reverts back to real boulevard status once again, this time as the outgoing lane for the Lazaro Cardenas Boulevard.

That's pretty much the end of the core of my fixed circuit. From that point, there's a variety of roads I can take back to Coromuel to close the loop. I have many options for what's next. One of the roads I've been taking lately, also called the Paseo de la Marina (the street, not the boulevard), takes me right past a restaurant called Gardenias. I like the look of the place. It's open and airy and often has a nice crowd but not too much of a crowd. Too many customers might interfere with my desire for reasonable service. It looks like everyone there is a tourist but that's okay with me. Sometimes tourists know what they're doing. Maybe I'll try it out. I decided last week that I can't be an immersion snob.

Another confrontation with the marina police - Wednesday, February 1

Four days after my last attempt to park my bike on the marina sidewalk in front of a tiki bar I decided to take another shot at it. The police chased me away last time but maybe they won't bother me again. Who knows, maybe a different cop. Maybe no cop. Once it's locked and I step away, no cop can tell me to park away from the marina. That was my logic. I rode to the marina in the late afternoon, dismounted and pushed my bike to Griseldas Smokehouse, one of the popular tiki bars. I liked it when I felt like watching sports. Griceldas has the most TVs and biggest screens. I locked the cruiser right to the restaurant's front railing, foot level, and pressed it up against the building's facade as much as possible, enough to be out of anyone's way. Two minutes later I was sucking on a bottle of Pacifico on the bar railing overlooking the marina sidewalk. No cops in sight. A minute later that changed. One came out of nowhere, stood next to the cruiser, which was only ten feet away from me, and looked around, for me no doubt. It is the only bike that is ever in the marina. Its distinct cruiser look is very memorable. I pulled back from the railing and slunk to a table a little farther into the restaurant, off the railing and out of the cop's line of sight.

After two beers, the cop was still standing near my bike, obviously waiting for me to show up. Why? To arrest me? Maybe. I didn't really think so, but I wondered if that was possible. Or, confiscate the cruiser? More possible. I didn't like either possibility, however slim the odds. I needed help. My waiter is Gabriel. I got his name when I walked in. He is also the manager, so he can make things happen. After that second beer, I told him about my predicament and that I was a little afraid to leave, fearful of a confrontation with the cop that was looking for me. Instantly, Gabriel took my side and then, unexpectedly, he took action.

On my behalf, Gabriel half-yelled at the cop, said something, but I don't know what. I did make out the words "tourist" and "good customer." One minute later, OMG, it worked. The cop said a few words to Gabriel, not nice ones, turned away, and sauntered down the marina. Time for my getaway. I thanked Gabriel. We bonded. I tipped him well and left in haste. I guess the cops were serious about not wanting to see the cruiser parked on the marina sidewalk. Stupid rule. Gabriel told me that he told the cop that I was a good customer, that tourists are important, and that the bike was on restaurant property by virtue of being locked to the restaurant's railing. Apparently, the spiel worked. I'd have to let the dust settle before I tried that again, maybe a few weeks later would I take another shot at parking on the marina. Or never.

<u>New faces, new places - Tuesday, January 31</u>

The cruiser gives me incredible mobility around town with ease and speed. I'm spending less time on the marina, or it seems that way, and more time running around other parts of town and in and out of the nooks and crannies of the *barrios*. Maybe it is more accurate for me to say I am branching out, expanding my world of possibilities. Going where no one has gone before. Okay, okay, not exactly that. It's also the only exercise I get. Which is probably not good. More would be nice, but a different kind. Something else to think about. And a reason to do even more explorations into the outlying neighborhoods of this tourist driven town.

Today I decided I need to interact even more with Spanish speaking people. Mexicans only. I am convinced it's the best way to learn Spanish. And it's not that difficult to go that route. I am constantly impressed how nice Mexicans are. They are quick to smile, quick with a greeting, and always polite. It all makes me want to work harder at learning Spanish, so I can feel closer in. *Poco a poco*. I am committing the afternoon to going face to face with some new faces. Fresh conversations will take me to the next level by testing me on what I've learned already and exposing me to new stuff.

Fishing update at Cabo Cantina - Tuesday, January 31

I was sitting at the bar at Cabo Cantina right after the lunch hour crush, by myself, when two people took over the bar stools next to me. An American couple. After a few minutes passed to let them get settled with their space and have the first few sips of their margaritas, I struck up a conversation with Judy and her husband David, a couple from Spokane, Washington. They were here for three weeks with only three more days left. They said they were not looking forward to going home, back to eastern Washington state's winter. It was cold in that part of Washington state, nothing like temperate Seattle.

This is a couple definitely committed to Cabo. Departure depression was beginning to set in, so they said. David and Judy have been coming down here for twenty years, always staying at the Terrasol Beach Resort on the Pacific side of Cabo, the resort over the hill that is closest to the Pacific beach and as close as you can get to The Arch. This year they booked a room overlooking the Pacific which was a splurge because budget issues usually kept them off the ocean side and on the land side. After twenty years of visiting Cabo, could they speak Spanish? No. Not a word of it at the bar. Pretty sad.

Judy reminded me of a frontier woman with a look and an air of plain ruggedness, but nice ruggedness. The look came from her thin, chiseled face haloed by short, thick brunette hair that was being invaded by a few strands of contrasting gray. She had deep smile lines that might be genetic because there wasn't much of a smile working on them. I knew she had an independent attitude, she told me as much, very specifically, in the telling of her determination to make a go at her landscaping business that was nothing but fifteen years of struggling. I think that's called a labor of love. She was mildly interesting, but talked too much. She quickly wore me down. I tried to interrupt her stride by finding out more about her chinless husband leaning back in his bar stool seated on her left. I was seated on her right.

David was not really into our conversation. He was more into his margarita. I don't think it was his first. Or his second. Of course, he knew his wife's history. They had been together long enough that neither of them had heard a story from the other less than ten times, maybe twenty. He appeared to be hiding from the world, almost invisible under his big floppy, top grade sun hat chosen, no doubt, for its practicality. My kind of hat. It was either two sizes too big or his head was a small head, not just in hat size. I figured him for a hiker. Maybe they both were. They both had lean bodies, unusual for Americans, which is why I guessed they were Canadians when I first saw them. Their lean, bony frames were the kind that one associates with hikers. Judy took a long sip of her margarita, which gave me a very short window to engage David. This was a good thing because after fifteen minutes of Judy's monologue I needed to switch channels. As it turns out, changing the channel was a lucky thing for me. I was about to discover that Judy's husband knew stuff that I wanted to hear about.

David said he loved coming down here to fish. His favorite fishing wasn't from a boat but from the beach. That caught my attention. He said every morning he's ever been here he's up at the crack of dawn with his gear and hikes down the slippery slope to the beach below the hotel. He loved fishing off the beach and Cabo was the only place he went surf casting. David has known about the dangers of the Pacific shoreline waters for twenty years. I could tell that from his initial comments. He was a veteran. Surf casting on that beach below his hotel is relatively safe as long as one doesn't get within a mile of the water. Kidding, but it is dangerous to stand in the surf. He said he stands in the surf. Also, everyone on the beach, fishing or not, needs to keep an eye on the horizon for rogue waves. That sort of thing can catch someone by surprise and suck them out to sea in the backwash. David said he was aware of the dangers. He was sitting there, in person, so he didn't have to tell me that he had never been sucked out to sea. Like most surfcasters, he was always surprised with his catch: surfcasters generally do not know what they have on the line until the hooked fish is relatively close to being dragged on shore. Personally, I love that kind of suspense. Maybe it's a small shark, it could be! Not a good thing.

We talked about the fish he caught, which means he mostly talked. I was all ears and staring at him, showing that I was fully captivated, afraid that his wife was going to interrupt. He was saying that all kinds of fish can be caught from the beach. I knew fifty pounders aren't all that rare. He said he hadn't hauled any fish that big on the shore but he might have had a few on a line that eventually broke. I thought about it. A fifty pounder is a lot of fish to drag up on the sand. He caught all kinds of fish over the years during his visits to Cabo, including Roosterfish, Sierra, Jack Crevalle, Groupers, Yellowtail, and even some reef manta rays, but not giant ones.

I asked David about manta rays. I think they are interesting but a little creepy, I imagine, if caught. I said I never caught one and hoped I never would catch one. Yep, he said, he caught some. Didn't like catching them. No surprise there. It's tricky getting the hook out of them, he said. He wasn't sure about venomous spines. We both think that just applies to giant mantas, the ones that can be big enough to have eight-foot wing spans.

On a dark note, a couple of days ago, in the Cabo Cantina, I met the cameraman who swore he witnessed the death of the Australian Crocodile Hunter, Steve Irwin. Irwin's crew was doing some underwater filming of him playing with manta rays. The cameraman said to me that a stingray that Irwin was holding onto, stabbed at him "hundreds of times." When they got Irwin out of the water and on the boat, they knew it was too late to save him. So did Irwin. Irwin's final words were "I'm dying." Another reason for any fisherman to hope that a manta ray is the one that got away.

Surf fishing was one of the things that interested me, and a reason I came to Cabo. I gave up the idea, too soon, because a tackle store manager said I had to drive over to the Pacific shore to catch anything. It sounded like his advice was contradicting David's twenty years of experience. I ask David about the conflicting advice I got. He let the tackle store manager off the hook when he said the fish weren't biting off the shoreline of Cabo this year. Nothing, no fish, maybe because the water temperatures had changed a bit. That's what a fishing guide told him as an explanation to his own bad luck this trip. My hopes rose at first and then were dashed once again for any chance of walking to a nearby beach to fish. A few minutes later I paid my bar bill for two Pacificos and walked out. Interesting conversation but time to get back to studying Spanish. I said goodbye to Jorge and smiled with a wave to a couple of the waiters I remembered seeing during one of my several visits since the Packers lost to the Falcons two Sundays ago. I left wondering if I should drive to the Pacific sometime in the near future for a shot at a fifty-pounder flounder. My luck to get a manta ray.

Gardenias restaurant - Tuesday, January 31

Today, after two post-lunch Pacificos at Cabo Cantina and my usual mid-day ride through *el centro*, I decided to try the food at Gardenias for a late afternoon lunch. It is my favorite time for lunch because sometimes I skip dinner because it's so late in the day. I locked up the cruiser on a lamppost close to the entrance. Moments later I got about twenty feet in before I ran into the hostess. I tried a greeting with her in Spanish, but there wasn't any time for more than that. No waiting for a table today. She walked me into the center and indicated that I had a choice of three tables. I took the one up against the wall and waited patiently for a server. I'm not in a hurry. I can use the time to think about my opening lines in Spanish and survey the restaurant.

Gardenias is a simple layout. The restaurant is contained in one large, rectangular room under a high ceiling. One end is open to the sidewalk. Above that opening, there is a big roll down metal sheet, like a garage door, for lock up at night. Along one of the long walls there is a small bar close to the sidewalk, with five stools, four are occupied. Then some kind of food preparation station next to the bar, separated from the large seating area by a low slung skinny wall with a tiny countertop, big enough for a plate. Farther in, toward the back, is a small kitchen where all the cooking occurs. It too is open to the dining area but separated from the dining area by a continuation of that skinny counter. Restrooms are in the back, way back, somewhere under an opening in the ceiling, judging from the sunlight pouring in.

It is basic in every aspect, no frills in this restaurant. It's the kind of place that attracts people because of the food, not the atmosphere. Even so, it is a pleasant atmosphere, just nothing to write home about (I'm not writing home). The decor is simple, almost austere. The walls are painted a soft yellow, with a tangerine accent on a couple of ceiling arches. The rest of the decor is all about white. Two dozen white plastic tables and white plastic chairs all supported by a nearly white tile floor. In unison, these elements create an impression of a clean, healthy, bright environment. It is not boring at all, hardly a white-out. The customers provide the color. So does a seven-foot Marlin mounted in the middle of the long wall opposite the kitchen. Five much smaller fish pose under the Marlin, hardly worth mentioning. Some odd sized framed photos run eye-high on the wall along the full length of the wall, but they're barely noticeable. That's the extent of the decor. Though the overall look is not minimalism, it strikes me as that. I like it. I am thinking I'll like the food too. What I see on the plates of the customers near me looks delicious. I have no reason to believe this will be anything but a great experience.

The Cock Cantina - Tuesday, January 31

Towards the end of the day, satiated from a delightful meal at Gardenias, I was cruising in and out of the back streets behind the Puerto Paraiso Mall, two blocks in from the marina, when I stumbled on a cool looking corner bar farther down the same street as the Mall's huge concrete parking structure. I leaned the cruiser on a skinny lamppost and locked it up within ten feet of this charming little corner bar with a memorable name, The Cock

Cantina. The place was tiny. The Tiny Cock Cantina? A total of eight bar stools, four on each leg of the bar wrapping around the corner of the sidewalk. No tables unless you wanted to hike up to its roof top. It was a very attractive layout. Small, even intimate because of close quarters, not because of anything else. Only two customers were seated at the bar, friends, chatting with each other. They drew me in when I cruised by, inducing a tricky U-turn without looking obvious about my interest in meeting them. Two blondes, each attached to a pair of long legs were chatting on two bar stools also with long legs on one leg of the bar. That's fourteen legs in all, with four of them being particularly attractive. The blondes had a case of beer between them, sitting on the bar. A case of Pacifico. I had a case of nerves. It was my shyness that kept me from sitting next to them on their side of the bar, but no big deal. The place was so tiny wherever I sat would seem like we were seated together, like one big table. I sat on the other leg of the bar, looking for an opening to break into their conversation. They looked interesting, besides being attractive, so why not? Speaking English to strangers was something I wasn't doing much of these days. I know, you're thinking I saw the two blondes first when I approached The Cock. Not exactly. Sort of, but it took more than two pretty faces to get me to stop. It took a case of Pacifico. That was something I could relate to!

The truth is, I saw the case of Pacifico sitting on the bar first, then the blondes, which closed the deal. I picked The Cock and it was a good time for a cold beer. Pacifico is my brand of beer on this adventure, so I pay attention when the name lands in front of me. I sat down, briefly smiled at the two blondes. Got the smile returned moments before I introduced myself to the bartender, a young kid in his early twenties. His name is José. His English is good, good enough for my purposes. However, as I've said many times before, I refused to speak English. I might even have said, *No hablo inglés*, to get a laugh out of him because clearly I am a gringo and The Cock must be a gringo bar. It's at the bottom of the gumdrop hill that goes up and then down right into the valet parking for Mango, a perfect location for thirsty gringos going to and coming from the beach.

José's bar is on a busy corner. That makes it an interesting place to linger as cars and taxi vans shuttle by constantly with beach goers and beach leavers. Along with the passing crowd of beach life as well. I chatted a bit with him when he wasn't tidying up the bar and checking on the other two customers. I turned away from looking at the bar's inventory of booze and switched my gaze to the two ladies. I was ready to try out my flirty English on them, a language that I hadn't used in weeks. I probably forgot how to do it but it didn't hurt to try. Be bold, I said to my inner self.

The ice broke with the blondes and the chatting began with the usual tourist banter. I quickly learned that the two women were on a beer run. I complimented them on their choice. They said they are two of twelve women down here for a girls' weekend to celebrate a fiftieth birthday. I love a party so I offered to carry the case of Pacifico for them, clever me, but I was denied the pleasure. I wondered if they saw my fangs come out. I haven't had a date down here and I am thinking chances are slim. No surprise there if indeed they saw my fangs. Of course, I'm not here to party. But it was a fun idea. I'm here to learn Spanish. They left. I guess that was my cue. The case of Pacificos left with them. Then I left on the cruiser riding in the opposite direction of the case of Pacificos. I waved *adios* to José. I liked him right away. I didn't expect to see the Pacifico blondes again. Clearly, the cantina was The Cock and I was not.

First day with the Bicks - Wednesday, February 1

My very dear friends Stewart and Londa Bick are here for a week. They are staying in their timeshare at a resort about ten miles north of town called Dreams. I was there five years ago with them for a couple of days. Dreams is dreamy. First class, on the beach, huge party pool with swim up bar, two other more private pools on the grounds, surrounded by eight championship golf courses, encompasses four à la carte restaurants, a buffet, a grill and a café to choose from. And all the food and booze is free for the timeshare guests. Because of all those amenities it was tough for me to talk Stew and Londa to meet me in town at a restaurant where you actually have to pay for food and booze. I talked them into coming into town for two of the three days we were sharing, a Wednesday and Friday. We three would spend the third day in each other's company for Super Bowl Sunday at Dreams. By the way, Stew and Londa stayed at my house in the south of France three years ago, so I happen to know they are great world travelers. And, they are a lot of fun.

Stew is a retired emergency room doc. Besides being a great guy, smart as a whip, a great athlete and old friend, it's good to have him nearby. I always confess that I am happy to be in the company of his capable hands. Especially if I get a heart attack. Or a broken bone. Or a headache. Or a hole in one. Or if I need a little consultation. In addition, he is a very lucky man because Londa Bick agreed to marry him, that was fourteen years ago. She's terrific, too. She is a chief administrator in overseeing twenty-two hospitals in Indiana. She is also the chief administrator in overseeing Stew. So, smart! And a beauty. I'm a lucky guy to have them as friends.

Our reunion in Cabo started at The Office restaurant on Medano Beach. Next to Mango. We three took a table for four in the sand, not far from the water. Fortunately, the tented restaurant was roped off from the vulture vendors roaming the beach. It was a beautiful setting. Turquoise table cloth, marine blue tented tarp ceiling, pale blue napkins, white tables and chairs all joined forces to deliver a fresh, nautical beach atmosphere that packed the house with tourists. Yes, we started with margaritas, of course, that caused a lightning storm of catch up stories. The pace slowed a bit over the Alaskan Crab and Avocado Quesadillas covered in fresh, cilantro salsa. Two hours of bliss with old friends in a perfect setting makes me say it doesn't get much better. A fourth at our table might have made it a little better, but having Stew and Londa all to myself makes me very happy.

Our afternoon didn't end at The Office. We three walked six blocks to the marina, strolled a bit and then parked at Cabo Cantina for a rest and to quench our thirst with more margaritas. I introduced Stew and Londa to my friends, pretty much the entire staff, who graciously welcomed them while taking a few cheap shots at me, all in the name of friendship, of course. Jorge was the great entertainer at the bar. A master at his craft. Mr. Entertainment. Nearly two hours later, after too many margaritas, we moseyed out. Stew and Londa grabbed a taxi back to their Dreams. I jumped on the cruiser. Our time together was non-stop stories, catch up, and a lot of reminiscing of our days at Indiana University. Londa went there too, so no shortage of shared memories.

Cabo Cantina every day - Wednesday, February 1

The week is over and if you ask me where I've been every afternoon this week, my answer is Cabo Cantina. It feels like home. I now call it CC for short. Which, if I say that aloud, it is the same sound as *Sí! Sí!* That's Spanish for "Yes, yes" and that's how I feel about CC. It is, hands down, my *bar favorito,* easily the best place to advance my skills in Spanish.

In the past five days, I've been caught up in a hurricane of conversations and lessons, mostly with Andres and Jorge, but I made many more new friends among the CC staff, like Ray and Guillermo who are both in managerial roles, Oliver in the lunch shift who is being trained by Andres, and Martin and Gabriel with the dinner shift. It's funny, these last couple of days, when I show up I am met with triple handshakes, crazy expressions in the greeting and fist pumping, like I am some lost hero who has been found, or something like that. These guys, and they are all guys, make me really feel at home, like I am part of the team. Dare I say family? They are so likable anybody would feel the same way in my shoes. Best of all, I am getting excellent support in learning Spanish. What a lucky break that I found CC. *Sí! Sí!*

An old friend gets in touch - Wednesday, February 1

A fantastically fun day ended with a surprise text when I was climbing into bed. A beautiful young woman by the name of Jennifer, who happens to be my old business partner emailed me tonight. She said she booked a room herself in La Paz for a long weekend the first week of March and asked me if I wanted to meet up for lunch on one of those days. I immediately wrote back and said yes to that. I haven't been to La Paz, but I heard some good things about it. This would be a good excuse to make the two-hour drive to see her. I hadn't seen Jennifer in over a year, that was over dinner in San Antonio, where she lives. And I've only seen her once every year or two before that over the course of ten years. She's not only smart but a lot of fun.

Jennifer's email told me she needed a break from the 24/7 demands of her franchise business. She was wanting a pure getaway, used the word "retreat" for some personal time away from her family and the business. Away from everything. She booked a terrific B&B in La Paz for four days and that's where I could find her. In my reply, I wrote I'd meet her at the Hacienda Paraiso, where she was staying. I suggested she make time for a nice long lunch by the water. We had a lot to catch up on. We could work out the details as the time approached. Can't wait. She's terrific.

Chapter Five

Week 5

Lunch again at Gardenias - Thursday, February 2

Repeat business is the sincerest form of flattery. I went back to Gardenias for lunch. I liked it so much last Tuesday when I went for the first time that going back was a given. I had the grilled shrimp and grilled fish tacos the first time I was there and saw no reason not to have the same order again today. If I follow suit on a return visit I can just start saying I'll have the usual. I'm definitely into that restaurant. The food was delicious again. I'll be back.

A prisoner in Ricazon - Thursday, February 2

I think from my adventures, one might conclude that I am a boozer. Well, I am not. I really don't drink much, rarely more than one drink at any one place. Only twelve to fourteen places in a night. Kidding, but I might stop at three in an evening. I like to go to bars in Cabo, an activity that puts me into the vitality of this tourist town. There are some real interesting ones. Mostly I go to the bars to strike up conversations with new people. Preferably in Spanish but English usually wins out after a long day of trying Spanish. Bartenders are particularly good for an exchange, if the bar isn't too busy. Bartenders are really good targets because they know enough English to get me through the rough spots of Spanish.

This evening, one of the bars I tried for the first time is Ricazon. It is an open-air bar, well off any mainline of traffic, which is to say it is not in the marina. The host hawker was standing just outside the open-air entrance when I rode up to him.

Of course, I did my thing about wanting to learn Spanish and took his temperature with that. He said, *Bueno!* His name is Carlos. He was encouraging me and invited me in. His restaurant was half full, which makes me an optimist. I would have entered even if it was half empty. The bar seated eight but no one was at the bar. The place was more of a dinner place and all the diners were tourists. Canadians, I think, filled at least half the tables. My accent detection skills told me that as I walked in. With all that space at the bar, I was optimistic about getting a little conversation going with the bartender. I ordered a Pacifico, no surprise. When it was set in front of me, I introduced myself. The bartender's name is Antonio. I sipped and he worked. He was busier than I thought, busy fixing drinks for all the dinner guests, so not much conversation floated between us. With that very minor disappointment I finished my beer, paid, and decided to use *el baño* before riding into the night once again.

The restrooms were off the back wall of the restaurant's dining area. A woman was standing in front of the door that said *Damas*. A man popped up from a table close to the door for *Caballeros* and cut in front of me. I was sorry to see that happen as I was beginning to feel a sense of urgency. I'd have to wait. The man in front of me discovered a locked door for *Caballeros*, so he had to wait too, ahead of me. Not good, but still not a serious wait for me.

Many restaurants in Cabo, especially the smaller ones, have one-person bathrooms, one for women and one for men, like Ricazon, and sometimes just one bathroom for both men and women, which can be stressful in a busy place. More than a minute passed while the three of us stood patiently outside the occupied *baños*. I said something stupid, like "There must be a convention in town." to get a chuckle. It didn't. And why should it? More importantly, why did I think that would be funny? That's what two beers does to me. Two! When I am starting to think I am really funny, I should know that's a good sign that I am not.

A long, poorly lit, skinny hallway ran away from the customer *baños* deeper into the back of the restaurant, like fifty feet deeper. I was curious what was down there because my experience in Cabo had taught me that bathrooms can be in the dangedest of places. Truly dangedest. After waiting another minute, I sauntered off into the darkness of that long hallway. At its end, I was rewarded. At the end, on the right, was a slightly open door to a small, empty bathroom. The light was on. Bingo! I stepped into the tiny room, barely big enough for a toilet and a sink, and locked the door with gratitude that the stress would be flowing out of me very soon. Done in a minute. Mr. Speedy. After washing my hands, I made a move to unlock the door by pinching that little button in the center of the door knob and giving it a twist. You know what it looks like; you've seen a million. When I turned it, the door knob's housing for it fell on the floor. That was a surprise. I barely touched it. Now that stuff was rolling around on the floor, by my feet. That's no big deal compared to the news that the door was still locked. Locked!

Okay, I said to myself, probably an easy fix. But it wasn't. I couldn't get that button back into the door knob without the housing and I couldn't get the housing back in place. Believe me, I tried everything. Nothing worked for me. The clock was ticking. I was now somewhere between five and ten minutes in my little prison, though it seemed like an hour. It was worth an hour of fear, at least, because it is easy to think of my predicament getting worse. I knew perfectly well that this tiny bathroom was at the end of a long, dark hallway, on the road less traveled. Nobody would be waiting outside my door for their turn. Of course, I tried turning the exposed knob apparatus every fifteen seconds, thinking some inner mechanism might give so I get my freedom back.

After about fifteen minutes, feeling like five hours, I could see that jiggling the door knob was futile. I was way more concerned about my predicament than I was willing to admit. I began wondering if my best chance of breaking out, literally, would be to bust open the door with my shoulder. Or my hip. Or both at once. The door was not flimsy. My shoulder and hip might be close to flimsy, hard to say. Bruising a bone was an ugly outcome, but not as ugly as spending hours and hours in this tiny bathroom. Or would it be all night? Maybe days. At least I had water and a toilet. Humans can go about three weeks without food, I knew that much. Starvation is an awful and painful death, so to avoid that remote possibility, I did the only thing I could do. I started yelling and pounding on the door. With the passage of every minute I upped the volume and frequency of my yells. I couldn't pound on the door any harder without bruising my hand. Like I said, this was not a flimsy door.

About half an hour later, which seemed like an eternity, the door of my prison cell suddenly opened into the now well-lit hallway. A very startled waiter greeted me from the hallway. Carlos stood behind him with his mouth open. I blurted something in English that I had been locked in. The waiter said the door knob was fine. I pointed out that it was fine on his side, but not mine. He asked me how long I had been in there. I wasn't sure, maybe the longest thirty minutes of my life. How do you say that in Spanish? I thanked them and said it was time for me to go. Carlos walked me to the front entrance. On the way, out he told me in English that a customer by the restaurant's main bathrooms for customers heard noise and reported it. Thank you Jesus, Mary, and Joseph. In my very best Spanish, I thanked Carlos profusely, laughed and then said, *No problemo, buenas noches!* and walked out. Stirred but not shaken.

The Cock Cantina again - Thursday, February 2

Late Thursday night, late for me anyway, almost ten. For the second time in a week, I rode the cruiser right up to the barstools of the Cock Cantina. A little closer than the first time. It's around the corner from Ricazon. This time I was close enough to lean on the back of a bar stool without dismounting. I am more inclined to think of this place as José's Bar rather than the Cock Cantina, a name I don't particularly like, for the obvious reason. Roosters don't come to mind. José, who I liked from the start, was still in the stages of opening up. I have ridden past it enough to know that it is not a day bar. Not exactly. It is an end of day bar sometimes and a night bar most of the time. I'd say he got off to a late start tonight, unless he is re-opening after a break from the afternoon crowd. José says it's always a late-night bar. Late means it's open as long as customers are buying. The end of day aspect is for the opportunity to attract the beach crowd leaving the beach for dinner or prepping at their hotels. The night part speaks for itself. I drive by in erratic darkness, getting strobed by the street lamps often enough to be visible for José to see me and wave back. I am generally not inclined to stop when I see customers at the bar, even though José is a good guy to practice my Spanish on. When he doesn't have any customers, I always stop.

This time I stopped. It was a good time to stop. I was a little rattled from Ricazon. I had the urge to chill over a beer and, besides, I'd have José all to myself. It's hard to resist that learning opportunity. When there are other customers, it is easy to resist, which explains my frequent drive-bys, which I think of as ride-bys.

I sat on a bar stool happy to have José's attention as long as I could get it. This time I didn't get it very long. After ten minutes of a nice conversation and only half way into my Pacifico night cap, two couples, still in their beach attire, walked up to the bar and said hi. To José' and to me. It wouldn't be the first time they walked up to a bar this evening. Tongues were a little thick. The two women sat and the men stood behind them. All four ordered a shot of tequila. That's what vacations in Mexico are for, I thought to myself. Mexico is the place for tequila. Constant hydration is important in Mexico. Tequila helps if it's consumed on a regular basis. Fortunately for this foursome, they were not suffering from dehydration.

José filled four shot glasses and placed them on the bar in front of the new arrivals. He then reached under the bar and pulled out a glass jar of very small scorpions. They looked dead. Must have been. Tiny things that could fit on a quarter, but easy to recognize the breed. The girls flinched. The two guys flinched. I flinched. The dozens of small dead scorpions piled up in the jar were disgusting, reminding me of marmalade, which I hate. José talked one of the guys into putting a scorpion into his shot glass and shooting it with his tequila. Some kind of macho man opportunity, I suppose. This called for a round of pictures before a single shot was fired. It was fun to joke about it, you know, the courage of swallowing a scorpion, a dead one by the way. The actual physical experience was probably a big nothing, but not enough of a nothing to get me to try it when José asked me. I'm already macho enough. We all chatted a bit, in English, except for my sporadic Spanish interventions with José. I finished my Pacifico to the last drop and paid up as José poured the foursome a third round of tequila shots. Maybe they were dehydrated. No scorpions this time, but it was evident that the foursome was developing a rhythm in tossing down those shots. I rode away without putting a scorpion shot on my list of things to try while I was in Cabo. My opinion on that is not going to change.

<u>A gecko intruder - Friday, February 3</u>

The day is just starting. It's Friday. I can see an erratic sliver of light at the periphery of my dark-out garbage bags. I'm sitting up on my bed, back against the headboard, reading light on, reading a really interesting book called *Humans Gone Extinct*. It's a compendium of theories about human evolution, particularly about our relatives in the distant past and who our predecessors were and theories about how most of them disappeared. It took place over thousands of years. When I was growing up and celebrating holidays in my parent's home, mom and dad never thought our relatives could disappear fast enough. Then, time was measured in hours. Side joke. It's a slow read, very dense with information, much like a text book. But, unlike any text book I've ever read, every page is fascinating to me. The Neanderthals were on this planet at least one hundred thousand years longer than we've been here. I didn't know that. Sounds like our predecessors were a pretty successful bunch of guys to me.

This is the second time I'm reading *Humans Gone Extinct* this year. Each time I repeat a chapter I learn something new because of something I missed the first time around or didn't understand. I know I will read it a third time, but probably not until next year. It's a keeper as a member in my library of reference books at home. This time around it was interesting to learn that almost all humans have about two percent of their DNA that can be traced to Neanderthals. I guess our ancestors partied with them once in a while. I'll bet you didn't know that! I didn't know that before I read the book. Unless you are from Africa, you and I have a little bit of Neanderthal in us

About the tenth minute into *Humans*, I looked up, for no reason at all. Above the door, I saw something move. It caught my eye. I zeroed in. I saw a eight inch gecko tiptoeing up the wall. Its slow movement didn't attract my eye at first, but the stark contrast between its bright green coat and my white wall did get my attention. I stared, waiting for it to dash someplace. It didn't. It stopped. A minute passed before he moved again. It scurried behind the door, out of my sight. Did he know I was watching him? Did he run behind the door because why? Was he frightened of me? Maybe just sizing me up and realized he was outsized? Was he doing a threat analysis? Was it smart to be on the move in front of me, a clear and present danger? Was he wondering if I had any gecko recipes? Maybe. Surely, he knew I was in the room. What he didn't know is that I didn't care that he was in the room with me.

I've seen geckos in my various bedrooms in my worldwide travels and know they are never harmful to humans. Happily, they eat bugs, which is an admirable quality of a roommate. I do know that you will never win a staring context with a gecko because you will be the first to blink every time. They always win that game because they don't blink. Ever. They can't. Geckos don't have eyelids. They keep their eyeballs moist by licking them. Oh, is that too much information? Can you do that?

In the past, when I've shared a room with a gecko or two I've named them. I prefer thinking of them as pets rather than reptilian intruders. They're harmless, of course. Sometimes they stick around and stick to the walls, and sometimes they are one and done. This little green gecko above my door is about eight inches long from its nose to the tip of its tail. That's how I chose to name it *Ocho*. In Spanish, the number eight is *Ocho*. I liked the name immediately, *Ocho* inches. Cha cha cha! I rose from my bed to look for him behind the door. *Ocho* was gone, didn't see him go, didn't see him anywhere. I looked around the room, double checked behind the door again. Geckos are like that, sneaky little bastards. They can disappear in the blink of an eye. Yours, not theirs. Remember, they can't blink. Maybe I'll see him again. Maybe I won't. I hope he sticks around. Get it? Sticks. Like sticks to the wall.

The flowers in the Ola Laundromat - Friday, February 3

It was early in the morning for me, earlier than usual by an hour, maybe two. Sometimes that happens. I dropped in at Ola to say hi to Juanie before I took off on my bike and before her day took off with the inevitable surge of customers dropping off laundry on their way to work. The bouquet I gave to her for returning all that money she found in one of my pockets had been on her front windowsill for over two weeks. I saw it every time I rode past her place. She said she was keeping it until the last flower keeled over. I think she overshot the deadline, but I didn't say anything. She walked to the window, close to where I was standing, smiled at me and showed me the only one that still held on to its petals. Petal is more accurate. With the morning's light coming through the window, I looked into her deep brown eyes and could see her pupils dilated with love for those faded flowers and her sadness for all the petals that had fallen on the window sill long ago. It was easy to see that the last flower had already faded. I could see, too, that her love for flowers would never fade. I think that's what the poet in me thought.

The second rendezvous with the Bicks - Friday, February 3

I'm just starting my sixth week in Cabo. Today will be the second time I'll be getting together with my friends Stew and Londa Bick since their arrival four days ago. Of course, it's a big event for me when a couple of my dearest friends are in town, so I was grateful for every minute together. I had a lot of fun in Stew and Londa's company two days ago. Today would be no different with more fun on the docket, with fun beginning on the dock.

At mid-morning, I met Stew and Londa on one of the fishing docks at the far end of the marina. They had just gotten off a charter fishing boat for some early morning fishing on the Sea of Cortez. They invited me the day before to join them on the charter boat, but I passed because of my propensity to spend valuable fishing time leaning over boat railings instead. And it was too early for me; I could not get myself up at five in the morning to meet them. As it turned out, Stew and Londa were happy to share their catch with me. They caught a dozen fish and did the catch and release thing, with one exception. They kept a three-foot dolphinfish, better known as mahi mahi. I saw it moments after I saw them. It was in a bag of ice in Stew's hand of white knuckles. A nice catch. Their catch of the day would be our lunch of the day.

We three headed for Captain Tony's restaurant located in the middle of the marina walkway. It is a restaurant that is well known for its motto "You hook 'em, we cook 'em." Captain Tony's is a open-air tiki bar with a great reputation for cleaning and preparing a customer's catch to serve it up fresh and delicious in any form: grilled, fried, or as sashimi. Thirty minutes after we were seated, the mahi mahi was presented to us on a beautiful platter as sashimi for an appetizer. For the main, we savored the grilled mahi mahi in two forms, blackened Cajun style and seared with zesty basil butter. Both, to die for. Londa and I indulged in both versions. Stew is sensitive to spicy hot foods, so he passed on Cajun style. He has to be careful in Mexico!

There were plenty of margaritas on the table but beer was my choice of beverage, Pacifico, and it would be easy for me to say it was the best meal I've had since I arrived in Cabo. Captain Tony's does a great job with exceptional food prep and service, but sitting in a tiki bar at a table overlooking Cabo's yacht basin with dear friends adds a lot of flavor to the experience. Afterwards, we slow-motion walked the marina sidewalk for forty-five minutes before Stew and Londa returned to Dreams. We split with a plan that I would spend Super Bowl Sunday at Dreams. Sweet Dreams in my future! That is a good thing.

Rude American tourists - Saturday, February 4

I was just pushing my cruiser around the marina on one of my typical mid-day cruiser adventures, when I spied a white middle-aged American male tourist walk right up to the host of a restaurant who happened to be standing on the marina walkway obviously doing what restaurant hosts do, inviting customers into the restaurant. I was fifteen feet from the host, on the leg with Señor Frog's, when I witnessed this interruption. Or should I call it a blitzkrieg? The tourist loudly directs a question, in English, at the host by blurting out, "Where's Dock H?" He throws his words right in the Mexican host's face. Just those three words. No greeting. No Spanish. No nothing. The host politely answers the American's question, of course, and points the way. I wanted to intercept that rude American and "accidentally" push him into the water. Sort of. I wouldn't really do that, of course. Unless I thought I could get away with it. I see that rude behavior all the time.

A couple of days ago, I was sitting at the end of the bar at Griceldas. I had a seat next to a very large woman. An American by appearance. After I ordered a Pacifico a conversation was struck, starting with hi and then into blah, blah, blah back and forth for a couple of minutes. She tells me she's been coming to Cabo for two months every winter for the last ten years. Loves it. She finishes her drink a few minutes into our shallow conversation then orders another one from the bartender. She did this by half-shouting the order to him when he was at the other end of the bar. Not one word of Spanish came out of her mouth. Not one word after coming down here every winter for ten years! And, of course, no please or thank you, not in Spanish nor English. The bartender was very polite and took care of her. I could sense he was irked, but you couldn't tell just by looking at him. I can read that, a consequence of my immersion radar. His feelings went unnoticed by the loud woman. I had a different idea of taking care of her. I remember how well I wanted to follow her out of the bar and push her in the water.

Oh, and yesterday, something else. I was cutting through a wide, tiled breezeway between two restaurants to leave the marina to get to my bike which was locked up inland per the cops' mandate. In the middle of the cut-through, some fat, white American male with belly bloat, probably in his late thirties and wearing a skin tight, belly-busting wife-beater shirt with his stomach hanging five inches below the hem, walks past me in the hallway heading for the marina. I noticed because I had to hug the wall to let him pass. A moment later, I heard him suddenly blurt out to the Mexican man who I knew to be walking behind me, "Where's the bathroom?" That's it, just those three words. Nothing else. Not a word of Spanish.

Am I being too harsh? No, but stupid me, I thought every American tourist knew the most important Spanish words for tourists in Mexico, *Dónde está el baño?* That's right, "Where is the bathroom?" There are other Spanish words on that list of the most important words. Some of them are: excuse me, which is *disculpe,* please which is, *por favor,* and thank you, which is *gracias.* Sometimes, I'm so embarrassed for my fellow Americans. I wish they weren't that way. I wish they knew how offensive their rude behavior is to the people who serve them in Cabo. It's offensive to anyone who lives in Mexico. And don't think the Mexicans are de-sensitized to this sort of intrusively rude tourist behavior. They are good sports about it. Always polite. I feel their pain. I feel for them because my efforts to learn Spanish have brought me closer to the Mexican culture. Oh, that last guy? I wanted to follow him to the marina sidewalk so I could push him in the water. I guess that must be my coping mechanism, to want to push rude people into the water. I wonder if I'll get to the point of actually doing it.

Gardenias for dunch - Saturday, February 4

Gardenias taco restaurant is the exception that trumps my reluctance to eat restaurant food, especially by myself. The food is usually light and healthy, but you can get the fried options if you're not into healthy eating. I ate there for the first time last week and then the second time two days after that. I love their grilled fish and grilled shrimp tacos. That's all I order, one or the other. Or both. I haven't tried the chicken. I won't. I'm a pescatarian. A cheatin' pescatarian, so maybe I will try the chicken some time. I love quesadillas, but not as much as shrimp and fish tacos so I can't say what their quesadillas are like. Yet. And might never be able to say. That's just like me, find a dish I like and I'll order it again and again. That sounds like a wonderful plan for Gardenias. I had a Pacifico for my first two visits. This time, I think water will be just fine from here on. Hold off on the beer until the evening. It's a healthier lifestyle that way.

I love the atmosphere there, too. At Gardenias I can sit comfortably by myself, for as long as I want, and well after my last bite. I like sitting in the back half of the room. It's quieter and a get a nice view of the whole place and then out onto the street life. My lesson book is almost always open on the table top. I can simply relax in this no-frills atmosphere. The space feels open, airy, and inviting. I happen to know that it draws a crowd that ebbs and flows with traditional meal times. If you are a traditional person, you might have to wait a few minutes for a table. Like twenty. But, if you are like me, you will never have to wait, not at the dunch hour. The joint can still be hopping even then, but not like the lunch hour. I ride the cruiser past it all the time, almost every day. I've observed that ebb and flow. It's a very popular place. Many people are repeat customers. A few have told me they have been coming to Gardenias for twenty years.

The grilled shrimp and grilled fish tacos are absolutely delicious, once again. It's hard for me to say *no mas*. As I said, there are fried options, but I will never know what they taste like. I've only ordered the grilled choices for my tacos. Each served to me on a flour tortilla the size of a slice of bread, but circular, of course. I don't like corn tortillas, too much corn in other food as a filler. Plain and simple.

It's up to me to dress my tacos. Two stainless steel garnish servers are placed on the table within a minute after my order goes in. Each garnish server has three stainless steel cups, thus comprising a nice variety among six options for topping the tacos. Hard to top that! One of the cups contains two-inch forest green, grilled *jalopeño* peppers. Today, I'll rip the stems off them and put two into each of my three tacos for a little extra kick. Like a kick from a mule. I like them a lot but they are too hot for most Americans. Stew couldn't get within ten feet of them.

Typically, I top my tacos with various combinations of different salsas or chopped onions, or guacamole, or coleslaw, or shredded cabbage. Maybe a little mayo that's in a squirt bottle on the table. There's also a squirt bottle on the table with liquid fire in it for the really brave. Perfect for anyone who wants to try some super-hot sauce on their tacos. It is triple X, like the label says: *XXXTRA Picante Habanero* sauce. Three X's is *ay caramba* hot. I use it in addition to the *jalopeños*, but I have to be careful that I don't put too much on my tacos. Very. Very, very. I mix and match and rarely duplicate an ensemble. The shrimp and fish are strong in flavor, but not fishy or shrimpy. Neither is ever overwhelmed by my potpourri of toppings, though once I set myself on fire when I overdosed on the extra hot table top sauce. I like the food so much at Gardenias that, in my first two visits, I asked for a second order of the same right after I inhaled the first. It was my mama who taught me that a request for seconds was the sincerest form of flattery!

My waiter is a tall, lithe Mexican named Gabriel. He's almost lanky. He moves with a certain amount of grace that conveys competence in what he does. I noticed that what he does, he always does in a hurry, but in an efficient way, not a klutzy way. Gardenias is a busy place. I made a point of introducing myself to Gabriel my first time at Gardenias, the first time he came to my table to set me up wth a menu and took my drink order. A

Pacifico. I did it all in Spanish. A snap. No English even though Gabriel used some English at first. I stopped him and said, please, no English, Spanish only. He liked that. We are friends forever.

Going to Super Bowl Sunday at Dreams - Sunday, February 5

I took a local bus to Dreams, about a thirty-minute trip north up the coast for twenty miles. It cost me two bucks. A cab would have cost me twenty-five bucks, thirty with the tip. Tourists rarely know about bus life in Cabo. I guess they forget that locals cannot afford taxis but have to get to and from work somehow. My bus driver dropped me off at the front gate of Dreams because I asked him to. They're that way. Buses here will drop you off anywhere you ask and, I am pretty sure, pick you up anywhere if you wave at the driver with the "pick me up" wave. You can figure that out yourself. How cool is that?

The high security at the entrance of Dreams was no secret. It was well known around town. For starters, you have to deal with steel gates, two uniformed guards in an enclosed booth, concrete ram posts to stop runaways and, of course, security cameras covering every inch. The guard asked for a picture i.d. which I did not have! I told him a guest of the hotel was expecting me. He called someone and let me through after a very long three minutes. I didn't have i.d. because I never needed it, until now. I don't need a driver's license for the cruiser. I don't need a car because I have the cruiser. Carrying an important document like a driver's license and/or a passport is asking fate for a loss of one or the other or both. A security guard intercepted me as I walked through the front gate and entered a long corridor of flowers, which was the driveway. He looked at me funny, like I didn't fit in with the typical Americans at Dreams. I probably should have shaved this morning. Maybe I look dangerous. I hope so. It's a good look in Mexico.

A different security guard took over at the main lobby entrance as my driveway escort peeled off. This one walked me to the front desk where, once again, I was asked for a picture i.d. of any kind. I guess the guard at the security gate called someone else because I had to explain my predicament again. The front desk people were actually reluctant to let me in on my word alone even after I named Stew and Londa as the Dreams' guests and said they were expecting me. I think my attempt at Spanish softened them up because they finally said okay and pointed to the lobby. Fifteen seconds later, I literally bumped into Stew in the lobby area fifty feet away. If I had to, I guess I could have called out to him to get me in. Stew, help! Help! Something like that. He had a glass of red wine. Not a drip was spilled in our grabby greeting. See, experience can teach us things and we get better with age. Our shared mission was to get a beverage in my hand as a means to launch myself into the spirit of Super Bowl Sunday. I had margaritas on my mind. Rocket fuel on the rocks, with salt.

Super Bowl Sunday at Dreams - Sunday, February 5

When I met with Stew in the lobby of Dreams, there was not a scintilla of doubt this would be a fun day. Today is Super Bowl Sunday. The kickoff is five hours out there and the buzz among the guests is already high. The lobby felt like the staging area for a big concert. One minute after my arrival, Londa showed up, so did my margarita. Our warm up for the game was underway. Londa led the way as she directed us to the lounge chairs she had reserved on the beach. We three, drinks in hand, wasted no time getting into a frenzy of conversation, much of which was initially directed at the crazy events going on in the States with our new president. Not surprisingly we three never run out of conversation about the past, the present, or the future.

Our lounge chairs were positioned to give us an unobstructed view of the Sea of Cortez and an opportunity for a little whale watching. It didn't take long. About a half mile out we saw a whale or whales breaking the surface of the water, silhouetted against the horizon of infinity, sometimes breaching the water. And, in one instance, I mean serious breaching. Londa saw it too. The leviathan my eyes were fixed on shot straight out of the water heading for the moon. Only its tail fins didn't break the surface. Think of the force it takes for a leap like that. Londa's mouth was open, mine too over the breech and the size of the splash. It is so unbelievable that we decided it must have been a leap of faith that made it happen.

The margaritas kept coming, I confess, and we kept sitting. Other guests that Stew and Londa had befriended in the course of their stay came and went with snippets of opinions tossed into our chatter. After two hours of acting like beached whales, we three opted for a pool session for a change of scenery and some fresh water refreshment to cool us off from the encroaching heat. The temperature was rising with the passage of each hour, keeping pace with the rising level of excitement for the biggest game in the universe. The energy of anticipation for the kick off was palpable. What a perfect setting to take it all in. Kick off was two hours out, giving us plenty of lounge time to watch the amazing parade of people partying poolside. The main pool was a very big irregularly shaped configuration with a jetty protruding into the middle, a swim-up bar that seats fifteen, and an infinity edge for a vista of the Sea of Whales. We committed ourselves to lounging for the next two hours close to the infinity edge that stopped at the swim up bar. This put us in position to easily maintain an endless supply of beverages. It was an easy walk across the pool to the swim up bar. Swimming to the bar was a fine option too.

At some point, don't ask me when or whose idea it was, we switched to Mai Tai cocktails. Poor recall is what happens when drinks are free. I do recall having a few while I circulated in the pool and I do recall that they did not have any alcohol in them. The inability to detect alcohol in a cocktail is a sure sign I had too much to drink. It didn't affect me that much because I was getting plenty of exercise going to and from the busy swim-up bar. I rationalized myself into having only a minor, but steady buzz most of the time, because the drinking took place over the course of five hours, punctuated by several runs to the bathroom. That's right. Not in the pool, please, a thought which gives me a good reason not to hang out at swim-up bars that have bar stools. Those people never give up their seats!

A giant screen had been set up outside on a grassy knoll close to the beach to accommodate hundreds of Dreamers. And I mean giant. *Gigante.* It had to be thirty feet long and twenty-five feet high. Hundreds of guests were milling around this communal area sampling food off of a dozen different grilling stations. The big screen was a great option for us but we three decided to watch the game on the TV in the room, preferring a less chaotic venue, one all to ourselves.

Then it happened! All of a sudden, game on! Watching in the room was a great call. We spread out on the beds and made ourselves comfortable in our little controlled environment. The score was lopsided at the end of the first half, but still it was the Super Bowl and anything could happen. We stayed glued to the set for the half show. Lady Gaga did not disappoint us. As it turned out, the second half didn't disappoint us either.

What a remarkable ending to Super Bowl Fifty-One! Everyone who watched this game witnessed the greatest come-from-behind victory in Super Bowl history. A real stunner. The New England Patriots beat the Atlanta Falcons 34-28 in overtime in a crazed, high suspense series of do or die plays for the Patriots that began in the fourth quarter, a quarter which had the Falcons scoreless and upped the Patriots total by 31 points. What an unbelievable game. The final outcome that came out of overtime: Tom Brady won the Super Bowl, his fifth, which probably secures his claim as the greatest quarterback of all time. He might have overshadowed Lady Gaga's performance, but not by much. I am a big fan of hers. Tom Brady, not so much.

I left Stew and Londa after the game with a gush of sad goodbyes on the heels of a gusher of fun. I don't know when I will see the Bicks again, never do, but wherever it is, we will have lots of fun. We always do. I walked out of their Dreams and returned to mine the same way I came in, sober. I crossed the poorly lit highway with excessive caution. Five minutes later, I was riding the local bus back into town still reverberating with excitement. It was a Super Bowl for all the ages and a super good time.

I met the owner of CC - Monday, February 6

Anyone that's been to CC once or twice a week in the past two weeks would recognize me as a regular by now. I usually sit at one of the four-person high-top tables close to the bar, within easy talking range of Jorge. Always nursing a bottle of Pacifico on my table, sometimes a second if I have to go into surgery. Never a third, is what I say, unless anesthesia is necessary. Or, for a change of pace, a margarita, salt, on the rocks. If the joint is jumping I won't take up a whole table for myself and instead sit at the bar. However, I prefer the table, where it is much easier for Andres and my other friends, like the two managers Ray and Guillermo, and the staff to hang with me by standing next to me and still look like they are in a work mode while chatting with me. They are all my friends and my teachers, one and the same. *Mis amigos y mis maestros.*

This was a busy night for CC, especially for a Monday, which is kind of hit and miss because every night in Cabo is a Saturday night for tourists. I walked up to the bar in the middle of the dinner hour and grabbed the only open bar stool, one that put my back to the sidewalk. I asked Gabriel, who works the evening shift, about the good-looking couple across the room from me. They were seated at one of the high-top tables on the far side of the bar, next to my usual table. I had seen them in CC before. Gabriel said the man is the owner and the woman is his girlfriend. This information given in Spanish, of course. I understood the words *el dueño y su novia.* That's all it took for me to go over to that table to introduce myself. I opened in English, though, on looks alone, the couple could have been Spanish. I introduced myself. The owner's name is Don. He looks like a movie star. Tall in stature, high in cheek bones, and silver in a head of thick, dark, wavy hair combed back. He introduced me to Maddie, his girlfriend. She is a thin, attractive American brunette who smokes a lot. I could see that

Don smokes a lot, too. Both are polite, pleasant, and create a very good first impression. It was a good start. Right out of the gate I told Don how much I enjoyed his place and how great the staff is. Don invited me to sit with them for a drink. I ordered another Pacifico right there rather than retrieving my half full bottle at the bar. There was no waiting at his table for service, of course. My beer at the bar was safe; it would be waiting for me when I returned. No one expected this to be a long conversation. I had the feeling that my Mexican pals did not particularly like to hear me slip back into full-on English. In a way, it felt funny to me, especially in CC where I was a dedicated Spanish speaker.

First off, I learned that Don and Maddie are a committed couple, having been together for over ten years, however not married and about the same age, she maybe a bit younger. Don was about sixty with a handsome chiseled face that had experienced a lot in life. In the course of our conversation, he and Maddie laughed when he told me he was sometimes mistaken for a very well-known Mexican movie star. It didn't surprise me. I didn't recognize the movie star's name, but Don definitely had the look of a Hollywood movie star. The next two hours passed quickly as Don thoroughly entertained me with the very interesting history of his life, a life that began as a kid in a very well-connected San Francisco family that have lived for generations in San Mateo, just south of the city and in all the places that right now are home to million-dollar homes on quarter acre lots. His grandfather had accumulated about a thousand of those acres at one point long ago, and held on to them for many years. Lucky guy. I don't know if I could have put up with anyone else's life story, but I confess Don's was really interesting. He was charming and could tell a good story, which took me into a fourth beer with a half of one waiting for me at the bar, maybe. A fourth! He was quite some storyteller!

Don bought CC ten years ago and fixed it up. He also owned the real estate agency across the street and had his finger in numerous real estate development deals in Cabo. Every bar owner knows that success is often dependent on being present in the establishment, which explains why I had seen him before and why he made it a point to drop in three or four nights every week. I would have seen more of him except most of my time in CC was afternoon time. Most of his time was night owl time. The tequila kept coming his way, one of the perks of being an owner. His glass was never empty, not even close as replacements flowed in a continuous stream. Concurrent with drinking, he'd work on some vaping. Vaping what? I don't know. I didn't smell weed, but maybe vaping can camouflage that. All fine by me. I just listened and enjoyed his monologue. And my never empty bottle of Pacifico. Service was top notch at his table. I turned down a fifth beer.

Don knew a lot about Cabo and its history so I asked him about the huge concrete structure behind CC on the marina, the one that was abandoned and looked so forlorn. I am referring to the five-story shell of an edifice of two hundred unfinished rooms that had been someone's dream of a luxury hotel. That must have been a long time ago. Now, it is worthless as a building, but sitting on two acres of prime real estate that ran a full leg of the marina. To my surprise, Don told me that it had been like that, untouched, for twenty-six years. Somewhere in that period the structure picked up the very fitting and apt name, The Gray Ghost. Its history was mired in financial disasters brought on by Mexico's roller coaster economy over the years and tortured by the whims of the market place. Most of the time it was a dust covered useless asset in some bank's portfolio of failed investment properties. Don told me that he even tried to buy it once for himself, for a song. The timing didn't work out when some competition showed up at the last second for ownership rights. The new owner did nothing to the building in the following years. All this wheeling and dealing talk told me Don was the real deal with some deep pockets and connections of his own.

Someone, Don said, should do something with The Gray Ghost. He sees a lot of potential in the lot, a lot. He wished he could be that someone but it had become way too pricey over the last couple of years and not without the threat of being a money pit. Clearly, the land that the Gray Ghost sat on had great potential as a building site, but cleaning it up was unquestionably an endeavor that could drain someone's banking account. It had special problems. Since it was so close to a harbor with dozens of multi-million-dollar luxury yachts, leveling the skeleton of reinforced concrete with dynamite was out of the question. That route simply meant too much dust and harbor trauma for the yacht owners. Poor boys. And, I assume, poor girls too. It had to be leveled by manual labor before any new construction could proceed on the property. The only way that would happen would be through the use of an army of men equipped with jackhammers. Even that was not easy. And it wouldn't be cheap. This vision is something that would have to occur in the heat of the summer when the tourist population is thin.

However daunting all the possibilities for The Gray Ghost were, it was in play. Don said it had recently been purchased by a Mexican billionaire, a man who owned many businesses, including the Modelo Brewing Company for many years. That's what he said anyway. I happened to know that Grupo Modelo brewing company was recently purchased by Belgian company Anheuser-Busch InBev. Mr. Modelo got a very nice piece of change out of the deal. Of course, I can't say if Don's news is true or not, but the idea of anyone replacing The Gray Ghost with a luxury hotel seems like a smart idea, if you can make the financials work. I say this because it is an amazing piece of real estate. Also, the residents of Cabo wanted to believe that the harbor's biggest generational eyesore would finally disappear. It's a big guess on what's going to happen with that property in the future. I guess it depends on whether or not you believe in ghosts.

I said goodnight to Don and Maddie after an evening of conversation that fully captured my attention. I paid for my beers. I looked forward to seeing them again, sometime on another night, though I know it would take me out of my slipstream for learning Spanish at CC. I was wrong about my abandoned bottle of Pacifico waiting for my return to my bar stool. It was long gone, as I should have been. As usual, I said personal goodbyes to each of my hard-working friends before leaving and making a beeline home on the cruiser.

CC is a great place to hang - Tuesday, February 7

I feel at home when I'm in Cabo Cantina. I can hang for a few minutes if I'm just doing quick break or for a couple of hours any time of day or night. I prefer the afternoon hours. When I'm there I am engaged in doing all sorts of things like working my way through *Spanish for Gringos*, mouthing Spanish as I read publications, staring mindlessly at nothing, listening to Spanish being spoken by the staff, watching sports on TV, and chatting up my working pals when they walk past my table. My chatter is almost always in Spanish with the CC employees but once in a while I chat up customers within my reach. Unfortunately, the customers are almost always Americans and there without it ever occurring to them to try Spanish, even a few simple basics. If they overhear me in a conversation with one of the waiters, in Spanish of course, sometimes they compliment me saying that my Spanish is "sooooo good." I tell them I've been working on it for five weeks and they're wowed. What do they know. I'm happy with the compliment but really, I'm still in the early chapters of *Spanish for Gringos* and my conversation skills are very limited. It's still all so new to me that I can easily freeze in place when unexpectedly confronted in Spanish. A deer in the headlights comes to mind as a metaphor. All that's fine, I guess, but it's not important. More importantly and most of all, I use CC for a place to have a nice little running patter of Spanish with my many friends that work here. Chatting with Americans is pretty much a waste of my time, especially in English. Especially in CC.

Ocho moved in - Tuesday, February 7

I've seen Ocho, my gecko roommate, every day this week, sometimes a couple of times a day, and in different rooms. He's made himself at home. That's nice. When I see him, I talk to him from time to time. He's a good listener. He never interrupts me. I like that.

The Ice Queen at CC - Tuesday, February 7

Early this evening, a six-foot-tall woman with long flowing blonde hair and wearing a floor length black gown and a broad brimmed floppy hat stood at Don and Maddy's high table with her back to me. Another American, younger than the owner Don, and bald like me, was seated between Don and Maddy. When I arrived, I saw the threesome but I didn't feel like intruding. The blonde showed up a beer later. From what I could see, she was someone I did feel like intruding on, though I could only see her backside, which sometimes is enough. From her relaxed posture and proximity to Don, I guessed she was a friend of his. I could keep an eye on her from my bar stool at the far end of the bar, just around the corner from them. I kept an eye on them while I was watching some soccer game on the tube. From that vantage point, I was at a bit of a disadvantage because I could not see the front of the blonde woman, or her side. And I could not even see any clues to her age, other than her long, flowing blonde hair, but that didn't stop me from finding out who this woman was.

I was due for my first date down here, maybe this tall blonde would be that person. Her long back and flowing hair were all I needed to see to motivate me to get up, saunter over to the table, and seek an introduction. It happened and then it happened quickly, and things went south. When I got to the table, it was the first time I was face to face with her. In less than a second, I concluded she was definitely not for me. With tired, dull blue eyes, she looked a lot older than me though she probably wasn't. Probably into drugs, just a sense I got. Certainly a smoker, that's what made her face that way. She had a pasty, dull complexion from too much nicotine. She also had that pinched lip look that heavy smokers have universally, especially north of sixty.

Don introduced me to Louise, the tall blonde, by my real name, T, not my Cabo name of Tomas. They got it out of me the night before, when I met them for the first time. No one else knew it in CC where I was known only as Tomas. Moments later her pinched, lackluster lips were aimed right at me, fish style, and she declared:

"Your first name can't possibly be T. What is it really?"

"T," I stated, "Just one letter, T. That's my name."

She rolled her eyes and said, "That's absurd."

That gave me the opening to just walk away, which was an opening I happily took.

Before I walked away, I said, "Nice meeting you, Louise. Pardon the interruption. I just wanted to say hi to Don and Maddie."

I turned and walked back to my seat at the bar without having said another word. I didn't need to talk to Louise and I certainly didn't want to look at her pinched lips again, spewing venom or not. Two minutes later she walked out of Cabo Cantina, my cue to return to Don's table and say WTF. I thought, too, that maybe I should apologize to them if I sensed they thought I was rude to their friend. I quickly learned from them that she's known to be a little icy. They suggested to me that it was not uncommon for a cold blast of air to come out of her mouth. From this, I easily inferred that no apology was necessary. Don suggested I should have simply said the T stands for Tomas and let it go, thereby sidestepping her offensively vehement objection beyond the usual disbelief that comes with a one letter name. I agreed, smiled, excused myself to re-join my beer in front of the TV. Never judge a book by its spine; you risk getting stabbed by some spines if you do. Or something like that.

The screaming cats - Tuesday, February 7

I'm hoping the screaming cats don't turn into a nightly event. And, lately, it has been nightly and at all hours of the night. I can't take it much longer. There's some serious screaming going on. I've never heard anything like that from cats in all my years. Maybe it's a whole herd of them getting gang-banged. I haven't a clue what's going on but I hope each night they go at it is the last night. How much longer? I don't know. Nothing I can do about it but hope that every cat in the neighborhood gets pregnant soon. Very soon. I'm guessing that would put an end to the screaming. For a while anyway.

Living at CC- Wednesday, February 8

I've been going to CC every day this week, usually the afternoons, but sometimes at night. The day shift is staffed by one set of guys and the evening shift by another. Ray and Guillermo, who are the managers, overlap the two. I like everyone who works here and every one of those guys helps me to varying degrees with my Spanish. In effect, I get free lessons and the pleasures of a little camaraderie. It would be perfect if I got free beer, but nothing's perfect. The first shift of the day ends at three. I like to arrive at two to catch the last hour of the day shift, which is Andres' shift, and greet the afternoon team when they check in as the next shift at three. The first shift is the one where I get the most help with my Spanish because there are fewer customers mid-afternoon.

Andres takes the lead with tutoring me. The managers Ray and Guillermo chip in as well, dropping in on my table for thirty seconds at a time, sometimes as much as a minute or two. They see the amount of time that Andres spends with me, which seems to be a lot to me, and I guess they don't mind. Oliver in the first shift and Edgar in the second shift know the least amount of English, which works for me, because I get to return the favors I get by helping them with their English. I'm thankful for the chance to reverse roles. I do that for everyone else, too, whenever the opportunities arise, but not as much for the other guys and to varying degrees.

Ismael, who is short, round, and the best schmoozing maitre d' in town is the oldest of the group. He is a roly-poly, lovable gramps type and a real charmer with everyone, especially the ladies. Especially the ladies. They love him, without exception. His English is really good. He is always smiling and friendly. And impish, in a good way. He is always nice to me as well. Though little instruction comes from Ismael in the way of vocabulary and grammar, he helps me from time to time, sometimes with my conversational skills and just by virtue of talking to me as he passes me to greet and seat someone. He always has a big welcome for me when I walk in. Everyone does. *Mi compadres*. I love it.

I'm now working on getting to know the kitchen crew. Ceci, a tiny, thin Mexican woman with sparkly, jet-black eyes is the first person I met in the kitchen. She is always smiling with wonderfully white teeth every time I see her from across the room. She may be a sous-chef, though I don't know the Spanish word for that role. *Chef Secundario?* She is always pleasant, even on a super busy day in the high heat of the kitchen. She speaks no English but we always smile at each through the bar set up that separates us. With the right angle and no bartender in the way I can see fairly easily into the kitchen, which means I often wave to Elio who is the head chef by day, as well as Ceci and the others who are all working hard in the kitchen heat and hustling to get the food out to waiting customers.

Sometimes I get to chat with the kitchen staff at my table too because they pass me once in a while on their breaks or on their way for a meeting in the back room with Ray. Sometimes I go to the open doorway of kitchen and shout out *hola* to the staff of four or five, often saying something funny to make them laugh, like asking if the special of the day is elephant burger with giant fries. I also tell them I like their giraffe burgers and their horse burgers, but not the dog burgers. It gets a laugh every time. That bit of craziness originated at The G Spot, but it's so funny, I can't resist saying it when I get the chance. I know all the words in Spanish. They are all very polite. Chef Elio looks like a chef, that is, a man who has been sampling the fare in the kitchen his entire life. You can't be thin doing that for very long. He is portly and I am being kind.

Totito, who is a very big kid, is also in the kitchen sometimes. He never is doing anything else there but washing dishes. When I see him towering over a sink perpetually full of dishes, I address him in a serious tone, calling him *El Presidente de Platos*, The President of Plates. He laughs over this because we both know his primary role in CC is bartender, which is an amazing job for a kid who is only fifteen. His real name is Martin, same as his dad, which is why he's called Totito, which means, I guess, the little one, as in junior, but not as in size because Totito is around six feet tall, almost a foot taller than his dad. He's good behind the bar but he's no equal to Jorge. No one is. Totito is a nice kid with a big round face and a tentative shyness about him. He is very big for his age, looks twenty, so customers think they're talking to an experienced, mature male mixologist, but they're not. He's only a kid, who has never shaved, and very new at tending bar. I've watched him from time to time. He's already good at what he does. Bartenders don't have to be eighteen in Cabo I guess. Maybe I've got Totito wrong, maybe he's been a bartender since he was ten. I want to call him Tostitos, which makes sense to me because he's a chip off the ol' block, his dad Martin. Get it? Chip?

Over a busy lunch hour, Andres is everywhere at once, but he always finds time to stand next to me at my table and deliver excellent advice on Spanish. He writes on a lot on napkins for me so I can see the words. He and I laugh a lot over my trials and tribulations. He is truly an excellent teacher. I always take the napkins home with me and study them. When I listen to him work a table of American tourists I am always impressed with his English, which he says is only good for the restaurant business. He is genuinely warm and friendly with customers and knows enough casual English and even some slang to make jokes and schmooze his American clientele. Other day shift waiters include Roberto and Leo. Roberto always has a big smile in his greeting to me, like we are the oldest of friends, though we don't chat much. Sometimes both Andres and Oliver stand beside me at my table. Andres is Oliver's mentor. Lucky Oliver for that but he is the target of endless chiding from Andres. I can see that Andres has a lot of fun teasing Oliver and, I confess, I get in on the fun once in a while. Fortunately for Oliver, it is all done in good spirit. Clearly the two of them are great friends. I like to pretend Andres and I are great friends too. It's easy to do that.

Elsewhere around the place, Leo lurks, stocky and steady. He is a man always focused on his customers. He's the quiet one who moves around the tables in the stealth mode while delivering timely service with few words of English. He and I rarely exchange more than a greeting, but we both know we're connected to each other in this unique network of friendship because of all the other connections we have. Yep, we are one big happy family. I'm not making this up. Guillermo often tells me that I am family at CC. Quote, unquote. It's so great.

In the evenings, my time at CC is usually under an hour and is spent often by myself because it is a busy time for the restaurant. When there is a quiet moment, however rare, Gabriel and Martin help me with my Spanish. I'll take whatever I can get. It's all helpful. Gabriel spent many years in the States, so no surprise that his English is very good. Gabriel looks like a leading man in the movies and is a very cool guy. Martin's English is good too. He likes to test me to make sure I really understood something that was just said to me. If I pretend to understand by nodding, he'll nail me for sure. They both find time to share some of their personal histories with me when they were in the States. And, they both make me wish I could spend more time with them. They are so interesting and kind and tuned in to my interest in learning as much Spanish as I can in the three months I have committed to Cabo. Every time I say goodnight to them I know that I look forward to seeing them again. We are truly *compadres*. I don't like to think that my time in Cabo will end. Gabriel and Martin and the others in both shifts are all people whose company I enjoy immensely. There is no reason we can't all be friends for a long time, regardless of my impending departure. I know I will be saying goodbye in less than two months, but I am saying that with the assumption that I will see all my new friends here at CC again someday. Isn't that funny to say that? After all, we just met. Go figure.

Busy or not, everyone has to work. I cannot be the center of their universe, of course. But I will say this, everyone is so nice and so attentive and so encouraging that at times I feel like I am the center of their universe. By the time I finish my second Pacifico in the sun-soaked afternoons, I am always sorry to leave but I can happily say see you again or see you tomorrow. *Hasta mañana amigos!*

After I nurse two beers through at least two hours, closer to three hours every day this week at CC I often decide on third beer at another bar for the finale of the day's entertainment. I needed to branch out a bit, see some new faces, try some new places, mingle with tourists, learn things about Cabo. A change of pace from CC is a good thing, no matter how wonderful Cabo Cantina is.

Every time I said goodnight to everyone at CC, I am grateful for everyone's kindness to me. Yes, I think of everybody who works at CC as a teacher, what the Spanish call a *maestro,* but I've got a solid friendship developing with many. However, after nearly a dozen visits in the past two weeks, everyone there is more than a teacher. They have become my friends and I am sure they know that I am their friend. And, already, I feel this friendship is a lasting one. Who knows? Maybe I'll return to Cabo for three months every winter to improve my Spanish and, more importantly, to see my friends. Most of them have been at CC for several years at least, so I expect they will be there next year. Like I said, you never know. I don't know about next year and I don't know what the next bar will be. I guess I'll do the usual and cruise around town and see what grabs me, see where I land for that third Pacifico. No one knows what the future holds.

Guadalupana becomes the G Spot - Wednesday, February 8

Sometimes after an afternoon at CC, I have a third beer and sometimes I don't. Sometimes I just ride around town, looking at things, feeling the heartbeat in Cabo and taking it all in with no particular agenda. More often than not, at night anyway, I ride aimlessly up and down the poorly lit streets until I call it a night and head for Coromuel. If it's after nine o'clock I don't get to drop in on Pedro and Facundo at Guadalupana because they close the place every night at nine sharp. I like riding my bike into Guadalupana, but no chance of that after nine. Lately I have been referring to it as the G Spot, in my mind only. I'd never tell Pedro and Facundo about that nickname. It would accomplish nothing. Yes, the G spot, my new name for Guadalupana. It's a great place to go hang and relax. It is now clear to me that the G Spot and CC have become my favorite places in Cabo for learning Spanish.

<u>Lupita, my Mexican neighbor - Wednesday, February 8</u>

This afternoon I was sitting poolside at a plastic table under one of the umbrellas in the shadow of my building. I was studying *Spanish for Gringos*, happy to be outside for a change of venue in that endeavor. I saw Lupita walk out of her building, heading for the gate. We exchanged greetings across the chilly water in the pool. Rather than exiting the complex to the right, she suddenly turned left, walked around the end of the pool, and walked up to me, to chat. How sweet.

At our introduction last week, I learned that she spoke some English but, of course, I tried to do my Spanish-only thing. She obliged me, with great patience. I invited her to sit, and she did. I showed her my book which she enjoyed paging through quickly enough to see what I was into. We chatted some more, mostly asking and answering basic questions about each other. The usual questions: family, where from, how long in Cabo, why etc. I learned the names and ages of her two children. Miguel is nine and Maria is eleven. About thirty minutes later, Lupita got up and left to get on with whatever she set out to do in the first place. I enjoyed my tutorial session with her. She was just perfect in explaining things to me in a patient and helpful way. I hoped I'd see more of her. I put my nose back into my book when I heard the building security gate slam shut. She was gone and I was back into page turning.

CHAPTER SIX

Week 6

<u>Some pros and cons of timeshares - Thursday, February 9</u>

Lots of people love timeshares and lots of people don't, even some owners don't. Of course, everything has its pros and cons. I think cons are always more interesting. Is that human nature or just my dark side in play? One couple, Dan and his wife Linda, who I talked to a couple of days ago when I was into people watching while hanging out at Griceldas, told me they felt like prisoners at their timeshare luxury resort. Granted, it wasn't really their timeshare but they were connected to it as if it were. They were there as guests for five days. Nonetheless, they felt imprisoned, their words not mine.

Dan and Linda were there as guest employees for a sales rewards meeting of a big East Coast company that was footing the bill. Dan, the employee, led the way in telling me things. For one, the food was fantastic and free drinks at every bar was almost too good to be true. Also, the swimming pools were great, one of which had an amazing swim-up bar with, of course, free drinks. They also said that the view from their room was of the Gulf in all its glory, including views of breaching whales not all that far out there. Linda liked the pampering and the luxury of the timeshare life at the resort. Nice for both of them.

But there are downsides to that life too. For example, Dan said they felt trapped because it was difficult for them to feel good about spending their own money in town when they could get all the food and booze they wanted for free at the resort. He also pointed out that the absence of free shuttles to and from the resort into town meant they had to pay cab fare if they wanted to go into town. I knew that was an ouch coming right at me. They were not happy that a taxi costs twenty-five dollars per person each way. That's a hundred bucks roundtrip for a couple that is not rolling in the dough. Today, their trip into Cabo was their only trip into town and they called it a big splurge. It was also the last day of their weeklong sales fest at the resort and they felt that they had to get away from their getaway to see "the real Mexico" and preserve their sanity. Pros and cons. Everything has both. A shame they didn't know about the local buses. The truth will set you free.

Eat it at Edith's - Thursday, February 9

Edith's might be Cabo's most famous fancy restaurant. It is on that gum drop hill overlooking Mango and Medano Beach. It is kitty corner from a cool looking bar called Esquina and directly across the street from some unfinished construction. Unlike that site, Edith's is very finished. I say finished because all the women look like they went to finishing school. Sort of. I'm just trying to be clever, but there's some truth in that. The women are well dressed, almost all of them. A lot of jewelry. David Yurmin is big. A lot of designer labels. A real mix. Most of the men are fairly well dressed, fairly, but never on par with the women. A few of the men are dressed like slobs. I see all this from my perch at the circular, granite-topped bar located in the heart of Edith's. A well-dressed woman just walked past me with her husband riding in her jet stream. She looked good. Coiffed and put together nicely with a chic ensemble. She was wearing a sleeveless, lime colored silk top, a tiny yellow scarf on the neck, along with a white skirt and white sandals. Tropical, airy, and form fitting. Very nice. In sharp contrast, he had crappy athletic shoes, though clearly he was no athlete, dirty khaki shorts, and I swear, a wife beater t-shirt or close to it, either way, micro sleeves. How does that happen? Did she just give up on his sloppiness, or is he a consummate slob? Or, is she picking her battles and his choice in clothes isn't a battle she's picking? In a nutshell, this is my way of saying Edith's is great for people watching. It has both ends of the class scale, but skews heavily in one direction. The right direction.

I'm not going to get to take the long route in describing Edith's, that's what TripAdvisor is for. However, I can say I love the indoor-outdoor jungle thatch decor. Bougainvillea in crimson and orange flowers intrudes everywhere as accents in this lush land of tropical plants. A jumble of seating areas in this simulated jungle make the different seating sections in this large restaurant seem small and intimate. Some seats even give the guest a peek at the Gulf through the canyons of the condo towers fronting the beach. Service people dressed uniformly with white shirts, black vests, and black trousers were high density and in constant motion. The food they served at every table looks delicious and it should with the *haute cuisine* prices on the menu. I saw a prime rib and some seared tuna shoot by me en route to some lucky guests. I see lobster and butterfly shrimp too, on many plates. I amuse myself in smug silence knowing that Edith in Spanish is pronounced Eat-it.

Of all the plates of photo-ready food on the tables in front of me, my eyes most often settled on the Caesar Salad being prepared table-side at several tables. The Saladeer knows how to make a real Caesar, something you don't see much of anymore. At Edith's it is made according to the original recipe from the Caesar's Hotel in Tijuana. It is probably the best-known dish originating in Baja. That would be my first item to order. The rest I can't say at this time, but it all looks good. Sure, nothing is perfect, but everyone who is interested in appetizing food should "eat it" at Edith's. Even with some steep menu prices, it just might be the best value in town.

I was the only one seated on one of sixteen bar stools at the restaurant's circular bee hive bar. It was buzzing with worker bees. It is a bar which is well placed deep into the interior of this big restaurant, just beyond its epicenter. Edith's is a dinner place, not a bar place, which explains the low profile of the bar and the presence of many open bar stools. I happen to like the bar very much, however, because I could practice my Spanish with one bartender in particular, the one taking care of me. His name is pronounced Es-lesch with a heavy slur but it is spelled Slenge. Don't ask me how that leap is made. There is no counterpart in English, he said, when I asked. I wondered if there's a counterpart in any language. Probably not. I had to say it five times with his help to get it right. I liked Slenge a lot. He is a very attentive and congenial young man. Maybe in his mid-twenties. And, he's pretty good with English. Best of all, maybe, he didn't mind me ordering only one beer in my hour of need. As I've experienced many times before, Mexicans in service positions serving gringos really appreciate it when a gringo is committed to learning Spanish. I think that's why they put up with my low consumption of DPH. That's Drinks Per Hour. After my hour of fun, I paid for the most expensive beer in town, twice the price of what I pay at CC. A hundred pesos did not cover the beer with a decent tip. I threw in another twenty bringing the total to one hundred twenty pesos, which is six bucks, steep for a beer in Cabo and for most places in the States. For me, it was worth every penny because I added Slenge's name to my roster of Spanish teachers and my roster of tongue twisters.

The start of my three-day water fast - Friday, February 10

After a week of way too much indulgence with my friends Stew and Londa, I decided to do a three-day water fast this weekend, the weekend after the Super Bowl. I liked the idea of losing weight, though mostly it would be easily recoverable water weight, but more importantly I liked the idea of a total body cleanse. For reasons I couldn't completely identify, this dietary adventure gave me a soft excuse not to go to Cabo Cantina for a few days. Not a perfect one, but good enough. At the heart of this goal was an interest in reducing inflammation in my body. I have felt some inordinate and scattered aches and pains lately along with a sore left hip that relentlessly delivers a low buzz of pain. It is hardly noticeable and I'd completely forget it were it not for the occasional interruption of a few hot, searing spikes of pain into my left thigh. It was disconcerting. Rather than ignoring it until I returned to the States, I decided to fiddle with pain relief myself. I wanted to see if three days of a non-inflammatory diet would help ease the pain. I thoroughly expected it would because I would be supplementing my water intake with twenty-four hundred milligrams of ibuprofen, at a rate of three rounds of eight hundred each day. That's a lot of milligrams, about a thousand over the daily recommended dosage. I thought I could get away with that heavy level for a few days without doing any damage to my kidneys. More than three days was probably not a smart thing to do.

Day one of my water fast - Saturday, February 11

Getting through the first day was a snap. I drank enough water to fill an Olympic sized swimming pool; it seemed that way. This high intake meant that my stomach was constantly at full capacity which reduced the hunger pangs. It also meant that I lost track of the number of trips I was making to the bathroom because I gave up counting after the sixth trip before noon. Water in, water out.

That doggie in the window - Saturday, February 11

Somebody's dog yaps at the worst times of the day, not that I think any time is better than the worst. Okay, five in the morning is the worst. I never like that kind of annoying yippy barking, especially after I go to sleep or before I wake up. This dog keeps track of my waking hours, so it can yap when I am sleeping. I just know it. The time has come. This afternoon I left my building to investigate the source of this annoying creature. The dog was yapping so much it was easy to locate. From across the parking lot, I could see its scruffy face four stories above me, poking out of the open window. I could also see its paws on the window sill. It's a big dog for a yip-yappy bark. Maybe a giant Schnauzer, which is notorious breed for barking, but maybe it's some kind of mutt because it looks pretty big for a Schnauzer to be poking its head above the sill. I looked carefully. An intense stare. My best STFU look that I could put out there. Yeah, a giant Schnauzer, all right. What could be worse in the world of barking dogs I don't know. I wondered if it would listen to my command? What if I yelled, Jump! Of course, I wouldn't yell that. The dog probably doesn't understand English. I need to look up the Spanish word for jump. Maybe that will work, sick bastard that I am.

I signed up for whale watching - Saturday, February 11

Today, I signed up for an excursion on one of the whale watching boats. A thirty-five-footer. It's scheduled for tomorrow. Pretty brave of me. I pray the day will be a calm, windless day. And I pray for the courage to show up at the dock when the boat was scheduled to leave at eight-thirty in the morning. That means I have to get up no later than seven-thirty. Early for me. The agent said I was lucky to get an opening on such short notice, so I took it. The weather forecast was good, another perfect day ahead, so I was good to go for the time being.

Day two of my water fast - Sunday, February 12

I was surprised that the second day of my water-only fast didn't seem like much of an ordeal. By the end of the day, I was thinking that this no calorie diet was so easy that I should consider making it a weekly event. To minimize temptation, it made perfect sense to avoid all restaurants and bars for this experiment, which might be a really sensible thing to do on a weekly basis as well.

Whale watching - Sunday, February 12

I rode the cruiser to the appointed Dock for the whale watching excursion, happy to feel no wind and see smooth water everywhere I looked, near and far out to the horizon. Lucky me. I didn't think I'd need Dramamine that morning but even so, I took one of the pills I bought yesterday just in case. However calm the surface, it could never be calm enough for me to sign up for a ride in an inflatable Zodiac, which was an option. An adventure in a super pumped up rubber dinghy like that would be jam-packed with minute after minute of regret. I'd be vomiting during those minutes of regret within minutes of leaving the dockside, even, I feared, with Dramamine. The excursion boat left at eight-thirty, on schedule, in the morning, I was comfortable on board with leaving the tranquility of the harbor and breaking out into the Gulf waters. So was my stomach, which notably has very little food in it because I'm in the middle of my three-day fast.

Two minutes later the semi-covered boat with its three-man crew and ten passengers passed El Arco on the starboard side, our right side for landlubbers. The excitement felt by all of us tourists was palpable. I surprised myself that I was so jazzed about seeing some whales closeup. I love animals and always marvel at the beauty and grace of whales in those Nat Geo specials on television. Already I felt my admiration for them was escalating to heights I hadn't imagined. I was actually giddy about the prospect of seeing these creatures up close. Captain Ricardo accelerated into the open water with a southwestern heading once we passed El Arco. He announced that his radio had picked up the news of a pod of Humpbacks just two miles off the coast due west for twenty minutes. Shortly after that, en route, some Bottlenose Dolphins picked us up, our own little escort service. Ricardo told us that there were over eighty species of cetaceans (could be a whale, a dolphin, or a porpoise) in the world and nine of them are found in the waters around Cabo. This was attributable to the fact that Cabo was in the middle of three oceanic currents supporting an abundance of biodiversity all year long. The big mammals come mostly in the winter months, but the density of sea life runs throughout the year. But, sadly, the density of shrimp and other big fish food is on the decline. Also, it's obvious that the density of humans on the water is increasing every year, a fact that did not thrill me. Nothing about this news makes the dolphins or whales happy either. Nor did it thrill all that other diversity under the water. I'm a big fan of diversity.

A cluster of whale watching boats was already on the scene. We cut through the smooth surface at a modest pace to join them. My stomach was doing surprisingly well. No hiccups, always a good sign. The absence of wind worked in everyone's favor as I am sure I wasn't the only one worrying about tossing breakfast.

The whole whale watching experience at the rendezvous point was over in sixty minutes. I can't believe how fast time shot by. The whales were easily visible with breaks in the surface long before we got with the other boats. The anticipation was electrifying but the voltage did not match the thrill of being in the thick of it all. Whales were everywhere, maybe fifteen in all, moms, dads, and their babies. Big babies. Before the trip I was afraid the boats would truly be on top of the whales, but they weren't. Clearly, there was some safe zone maintained by the various captains so as not to threaten or endanger the whales. Nonetheless, despite the sensitivity of the captains, the whales seemed to be moving in on us more than we were moving in on them. Their natural curiosity sometimes brought them so close to the boat that I wanted to reach out and pet them. Hardly possible, of course, it was more an expression of love that I was interested in. I was happy just to see them so up front and close. It was hard for me to say who was being observed more, us or them.

In this experience of mingling with the whales I actually find myself at a loss for words to accurately describe my feelings. It was all so indescribably exciting as the word "awe" kept coming to the forefront of adjectives. In this bobbing boat in the endless ocean sitting miles off the coastline, I felt so incredibly close to the whales in our fellowship as mammals. Besides the oohs and ahhs from witnessing an exhilarating breaching of these monstrously wonderful creatures, they rolled on the surface unexpectedly in many places all around us with such slippery grace and power that I can only come close to defining my feelings as spiritual for this life form mixed in with a great reverence and sadness at the same time, the latter for the damage we humans have done to the oceans and all of its miraculous life. It might be too late for all the big fish around the world. Their populations have been decimated in the last two decades.

Every time I got a good glimpse of a whale, be it near or far, I silently apologized to it for man's cruelty over hundreds of years of harvesting them and their ancestors. If any of the other passengers were lip readers, they would have seen my lips forming the words "I'm sorry" over and over and over again, for a good part of our shared hour. However bad I felt for mankind's cruelty, my feelings for the majesty of these animals was uplifting enough to easily overwhelm the sadness I felt inside of me. I keep to myself for the entire return to our slip in the harbor. Saying nothing was all I could say and listening to the reactions of the other whale-watching tourists gave me hope that love and respect for these animals, and maybe all animals, is still out there, in the hearts of most humans, if not all.

Sea sickness didn't happen to me, not even the threat, even when I looked overboard and downward earlier at the dolphins that ran with us just off the side of the boat. Must be the empty stomach. When I looked over the railing a couple of years ago in the Mediterranean, I threw up instantly. So not tossing breakfast this time was a really good sign. Fortunately, I didn't lose my stomach but the experience did take my breath away. I left the dock feeling light headed from what I witnessed out at sea. A real wow.

As I mounted the cruiser for my ride back to my condo, I easily recalled how I felt so grounded the entire time, grounded and humbled during my time on board. I slowly pedaled the cruiser back to the condo, bypassing The Cabo Cantina, not wanting to break out of my silence of reverence until I was good and ready. I like to think of my experience with the dolphins and the whales as "mixed mammal mingling" instead of simply "whale watching." The interaction I felt was way beyond simply seeing, beyond simply watching. I'll never forget that experience. It was a real reminder that we humans are mammals too, like millions of other creatures who are all deserving of our respect and hope for a healthy environment. And healthy babies.

<u>Day three of my water fast - Monday, February 13</u>

When I woke up on the third day of my fast, I wanted to eat the kitchen counter. Getting through the third day was going to be rough. Filling myself up with water probably wouldn't be enough to get food out of the picture. This is a day that would require an enormous amount of will power. I was really hungry and my stomach, full of water, felt depressed when I lay on my back, like it was caving in on my spine. I was also experiencing hunger pangs, though hunger fangs were more like it.

By mid-morning I was doing some serious menu planning for the next day. Gardenias dominated my thoughts as front runner for food sourcing in my recovery plan. In particular, I easily envisioned two grilled shrimp tacos and two grilled fish tacos, and a Pacifico. Maybe three Pacificos. By mid-afternoon, I upped my desires for the shrimp and fish taco count to three each with growing consideration for four of each. By dinner I would be ravenous. For the first time, I was also feeling weak from food deprivation. My body needed fuel to function. I decided that I would go to bed early tonight, really early, like at seven, so a state of sleep could mask my hunger. This meant that I could wake up to a successful three-day fast.

<u>An afternoon hanging out with Ocho - Monday, February 13</u>

I'm feeling too weak from hunger to do much. Rather than riding my usual routes, I chose to go back to my condo in mid-afternoon and relax. The daily temperatures have been slowly climbing. When outside, it is easier than ever to feel the sun burning my exposed skin. Nope, no riding for the rest of the day. Good call. Being indoors all afternoon is the right thing to do. Maybe a good time to get a nap in. I needed a nap but I am never good at them. Too many times I nap for too long, like a couple of hours, which absolutely kills me for the rest of my existence that day. I wish I could be one of those people who take a twenty-minute nap and wake up super refreshed, as if it was as good as eight. There are people like that. I am not one of them.

I plopped down on my queen size bed knowing right away that this day would not be a good day for a nap, regardless of my fatigue. It was too hot to sleep and I was too hungry. The fast and the hot weather combined forces and beat me up today. This was a new experience for me. A really hot afternoon, the first one for me in Cabo. After five minutes of nap failure, I got up for a better option: I wandered around the condo in search of Ocho. He was easy to find. I spotted him in the ceiling corner where the two walls meet just right of the stove. He was staring at me, expecting me to say something brilliant in Spanish, as usual, but I couldn't think of anything witty in my fatigue. I settled for, *Buenas tardes amigo. Como estas? Te gusta el clima caliente?* Ocho didn't respond. No surprise there. I took his silence as a yes for my question about liking the hot weather. I waved to him and then I walked into the living room alcove, grabbed the remote, and settled in for a couple of hours of Spanish *telenovelas*, which are equivalent to our soap operas on TV. Sort of.

I try to watch the *telenovelas* for at least an hour every day. It's just one more way I can help myself in my quest to learn Spanish. It's good for developing one's ear to Spanish by listening to the nuances in pronunciation and the cadence of the language. I'm understanding more words and phrases than ever before but I still don't pick up enough of the sentences to follow the plot. Of course, I don't need to speak the language to follow the story. Almost anyone can just watch a *telenovela* or soap opera on TV and get it without speaking the language. Actually, I like to watch. It's relaxing and probably as close to a nap as I can get. Besides, it's a series of visual treats. Maybe someday I'll suddenly understand the conversations, like instantly, but it won't be this week.

<u>Mexican telenovas aren't the same as our soaps - Monday, February 13</u>

I've watched enough TV to know that Mexican *telenovelas* are definitely different from American soaps. Here are some of the differences I see. First, because the word *telenovela* includes the word "novel" within it I believe that's a clue that the Mexican productions are more like mini-movies than the shallow patter on American soaps, though clearly both styles have limited production budgets. Second, the music in *telenovelas* is more engaging and hotter. It's catchier, and it's way more fun and upbeat, which makes it more memorable. There's nothing serious about it, unlike the music for American soaps, music that is often heavy, dark and full of drama. Third, the women are better looking. Like the music, women in *telenovelas* are hotter than the women in American soaps. Fourth and my final observation, all the men have their shirts unbuttoned, sometimes to the navel, but always enough for chest exposure. I guess fewer buttons means more *macho*. Pass the cheese, please. Or something like that. Oh, the women often have their blouses unbuttoned too, nice, but not enough for my desires. All this unbuttoning creates an overall impact that Mexican *telenovelas* are steamier than American soaps in general, even steamier than The Hung and The Restless. Even steamier than this afternoon.

<u>The three-day water fast is over - Tuesday, February 14</u>

I slept well and through the night. I woke up bright-eyed and bushy-tailed. In the three-day run, I dropped eight pounds, which I'm guessing was mostly water. Best of all, for a few hours I actually felt skinny. This sort of delusion may have been generated by hallucinations from food deprivation, but the thinness sensation felt pretty damn good. Besides feeling zippier this morning, I actually felt younger. Fat is not where it's at! The best news of all was that all the hip pain I had been experiencing leading up to this fast was gone. This meant that the problem was inflammation and not something horrible like, like, like what? Bone cancer?

The absence of inflammatory food like sugar and the presence of a heavy up on ibuprofen did the trick. Of course, the fasting experiment had to come to a close, and just in time as I was beginning to accept my mortality or expecting to go through intense suffering the remaining days of my life from food deprivation. Could I handle that? Could I face a terminal illness? Would I off myself ahead of it and beat the Grim Reaper's own timetable? Oh dammit, what would I do? Then I came to my senses after being, perhaps, a bit delusional from hunger. Screw all that unknown stuff, more importantly, all I could think about now was eating everything on the menu at Gardenias until I was stuffed while washing the works down with one cold Pacifico after another. Life was looking up. All I had to do was muster enough strength to ride my bike to Gardenias. Two eggs over easy for breakfast with Ocho gave me the strength to ride to Gardenias to fulfill my fantasy.

After three days of fasting and by the end of my first day back on food, with three meals behind me, including one massive pig-out at Gardenias, I was hoping the pain would not return. It felt so good to be pain free. Of course, I was hoping that it was gone for good. Dammit, no such luck. I went to bed feeling stiff in the hip once again. Dammit to that. When I get back to the States I'll get a much better idea of the cause of my hip pain with an MRI. When I talked to Stew about it he said the MRI would reveal what the cause was in a heartbeat. I'd have to wait to return to the States for that, hopeful that my heart was still beating. Pain is not a good thing to live with. It makes me cranky.

Too much pressure - Tuesday, February 14

Something weird is going on in my head. It has nothing to do with Valentine's Day which, by the way, is today. And, by the way again, Valentine's Day always makes me uncomfortable. So factor that in, if you want. Regardless of a man's situation in the dating world,

Valentine's Day is a holiday that most men want to ignore, thus it is of no consequence or, if it is, it causes a forced declaration of a man's feelings for someone else, which has consequences. Totally different for women. I think it's a holiday that women love if they have a boyfriend or one in the making. Not so for a guy because it makes the guy put his cards on the table. I don't like to play cards. I associate playing cards with gambling. But enough of that. More importantly, as I said, something weird is going on in my head, about Cabo Cantina.

I've been intentionally ducking Cabo Cantina these last four days. Fasting is not really a valid excuse, though I used it as my excuse not to show up. I wasn't so much avoiding food and alcohol as I was avoiding my friends at CC. I had plenty of time to think about it. I could sense my frustration with my lack of progress in learning Spanish. I don't exactly get what this feeling is but I feel it. I have been experiencing a growing anxiety about showing up at CC, taking my usual high-top table, hanging with the guys, and all the while stressing over the constant and frantic searching for the Spanish words I want so badly to use in my conversations. I need so many more words than I know. I didn't feel like I knew enough words to have a decent conversation with my buddies. It was like being tongue-tied. I am the one wanting conversations and that desire is enough to create brain freeze. And anxiety. That's what is going on, anxiety.

The last couple of times I actually went to CC, I pretty much kept to myself. I looked a bit on edge, I think, and maybe even borderline depressed, which means I did not send out welcome signals to my *amigos*. They picked up on that and pretty much steered clear of me. I was giving off bad vibrations. It really bothered me, so I stopped going. That was four days ago. Four days away from CC was an eternity.

I just couldn't skip CC a fifth day in a row. I thought that would feel worse than the anxiety I felt at the table last time I was there. I pulled myself together after the lunch hour and found the courage to walk in. I shouldn't have been more surprised by the welcome I received. These guys are all so great. They greeted me as if I were an old friend, long gone and finally home again. The prodigal son. It was so sweet. They asked me where I've been these last four days. Like, who's counting? Actually, I was very moved by all this attention. I really like these guys and was sincerely happy to see them. Andres was the first to come up to me and say hi, slap me on the back, and ask what's up, as he always does. For the first greeting in Spanish, close friends use the most familiar form of speech, *Como estas?* I like to get it out first. Andres countered and added something I didn't understand. It was a hit and run for him this time because the tables were full of customers. It was Ray who pulled up to my table next. He's a smart guy, plugged in, and has some real radar for feelings. He's a good manager and a good read on people. He knew something was up with me, so he asked.

Ray and I talked for about twenty minutes. It turned out to be a pep talk. For me. He understood my self-afflicted pain after a minute of me trying to explain my anxiety. It was the same stuff, he said, that he experienced when he was learning English in the States. He told me that everyone at CC was supporting me and thought it was great that I was so committed. They knew it was hard. More than anything, Ray wanted me to know that no one was judging me. Everyone understood the challenges. He said I was being too hard on myself. I know he was right. He reminded me of the magic words, *poco a poco*, and said knowingly to me, *paciencia, mi amigo, paciencia*, which means "patience, my friend, patience." I felt better after our conversation and re-committed to being there daily once again.

Ray also had a great suggestion for me in my quest to learn Spanish. Music! Ray told me that when he was in the States, he constantly listened to American rock and roll and before long, could sing along with all the top hits when they came up on the radio. He went on to explain to me that pop song lyrics are often repetitive and simple and because they are set to music they become very memorable quickly. He suggested I try the same tactic in Cabo with Mexican music. The idea struck me as perfectly sensible because it was exactly that. My problem? I didn't have an iPhone or ear buds or a clue how to get the music into my ears. Maybe this would have been easy for most people, but organizing the electronics of it seemed to be a great a challenge for me. Too great. Besides, I hate ear buds. I told him I'd look into it but, frankly, I knew it wasn't going to happen.

A downpour at CC - Wednesday, February 15

I was coming to the close of my sixth week and a six-week history of non-stop perfect blue sky sunny days. Daytime temperatures were always in the mid-seventies and the nights were warming up enough to consistently be called t-shirt weather in the early part of the evenings. Not a drop of rain had fallen since my arrival, which is understandable because there hasn't been a cloud in the sky, ever. This morning was different. A blanket of soft gray clouds covered Cabo, making for the start of an overcast day of diffused light. When I stepped out into the parking lot for the second time that morning, I could see no threat of rain in any direction, just a light grayness, so rain didn't occur to me as even a remote possibility.

On my ride back from Walmart, late in the morning, I began to feel the faintest of mists on my bare arms. Tingly, misty rain, rain that was almost unseeable. And just on my arms because my big floppy sun hat shields my head from all the elements. I also felt a bit of a chill in the air, even though the temperature is already seventy. Everything is relative. I unloaded my groceries and jumped on the cruiser for a ride through town and then Cabo Cantina for lunch. I arrived before any clouds on the western horizon could possibly be taken seriously. When I walked in. I put out a warm *hola, que bueno verte otra vez* to Guillermo, Jorge, Ray, Andres and Oliver and Ismael. An extra shoulder slap to Guillermo who I hadn't seen for a week because he referred to me as "family" *Ay caramba!* But I liked that. I feel the same way about these guys. They all greeted me with the same enthusiasm. I wasn't feeling any anxiety at all. None. My positive attitude was back and my smile was big. Twenty minutes later, the downpour began, medium sized droplets at first and then quickly to big, heavy drops.

I joked with my friends about this unusual absence of the sun, adding something in my bad Spanish about *el fin del mundo,* the end of the world because it was the first time I've seen rain in Cabo. They said clouds show up sometimes, but not often. And we laughed over the way they said that. Or maybe we laughed over the way I was saying things. Probably that. Andres placed a bottle of Pacifico on my table, signifying that Spanish 101 was underway once again.

Well into my first Pacifico, seated comfortably at my usual table, I was able to see that all the other tables that were filled with tourists. The rain became relentless. This was no passing cloudburst. The gray blanket that was overhead thirty minutes earlier suddenly turned black with a perilous pattern of clouds whirling into wildness in competition with rippled streaks of gray knifing through the western sky. Exactly at one o'clock in the afternoon, just when I was sitting at CC contemplating the possibility of a second bottle of Pacifico, the sky really opened up. It created a momentary silence in the restaurant from the shock of the volume. The rain came down thick and heavy, as big as droplets can get. It was crazy, crazy rain. Sheets of it suddenly made it difficult to see across the street. Sidewalk pedestrians trapped in the open dashed into CC and slipped between CC's busy tables seeking shelter, partially blocking my view of the deluge going on outside the restaurant. I didn't have to see the downpour; hearing it was enough to know that this wasn't a passing shower and it wasn't going to let up anytime soon.

The water show was underway. Cabo Cantina was full of American customers, all of us watching the rain. Almost speechless over its power. No one was going anywhere. Ten minutes since the first heavy droplets hit, customers knew they were all staying longer than they expected. The water level on the street was rising and starting to move fast enough to challenge pedestrians crossing the street. It rose quickly and with a current that could not be ignored as it lapped above the curb, spilling over onto the sidewalk. Four-inch wide rivulets of water started to cut through the restaurant's red tile floor. I looked up at the ceiling and could see that a couple of thatched roof leaks graduated from drip drip drip to a steady trickle, one almost directly over the cashier's computer. A Mexican man walked into CC wearing a fifty-five-gallon garbage bag while waving five more in his hand. He said he was sent by the hotel across the street to help hotel guests back to the hotel. No one moved. It was all so interesting.

Everyone, myself included, was mesmerized by the volume of water filling the streets. After twenty minutes of this never-before-seen amount of heavy rain, the street turned into a turbulent river of brown froth and competing currents. Sheets of brown water spilled over the sidewalk and began lapping the step-up onto the restaurant's main floor. Street traffic was gone, the street was a river, the river looked dangerous and nobody believed all that could have happened that fast.

The crowd of customers let out a collective gasp and cell phones rose up at the end of outstretched arms when some daring driver of a big old Chevy Blazer plowed down the street, moving downstream, barely faster than the flow of water. The Blazer put up a spectacular spray off its bow and garnered hundreds of photos from the landlubbers of CC. It was quite an aquatic display and fun to see. It gave us a good measure of the depth of the water on the street. It was as high as the base of the Blazer's doors. Any regular car would have been swamped and, possibly, swept uncontrollably downstream. We all hoped to see something like that, of course.

The Chevy Blazer's wake flowed into CC and upped the volume of noise as customers at tables close to the sidewalk reacted unfavorably to the sudden wash of water over their shoes. Andres stood by my table. We were toward the back, secure on higher ground, one step above the main floor. No one moved, all of us were stunned by the event.

We waited it out. There really wasn't any other choice. Happily, I wasn't in a hurry to go anywhere. I never am. I had finished two Pacificos and was contemplating a third as I realized I might be in for the long haul. I nixed the idea of a third beer and ordered a margarita instead. *Con sal, sobre hielos.* Salt, over ice. And *una hamburguesa, rosa en el centro* was the closest I could come to saying a hamburger medium rare. The amount of water everywhere was so amazing that it was shocking. I didn't want to leave and I don't think anyone else did either. We were all having fun commenting on the brown river that completely replaced the street. The mocha river seemed never ending as it continuously ran over the sidewalks and licked the doorsteps of one shop after another on its way into the harbor basin.

Well into thirty minutes of cats and dogs, Andres confessed that had never seen a downpour like this in his five years at CC and maybe never. Then it stopped, as suddenly as it started. The sky went from black to gray to blue in five minutes and it was over. The sun came out and presto! We all survived. For many of us, lunch was liquid, with salt on the rocks. It was exciting and the crowd loved being part of it. The sidewalk water eventually drained back into the swift current running down the street, harbor bound.

Time to go. I paid up, *adios*-ed everyone, and pushed the cruiser along the sidewalk, moving downstream, northbound, in the direction of Coromuel. It was the wrong direction. With each block, I could see that the street water merged with the water from other streets creating an even bigger flood of water that was coursing toward the boat ramp for easy entry into the harbor. It was roiling water and fast enough that no one made an attempt to get across it. For only a second, I foolishly considered pedaling through it but changed my mind when I saw that my lower pedal would be entirely under the moving water. By the time I got to Señor Frog's, I ascertained that moving downstream was a mistake. It just got deeper and deeper and flowed faster and faster.

I turned around and pushed my bike back up the sidewalk, upstream, and past CC's street frontage, waving once again to all my sheltered friends and pointing out my intent to move uphill. A river of brown fast-flowing turbulent water still roiled down the street, as high as the curbs, even though the rain had stopped. It smelled bad, sewage bad. I saw that the only place that I could cross the street without getting my feet wet was just up ahead. I could make it across the river with dry feet if I rode the ridge of a speed bump I knew to be at the crosswalk. I took it and got to the other side in good shape. This maneuver made it much easier for me to move to higher ground. The main street, now behind me, was a torrent of calf-high water but with my gradual uphill climb I would be moving away from the deep water into rivulets no more than a couple of inches. At that point, I could head north safely by going a bit more uphill and then across town on higher ground while staying out of the bottom of the bowl-shaped geography to make it home dry and ready for a nap. That's what I hoped for anyway.

Three blocks up the hill, I was finally able to turn right and take the high ground back in the direction of Coromuel. A couple of the downhill cross streets were still shallow rivers of water from the surrounding hills, somewhat daunting in their fast flow toward the harbor. They were not nearly as deep as the in-town currents so it was an easy challenge to get across. I pedaled through them cautiously and after five blocks I was out of the basin of the marina, clear of all flooding. That water smelled really bad. I was extra careful to avoid getting my feet wet when I was jiggy-jagging through the streets to get home. By the time I got home, the blanket of gray had been completely rolled back to reveal nothing but blue skies from horizon to horizon. Time for a shower and a nap.

Ocho again - Wednesday, February 15

When I got home after the deluge, Ocho was stuck to the ceiling above the stove, watching me. Staring as usual. I said hi and got nothing in return. Typical. That's Ocho. He's not into reciprocity and he certainly isn't a drama queen. He was way out of reach so flailing my arms once did nothing to inspire movement out of him. Such movement had been ineffective in the past, even when Ocho wasn't so high and out of reach. I'm sure he thought I was annoying when I did this. Even so, I never stop trying to get a rise out of him. He must think I'm crazy for waving my arms time and time again. He might be right, to some extent.

Cats again and that insane dog - Wednesday, February 15

Cats again, night after night, early and late, and in the middle of the night. Screaming beyond the pale. I wish I had a pail I could throw at them. It's crazy. I'm not sure I can get so used to it that it won't wake me. It does sound like violence against a woman, maybe long term wild sex, but more like violence. I can't ignore that in my sleep. There's something else I haven't been able to ignore, sporadic yip-yapping from across the parking lot. It's the doggie in the window. I know where he is because I've investigated the source. I've even walked outside to double check its locations, often at hours when you don't want a dog barking, like two a.m. It's easy to spot the barker: some big Schnauzer-type doggie in the window stands with its paws on the sill of four stories up across the parking lot of my building. It goes into spasms when it sees another dog outside. I thought about emailing my landlord but that would be stupid. Really, what can she do? Or I should say what can she do that I can't do? When it woke me up at four in the morning yesterday, or maybe that was that today, I promised myself I'd leave a note on the door sometime this week.

Really? *Ron* means rum in Spanish? - Wednesday, February 15

Tonight at Guadalupana, I made my last stop of the evening. I learned that I have been carrying a misperception with me since I was a freshman in college. I learned of my folly when Facundo and I were talking about the various liquor bottles on the shelves behind the bar. It was a fun conversation and all undertaken for the sake of having an easy conversation with objects in hand and simple words for comparisons. He was being my teacher in a subtle yet practical way. He told me that "Ron" on the bottle labels means rum in Spanish. Maybe you know that, maybe everyone knows that, but I didn't know that. I thought Ron was short for Ronald. Just then, I learned that it meant rum when I asked Facundo how to say rum in Spanish. Of course, I've seen the label Ron Rico my entire adult life. At first, I thought he didn't understand my question. But he did. I just didn't understand his answer right away. Poof! Misperception gone! And I lived my entire adult thinking Ron Rico was some cool Latino heavily invested in rum, when it is actually Rico Rum. I thought Ronald "Ron" Bacardi was a person's name, too. Am I the only one?

CHAPTER SEVEN

Week 7

<u>My fifth flat - Thursday, February 16</u>

I saw it coming. No surprise. When I got out bed this morning and walked into the kitchen, I glanced at my front bicycle tire fearful that yesterday's expectation would be fulfilled. It was. I could see the tire was almost completely flat. I think it was my fifth flat. I wasn't surprised. Just by looking at it I could tell it did not have enough air to ride but it did have enough for me to roll it along the sidewalk easily enough with that blup blup blup sound that doesn't exist with an all-out dead flat running on the rim. The tire has been leaking all week. It has been a very slow weak, which tells me it is a very small thorn. I knew it was happening. Like I said, I saw it coming. Once again, a leak derails my fine-tuned machine, plunging it into a useless state and me into despondency. Well, not exactly, but I'm never happy about getting flats.

Once I stepped outside, I could see it was another perfectly sunny day, like all them since my arrival with one exception, yesterday. The impact of yesterday's downpour and subsequent flooding was evident in the accumulation of sand and debris in the roads, not just curbside but, in some instances, ankle high heaps of sand and silt appeared in the low spots, the last vestige of the trails of rivulets from the torrential rain. An army of civic sweepers was everywhere. Workers, up and down the streets, were bent over their worn straw brooms pushing detritus into neat little collectible piles curbside. The sweepers wore matching uniforms of sun protective clothing from head to toe. Broad brimmed hats and thick clunky rubber boots were the book ends to olive green full body jumpsuits, a body wrap concept that made no sense to me. It was insulation, I suppose, from the heat but how did that work? Those suits had to be sweat inducing and debilitatingly hot. I wanted to pay every sweeper's wage for the day and tell them to go home and sit in the shade, a show of mercy that would accomplish nothing in the clearing of the mini-dunes from the streets. I saw all this in the first few blocks walking the cruiser to Fernando's, but I knew the cleanup effort was underway city-wide. Cabo's town fathers care about their town's image.

I was pushing the cruiser past the Pemex gas station where I stopped three days ago for a hit of compressed air, for the tire, not me, to bring the leaking tire back to snuff. I knew it was only a temporary fix. That got me a good front tire for three more days, though it was noticeably softer on the third day, yesterday. Today, a flat was no surprise. I could have pumped it up at Pemex again this morning to get another three days out of it, but I passed. Or just to make getting to Fernando's easier. Instead, I walked my bike past the gas station without stopping, waved and said *Hola! Buenos dias!* to the attendants who had pumped my tires on other occasions. They remembered me and waved back. I don't mind walking. This time I'd walk my bike all of fifteen blocks to Fernando's open-air tire garage. The walk was relatively easy and quite enjoyable because it gave me a chance to say, *Hola! Buenas dias!* or some variation of that to the people I pass along the way. All of them must think I'm a loon, but they respond in kind.

The late morning sun was already hot and the half mile walk to Fernando's place drew a little sweat out of me. It felt good. It was exercise. When I pushed my bike up the gentle slope of his driveway Fernando was hard at work in his shaded workspace, crouched over an old tire making it look new again. He didn't hear me come up the drive. His son Ivan, hunched over on a six-inch-high stool, was assisting him, and lost in the job as well. Like father, like son. I got their attention when I called out *De nuevo, ayuda!* This greeting means, I think, It's me again, help! We exchanged warm greetings and I stumbled through an explanation even though one wasn't necessary. He could see for himself that my front tire was once again flat. Anyone could see that at this point.

Fernando is a gem. He is always happy to see me. I think he is naturally a cheery person. It's in his genes. He always stops what he's doing to talk to me, to help me. And I am happy to see him, not just because of his very capable services, but because he is a genuinely nice person. He is attentive, knows what he is doing, and he is patient with my Spanish while teaching me a few words along the way. The word he taught me four weeks ago was *espina*, means thorn, which is what was undoubtedly in my tire once again. Since that lesson I have used that word every time I needed his services even though once the culprit was *una pieza microscópica de metal*. This time I said I don't know for sure what caused the flat. I could not find the enemy. I used the word *enimiga* for enemy because I don't know the word for culprit or cause.

Ivan, at fourteen and big for his age, thinks everything I say is funny. I'm not saying funny things, of course; he's laughing at my pronunciation. It's hard to get Ivan to respond to me, maybe because he's a kid. Or, more likely, he has trouble understanding my pigeon Spanish. I'm sure I maul it and my hand gestures make no sense to him. He is not like his father in this regard. His father is an excellent communicator. I always understand what Fernando is saying to me, maybe because he is willing to say it a few different ways and slowly until he thinks I understand him. Another reason to like him.

As always, Fernando repaired my flat in less than ten minutes. He's speedy. He's a man who knows exactly what has to be done and he does it with the precision that comes with years of experience. We are about the same age, so he must know a lot about tires and has seen everything in the tire world. He is always focused and orderly. He pulled out the inner tube, filled it with air, dunked it in a tub of water and rotated the tire around in his skilled hands until he spotted bubbles coming out of the latest hole. I was standing over him. We saw only that one leak. He then lined the tube up with my tire to identify the location of the leak on the tire. Within seconds, he found the enemy, yep, a thorn. *Una espina.* Of course. It was not only difficult to see because it was so tiny, less than a pinhead, but it was also difficult to pull it out of the tire for the same reason. We agreed it was the smallest enemy thorn we had seen so far. Of course, we dramatized our mutual shock and shared a good laugh over it. I am always in danger with millions of enemies. Millions of them, all over town! Fernando laughs at my hyperbole, so do I.

As I held the thorn in the palm of my hand, Fernando and I couldn't believe it was long enough to punch through the tire. Moments later, I saved it in a carefully folded fifty-peso bill for tomorrow. It was the only paper I had on me. I want to show this treachery to my friends at Cabo Cantina and Guadalupana. They know I have had many flats because I am always complaining about the condition of the streets. This time I can show them the culprit or, rather, the *enemiga*. They will commiserate with me over the likelihood that there are five million thorns just like this tiny one on the road, all lying in wait for a bicyclist. Since I am just about the only bicyclist in town, they are waiting for me. Hungrily. And mercilessly.

I don't think Fernando ever expects me to pay him. He always acts surprised when I insist. I can tell he is happy with any payment. I gave him three hundred pesos for the repair. That's about fifteen bucks which is what I've been paying him from the start. I think he's happy with that amount.

Bob and Laura at Solomon's Landing - Thursday, February 16

Tonight was fun. I met a very nice couple at Solomon's Landing, Bob and Laura from Albuquerque. It was my first time there since the *huevos rancheros* breakfast I had on my first full day in Cabo over a month ago. The evening started about five thirty. It was happy hour, which doesn't tell you anything because happy hour is every hour of the day in Cabo. Seems like it anyway. I sat on the backside of the bar, facing the marina, so I got a good view through the bar, over the crowd, and into the world of yachts. The two barstools to my right were open.

Laura showed up first and sat next to me, leaving the one on the corner open. Bob showed up five minutes later and sat in that corner stool. All three of us had a nice view. Of course, I didn't know their names at first, but introductions happened shortly after Bob sat down. I liked them both right off the bat. They were so friendly and relaxed and interesting that I felt I was with a couple of old friends. They made me forget the challenges of learning Spanish. A break from that intensity is always welcome, though I rarely have them.

Bob and Laura are from the Sandia area of Albuquerque, just four hours south of my home in Durango. For some reason, maybe because we three are sitting at a bar at the bottom of the Baja far from our homes that are relatively close back in the States, we yik-yak like neighbors. We agree that our hometowns are similar in livability and fairly well-kept secrets on that measure. Both places are a nice size, have some history, and good people. And four seasons. I didn't realize Albuquerque had four. Bob was telling me about the weather and enlightened me with the fact that Albuquerque was a little higher than five thousand feet, not quite as high as Durango, which explains the snow, however light and infrequent it is. As I was listening, it was easy for me to remind myself that snow in Durango is not light and infrequent, but the opposite. I wasn't missing Durango's cold weather sitting there, at Solomon's Landing in shorts and a t-shirt. Nonetheless, both places have four seasons, which we agreed we liked.

Bob and Laura have been married for twenty-eight years. I'm sure it was mostly bliss because it is easy to see *and feel* that they get along so well. Bob said he's an introvert and Laura is the extrovert which they said worked for them all those years. Laura added that they didn't have any children. In my head, I said to myself that might be another reason that have been happily married and still together. Sorry, but children take a toll on a lot of marriages. I don't know that from personal experience because not only do I not have children, which is something I have in common with this couple, but I have never been married, something I don't have in common with most people. Also, we three share a love for Jimmy

Buffet. I confessed that if I could swap my life for anyone else's, it would be for Jimmy Buffet's life. Who would you swap yours for?

I introduced myself as a writer and briefly explained my reasons for being in Cabo for three months. Their stories were much more interesting. Bob owns numerous hotels around the country, so, like me, he's familiar with a lot of great cities for hotels, like Napa. He owns one there. He creates ownership with his investor partners and then is heavily involved in their development and the actual design elements. I love talking about hotel design, such as lighting and location and the marketing sensibility behind everything. That stuff is right up my alley of interest so I had a lot of fun listening to his experience.

Laura, too, had great stories about her life challenges, like being a cancer survivor. She's had to fight it off a couple of times, including when she was nineteen, and is still on top of it. Somehow, over the years, she has integrated her battle into her life to have made a very successful career with Mary Kay Cosmetics. I knew a lot about that business, too, from my business experience in Dallas. In the eighties, I actually met Mary Kay a few times. She had a look that no one could forget. Laura had some great stories about Mary Kay and that whole experience too, also right up my alley. They gave me a fun evening at the bar. It was so much fun that we agreed to meet again, same place, same time towards the end of the week.

On my way home, I dropped in on a restaurant by the Bahia Hotel called Esquina, the Spanish word for corner. It's the only bar that Bob and Laura recommended over dinner. They said it was kinda hip and a good looking late-night singles sort of crowd. That concept appealed to me, so I pedaled on to the base of the gum drop hill and pushed the the rest of the way to the top. A minute later I was overlooking Mango, The Office, and the other beachy restaurants. Edith's was across the street from me. I locked my bike to a post across the street from Esquina.

When I walked into Esquina I liked it immediately. It made a strong first impression on me. Excellent soft lighting, sectioned for different kinds of seating choices, a lively bar, live music in the outdoor section, and a tony looking crowd of Americans. It was the hippest looking restaurant I've been in since I got here. I leaned against a wall in front of the bar for a few minutes and chatted with a married chick in her late twenties from Iowa. She said it was highly rated in TripAdvisor. I walked out after ten minutes, content with getting a flavor of the place and making a mental note that I should go back there some night, even if I am the oldest guy in the joint. I certainly was tonight.

Locked out - Friday, February 17

I've been noticing home security "systems" lately. Security is an important issue in any foreign country. The most common system in Central and South America is jail cell iron bars on windows and doors. In some of the denser, low income barrios of Cabo, every home has them. I never liked that system, not just because it is ugly and interferes with the view, but because it makes it difficult to jump out the window if you find yourself inside when flames are licking the walls and everything else. I noticed that my condo has bars on all the windows, except one. The double sliding window in the kitchen doesn't have bars. It opens into the alley-like separation space between my building and the building next door. Looking out, the left end of the space is a parking lot wall, about eight feet high spiked with razor blade wires and broken glass, which must be effective because I see that arrangement atop a lot of walls everywhere south of the border. The other end, to my right, opens to the courtyard only twenty feet from the swimming pool. My unguarded kitchen window makes the bars on all the other windows irrelevant. You either have bars on all the windows or none of them. Just having bars on some is pointless. Burglar school 101.

I was a little concerned about the break-in risk this oversight posed but I let it go because the kitchen window overlooks the courtyard, not the very public parking lot. I made a mental note to let Ale, my landlord, know about my concern after I returned to the States. As it turns out, the day I locked myself out of my condo was the day I discovered how ineffective the kitchen window is at keeping out intruders. That happened today.

Around ten o'clock in the morning, I left my condo to ride to Walmart for a frozen vegetable run and some other basics. I was distracted by my thoughts about my shopping list. The instant the lock clicked as I closed my front door behind me, I realized that I left my key on the kitchen counter. Locked out! I wasn't happy about this situation, but I immediately recognized that it was a lot better situation than if I had locked myself out late at night. That's a major league unfortunate disservice to Ale that I never wanted to happen. My mid-morning problem didn't seem all that bad.

I went right to the building office in search of an extra key. They might have one, but if not, they could call Ale for me. The latter happened and I was told that Ale would show up in an hour to let me in. The office person who helped me is a babe, the babe, the one that catches my attention the most in that office. The one that I'd never really say anything to other than *hola*. Or for an emergency, which this lock-out was to me. She was helpful, besides being so attractive. My Spanish wasn't particularly good, but I was able to put together a sentence that was good enough. I said, *Quiero una llave para mi puerta, for favor*, which was the best I could do at requesting a key for my door. Along with some shrugging from me and a little pantomime, she understood that I locked myself out. She said she did not have a key, but would make a telephone call to Ale. I waited, she called. I listened to some super-fast Spanish with Ale that I couldn't follow but I recognized *llave*, the word for key. The babe hung up and told me that Ale would come to my rescue soon, maybe an hour, maybe two. I thanked her for her call to Ale and then went to the pool to wait.

But I didn't wait. As soon as I sat down on a poolside lounge chair, my salvation hit me right between the eyes. I got up with the idea that I could break into my kitchen window! A burglar strikes in the middle of the day! Me, sneaky me! I suddenly became concerned that someone might be watching, however silly that was because anyone who might see me fooling with the window surely knows that it's the window to my place. Thank goodness I was on the ground floor. I felt I had to be sneaky and fast about my attempt at a break-in. I played it like it was really a break in, clearly empathizing with the burglar, the one I imagined thirty minutes ago when I was inside my kitchen looking out through a window without bars. I wanted to beat him up, but of course, that made no sense.

I didn't want to be seen in this caper, so I scurried into the small space between the two buildings for quick access to my kitchen window. The window had a cheap aluminum frame around two panels of glass. Even the manufacturer had to see it was cheap enough for an easy break-in. It was as cheap and flimsy as frames can get, which is good for a first-time burglar. I gently, but firmly pushed one frame of glass in, being careful not to break it, while hoping to force the frame's clip lock on the inside between the two frames to unlock. It took thirty seconds to unlock the window, slide one panel open, and climb through the opening. I was in and it was easy to get in! I closed the window behind me, and locked it. I was happy about my break-in, but a bit undone over how easy it was. I would not want my computer stolen. I put that fear aside and gave some thought to the next step.

Ale was on her way, fighting nasty traffic no doubt, probably at least a half hour away. She'd arrive to discover that I was back in my apartment. I felt bad about her inevitable disappointment upon learning that her effort turned out to be unnecessary, a total waste of her time. Also, I didn't think she'd be happy to learn that it was so easy for me to break in. I wanted to postpone that unhappiness until my return to the States. There was only one thing I could do. I locked myself out again, this time intentionally, and then would say nothing about my break-in. An hour later, Ale's husband showed up instead. He had a set of keys. He was very nice. We chatted for five minutes after he let me in and, on his way out, informed me that he would leave a set of keys with Juanie in the laundromat for future mishaps. Good to know, but only I knew it was not necessary. Next time, if there is a next time, of course I'll break in again; it was too much fun! It brought the sneaky out of me.

I love the smell of Gardenias - Friday, February 17

Ever since the first time I met Gabriel as my server at Gardenias, He and I always exchange a few words in Spanish beyond the basics in a greeting, but not much else. *Poco a poco*. He's busy gliding from table to table, about twenty of them, sometimes more. He moves with equal grace back and forth from the kitchen to keep the American tourists happy. He and the other workers are nice, but while there is some growing recognition of me, I can't tell yet if any friendships with the staff are in the making. I am guessing not. That's not a criticism. After all, I can't imagine finding another place that offers the camaraderie of CC and Guadalupana, so I don't expect it at Gardenias or anywhere else.

I must say, the food at Gardenias always smells so good to me. It whets my appetite the moment I walk in. Even thinking about it. It's the smell of deliciousness, if there is such a thing. Surprisingly, it is not the smell of fried food. It's the scent of intrigue and it creates the anticipation of impending gustatory nirvana. It's not complex. It's simple, like the food. It's a smell I really like, almost as much as I like the smell of lilacs and lavender. It's not the smell of gardenias. It is the smell of Gardenias' food.

My time at the table passed quickly. I was focused on eating, not studying. Today, I inhaled three grilled shrimp tacos, two grilled fish tacos, and a Pacifico. I was hungry. And I was celebrating my ability to break into my condo. It was a splurge. All that food, including a very generous tip for Gabriel comes out to twenty-two bucks. A feast. That will be my dinner. On my way out, I stopped at the counter by the open kitchen and personally thanked the cooks. I get to say things in Spanish like, *Gracias por tacos muy deliciosos*. And I always walk out happy and I make them smile. I'll probably have more meals there in the weeks ahead, probably every week I'm here. Every day wouldn't be a bad thing. And every time, I'll order the grilled shrimp tacos. Or the grilled fish tacos. Or both. I'm the kind of guy that doesn't let go of a good thing.

Esquina on a Friday Night - Friday, February 17

Just got back from Esquina, that hip little L.A. style bar on the crest of the gum drop above Mango. Bob and Laura recommended it yesterday. I checked it out that very night. They made a good call. Now, it's ten-thirty p.m. and I now know where the hip people in Cabo spend their Friday nights. Packed, a mixed crowd, mostly Americans, probably out of the hotels right there on the hill, specifically the Bahia Hotel and Beach Club. The men weren't impressive in their attire but, as usual, the women were, many dressed in cocktail attire and were very put-together. Mix of ages too, a real mix, twenties to sixties, putting me on the far end of the wisdom side of the life experience scale.

I was not feeling particularly talkative, for no reason. Sometimes I preferred the role of quiet observer which was made possible by assuming the lean-against-the-wall-silent-observer-position. I was the guy just scoping things out, with a bottle of Pacifico in hand. One beer was enough for me, but on my ambling departure, I got side-tracked. I stopped at the corner of the bar closest to the front door to take in another minute of the the live music across the dining area. That area was dark so it was hard to see the trio, but I liked their music. I turned to face the bartender with a change in heart. I was thinking about another beer when, suddenly I blurted out "hi" to a very attractive woman who was two feet in front of me after my semi-pirouette. A half second later, I made eye contact with the man she was attached to, who turned out to be her husband. I said hi to him, too. Allen and Alissa.

Right away I learned that Allen and Alissa are from North Dakota. They got in this afternoon and would be staying for five days. Married for twenty-seven years. He's a third-generation farmer, quiet as in low key, but definitely a nice person. Alissa, I learned, is a state representative who must have won some Meg

Ryan lookalike contest at some point in her life, per Meg Ryan's younger days. What a doll and a great conversationalist. They were both happy to be out of the all that political noise and the relentless cold that was subjugating North Dakota. The political noise in their state government was emanating at all levels, mostly in the context of a lot of partisan bickering. We didn't want to make that the subject of our first conversation. Alissa liked my artwork when I showed her one of my business cards. Sweetly, she expressed an interest in my paintings, enough to say she'd like to buy one. Maybe I'll hear from her when she gets back to the state whose license plate says, Discover the Spirit. Who knows, maybe she'll discover the spirit in my art. That'd be nice. I said goodnight after thirty minutes and continued my walk out of Esquina.

I'm here on my own for three months. I just passed the half way marker. Talking to Alissa was a pleasure but I generated a flash of my own loneliness out of it. It's tough sometimes being by oneself in a crowd of people who are caught up in vacationland intent on having the most fun possible in a very short getaway. It's okay though, I told myself. I'm in Cabo for two reasons. One, to learn as much Spanish as I can. Two, to write as much as I can. Of course, enjoying myself is part of the experience too, but getting into a relationship is not one of my objectives. Hmm. There's no reason fun shouldn't be the number one objective. What's with that?

Nonetheless, it is easy for me to say that interaction with nice, fun, interesting people like Bob and Laura last night and, however short a time it was with Alissa and Allen tonight, is a nice break from the isolation that comes with the life of a lone wolf writer. No howling tonight, however. Maybe another night and now I know the place where the "it" thing is happening in Cabo. That would be Esquina on a Friday night. Maybe Saturday night too. I might check it out then, too. It's been a fun week.

<u>A tough hour at Cabo Cantina - Saturday, February 18</u>

No customers when I walked into Cabo Cantina at two in the afternoon. None. Not really a huge surprise because it was mid-afternoon, usually a slow time, even on the weekends. You might say the place was dead. I certainly would. My arrival didn't go unnoticed. This time I sat at the bar, a change from going to my usual high-top bar table for four. I was perfectly aware that I walked in feeling a little anxiety. I don't know why I feel so nervous about walking into the CC these days. Everyone who works there is my friend. It's a great group of guys: Jorge, Andres, Oliver, Gabriel, Martin, Edgar, Ray, Ismael, and Guillermo all support my interest in learning Spanish. Of course, not all of them were there at that moment. I didn't see Edgar or Martin.

If it was obvious to me that I was feeling anxious, it must have been obvious to everyone. I wasn't my usual congenial self. Jorge was tending bar, but had little to do when I showed up as his only customer. His grasp of English was tops in CC, on par with Ray, maybe a little better. He asked me in Spanish, what's the problem. He could tell that something was bugging me. I wasn't my usual cheery self. I guess I was acting like I lost my mojo or something. That was the problem. I was having a setback since my pep talk from Ray. The light bulb went off. That was it, my mojo was gone. I wasn't feeling the mojo I use to speak Spanish, different from the other mojo reserved for the opposite sex, though that might be gone as well.

Some customers walked in, two couples, not together, took two tables close to the sidewalk. Good, I had still had the bar to myself. Anyway, after a half hour of chatting about nothing in particular in Spanish and English, mostly the latter, it was Jorge's turn to give me a pep talk. There never would have been time for this on any other day that I recalled. Anyway, it was the same one I got from Ray a week ago. Clearly, I needed to hear it again. I think they're comparing notes on my mental state. I get it, and I agreed with everything Jorge said, which is pretty much what Ray said. Did Ray's words change my behavior? I wish I could say yes, but the answer is apparently not. Today was Jorge's turn to tell me to relax. Maybe have a shot of tequila. Maybe have two. Maybe get laid. That's what he said. I told him that the tequila part is easy. The other, not so much. Maybe his advice will connect with me if I connect with someone.

I finished my bottle of Pacifico and didn't order a second. Paid my usual one hundred pesos, double the cost of the beer. I stood up and thanked Jorge and said, *Hasta mañana!* to my amigos. As I walked out the door, the last words spoken came from Andres, in English. I guess it was advice. He said, "Amigo, you are not the same person when you first came here. You talked a lot of Spanish then. Now, not so much. We're your friends." I smiled, kept walking, maybe with my head down a little bit. And my tail between my legs. I don't know why but I felt like an idiot.

He was right. I am not the same person. I am now Mr. Nervous Nelly at CC. Why? Who knows? What I think has happened is that I have placed too much importance on speaking Spanish. And, worse, I have created an expectation that I will be able to speak it before I leave Cabo. That sort of thinking is wrecking me. It's an insanely unrealistic goal. My friends are right. I have to lighten up. There is no deadline to learn Spanish; it could take years and years. And, for that matter, I don't even have to learn Spanish. No one is making me learn it. It's a self-imposed goal. I could fly out of Mexico today, happy to have been here and forget ever speaking another word of Spanish. There is no job requirement to speak Spanish. It's just supposed to be a fun thing that I thought I'd try for three months in Cabo San Lucas. I've turned it into a monster goal that does nothing to me but make me frustrated and uptight. This has got to stop.

A little extra for Fernando - Saturday, February 18

On my way home after Jorge's pep talk at CC, I swung by Fernando's garage. I wanted to pay him a little more than the three hundred pesos I forked over a couple of days ago. I decided not to wait until next time to duke him and rode the cruiser to his garage.

He was kneeling by the right rear tire of another customer's car, a big tan SUV, with the customer standing over him, when he saw me at the end of his driveway. His brow wrinkled and he looked concerned when he saw me. He said, *Otra vez?* Again? Meaning another flat tire? He stood up and I waved him toward me to get him out of the other customer's sight line, while asking the other customer to pardon the interruption of a moment. I did that in Spanish. As quickly as I could, which sometimes isn't very quick when I revert to Spanish, I thanked Fernando again for his service and being so kind. Then I said, *Aqui hay un poco mas*, which means, "Here is a little more," as I handed him two hundred pesos, an extra ten bucks, bringing the total to twenty-five. His thanks came with a big smile and then we both knew he had to get back to his important Mexican customer. It was a small, speedy, and sweet gesture. I rode off into the sunset, happy I did that, but still feeling the malaise I had when I left CC earlier.

<u>Saturday night at Esquina - Saturday, February 18</u>

It's Saturday night! Live. I decided to cruise to Esquina tonight, to cruise the scene, you know, see what's up. My third night in a row. Why not? Nothing else going on. There are only so many hours I can devote to Spanish before my mind turns to mush. I continued my push up gum drop hill and passed Esquina's open entrance on my way to the lamppost for my bike just over the crest. I locked the cruiser up, as always. I confess that I dressed for Esquina tonight, which is saying a lot because I don't really have clothes that would count for dressing for anything other than a day at a beach bar. Same black, cotton, short sleeved shirt I wore last night but I swapped out my khaki cargo shorts for my skinny blue jeans. It didn't even occur to me to wear one of my Tommy Bahama shirts. If not here, then nowhere I suppose, unless I get invited on to someone's yacht for a couple of cocktails. I wouldn't turn down that invitation, whatever the dress code.

At the threshold, I could see that place was packed once again, which is a good thing. I walked into the candlelit entrance, paused long enough to get the vibe, said hi to the hostess who was seductively tricked out in a black pantsuit with a lowcut v showing off a beautiful neck. I smiled at her and beyond, aimed for the bar, and said to myself this could be an interesting night, even if nothing happens. I just thought it would be interesting because I was feeling good. I was happy to be in Cabo and lucky to be able to be here for three months with no responsibilities. Shoot me if I ever complain.

Don't give up - Sunday, February 19

I slept in this morning, which means sleeping until eight-thirty. Not much of a sleep-in, but good enough for me. I actually didn't get out of bed until ten because I studied Spanish for an hour and half before I threw the sheets back. I have wonderful days like this with a schedule that is no schedule at all. I am sure there are plenty of people that would like my schedule. I don't take my situation for granted. I'm doing well, even though I seem to stress a bit with my self-inflicted pain in Spanish lessons. Which is funny because there is nothing at stake. I can walk away anytime if that will make me feel better. I was stressing a bit lately over my recent weak performance at Cabo Cantina. I awoke saying to myself no more because it is not a performance. I don't have to perform. I can just be myself. That should be the ticket to getting me back into a happy space at CC.

When I climbed out of bed, CC was on my mind and I asked myself, go or no go today? It was an easy decision. I thought of Jorge's words. And Ray's. And Andres' advice, too. Go! CC is where my friends are. I am always welcome there and every single person I know there is kind to me and always happy to see me. To date, I have never done so many high-fives in my life as I have accumulated so far at CC. By the end of my stay in Cabo, I will have attained a number that is so astronomically high it will never be challenged by any future activity in my life. What a great bunch of guys. Truly. Of course, I'll show up today.

I'm up fixing breakfast after my shower and shave. It's the usual. I steam two handfuls of frozen mixed vegetables from a package right out of my freezer. Bought at Walmart, in the frozen section, best deal for vegetables on a cost per ounce basis. It is Sunday and I am thinking I need to get out more, get a little more variety into my schedule, have a little more fun. Beyond making plans to go to CC after the lunch hour, I'll just let the day take me where it wants to. Wherever that is, is okay by me. I think this is a reflection of slipping a little deeper into the culture here. Yes, people work hard here and, yes, not everyone makes a lot of money, but I am thinking they have a nice balance going. When they work, they work hard. After that, they put the work behind them so they can do the things that really matter, like spend time with family and friends. That's what I think. I don't have a behavioral study in my hip pocket to prove it. It's just my opinion. I don't know how else to explain the general good nature of Mexicans.

When I walked into CC, I went up to every server and greeted him in a personal manner, as usual. The place wasn't packed, maybe only a dozen customers, which is how I like it. I spent a bit more than an hour at CC, knocking down two Pacificos at lunch time, but not ordering food. A liquid lunch. I talked to every server in that shift, but only briefly in passing because they were all busy with tables. Even so, they all found time to say hi to me after I got comfortable at the bar. I may have looked comfortable, but I still wasn't feeling comfortable. I didn't feel like I was connecting. The Spanish just wasn't flowing out of me. I was shutting down again from expecting too much from myself. This was turning out to be a tough hill to climb. I tried to put the worry aside.

Instead of doing the Spanish thing with my working friends, I chatted up an American couple sitting to my right. From Oregon. We talked about the thrilling victory Oregon had over Stanford yesterday in a Pac-12 conference basketball game. It was a real squeaker, down to the last second for a 75-73 win for Oregon. David and Mary Jane are big Oregon fans from Portland, so the buzz of that win hadn't worn off. Nice people, but we weren't speaking Spanish so it was time for me to move on. I didn't feel like hanging another minute at CC. I was stressing out over my inability to put sentences together in Spanish.

I left CC to study at home, but somehow got distracted en route. I rode my bike through the gaping entrance to Esteban's and right into an open space on the outdoor patio. I was hoping to see Lourdes for a little harmless flirting, if I could do such a thing. She wasn't in but that didn't stop me from parking the cruiser against the wall in a vacant corner of the patio. I skipped lunch at CC, so I was hungry. That said, I decided to order the lunch special: three fish tacos, rice, beans, a cup of salsa, a beer and a shot of tequila. I passed on the tequila but happily ordered my third Pacifico of the day. I settled in and watched the insane traffic on the boulevard, somehow comfortable with eating solo at a restaurant table.

I know the three servers at Esteban's. Hector, Saul, and Toney. All three are super nice and speak very little English. No surprise. Hector the most. And all three know I flirt with Lourdes, especially Hector who has an all-seeing eye. I think it is more accurate of me to say I flirt with the idea of flirting with Lourdes. Hector and I laugh a lot over my infatuation. He is encouraging me to make a serious move on her. He told me she isn't married and currently doesn't have a boyfriend. He is telling me not to be shy because.... but I didn't understand what he said in Spanish. I didn't ask him to clarify it because nothing would ever develop between Lourdes and me. I'm the only one who knew that. Maybe he wants me to live his fantasy, ha. I asked Hector twice if he was sure she was single. This is a very important question because, earlier, Toney told me a different story between the pep talks I got from Hector. Toney told me the same, that Lourdes doesn't have an *esposo*, which means a husband, and doesn't have a boyfriend either, a *novio*. Okay, got that. But, Toney added that she did have an *esposa*, which means wife. I thought we ran into a language barrier with that news so I triple checked the choice of words with him. Yes, he confirmed his choice of words, that Lourdes has an *esposa*, but not an *esposo*. Interesting. In my next conversation with

Hector I reported Toney's news. Hector said that's absolutely not true. He was certain. Just before he walked away he said to me, *La puerta está abierta*, which means the door is open.

One minute after Hector advised me to go for it with Lourdes, which is how I interpreted his open-door comment, Lourdes walked onto the patio making, in my mind, a surprise entrance. She was looking just north of terrific. She saw me, smiled, and headed my way. Gulp. My tongue started to swell and my mind went blank. It was easy to forget every Spanish word I know except *adiós* and *ay chihuahua*. It would have been dumb to say the former and dumber to say the latter. Silence could be the cool way to go, you know, a man of few words. Sure enough she stopped at my table, stood across from me, her beauty towering over me, to say hi. I stood up, playing the perfect *caballero*, shook her hand, swapped a mutual greeting, and then sat down, clueless beyond a sentence or two, of course, as she walked away. So much for practicing Spanish. As it turned out, some words actually did come out of me, like telling her it was nice to see her and something like I didn't think she would be arriving until nine o'clock. She was surprised about the nine o'clock thing, which made me realize I misunderstood Hector earlier. He said she was "leaving" at nine o'clock and I heard she was "arriving" at nine o'clock. And that was pretty much my excitement for the day. When she walked into the interior of the restaurant, out of sight, I went into the interior of my head, out of mind.

I reviewed my conversation with her in my head. It didn't take long and it wasn't pretty. Then I looked down at my crotch with the fear that I still had a big water stain there from my attempt thirty minutes earlier to clean up a sizable chunk of salsa that dripped off a chip into my lap. Great if she saw that when I stood up. Thank goodness the air is dry here. My pants were too, at that moment. I don't know what to do with Lourdes. I have no idea what she thinks. Me? What should I do? I am reasonably sure I'll simply try to minimize my pain and suffering by doing nothing.

I rode the cruiser out of the confines of Esteban's patio for *mi casa*. I had to go home to practice Spanish, so I could say correctly, it's nice to see you again. Or how about this sentence for Lourdes: Come to my place so we can make passionate love to each other. Now that is funny! The evening was still ahead of me. Maybe another visit to Esquina is in the near future. Very near. Like about nine tonight. It'd be nice to see Alissa and Allen there, the couple I met at Esquina's bar Friday night. It would be especially nice to see Alissa. What a babe. Lucky Allen. Dang it, farmers have all the luck.

Sneaky gringo leaves note on a door - Monday, February 20

What should be a relatively quiet Monday morning, wasn't. I stood just outside the front security gate of Villa Paloma, my five-building complex. I was looking up, staring at the dog in a window on the fourth floor of the building across the street. It was staring back at me, barking up a storm. It's the one that had been barking since five this morning and showing no sign of fatigue. It barks a lot, on most mornings, sometimes as early as five and even earlier on more recent mornings. I am sure about the time. I kept looking at him and tried to think of some great dog recipes, but none came to mind. The time was now. I was prepared. I looked across the parking lot, confirmed that no one else was around and then scampered across the lot to the dog's building. My mission was to deliver a scribbled note to the owner of the dog. I didn't think anyone was in because the dog was on a run of incessant barking. I did not want a confrontation, with the owner or the dog.

I speed walked across the parking lot and climbed the four flights expeditiously. When I got to the fourth floor, panting like a dog, the barking dog heard me outside his front door and went into even bigger spasms of barking. It was a bit like the stuff I've been hearing on a regular basis but with a little more edge. With a little more bite. This time it occurred to me that it wanted to bite me really bad. Maybe start with my hand. Or my foot if my hand wasn't within easy reach. Maybe my everything. I taped the note to the door with a thumb nail size piece of duct tape, thus putting my privates probably a mere six inches from the monster's lethal muzzle. I was very thankful a solid core door was in-between us. I got out of there in a hurry, taking two steps at a time down the never-ending four flights of stairs. I didn't think my note would do any good, of course, but it made me feel better. Of course, the note was in Spanish. And, of course, the dog owner would know it was written by a gringo. I'd be a suspect, but he'd never know for sure. Good luck to my request, but it made me feel better with the effort.

Coming out of that building like a thief on the run, happy with a clean getaway in mind, I ran into Martina in the middle of the parking lot. She witnessed my hasty departure from the building. She probably saw my stealthy entrance as well. She knew I was in strange territory and her face needed an explanation. I told her that I left a note on the door of a fourth floor condo that housed a dog that was waking me up every morning with its incessant barking. She said she was aware of it too. She said I cannot shut the noise out because I must have a bad conscience. Where did she get that notion? She's my neighbor, not my shrink. Anyway, Martina and I chatted for a minute about the cacophony of nocturnal life in our neighborhood. She told me that cats have been keeping her up. I laughed, then she laughed when I said it's because she must have a bad conscience.

Bill and Lisa at Solomon's Landing- Monday, February 20

Today is President's Day in the U.S. This is a holiday that is not celebrated in Mexico. None of our national holidays are celebrated in Mexico. On the other hand, Americans celebrate Cinco de Mayo, a very big Mexican holiday. What does that tell you? Mexicans know how to party! This is true. They have fiestas for every possible reason. It is another manifestation of their happy culture.

For me, today is business as usual; every day has the same significance to me. The morning passed in a flash from sleeping in and then filling the first four hours of the day with a trip to Walmart followed by some in-home studying and writing. By one o'clock, I needed to get out of the confines of my place, however nicely it works for me. I was hungry, time to eat. Fearful that I would pick a restaurant, any restaurant, and pig out on tacos or succumb to some restaurant's five course lunch special, I decided to steam some vegetables to head off the threat of bad judgement caused by ravenous hunger and, importantly, to meet my daily vegetable quota. I don't really have a quota per se, but I try to get a big serving of mixed vegetables into my daily diet. Doing that now seems like a good idea, along with fixing a new round of my usual green smoothies. After that, I'd head into town, cruise around for exercise and people watching, watch the boat traffic at the harbor entrance, and peruse *Spanish for Gringos* on a marina bench while pondering life. All this before going to Solomon's Landing for happy hour.

I walked in perfectly aware that I wasn't giving myself much time in the joint. Happy hour for me was about an hour, which is all I needed for a beer. I went to the far side of the bar and took the same seat I sat in last week. It was a good seat for on overview of the whole restaurant and, beyond that, it overlooked the marina walk and the harbor. I brought *Spanish for Gringos* with me out of a deeply entrenched habit of taking it with me wherever I go. I plunked down on a bar stool surrounded by other empty stools and opened my book. After I ordered a Pacifico, I scanned the bar for talent and saw no possibilities. Maybe that would change. One minute later a nice looking American couple in their fifties sat next to me, in the same seats that Bob and Laura sat in the day before.

For the first ten minutes at the bar I kept to myself, mostly studying infinitives off a list in the back of my book. The American woman sat next to me, her husband, I assumed, on the other side of her. It was a safe assumption, not one of those "assume makes an ass out of u and me" things. She had some big diamonds on her wedding finger. But maybe not, who knows, and I didn't care. My mojo wasn't going to be tested this time around. The couple was well dressed and fit, a compliment to them given America's shocking numbers for obesity. In every foreign country in the world, it is easy to identify Americans: they're the fatties.

This couple ordered two draft beers, Dos Equis Ambers, and chatted between themselves a bit before the woman interrupted my straightaway stare into the infinite distance by making some friendly comment about my Spanish book. A minute later the introductions followed. I was talking to Lisa and Bill from the Boston area. They were vacationing in Cabo for two weeks. They were both professionals in health care and they both professed their love for Mexico. They had been to Cabo several times in the past few years for vacation and were now contemplating retirement here.

For the most part, they talked. I listened to them tell me about their arrival in Cabo, specifically about the room and the place they were staying in. This was their fourth day and last night in the B&B they found on Airbnb and booked for ten nights. I think they said it was called Robin's House. They chose it for its location. It was in town, just a couple of blocks off the marina. They also told me that they liked the price which was a good segue for them to be able to say, "You get what you pay for." For the next twenty minutes, they took turns telling me what they got for their money. Which wasn't much. The one-word answer is, screwed. Right up front they made it clear that they couldn't wait to get out of that place. They could not stand another day in their B&B so they bit the bullet on the full amount they paid for their ten-day stay. It hurt, but they were thankful they were able to book a room on short notice at the Solmar Hotel, as refugees. Their check-in at the Solmar Hotel was tomorrow. Now, they were drinking heavily to fortify themselves for their last night at the birdhouse B&B, their words, not mine.

When Bill and Lisa checked into the B&B three days ago they had a feeling right off the bat that it wasn't going to work for them. They said their initial fears were confirmed by a Canadian couple staying in the only other room in the B&B, across the hall from them. When they met, the Canadians said they hated the place from the start. Like Bill and Lisa, they too wanted to leave. Unlike Bill and Lisa, they couldn't afford to leave and pay for another place. It was simply too painful for the Canadians to give up the vacation money they paid into the B&B for two weeks and then shell out some more dough for a room at another hotel. They were very upset. And sad. And mad. It was ominous news for Bill and Lisa who nonetheless tried to give it a go at first. Maybe they would have a different experience from the Canadians, but that turned out to be wishful thinking. This morning, after three nights, Bill and Lisa decided to pull the plug on Robin's House. Of course, I asked what was so bad about the place. Of course, they were going to tell me whether I had asked or not.

Photos don't always line up with reality. I know that and I even experienced that myself when I got here. Lucky for me, it was easy for me to toss my first impression and conclude that I liked my condo quite a bit. Bill and Lisa weren't as lucky. They said their room was way smaller than they expected. They told me they had never stayed in a B&B before so I know there's some shock for that adjustment compared to hotel rooms. The close quarters of B&Bs are not for everyone. Especially when your room rate comes with a shared bathroom. Nope, B&Bs are certainly not for me. I wish I could have warned them.

They also didn't like the idea of a long walk down the hall to the shared bathroom. Another reason I'm not wild about B&Bs; a lot of them are like that. There's more. The advertised "balcony" wasn't big enough to stand on. The photo tricked them. One could hardly call it a balcony, Lisa said. This photo trick was surely disappointing but, she went on, not as disappointing as having a TV in the room that was not hooked up to a cable nor a satellite. Local stations, which would have been in Spanish (something I know from my condo), was the only programing available. True, the B&B delivered on its promise that the room had a TV, but Bill and Lisa saw no point in turning it on, to what? They complained to the B&Bs owner and got the brush off as the owner reiterated that she advertised the room had a TV and there was, in fact, a TV in the room. Bill just about blew his stack recalling the owner's words. The owner, in self-defense I suppose, countered with the news that the room had a DVD player they could use. Lisa pointed out that there were no DVDs in the room to play. She then asked to see what DVDs were available to guests. The answer was "there are none here but you probably could buy some." I could see that Bill's eyeballs just about popped out of their sockets with that little bit of reminiscence. But wait, there's more.

On the second day, after a lot of exploring around the marina, Bill & Lisa returned to the B&B exhausted and over-dosed on margaritas. Upon bumping into the owner who they now referred to as "the crazy lady" with some added description about drugs that I didn't exactly hear, they told her they were going up to the room to take a nap. Before that could happen, the crazy lady asked Bill to help her carry some water bottles upstairs. Bill, who was indeed exhausted and over-fueled on drinks, nonetheless agreed to help her. She was happy with that and had him follow her to the back of the house, down some stairs, out the back door, and into a shed in the backyard yard where the bottles were stored. I think Bill said something about expecting to see a case of plastic wrapped 12-ounce bottles, not two thirty-pound water cooler jugs. He's a good guy, definitely went above and beyond the call and carried the two jugs upstairs, making two trips to do it. He subsequently learned that the Canadian guy had already said no to the request. Bill certainly earned a nap. Fifteen minutes later, Lisa and Bill awoke to the sound of some serious metal drum music right below their balcony. The crazy lady was whacking an old outdoor grill with a metal rod to do what? Knock some rust off of it? She knew they were napping, of course. That wasn't music to their ears. That's just one aspect of crazy.

As Bill and Lisa continue with their traveler's horror story, they already have my full-on sympathy. No one wants that experience. They also told me about their discovery that the crazy lady sleeps on the couch in the living room every night, which is right off the front door, completely taking that room out of action for any possible usage by the guests. They stopped tip-toeing after the second night.

I was glad to hear that this nice couple from Boston would finish out their vacation at the Solmar Hotel. I felt sorry for them, but I felt sorrier for that Canadian couple. I wonder if I'll meet them at Solomon's Landing tomorrow. Eh? Or maybe I'll meet another couple, or a solo traveler, like an attractive single woman looking for a good conversation with a writer who likes to drink Pacifico. It's turning out to be a pretty interesting place, granted, but lady luck won't happen.

Woe is me at Guadalupana - Monday, February 20

I stopped at the G Spot on my way home, unable to completely shake my frustrations over my assessment of slow progress with the language. I know I was making progress, but I just didn't feel it was enough. This is a self-imposed criticism that I don't need, but that didn't stop me from expressing my disappointment to Facundo who was behind the bar as usual. Pedro appeared briefly to say hi to me. Lately he really hasn't been joining Facundo and me at the bar. Don't know why. Maybe Facundo has the patience to deal with me and Pedro doesn't anymore. A shame because I like both of them very much. Of course, this is my imagination at work. I know it's a struggle for everyone to exchange ideas but Facundo is probably a little more patient with me. I tried to complain but he wouldn't let me. He assured me that my Spanish was a lot better since my arrival seven weeks ago. I guess that's what I wanted to hear.

I was only there for twenty minutes, long enough to enjoy a Cuba Libre. It's my drink of choice, but only at the G Spot. I always pay Facundo one hundred pesos for a drink that costs only fifty-five pesos. That's a total of five bucks. What a deal. I got on my bike and rode out the door feeling a little better, but not first without taking a lap around the room. No customers were there at that moment. Only me. So it seemed okay to do that. Facundo didn't object, but probably wouldn't say if he did. It might have been disrespectful of me. I hope not. I did it to be amusing. It's easy enough after one Cuba Libre, not so easy after two.

As for my Spanish, Facundo's finals words to me were, *Poco a poco, amigo!* Words I don't always remember but definitely words I should never forget. I waved on my way out the door and rode off into the night. Thankfully, Coromuel was across the street, so it was a short ride into the night.

<u>I won't ride my bike to Walmart for a week - Tuesday, February 21</u>

My string of flat tires is annoying me. I am sure Fernando is not annoyed by that string. It's a nice steady piece of business he's getting from me. It is a string. And now I've got a string theory of my own. I noticed that all the thorns pulled from my tires look alike. They are very small, even tiny, about the size of the broken tip of a stick pin, only an eighth of an inch long, that kind of small. All the same color and shape. The point is, they look alike. That tells me that they may be coming from the same source. So, what is the source?

My best guess, the source of those nasty thorns is "the chute." That's right, that narrow stretch of shoulder that runs like a gauntlet for a hundred yards on the frontage road. That's the strip I have been hustling through to get to and from Walmart. On one side, the desert side, a line of prickly bushes mixed in with various cacti forms one wall of that skinny chute, maybe the source is in that jumbled mess. That shoulder of the frontage road collects a lot of debris that never gets pushed off by the cars or washed away by the rain, whatever rain there is. It's a hundred-yard run of a carpet of dust. But I am thinking it's not just dust. I bet thousands of tiny thorns are embedded in that carpet.

I suppose I could ride my bike up to the beginning of the chute, dismount, park it, and investigate on foot to see if my theory is good. It would take a long time to search for thorns, besides, it's more dangerous in the chute on foot than on a bike. I'd have to be on my hands and knees. Not a good idea, at all. To bolster my hypothesis, I've decided that I'm not going to ride my bike to Walmart for a week, thereby avoiding the chute on my bike. If I don't get a flat tire within the week, I can assume the chute is the source of the thorns. Alternatively, I can walk to Walmart or take a taxi. Or not go to Walmart at all.

I walked to Walmart my first day in Cabo. It wasn't a bad walk. I got a nice bit of exercise out of it. Also, it would give me the chance to search for thorns in the dust of the chute. It'll be a quick search, almost impossible without kneeling. And I'll be alert about it. I do not want to become a statistic as a pedestrian fatality on Federal Highway 1. I'll still have to be quick about getting through the chute, maybe forego any chance to look for thorns. My theory isn't dependent on finding thorns. It is dependent on not getting a flat tire. Flirting with death like that is not a good idea, but if I am extra careful, it is doable. I walked it the first day I got here. I can do it again, even though the weekly temperatures have been climbing. It's only for a week.

Bob and Laura again at Solomon's Landing - Tuesday, February 21

I had the best time tonight with Bob and Laura. I needed that. I haven't really been out for a full evening of fun like that since I got here. What's wrong with me? I think that sounds horrible to confess that. Bob and Laura are the couple I met five days ago, from Albuquerque. We met for the second time at Solomon's Landing in the marina at six o'clock and said goodnight at nine. We three preferred back of the bar seats, where we were seated when we met, over the tables above the walkway. We all liked the crow's nest view over the dining room tables and out to the marina.

Our evening started with drinks, of course. Laura ordered white wine. Two orders of calamari kept our hunger at bay, but not for long. After my opening order of a Pacifico I switched to margaritas, same as Bob. Between the margs, dinner showed up. Bob and I ordered the seafood risotto. I can't remember what Laura ordered, but we three finished off every bite on our plates. It was delicious food but way too fattening for my palate. After two margaritas, I quit and agreed with Bob that the last round didn't feel like it had any tequila. That's when we both knew we were bombed. Actually, I insist we weren't, but we didn't feel like any more drinks. However, stopping the drinks didn't stop the stories.

They flew back and forth over the bar the rest of the evening. I hated to see it end.

Bob and Laura are the nicest couple I've met in years. We got along like great old friends. It isn't me just saying that. It was really great chemistry among the three of us, no denying that. We parted ways after exchanging invitations to visit each other any time. I can't believe three hours went by so quickly.

On my way home, I stopped at the entrance of Esteban's to flirt with the idea of flirting with Lourdes, but she was gone for the night. I just missed her. Saul, the stand-in host, told me that she typically leaves at nine. He smiled and told me they called her Lulu, not Lourdes. I think they've been talking about me since my drive by on my bike a few hours earlier when I called out to Lourdes, *Tu eres muy bonita*. She was just inside the entrance and I was past her before I could tell if she blushed. She is pretty so I wasn't wrong in telling her that. *Sinceramente*. I'm sure my drive-by flattery was of no consequence with Lulu. After a one-minute conversation with Saul, I moved on to Guadalupana. I could see the G Spot was lit up, so it was obviously open, but when I bumped into Pedro walking out of the swinging doors he told me they were closing. No surprise, I knew they closed around nine. Definitely time for me to call it a night. Nine is usually the beginning of the end for me, the end of my evenings out.

As I nodded off in bed, I told myself it was a good day. And a productive day. I spent most of the day writing and studying Spanish, which is a typical day except for the fact that I didn't go to Cabo Cantina. I would go to sleep feeling bad about that conversation with Jorge. I couldn't shake it from my thoughts. I know Jorge is right on every count about me being afraid to stick my neck out speaking Spanish. Weird because I was perfectly comfortable taking my best shot at Spanish with the staff at Solomon's Landing tonight. So, why uptight at CC? Maybe I'll go there tomorrow afternoon. Maybe I won't. Maybe I'll be able to answer that question sometime soon. The sooner the better.

They won't believe this in Minnesota - Wednesday, February 22

I managed to stay on my bike on the sidewalk as I navigated Coromuel's series of ninety-degree narrow corners to get from my building past the security guard. I always took the side-walk, the parking surface was cobbled stones making for a very uncomfortable ride. On the sidewalk, I had about an eighty percent success rate of making it without dismounting. I almost always succeed. I did this morning. When I succeed, it makes me feel like I'm getting the day off to a good start. I left my place as soon as the weekly maid showed up to clean my place. That's unexpected service that comes with the Airbnb contract with Ale. Nice. And necessary, but not scary for the maid because I'm pretty neat. It's nice to get fresh towels and new linens on the bed. Anyway, I rode out of Coromuel under the bright sun just before noon. One hundred yards later, a young couple, probably late twenties, coming towards me on foot, waved and said hi to me. I quickly recognized them and stopped in time to say hi and chat, leaving them with no doubt that I recognized them back. I've seen them in and out of my complex for the last several days.

We chatted on the sidewalk. The couple is from Minnesota and they are returning to the land of ten thousand frozen lakes in the late afternoon. I didn't get their names. They were very friendly, which is required of all Minnesotans. I told them that their freezing friends back home would be envious of their tans. I wanted to remind them that the last five letters of Minnesotan spells "so tan." But I didn't. Instead, I asked them about the morning, their last morning of their vacation. They said they were coming back from a little charter fishing. My inquiry took the lid of their contained excitement so they told me their fishing story. It's a good one. I never heard anything like it before.

The woman, a tall brunette undoubtedly raised in the Midwest, said she hooked what felt like a pretty big fish just about when the charter time was up. She was excited about this because the fishing all morning hadn't been great. In fact, she said it was really poor. Her husband didn't catch anything because he didn't fish much that morning. I think he said something about spending much of his time leaning out over the side of the boat and inspecting his breakfast. I felt for him, because I inspect my breakfast too, whenever I'm in the open water. Anyway, when she suddenly got a fish on the line, she thought it was something big, but she couldn't get it to the surface to reveal its identity. For the most part, reeling it in didn't seem to be that tough after the initial strike. Still, it felt big and it seemed to be moving toward the boat as she reeled it in. The guide didn't know what it could be, but whatever it was, it was unusual. Eventually, she did reel it in, right up to the back of the boat. She gasped when she saw her catch of the day. Of the year. The catch of a lifetime. She caught a seal!

Her Mexican guide had seen this happen only once before in years and years of fishing. When the seal spotted the woman, her husband, and the Mexican leaning over the stern, their mouths agape, he gave the bait fish on her hook one more futile tug. Unable to get the entire fish, the seal let go, tossing the fish and the hook. It flipped its tail in their faces, and disappeared into the deep. That foxy seal had done this sort of thing before because it didn't hook itself. I was glad to hear that it made a clean getaway. Of course, no one in Minnesota will believe her. It's a tough crowd of doubters up there when a fellow Minnesotan tells a fish story like that!

Someone else caught a seal - Wednesday, February 22

Mrs. Minnesota's seal story was such an usual fish story I had to immediately Skype my very close friend Dr. Dan Rodriguez in Portland, Oregon to tell him about it. He is the best dentist I have ever had, which is how I got to know him when I was living in Portland six years ago. Over the years, wherever I am living, I visit him every four months to have my teeth cleaned and taken care of. I did this even when I lived in France. He is brilliant at everything he does, including fishing. He's a world class fisherman, fresh water and salt. He's also the one who introduced me to surf fishing.

On Skype, Dan told me the Minnesota woman's seal experience was very cool, especially because the seal got away unharmed. He had heard of seals "mouthing" bait fish like that and tracking them right up to boats, but it was a very rare event. Then he told me something like that happened to him about fifteen years ago.

There are a lot of seals hanging out in the Pacific off the Oregon coast where the mighty Willamette River flows into the sea. The area is rich in sea life and a great food source for countless species. Dan said that's where he hooked a seal once, which was never his intention. Unfortunately for the seal, it was indeed hooked, which wasn't the case for Mrs. Minnesota. I cringed when I heard that part of his story. Poor seal, to say the least. Dan went on to tell me that the seal tried to steal his bait fish just as Dan was lifting it out of the water for his next cast. He saw the seal surface and grab the bait fish, hook, line, and sinker as it broke the surface ten feet away from him. The hooked seal took off and Dan's line zinged out. He said the force was so powerful and sudden that he was very lucky he was able to hold onto his rod, in which case he was also lucky he didn't get yanked overboard. This situation was not good. This, he said, had never happened to him. He said having hooked a seal lion was, and I quote, "like having a freight train on the end of the line." The only thing he could do was cut the line and hope the seal survived. It was horrible, we agreed. His story made me happy that Mrs. Minnesota's seal got off lucky, even if it didn't get the whole *enchilada*.

The doggie in the window - Wednesday, February 22

My note was ignored. The doggie in the window is still barking at will. No surprise there. I would just have to shut out the barking with pure mental effort before it drove me mental. It might be easier than I think because my conscience is clear.

No Ocho this week - Wednesday, February 22

A week has passed without seeing Ocho. I missed him enough to stretch my neck out and press my face against the wall to get a decent look behind the refrigerator, one of his hideouts. Didn't see him. Maybe I bored him. Or I didn't give him enough attention. Now I miss him. I know, I know, sometimes you take someone in your life for granted, and don't appreciate them enough until they're gone. Ocho triggers in me deep thoughts. We're a lot alike, but different too of course. I blink, he doesn't. There are many facets to him that I admire, including being able to walk up walls and stick to ceilings. I called out his name a few times today. Nothing. No response. No head peering out from behind the TV cabinet either. *Nada.*

Making friends with the marina police - Wednesday, February 22

Even though the police warned me four weeks ago not to ride my bike on the marina sidewalk, that admonition did not preclude me from pushing the cruiser up and down the sidewalk. That's how I translated their words of warning. I've been doing that almost every day. It is exercise, which is good, but more importantly it allows me to speak some Spanish with the vendors and restaurant hawks that have become familiar faces to me. They all know me and often call out to me by name. I know some names too. They like my cruiser. They are forever telling me it is a nice bike, in English. I thank them of course, in Spanish, and the we go back and forth with some English and Spanish. Good for them and good for me. These walks also give me a chance to say hello to all the police and security guards who stand at various and carefully spaced places along the marina, usually behind an advertising poster or in some spot of shade to keep them out of the burning sunshine. They know me too. I am being devious with them because it is my plan to attempt a ride on the marina again in the very near future. I am thinking that if they know me and respect my desire to speak Spanish they might cut me some slack and look the other way when I mount the cruiser and pedal through the marina. Soon, I say to myself, soon.

Mario at poolside - Wednesday, February 22

With a delightful day behind me, mostly spent engaged in Spanish at CC and then Esteban's. My afternoon of venturing out and about town came to a close when I rode up to the metal security door in my building complex, but the day wasn't over. Mario, my neighbor, was at the gate at the same time. We entered together and chatted a bit, as always, until I had to veer off to my condo. His was in the next building. But this time, before we broke it off, Mario asked me to wait for him. He said he has something for me, *un regalo*, which happened to be a word I learned earlier in the week. It means gift. I was happy to wait. The pool area is always beautiful and a perfectly suitable place to pause and enjoy the end of a warm sunny day in a quiet moment of being lost in one's thoughts. Mario returned in a matter of minutes. He presented me with a key chain which featured a small rubbery tricolor square which had the Mexican flag on one side and some words imprinted on the other. The words were *Mexico, no hay dos,* which idiomatically means, as Mario explained: Mexico, there's no place like it. It was a gift out of the blue. The best kind? I say yes. I put my keys on it right away, right in front of him. He liked that. I thanked him and really appreciated the gesture. What a nice thing to do. It made me feel good and for the umpteenth time it reminded me how nice the people of Mexico are.

I passed on CC again - Wednesday, February 22

I didn't go to CC today, third day in a row. Hard to explain. I felt kinda bad about that, and opted instead for four tacos at Gardenias in mid-day with a study session built into the visit. I'm still a bit on wobbly legs from Jorge's candor at CC four days ago, though I shouldn't be. I have been uptight at CC lately and I don't know why. I didn't feel like going there yesterday or today just to sit there and feel uptight. What is that all about? I'm putting too much pressure on myself while being surrounded by a handful of terrific guys who I sincerely feel a friendship with. Their support is undeniable.

It's some kind of funny feeling I'm getting at CC this week. The nervousness of speaking in Spanish there is exactly the same uncomfortable, internal feeling I had when I used to be on-camera as an actor in TV commercials. That was a long time ago, thirty years to be exact. I had forgotten that amped up self-conscious feeling of the self-inflicted pressure of having to remember lines. Could that be what's happening to me at CC? Maybe that's my problem. I am trying to memorize phrases and sentences for CC, but that's not the right way to do it. I should just go there happy with what I already know and see what I can do with it. As Ray and Jorge both said, no one is judging me just as I don't judge them with their broken English. In fact, they are all rooting for me. I wonder how I'll feel about this revelation tomorrow. I'll sleep on it.

Ocho is back - Wednesday, February 22

Ocho disappeared for a while. Then he reappeared. I saw him when I was getting ready for bed. He was on the kitchen wall three feet above the stove top. It's one of the places he likes to hang. It's the first place I look to when I enter the room. I am expecting to see him. Maybe it's a good vantage point to surveil the counter for some crumbs. I'm not sure what he likes to eat. Maybe not crumbs. Probably bugs. Ants, I bet. I have a few ants, tiny ants, around the sink. So tiny that they would be *aperitivos*, at best, but he would have to eat a hundred to get any volume. I wonder what he eats for his main course? Stray peas and kernels of corn? Plenty of them on the counter and the floor. That's probably what he dines on. Maybe he's a vegetarian. Upon seeing him, I realized that I missed his presence. Already I know I'll miss Ocho after I leave Cabo. Sounds funny, I know, but he is an animal and I love animals. Even lizards. He is my roommate and he has become my lizard friend. This is good. This is better than having friends who are snakes.

CHAPTER EIGHT

Week 8

<u>Cabo Wabo - Thursday, February 23</u>

I had to investigate Cabo Wabo, perhaps the most famous bar in Cabo, only because of its reputation as the most famous bar in Cabo. It is just one of many popular Cabo bars owned by L.A. personality Sammy Hagar. It is fairly famous for its Mexican food, DJ and live bands, every kind of *cerveza* and tequila, and many different interior rooms along with an open rooftop for partying. Also for its craziness. I kept putting a visit off because the place was so touristy and probably not a great place to practice Spanish. Rather than a night time visit, one afternoon I rode the cruiser right up to a tree in front of Cabo Wabo thinking it was a good place to lock her up. Where have I heard those words before? Anyway, I was off to a bad start. Within two seconds, a security guard materialized and said no to parking the cruiser on the tree. I pushed back with a shrug like there's nowhere else. My pointing helped too. I indicated that there were no good places for the cruiser. I repeated *donde, donde, donde*, which is the word for where. I said I was a customer. That's the argument that got his attention. He contacted some Cabo Wabo manager on his walky-talky thing to get permission for me to use the tree. No one wants to turn away a paying customer. No surprise, I got a green light. I smiled, of course, then locked the cruiser to the tree and went through the front door.

When I crossed the Cabo Wabo threshold, I entered the sacred darkness. The front room was a relatively small space with some live music underway. Once my eyes adjusted, the darkness went from dark to dim and revealed a very thin crowd. It was three o'clock in the afternoon, a quiet time in any Cabo bar, but live music played in this one. I walked right through the main room, unimpressed. Maybe there was something else going on in the back rooms. Seconds later, I could see that the rest of the place was dead empty. Lights out in the back, except for a television suspended overhead that no one was watching. That interested me. I took a seat in a booth, where I knew I would be unmolested by servers, to watch that TV, which was airing a college basketball game interesting enough to learn if it was interesting enough to stay seated. Three minutes later, I was kicked out of my backroom booth which, granted, was roped off but with a TV that was on, I took it as an invitation to make myself comfortable.

For first impressions, it wasn't going well for Cabo Wabo. Or me. First cruiser parking, then the hassle for sitting in a booth in a roped off section. I returned to the music in the main room, took a seat at a small table up front and ordered a margarita from the server, a young Latino male with slicked back hair. A young Antonio Banderas. He said no and told me I'd have to sit at the bar. The table, he explained, was reserved for two or more people. He was emphatic about me taking a seat at the bar. All I could see was a crappy bar stool behind a pillar at the bar. At that point, I gestured I was leaving. I said one word and walked out. *Adios!* That's the word you use to say goodbye in the context of never coming back. It was the right word.

I told some of my friends about my experience at Cabo Wabo. My afternoon experience didn't surprise them. My mistake in assessing Cabo Wabo was made by visiting it in the day. I was told the place comes alive at night, with all kinds of craziness, which is how it became so famous. I get it. Wrong time of day to be investigating. Maybe I'll investigate it some evening in the next week or two. Or three. Some night when I can stay up later than nine o'clock. Or maybe not. Sometimes I can be a real geezer.

<u>The cause of my flat tires - Thursday, February 23</u>

For the past week, I have assumed that the source of the thorns pulled from my bike tires was somewhere on the frontage road between Coromuel and Walmart, which is why I decided not to ride my bike to Walmart and, instead, walk there. I would continue to ride all over Cabo, just as I have been doing for the past seven weeks, but not on that frontage road. If I did not get anymore thorny flats in the week, then I would conclude that I was right with my hypothesis that my tires were picking up the thorns somewhere on the frontage road. The test would start today with my first walk to Walmart since I arrived.

Late in the morning was the time I picked for this first walk to Walmart, after rush hour. I stepped out of my condo and passed the pool on my left. Before I stepped up into the foyer to leave my building I stopped. I could feel the heat already and I had only travelled a hundred feet. A hot day was underway and it would be getting hotter before it got cooler. I couldn't do it. I just couldn't bring myself to walk to Walmart and back in the heat. I went back into my condo to retrieve the cruiser. Screw walking. I decided I could still test my hypothesis if I rode my bike in the middle of the frontage road, instead of the dusty, probably thorn-infested shoulder. I'd scan the shoulder, not the middle of the road, for culprit candidates. I didn't think there would be any thorns collecting on the road because the traffic would blow them off to the shoulders. It was a significant modification of my test, and even more dangerous than riding on the shoulder. Down the middle of a busy frontage road did not sound like a smart alternative methodology. I had to try it and I was willing to do it only when I could see absolutely no car on the road that could threaten me, an impossibility during morning and afternoon rush hours. Mid-day was pretty busy too. That left me with mid-morning and late night. Late night was quickly eliminated as a possibility for obvious reasons. The mid-morning window would be it for me. My new plan!

<u>Cindy and Bill - Friday, February 24</u>

I met Cindy and Bill today, mid-morning, poolside. A long-distance dating couple, in their late forties, on their fifth trip together. Bill is a handsome, fit guy with a boyish face and an infectious laugh. Cindy is a curvaceous blonde who clearly has a sense of humor and carries a lot of confidence in what she says and does. From the start, they struck me as a good match, like a couple who has observable chemistry. They were sunning side by side on lounge chairs across the pool from my doorway. I wanted a little sun, too, so I grabbed a chair fairly close to them. That's where the sun was, everything else in the courtyard was in the shadows of the buildings.

I liked Cindy and Bill right away. It was an easy first conversation. We swapped basics, laughed a lot, and knew we'd be friends right away. I learned that they met on the dating website *Our Time* two years ago. Later, when the topic switched to dating and my single state, a rather pathetic state, Bill recommended zoosk.com to me. He said it was a better option to get for men into and beyond their fifties. The latter is me, the beyond. We agreed I shouldn't go over fifty-five in seeking desirable women. I was pleasantly agreeable about that but I didn't really buy into it. A difference of ten years sounded like a stretch to me. I'm sixty-five. Shut up, please don't tell me that my skin looks great. From experience, women under fifty-five is an age range where women stop getting my jokes and can't name the Beatles.

We three decided that alcoholic beverages at poolside was a good idea. I offered to fix something out of my kitchen. I prepared a concoction for us consisting of Kahlua, vodka, and pineapple juice. Tasty and lethal, wicked good. We each downed two of them faster than anyone could jump in and jump out of the pool. Here for a four-day getaway, I learned that Cindy and Bill leave the day after tomorrow. They'd already been around town a lot, been to a lot of places I hadn't even heard about. Like The Roadhouse, which they described as a cool place but snooty with mostly locals. They had also been to the rooftop at Baja Brewing company for a view of the gulf as far as the eye can see. They liked that a lot. And, they also tried a beach resort called Blue Marlin Ibiza on the beach just beyond Mango. Why Ibiza is in the name I don't know. It should be Blue Marlin Cabo, but it wasn't. Bill and Cindy raved about the Blue Marlin's pool, huge with a water bar with underwater seats so people could pee without giving up their seat. You gotta love that. Actually, I hate that. Coincidentally, I knew the place from a scouting trip the day before.

Our conversation came full circle and got around to dating. Since I had nothing of recent interest to talk about in that category, we discussed dating in general and mostly its pitfalls, of which there are many. Cindy and Bill know they have a good thing going. They have been dating for almost two years. I got a different length of time from each but I didn't say anything. I guess it's serious, given that amount of time, but both are still active on the dating sites, still. Keeps each other from taking the relationship for granted, I guess. Or something like that. We split after a couple of hours and who's counting drinks. We agreed to meet up in the late afternoon for a walking adventure on Medano Beach. I think they had something more in mind, like a drinking adventure.

The first night out with Cindy and Bill - Friday, February 24

I was ready for a night out. It began at my place, in my condo, door open, Bose wifi speaker off my MacAir blasting out Jimmy Buffet singing his pencil thin mustache singalong song with his parrot head fans in full participation in a live concert. I like to sing along, too. The lyrics right then went something like this:

> *Then it's flat top, dirty bob, coppin' a feel*
> *Grubbin' on the livin' room floor (so sore)*
> *Yeah, they send you off to college, try to gain a little knowledge,*
> *But all you want to do is* (full audience participation) *fuck on the floor*

While I was waiting for Cindy and Bill, I recalled my solo visit to the Blue Marlin resort the day before. I liked the idea that we were headed there for happy hour for openers. It's a cool place, worth return trips. Yesterday, a late afternoon walk on Medano Beach got me into the spirit of Cabo craziness. I invested in a Tecate beer for beach walking when I cut through The Office bar. With libation in hand to mouth, I stopped behind Mango to ogle scantily clad, heavily drunk college girls participating in Mango daily game of musical chairs. After two minutes of feeling really old viewing that craziness, I then walked down the beach for an hour or two to explore the Blue Marlin Ibiza Los Cabos Beach Resort. It was up the beach about two hundred yards and then up the wooden stairs about twenty steps to get to the bar there, just beyond the threshold. I was ready for another Tecate when I reached the top of the stairs. With my foot pushing off the top of the wooden stairs I could see a large outdoor bar on my left and the resort's colossal swimming pool in front of me, surrounded by two hundred lounge chairs. The view from the top of the stairs presented a fantastically impressive layout. I lounged in one of the poolside chairs, worked a couple of Pacifico, and totally went veg.

Unbeknownst to me at the time, four hours earlier in this same day, Cindy and Bill were in the pool hanging out under the hot sun at the Blue Marlin pool's submerged bar stools and loving every minute. Tonight, we three revisited the Blue Marlin after cutting through The Office bar where we stayed long enough to pick up a Tecate. I experienced a little déjà vu on that one. We three, comrades in arms, then walked out onto the beach for the walk to the Blue Marlin for the next round.

Cindy and Bill were on vacation, so drinking was on their menu. I was okay with that. I went with their menu. It was different from my usual routine so I found it as refreshing as a cold beer, and enjoyed their company as well, of course. We wandered around the Blue Marlin pool, a whole lap, which at a leisurely pace took about twenty minutes. It was that big and we were that slow. Then, we took over some poolside lounge chairs, chatted, and went through two rounds of Tecates before going down the wooden stairs back onto the beach as setting sun spread its golden light over Cabo.

Picking a restaurant for dinner was easy. We picked the first one we ran across after turning right at the base of Blue Marlin's beach stairs. The name of the restaurant was Sand Bar, a casual looking place with a bar on the sand. Perfect name. Sand Bar. Of course, the real meaning of the name wasn't lost on us. A sand bar is a low ridge of submerged or partially exposed sand built up in the water along a shore or beach by the action of waves or currents. This is foreshadowing. It's a nice name however you see it. The tabled area on the beach already had an open fire going in a giant wok-like fire pit surrounded orchestrally by twenty empty tables. We beat the crowd, apparently, or perhaps the restaurant's reputation wasn't very good and the crowd wasn't coming. Either way, fine by us, no big deal. We seated ourselves at one of those universal white plastic tables, the only one that was between the fire and the surf. It was close enough to the fire to feel some heat, which was a good thing because the temperature had been slowly dropping for the last hour. It would continue to drop a bit into the night. Our table was close enough to the water's edge to give us the full force of the beach's beauty. Also, because it was surfside, it was a table that gave us a great view down the beach, well past Mango and The Office, and right into the lit-up outline of the Cabo marina's silhouetted harbor entrance as the town morphed into its nocturnal identity.

The edge of our hunger was quickly removed with chips, guacamole, and salsa, which required another round of Tecates. Then the main meal arrived and we three jumped on a shared platter of eight fish tacos. Satiating ourselves, quenching our thirst, and enjoying a fantastic view over a lively conversation made it easy to ignore the water from the rising tide that was suddenly lapping over our toes. How perfect. When we left the Sand Bar, the harbor was fully lit up and so were we, all in the name of fun and new friends. Shoreline lights over town became brighter with the now faded natural light causing a golden halo hovering over countless bars and a shimmer coming from the reflections off a million margarita glasses. That was our first night on the town, but it wasn't the end of fun as a threesome. We strolled home, happy, sappy, and ready for a good night of sleep. We agreed to meet before noon tomorrow for another adventure and our second evening together.

<u>A trip to The Arch next day - Saturday, February 25</u>

Yesterday was so much fun with my new friends Bill and Cindy. I can't imagine three people hitting it off better than the three of us. Cindy and Bill are a rock solid fun couple. It was fun getting to know them better. Bill lives in Eugene. He is a successful regional sales manager for a landscape company. Cindy's a retired American Airlines flight attendant from Dallas. She has free flights for herself and her companion, which is a fantastic deal for their mutual vacation interests. Lucky Bill. They've had a long-distance relationship for a couple of years. They have so much fun flying off to different adventure every two or three months that it's hard for either one of them to think about not being together, so distance doesn't get in the way. I guess that's how it is. I had my eye out for them since I got up; we agreed to meet in the morning, skewing to the late morning hours. By mid-morning, I was saying to myself, let's get this party started!

When we finally bumped into each other around eleven in the morning of the second day of knowing each other, that was several hours after my trip to Walmart via the middle of the frontage road, both ways. I was still alive having survived the chute for the umpteenth time. They were sitting poolside, possibly waiting for me to show up. I showed up in the agreed upon window of time, confronted with another beautiful sunny day of perfect t-shirt weather. It was quickly agreed that we should go to The Arch at noon, in an hour. We could do that via a water taxi off Medano Beach behind Mango. I happily said game on.

Our action plan gave us an hour to get ready. I prepped by setting up myself with as few things as possible to lug with me. There would be no lugging. Zero. I hate lugging. I stuffed the one key I need into a special key pocket on the inside of my swim suit waist band. I took out one-hundred dollars' worth of pesos, which was way more than I thought I would need, and folded the money into a plastic, air tight baggie which, with the air pressed out of it, fit nicely into my suit's back pocket, a pocket with a Velcro flap. These are the kinds of features you get when you cough up some dough for a Ralph Lauren bathing suit. I confess, I didn't pay top dollar, never do. It is florescent lime green, which is probably why it was on sale at Macy's for twenty-five bucks, a mark down from eighty-five. Oh, I grabbed a towel too and stuffed it into Cindi's bag, only because she offered to carry it. I contributed a water proofed lined beach bag, purchased at Walmart that morning, which was perfect for ice and twelve cans of Tecate. Bill carried that load for starters, but I knew we'd be passing it back and forth for the one mile walk to Medano Beach.

When we got to the Medano beach enclave of bars and shoppy-shops we rested on the bench by the entrance to Mango to pop a couple of Tecates. You know, lighten our load. Cindy took some iPhone pics while Bill and I quenched our thirst with our first beers of the day, for me anyway, not for Bill. Sometime in the mile-long hike Bill had lightened the load by two beers. Cindy disappeared and re-appeared after five minutes with a Cuba Libre in hand along with the news that it was only a buck at the bar. That price rang my frugal bell so I chugged my Tecate and walked back to the bar with Cindy to order one for myself and close out her tab. She didn't have any money with her, which was fine because I had plenty. At the bar, when I was served my drink we discovered that each Cuba Libra was five bucks, not one buck. *No problemo*, I was happy to pay, still a steal, even with a memorable tip for Macky, the English-speaking mix master behind the bar. I put the change in bills back into my baggie and Velcroed it into the back pocket of my bathing suit. In the forty seconds it took to walk back to the front entrance, I had finished my Cuba Libra. Hey, c'mon, it was really good. I rationalized the chug by telling myself that I would need the caffeine to stay perky for the Arch trip. I also felt I had to catch up with Bill. Don't know why, must be some inexplicable male thing. Maybe some kind of subliminal competition underway? I was a little worn from the night before. Bill popped another Tecate, handed it to me, and popped one for himself as well. He and I rose, collected Cindy, and we three cut through Mango while taking turns posing for a few pics inside the restaurant en route to the water's edge where the taxis were beached for Arch trips.

I usually don't drink much. Suffice to say, I was feeling no pain by the time I was ankle deep in the water, holding onto the bobbing bow of glass-bottomed water taxi, while Bill negotiated a fair price for a round trip. He tried. We paid the going rate, what everyone paid. Fair enough. The taxi drivers don't budge on the rate, so despite Bill's persistence and his fake walk-away from the deal, the driver got his rate. Ten bucks a person roundtrip. Not a bad deal. In the context of what things cost in the States, it was a steal of a deal.

We had the taxi to ourselves and *Capitan* Juan started giving us the tourist spiel right away. He was a good kid, a smile full of bright white teeth, full of energy, engaging, maybe eighteen years old with a decent grasp of tourist English, enough to explain where we were going. A glass bottom is supposed to be a big sell, I think, but all it really is are two small narrow windowed openings in the bottom of the boat. I was thinking the glass windows were too narrow for me to rave about them. We three ignored them. Nothing could be seen through them. Besides, why look down when there was so much to see in front of us. We wanted to see the famous Arch, of course, like every good tourist. After all, it is the defining landmark of Cabo San Lucas.

Cindy got plenty of touristy photos on the way and Juan even took a couple of the three of us without capsizing the boat or going off course. I was a bit surprised how magnificent the rock formations on the approaching coast were, but why not, it was nature's power at work. Nothing holds steadfast against that kind of wave power we faced along the rocky shoreline, so Juan's skills at the wheel were appreciated. Before our drop off at Lover's Beach, Juan took us as close as a boat can get to the Arch for a tourist shot, as close as anyone could get. None of the boats went under the Arch and into its frothy epicenter, maybe because it ruins the purity of other tourists' photos. Or maybe it looked like a sure way to sink your boat. Keeping a bit of distance was a good thing. It was rough water because it was where the Gulf water collided with the Pacific water which made that archway simply too dangerous to navigate under. I forgot to ask Juan the reason no one goes under the arch, but I'm guessing my call on danger is the reason. Besides visiting El Arco, the Spanish name for The Arch, we also arranged for Juan to drop us off for an hour at Lover's Beach. He was happy to oblige and assured us that he would return to pick us up, even though he already got our money.

For the drop-off, Juan masterfully took us close in to a very specific and small, one-boat-at-a-time drop-off point on a tiny landing zone. He demonstrated great capability at the helm as he maneuvered his fifteen-foot craft like a pro around some very rocky formations in some pretty wavy water. Two Mexicans on the beach were working as boat greeters. As Juan approached the shore, they stepped into the surf and grabbed the bow in the iffy water long enough for we three *americanos* to jump into the roiling surf leading up to the beach. We jumped off the bow of the low-slung taxi into a foot of water. Well, Cindy and I did that. Since Bill had his iPhone in the pocket of his shorts, fate's fickle finger directed him to jump into four feet of water off the side of the boat. The depth caught him by surprise. And shocked his phone. He took the battery out right away and prayed it would work when he tried it after it was dry. I hope it survived.

From the shoreline of Lover's it took us five minutes to walk to the Pacific side, which was Divorce Beach. We went from Lover's to Divorce in less than five minutes. Who'd a thunk? It was a blue-sky-drop-dead gorgeous walk of a hundred yards on soft white sand through a narrow and rocky canyon to get to the Pacific from the Sea of Cortez. We accomplished the passage in two minutes and threw our towels down on the isthmus of sand between the two beaches. We propped ourselves against a rock wall facing west to watch the raging Pacific on our left and the Sea of Cortez on our right. It was a perfect setting for us to toss down a couple of more beers. You can't imagine how great those cold Tecates tasted while we bathed in the warmth of the Cabo sun in a transcendent state. Nirvana. Perfection for *tres amigos americanos.* For the remainder of our time there, we three laughed, marveled together, and talked about stuff as if we had known each other for a lifetime. I even told Cindy and Bob my Eiffel Tower story, a story which only the closest of friends have gotten out of me over the years. It's one for the ages, but not one for this book.

Our time had been pre-set with Juan, so we were committed to getting back to the drop off point on Lover's Beach. Sure enough, Juan was waiting for us just off shore in a holding pattern, about fifty yards off the edge of Lover's beach. We hailed him, mindful that we ran a bit over the hour, like a half hour over but that would translate into a nice tip, which Bill paid just before we returned to the white, tourist-infested sands of Medano beach. I couldn't have paid Juan if I wanted to. Before we landed on Lover's Beach, I had given Cindy my plastic baggie, the one with my money because she wanted to protect her cell phone, so I didn't bother with the tip part. Bill and I work harmoniously in paying for things. He covered the tip. Time for another cold beer. None of us were in the bag, so to speak, but no beer was in the bag either because it held only empty cans.

We loved every minute of that archy-beachy adventure. It was time to move on for the next adventure, location yet undecided. We left Medano the way we came, through Mango. This time we walked uphill with a much lighter load. No more Tecates. This was a problem that needed a solution. The empty aluminum cans got tossed into a garbage can outside Mango before we three charged up the hill. More accurately, we were weaving up the hill, slowly at that, but in no hurry. To where?

The Baja Brewery - Saturday, February 25

We made it to the top of the hill above Mango after our water taxi adventure to El Arco. It wasn't a physical challenge because it's only a gum drop hill, but it was hard to get to the crest because we kept stopping every few steps to contain our laughter. At that point, everything was funny. The absence of stress facilitated that state of mind. So did the presence of a good buzz. Tecate is fantastically refreshing on a hot, sunny day in Cabo. Maybe every beer is. A pow-wow at the top of the hill concluded with the decision to go to a terrific roof top bar, seven stories up, overlooking the Gulf and all of Cabo. It was right around the corner, which influenced our choice. The place was the Baja Brewery's rooftop bar, where Cindy and Bill were yesterday. The entrance started with some obscure doorway and then a cut through a tiny courtyard to an elevator bank in an adjacent hallway. The elevator took us five stories up and we used a stairwell for getting up to the sixth floor. Eureka! The view made the maze worthwhile.

We three settled into three cushy seats on a banquette close to a railing in the open seating area of the bar. After thirty seconds of some very important decision making, I got up and went to the bar and ordered two Cuba Libres and, for Bill, a glass of one of Baja Brewery's specialty beers. No stopping us now!

Sometime into the first hour on the rooftop, Cindy spied an old acquaintance from her airline days who was dancing by herself on the dance floor, moving and grooving to the rooftop's live music coming from a nifty jazz trio. Cindy pointed her out to us. Bill and I pretended we were seeing her for the first time, as if we didn't notice her. As if the whole place hadn't noticed. Bill and I already knew her name, it was Ms. Boobalicious. C'mon, cut Bill and me some slack. Any guy would have tagged her with that objectifying name or something close to it. Cindy couldn't remember her last name but said her first name was Theresa, in which case she quickly became Theresa Boobalicious. Easy to say she was a hot and sexy woman in her early or mid-forties. And she knew it and played it out there for everyone. That kind. She was grooving and swaying and twirling to the beat on her four-inch heeled sandals, strap purse in one hand, legs wrapped in tight black skinny jeans and a body hugging light blue, furry sweater that justified the surname she was just given. The sweater was appropriate at that altitude on a day that was cooling off, but maybe not for that establishment. This woman was succeeding as an attention seeker for the entire place, not just the men. I tried to take my eyes off this alluring siren, of course, but failed. Instinct is undeniable. After a few minutes alone with her, my ship would be floundering on the rocks. Of course, that would never happen, I'm just sayin'. A cool onshore breeze kicked in with the late afternoon light. The sweet breeze brought me back to my senses. The day was moving along nicely.

Cindy wanted me to meet her friend, Theresa. This would be very possible according to Bill, who quickly described Cindy to me as socially fearless and now I know why. Cindy stood up and smiled at us then snaked her way through a dozen tables to get to the dance floor where she started dancing in sync with Theresa Boobalicious, a name Bill and I freely used, but only in Cindy's absence. The two girls looked cute on the dance floor. I was ready for Cuba Libre number two, though actually it was number three if you count the one I gulped down at Mango. Bill was fine with his beer so I made another trip to the bar for my purposes only, which in part was to get a better view of the dance floor. I sat on a barstool just off the edge of the dance floor waiting for my drink and unavoidably staring at Theresa Boobalicious. Staring like everyone else there, so don't give me a hard time. Cindy leaned into Ms. B and said something and then pointed to me. I smiled my best Elmer Fudd smile as Ms. B started walking toward me. I prayed to the vacation gods that she wasn't going to ask me to dance. I was inebriated but not liberated enough to dance. I needed another Cuba Libra to liberate myself but there was not enough time for that. She walked right up to me and introduced herself. First name only, which was fine for starters, because I already knew her last name.

Ms. B and I exchanged a few words. With the introduction, I stood up like the gentleman I am but quickly fell back into my seat, not wanting to be whisked onto the dance floor. She didn't ask me to dance. Instead, she asked me to watch her purse for her as she set it down on the bar inches from me. Of course, I said sure, thinking it was the promise to return to me for an excellent conversation in which I would charm her pants off. Of course, I could never be charming enough to get those skin-tight jeans off of her. No one could. I'd have to hang her by ankles and shake her by her cuffs but even that couldn't possibly do the trick. I let the image go. Ms. B sashayed back to the dance floor at which time, Cindy's bold move became infectious and now ten women, but no men, were dancing to the music. It was just about the cutest thing I had ever seen. It was a good show for everyone hanging out on the Baja Brewery rooftop.

Theresa continued to dance, well into the back half of an hour with no sign of letting up. Not a glance my way, by the way, She continued to be the focal point for just about every male on the roof. I tired of being keeper of her purse. Actually, I was feeling a bit used. Forty-five minutes had passed, which is about thirty-five minutes too many. This was going nowhere and I am sure Bill was missing me. Even Cindy had left the dance floor. I picked up the purse, walked a little light headed onto the dance floor, handed it to Ms. B, smiled, pointed my thumb to the door where I came in and walked away. Nothing said to me, but one word, thanks. Which for me, was enough. I had no interest in this show. I was not about to buy a ticket. A minute later, I happily plunked myself back into my seat at our banquette, fully into a comfort zone with Cindy and Bill and commenced where we left off, meaning mindless chatter that was nothing but lots of fun.

While I was guarding Ms. B's purse with my life, unbeknownst to me, Bill had entered into a feisty conversation with a thirty-year-old timeshare salesman who recently moved to Cabo from the States. With my return to the banquette, I found myself in the thick of their conversation. The guy was a bit of a greaser, right out of Saturday Night Fever, maybe a real Vinnie. I learned his real name was Cortez. He repeated over and over saying it was like the Sea of Cortez. Good linkage, but so what. I wanted to call him Sea for short. Or Sea of. Why was this guy selling so hard on the rooftop of a very cool bar? After hours, too.

Desperate maybe. Certainly cheesy. I listened in and picked up on some static and vibes going south. Bill knows a lot about timeshares. More than most people, certainly more than Vinnie, oops, I mean Cortez. But Cortez wasn't listening, like all bad salesmen. Bill shot him down so many times that I was becoming afraid that I'd become collateral damage. It was time for us to leave. Ms. B was nowhere in sight because I didn't even bother to look for her. We three needed some food and named the marina as our next neighborhood. That's pretty much the last of what I remember from that night other than over-eating at some no name tiki bar that I'd never been to somewhere in the marina.

Who you speak to makes a big difference - Sunday, February 26

I go through so many emotional ups and downs with my attempts at learning Spanish. Sometimes I feel that I am making progress. At times like this, certain elements are working for me, not the least of which is a sunny disposition in the sense of waking up every morning with the belief that I can do this. The topic in every conversation makes a big difference too. I can now discuss family and most personal interests at a pseudo conversational level, however choppy. Certainly not politics which is what a lot of Mexicans wanted to discuss. They wanted to tell me what they thought of our new president. In addition, I have learned some of the basic transitional words, like therefore, however, and in addition to, along with the words for coming and going. The transitional words are helpful for moving a conversation along and, I think, they give me the sense that I am actually speaking in conversational sentences. Also, I can now comfortably walk into any room with a simple greeting as well as I can leave a room.

My favorite expression for both coming and going is, *Que bueno verte otra vez*, which means, "It's good to see you again." Of course, that line is for people I've already met. Strangers get only the basic every day greeting of *buenos dias, buenas tardes,* or *buenas noches* depending on the time of day. Those three greetings are good for good morning, good afternoon and good night. Close friends get *Como estas?* which is the familiar form of how are you. When I've leaving someplace, I'm always tempted to say *Adios*, regardless of whom I am talking to, but as I learned early on, it's a word that is supposed to be used only for final goodbye. Like maybe forever. I need to say something else if I want to imply that I will see that person again. Of course, I don't always know if I will see someone again.

This sounds all so tricky. It isn't. I'm just making it sound tricky, which is why I sometimes stumble with my efforts to learn Spanish. I probably stumble too much. That's what I think. It doesn't have to be that way. All in all, I think Spanish is relatively easy to learn, easier than French and Italian and way easier than English. And, of course, every language becomes more of a challenge for the beginner with a move into a technical realm. That realm, which requires more than everyday words, leaves me speechless, literally. I'm not going there, ever. I just want to be able to get to the conversational level for travel purposes. I am getting closer and closer to that every day.

Spanish with Mexicans who speak some English as a consequence of the experience they have from interacting with tourists is the easiest way to learn Spanish. This is true not only because they speak some English but, more importantly, they have an ear that can make sense of a tourist's butchered attempts at Spanish. Also, the topic is very basic. They also have had tons of practice understanding someone's question or statement just from being able to pick up on a couple of the words within the sentence. Another reason the Spanish is more likely to flow in this case is that the Mexican knows that it is helpful at times to say something a different way or put the thought into different words if the first attempt doesn't work. That kind of flexibility can make a big difference; it is a time when knowledge of synonyms can be really helpful. Oh, one more reason that Spanish with Mexicans who interact with Americans is easier is because the Spanish speakers know automatically that they have to speak slowly when talking to gringos.

Speaking Spanish with Mexicans who have little or no interaction with Americans is usually a real challenge for me. And most people, I assume. And, sorry to say, hugely frustrating because it brings my inadequacies to the forefront. Sometimes it is impossible to communicate even the simplest of thoughts beyond a word or two, in which case a huge fall back into a pantomime is my only hope. Of course, just about any simple transaction in a store for the purchase of something like food doesn't require an exchange of more than a word or two for the deal to be done. By the way, *trato hecho* means, done deal! I happen to know that from my book *Spanish for Gringos*, but I haven't used those words. There are a lot of words I know that I haven't used. I guess it's better to learn the necessary ones first, the ones that are used most often. I just am not always sure which ones those are, beyond the most basic words.

Couldn't go cold turkey - Sunday, February 26

Sunday night, on my own once again. I had a lot of fun with Bill and Cindy this weekend. I was sorry that they were leaving Coromuel for their return to Oregon at noon. By late afternoon I was having withdrawal symptoms from them, or was it from alcohol? Both! With the sun tumbling into dusk I went back to the top of the Baja Brewing Company to try to recapture that fun feeling I had with the two of them. I couldn't, of course. And in fact, it was worse, a lot worse than I thought.

When I walked in I went right to the long bar in a reenactment of the day before when I ordered a Cuba Libre, with Coke, not Coke Light. I guess I'm determined not to lose weight. With drink in hand, I walked up to the upper outdoor deck overlooking the archipelago that leads to The Arch. I couldn't see The Arch from the angle, but the rocks were pretty enough. I took the closest table for the view because all of the railing seats in front of me that were all looking out over the water were taken. One sip later I realized I was directly behind the Self-Absorbed Buxom Babe I met yesterday, the one Cindy knew only in passing from her airline work. That's right, Theresa Boobalicious. The one who danced for forty-five minutes while I, stupidly, watched over her purse and cell phone. I had no interest in even saying hi to her. The back of her head was directly in front of me, which is why I didn't recognize her at first, and not confirmed until she turned to talk to her girlfriend. They discussed the bill. Ms. Boobalicious rose from her seat, turned and looked directly at me, or should I say through me, and walked to the bar, bill in hand. Not a blink of acknowledgment. Not an eyebrow. Not a *nada*. So much for watching her phone and purse at the bar while she danced solo on the dance floor. I didn't blink either. When she came back to get her girlfriend and settle the bill between them, the two women turned to walk out, right past me, again within two feet. I was invisible. So was she, to me.

Twenty minutes later I got up and left. Great view but I had enough, especially since I was getting chilled by a sudden, brisk on-shore breeze from the north. The place wasn't the same without Cindy and Bill. I remember Cindy's words from yesterday when I told her I was snubbed by Theresa at the bar. She said, "Don't take it personal." For the second day in a row, I didn't. Next stop? Esquina, for one beer at the bar before cruising home on the cruiser. Darkness was descending, time for me to descend in the elevator. I'd need my front and rear blinkers for the ride to Esquina.

Where have all the big fish gone? - Monday, February 27

I've chatted up fishing here and there with some locals along the marina and with a few tourists too about their luck out there in the wild blue yonder. That's the yonder underwater not the yonder above the water. I consistently hear two things that sync up with each other. One, fishing this year has been pretty poor. Some attribute this to a change in water temperatures. The oceans are warming up, but is the impact on sea life real? Two, there are a lot fewer fish in the sea than ever before. To me, that means our oceans are being fished out, depleted of life. I investigated that very real possibility and I am embarrassed that I used the word "possibility." There is no doubt that there are a lot fewer fish on this planet since we were kids, regardless of our age.

The Sea of Cortes, a.k.a. the Gulf of California has a reputation for being one of the greatest bodies of water for sport fishing, notably world-renown for its concentration of sailfish. Intuitively, I know the size and quantity of sailfish are down. Anyone who has any interest in fishing can easily recall seeing those old black and white photos of some fisherman posing with his marlin catch, a catch which happens to be dead, hanging from its tail from something resembling the gallows. The fish is huge, probably twelve feet stem to stern. Nobody catches those big ones anymore because there aren't any big ones out there. Okay, maybe a few but nothing like the density of big fish that existed thirty, forty, fifty years ago. Nothing like the fish the Ernest Hemingway posed with, the same that gave him the inspiration for his book *The Old Man and the Sea*. These days, the sailfish are mostly five to six feet in length. Not all of the ones in that size range that are caught get lucky with catch and release. They're all doomed, is what I tell people. Which means we are all doomed.

As an aside, I have to add that the big game fish and sea mammals aren't disappearing just because of over-fishing. Another factor is the reduction of breeding grounds that are typically estuaries and other wetlands. This sea, incredibly rich in sea life, once had the Colorado River flowing into it with tons of water non-stop, an action that supported vast areas of the breeding grounds for all kinds of sea life. Now the Colorado River is one of a handful of the world's major rivers that no longer reaches the sea, unless you think a trickle counts as a river flowing into a sea. That loss has meant a loss in shallow breeding beds for fish. Its impact has been devastating.

I did a little research. The demise of sea life in the Sea of Cortez by man's hand began in the 1940's with commercial shrimp fishing. You know the importance of shrimp in the food chain. Big fish like to eat shrimp. Who doesn't? That population was quickly decimated. That's one very big link that was adversely impacted rapidly. The introduction of outboard motors in the 1970's gave the local fisherman, especially those using gill nets, a real boost in the on-going decimation of sea life. From there, the hits keep on coming. Thus, it is easy to believe that decades of commercial fishing adds a lot of credibility to every fisherman in the Sea of Cortez who says fishing just ain't what it used to be. Enough said.

Martina walks in on me - Monday, February 27

Sometimes I hang out in my place with the front door open by necessity. That's about the only way I get fresh air into this place because my windows are covered with garbage bags. Generally speaking, I'm fine with that stagnant smell because, ha, it's probably me. But anyone else, might think my place has been sealed up for two thousand years. When the door is open I am always sitting at the kitchen counter with my back to the door. This way I am not distracted by people who walk past my door. If it is open, it is also a good idea for people to see right away that I am home, so they are not tempted to walk in and explore my possessions. Yesterday afternoon I got an unexpected visitor.

Yesterday, the door was open, my back to it, and in walked Martina, as effervescent as ever. We chat enough in passing outside that we are comfortable around each other. She must feel the same way because she's never just walked into my place before. I stood up from my chair and she was face to face with me before I could take a step. Her usual high energy expenditure was instantly evident. I didn't know why she walked in until she spun around and asked me to zip up the back of her dress. Happy to do a favor, I zipped it up, but not without a comment. I laughed and said to her, "Next time, walk in and ask me to unzip it. I'm much better at that." She thanked me, laughed, and was out the door before I could say anything else. All that was less than a minute. I wondered about that event for a few minutes. I wondered what it meant, if anything. Martina is an attractive woman who moves so quickly I never imagined slowing her down for a little flirting or socializing.

Shortly after I met in my first week, we encountered each other just outside my door when she was on her way out of the building. She said we should have dinner sometime and followed it up with the suggestion that I could have her over for dinner. At the time, it never occurred that she might have some interest in me. I'm not very good about interpreting statements of that nature coming from women. I simply didn't feel a single vibe coming out of it. I laughed off her dinner suggestion claiming I didn't have the pots and pans to do a decent job. I also said my place wasn't much for entertaining. She seemed to be fine with that, said she had to run, and she ran off, as usual. That was six weeks ago. Nothing came of it. No invitations, either way.

Marlin fishing - Monday, February 27

I like fishing, but I like catching better. Most of my friends know I like to fish. I prefer fresh water fishing, especially fishing for trout, but saltwater fishing is fun too, as long as I don't have to get on a boat. Go figure. It's that throw-up thing that keeps me off boats on big open water. I am also perfectly aware that anyone who fishes would find it hard to believe that I spent several months in Cabo and didn't go marlin fishing. In a way, it surprises me too, but like I said, throwing up trumps marlin fishing. But it doesn't have to be that way.

Emboldened by Londa's success on the water while under the influence of Dramamine, I decided to go for it. Not an all-day thing, but I was willing to take a shot at being on the open water for a half day, on a decent sized boat, not a dinghy. I would have to be a little dingy to go out on that water in a dinghy. Dramamine could not save me in that case. I needed a regular charter boat which meant I would be a tagalong on someone else's charter.

I got a seat on a good boat, good enough for me. It is a 1985 thirty-two-foot Blackfin Flybridge, a solid fishing boat. I didn't know the cost when it was new, but twenty years ago you could have gotten it for about one hundred and twenty thousand. Today, I don't have a clue about its cost. This boat was called the Dream

Catcher, a perfect name for a charter fishing boat, in my humble opinion. Clearly it is referencing tourists, not fish. I found it at Gate C3 by the corner of the Puerto Paraiso Mall. This is a boat with an open deck on the back half, where the fishing and throwing up take place.

The deck of the Dream Catcher has an anchored fighting chair centered toward the rear. It's only a fishing chair if you get a big fish on the line. If you don't, then it's just a very expensive, tricked out deck chair. Practicality aside, fighting chairs are often viewed as functional works of art. I can see that. I am a big fan of functionality and art, especially when the two work in combination. A good chair allows anglers to use heavier tackle with heavier drag settings. This means shorter fight times which is better for the fish. I favored the art aspect of the chair. In simple terms, it was a beautiful piece of work. The chair I'd be sitting in looked like the real deal. It was teak, the overwhelmingly most popular choice in hardwoods. Injection molded resin is also a very popular option because it is less expensive to produce and requires less maintenance. It had a foot rest, seatbelt, and it was upholstered with dreams of catching big fish. In the past, I once fished from a boat called Good Luck. I learned that the name had some attitude, like good luck if you catch anything! The name Dream Catcher gave me hope.

The Dream Catcher has a brochure with some pretty hefty claims about its amenities, including: electric head, fresh water tank, thirty-two -oot outriggers, dual ICOM radios, eighty-gallon live bait well, Furuno NavNet II GPS, Furuno fish finders, Sirius Satellite Radio, cruises at twenty-two knots. The price included water, ice, and all fishing tackle. I would have to fork over a hundred and fifty bucks to be the fifth wheel for a foursome of guys from Denver. Our Captain, who also happens to be the owner, is Captain Ramon. He's in his early thirties, I'm guessing. What I am not guessing at is that Ramon was the captain on the boat named Extraction which won first place in the 2013 Los Cabos Billfish Tournament with a 625-pound Blue Marlin. His tournament winnings easily exceeded one million dollars in the last few years. He knows what he's doing when it comes to marlin fishing. I don't. My tournament winnings do not exceed zero dollars.

My turn in the chair came up with maybe twenty minutes left in the charter. I was last. No one caught anything up to that point. That's four guys fishing, not catching. That made for a lot of disappointment. Captain Ramon clearly felt it. I did too. Four down, one to go. Me. I wasn't expecting to break that streak, especially since I believed that the fish population has been on the decline in big water for years, for decades of years. Five minutes after my baitfish went into the water I had a marlin on my line. This made for a lot of excitement for me and, possibly, a lot of jealousy and resentment directed at the fifth wheel.

When the marlin hit, my line went out, making that wonderful zing sound against the reel's drag. Zinnnnnng! Music to a fisherman's ears! One minute later, confirmation that it was a marlin occurred when it jumped out of the water, doing that marlin dance on its tail fins that makes for good film. With that leap, my foursome switched into overdrive and started rooting for me. It wasn't a big one, but it was one. Maybe five feet. It would be released, of course, regardless of the size. It only took about forty-five seconds for my arms to turn to rubber. It showed, which is a good thing, because Ramon stepped in behind my chair and two handed my rod to give me the support I needed. For the next six very long minutes, Ramon provided the muscle I needed as a wuss to bring the marlin to the stern's platform where we could all see it up close. The fish was so damn beautiful, a rainbow of iridescence with a force of color that caused me to gasp. Nothing, I thought, that beautiful should come to an end by my hands. The boys on board would have been disappointed if they were able to read my thoughts. I felt horrible with this catch, especially seeing it up close, especially seeing its boat side eyeball with what could only be a panicked look. It was a look that was fully revealed to me by its highly dilated pupil. I don't know how long I was shouting to one of the crew, the one who suddenly held the fish's four-foot bill in his hand for purchase on the fish to free the hook from the marline's mouth, but the words that kept spewing out of me were "Don't hurt him! Don't hurt him!" Miracle of miracles, it was a clean release. The Denver boys must have thought I was nuts.

I endured a lot of back slapping on the way back to the harbor. My back, of course, was the only back that got slapped. I hated every whack but I had to smile to further add to the mix of feelings I was going through. I have to admit it was exhilarating to have the marlin strike. It was absolutely electric and my primitive brain circuit board lit up with the catch. It truly surprised me. Something else that truly surprised me was how fast my arms wore out in the fight. But the thing that surprised me most was the vibrant colors of the marlin. I will never forget that. And I never want to catch another one again.

The hot office manager in Coromuel - Tuesday, February 28

So what? I'm entitled to an imagination. I think the shapely manager in my condo complex office is really hot. *Muy picante*. She makes me wish I were fluent in Spanish. I can describe her that way, guilt free. What makes me different from others is that I put it into writing. In the middle of the afternoon, a couple of hours after my marlin adventure, I bumped into one of the four women who work the office when I was walking out the building's front security gate. These four women work in an office just inside the gate as administrators of all of Coromuel, five days a week, but just mornings. One of them is *Señorita* Shapely, not just a beauty but a knockout actually. She's the one I bumped into. Which caused a flash back, a sorry assed one from my recent past.

Eleven days ago, I walked into the office seeking help because I locked myself out of my condo. I went to the office right away, thankful that someone was even there. Maybe there was a spare key in the office. Or, if not, someone could call Ale for me to ask her to help me. It turned out to be the latter. The knockout was the only one who spoke some English, so she had to deal with me. Lucky me. I remember that I got flustered talking to her, of course, but I was able to communicate my situation easily enough, in Spanish. She called Ale. Problem solved, though I had to wait two hours. You know the story about this and about my break-in from an earlier chapter.

Anyway, as I was saying, this morning I bumped into *Señorita Knockout* as I was trying to get my bike out of the lobby gate. I noticed from the first time I met her that she didn't have a ring, so my assumption that she's a *señorita* was right on. She looked great, even better than before. Dressed full bore with a short black skirt, a print Hermes blouse with a pattern of golden scrolls and plenty of jewelry. Very well put together. Made me wonder where she was going that afternoon. At that moment, she was going into the office, but she surprised me by stopping, turning around to face me, and saying hi. Okay, she didn't say hi, she said *Hola* like she remembered me from the lock out. I was breathtakingly awesome in stumbling through a few words at a time, a total embarrassment to myself, but she stuck in there. She seemed to be interested in having a conversation. This is what my wishful self said to my doubtful self. We exchanged a few sentences, at the pace of me walking through a mine field, until we were interrupted by a call coming in on her cell. She took the call at the office door. I was hoping she'd hang up in a heartbeat so we could continue our scintillating conversation. She didn't, must have been important. Or maybe she faked the continuation of the call after foolishly engaging in a nowhere conversation with a bumbling, stumbling gringo.

It would have been silly for me to wait more than a few seconds for her to hang up, as if she were really interested in talking to me, but I did, being a guy. I stood alongside my bike, me with it, it with me, caught up in the middle of the press of the swinging security gate for more than a minute before my senses returned to me. I pushed my bike out into the real world, ready to get on with my day. I must be crazy thinking that was an encounter that could lead to another conversation, but that's what I'm telling myself.

Maybe I'll see her again and pick up where we left off, you know, the part that had me groping for a word, any word to say in

Spanish. All this happened while I was rolling my eyes upward in frustration hoping a teleprompter would suddenly appear high up on the wall behind her to feed me all the right words. Bikes are good for working off a little frustration. The ride to Walmart would do me good. My routine would get me through the day nicely. And the next. And the next after that.

Tough place to be a single guy - Tuesday, February 28

I've been here for two months. Not a single date. I haven't even seen a woman who might be available for a date. Don't get me wrong, there are plenty of American women here but they're busy. They are either with the husband or the boyfriend or a handful of their friends for the big 5-0. Or the big 6-0. Or a lesser birthday, but that's way out of my range. No single women in my age group, but maybe some under fifty, which, like I said, is out of my range. In a way, I'm not surprised because I might pick a different place to visit if I were a single woman, something with a little more glam and less focus on fishing. But that's a total guess, so surely, I'm wrong. Still, there are a lot of single men here for the fishing. And maybe for the golf. All those single men doing expensive things might be the kind of man a single woman is looking for. Not to mention the draw of dozens of yacht owners.

Me, dating here? Not really interested. Could get too complicated or too messy. Besides, I'm too busy writing and learning Spanish. Also, my time here in Cabo is limited. I'm gone the first of April, so, to me, that means it's pointless to start up a relationship only to have to break it off. American or Mexican. Breaking up is hard to do.

Zip it up, baby! - Tuesday, February 28

On Tuesday around noon, there was a knock on my door, something that never happens. I think the maid is an exception to that never, but that was only once a week. I just had my khaki shorts on. No shoes, no shirt, my usual nearly naked indoors attire.

I opened the door not caring how I looked. It was Martina, looking dressed for a ladies' luncheon as usual, with some rapid-fire request. She turned her back to me with a perfect pirouette. The zipper in the back needed a lift. Looking at her bare back was suddenly giving me a lift. I unexpectedly turned into a lecherous old man. Her exposed neck was getting my attention, too. A little. Maybe more than a little. I zipped the zipper up the rest of the way, instinctively thinking I was moving it in the wrong direction. With that accomplishment, I teased her again by repeating something I said last time, "Next time you knock I want to pull your zipper down, not up." I laughed a very harmless laugh, or I tried to, not wanting to sound like a rake.

By the way, I think saying those words seems a lot more innocent than seeing them in writing. She laughed too, which was good, and in an instant, she was out of sight of my smiling eyes. Again, I told myself I never know how to interpret stuff like that. Maybe I'll get some more insight into that in the next week, if I get another chance at zipping. Nothing will come of this, but suddenly it is a little fun to think that maybe something will. Instinctively, I checked my own zipper. It was up. If it ever gets stuck, I'll knock on her door. With that insipid fantasy, I got back to my laptop. Probably the best advice I can give myself on Martina is to keep my mouth zipped.

Getting bombed at Cabo Cantina - Tuesday, February 28

I walked into CC at two in the afternoon today, pretty much my usual time. I have been stressing about showing up there since I woke up. I know the guys are trying to help me through my stress. What they don't know, at least not yet, is that CC is the only place I feel this tension. It's been building gradually over the past few visits. I kept thinking it would go away, but it continues to grow. I created it by my own heavy demands on learning Spanish. Last week, I knew Jorge sensed it. He's a sensitive guy, comes with being a great bartender. At one point, out of the blue, he said I need to loosen up. I think he meant I need to get laid. I get it, the best stress buster of all, but spending any time with a date here in Cabo just isn't on my docket. I don't want to get into a relationship and then say *adios* forever a few weeks later. The woman wouldn't like that either, I'm guessing. No, take that back, I am not guessing. I am sure.

At the moment, loosening up means to me that it's time for a margarita, a big one. That's what I ordered, not my usual Pacifico, which was waiting on my table when I sat down. The guys know the drill but this order for a marg was a curve ball. Since I was thinking of it as a remedy, I gulped it down within minutes and sat there with a "Now what?" look on my face. Jorge knew what, he knew exactly what the solution was. Yep, another margarita. This one, he said, was on the house. How could I refuse his kind gesture? I said the only thing I could say, *muchas gracias amigo!* I had skipped breakfast so it went right to my head. The first one and the second one. Numbness in my face already kicked in so I think I slightly slurred my *muchas gracias amigo*. I probably said *moooshish grashus smeego*. I'm pretty much a beer guy so that first bit of tequila hit my head like a heat seeking missile and blew up all resistance to more.

It was nice of Jorge to buy me a second margarita. I never would have guessed that he was giving me doubles with his strongest stuff. That possibility never occurred to me. He did however, unbeknownst to me. Given my inexperience with tequila, I couldn't tell the gun was loaded until after I emptied the glass. That was his idea of loosening me up. In theory, it was a good idea. In practice, my tongue stopped moving. I liked sitting on my barstool doing nothing, so I stayed for a while and smiled like an idiot at everything said to me while understanding nothing. I don't recall much of the next hour, but when I was leaving everyone was saying something about me being very funny and very good with Spanish. I think I might have been lucky getting home safely on the cruiser after Jorge's generosity. I forgot about the stress I felt when I walked in, but I know it was still inside of me, I think. A splash of water, a little brush-a-brush, and a few moments after that I sat on my bed, I didn't worry about it because there was no time left to think. I don't remember my head hitting the pillow.

Where's Ocho? - Wednesday, March 1

Ocho, my reptilian roommate, has been away entirely too much. It's been almost a week since I've seen him. Maybe two weeks if I only dreamed seeing him last week. He's up to something, but what, I don't know. Maybe vacationing next door? That's a long vacation, especially if it's been two weeks. Or sunning in one of the planters around the pool? Right, but I haven't seen him at night lately. Or maybe he's behind the refrigerator just playing hide and seek. That's the most plausible explanation. I should look everywhere for him, play his game. Or, maybe he's become a lounge lizard running around the joint with lady lizards when I'm in dreamland. I must like him, a lot, otherwise I wouldn't notice his absence. Since I've come to think of him as a pet, I can unabashedly say I hope he shows his cute little snouty face again.

In CC the day after - Wednesday, March 1

I returned to CC this afternoon feeling somewhere between a bad hangover and a near death experience. Without question, I've been out of it all day, Zombieland, useless, from Jorge's parade of margaritas the day before. Sadly, it was a parade I don't really recall. Again, I sat at the bar for a chat with Jorge. I think I wanted to scold him, but I couldn't bring myself to raise my voice. Andres was busy with customers who had taken my usual table. Jorge has appointed himself my shrink. He's been good at sensing my recent wave of melancholy and tried to boost me with the suggestion that I order a margarita. He said they really helped to loosen me up. He emphasized "really" and laughed about me being bombed at CC yesterday. What? I told him I didn't recall being bombed. Me, playing innocent. He said I definitely was. Said I had a regular margarita and three doubles. Three doubles! Three was news. I thought I only had two. That's so funny because I only remembered the one I bought and the one he comped, nothing more after that.

Jorge was laughing at me. He laughed loudly, mocking me, and called across the room to Andres and Guillermo and told them to tell me if I had anything to drink yesterday. Aha! Witnesses that would vouch for me! I looked at them and said, well? They laughed when Andres' pointed directly at me and said it all in one word, *borracho,* which means drunk! I steadfastly denied it as a possibility. The three of them ganged up on me and assured me that I had all those drinks. My disbelief was real. When I turned to Jorge, still shocked but convinced now that I must be guilty, he assured me that my Spanish was pretty good when I was inebriated, which is amazing because when I am inebriated, even a little, I too am likely to think that my Spanish is pretty good. I thanked him for the recap and said I had to go back to my condo to work on my book. What I really needed was a nap, that's what I'd work on.

I had to go all right. I wasn't happy about all that booze. Truly, it was a lot. I think I have to come to grips with what he swears was true, that I was bombed on margaritas and didn't remember it. Tequila at work. That's what did it. Tequila, to-kill-ya. Almost the same words. I won't do that again. Of course, if I did, I suppose I wouldn't remember that either.

CHAPTER NINE

Week 9

<u>Going to La Paz -Thursday, March 2</u>

When I was running a small company, it was so long ago that it's challenging to remember those days. Indeed, they are way behind me. I don't reminisce about them much, maybe because there is hardly anyone around I'd want to reminisce with. However, I haven't forgotten a few of the highlights. One employee in particular was a young woman who I can say was the highlight of my experience in having employees for twenty-five years. She worked for me for ten years and everything about her was a sharp contrast to everyone else, almost all of them low lights. Maybe I'm being a little harsh about the others, but this woman was the only truly great employee. Her name is Jennifer. She was the Director of Sales & Business Development. It was a big responsibility for someone that young, younger than me by twenty-four years. At the peak of my business, I had twelve direct employees. Plus, over a hundred suppliers. If I had another two or three Jennifers working for me in those years, we could have grown to become a much bigger company. Of course, that would have meant more employees, which might have driven me completely nuts.

Jennifer was fantastic at sales. She knew her stuff. She could quote Zig Ziglar and all the other sales and management gurus to me and to our clients. I remember that, which makes me say, funny what things we remember from our past. Speaking of which, I shut down the business ten years ago in order to pursue other less stressful interests. Jennifer moved on to a similar company before changing careers and becoming the most successful multiple store owner in a major U.S. franchise year after year. Somehow, I am not surprised over that outcome.

Happily, Jennifer and I stayed in touch with a few email exchanges over the years. If the stars lined up, we'd have lunch every two or three years when our travel plans put us in the same city. Since she left me she has become a star in business, which has kept her super busy, along with running a household that includes her only child, a teenage girl in a whirlwind of all those things that come with being a teenage girl. Last year, Jennifer told me that her daughter is a handful, but usually a delightful handful. She amended her choice of usually to sometimes. What teenager isn't a handful?

With all the things Jennifer does in her many different roles in the past year, she needed a break from it all. She said it would be the first for her in many years. She picked a four-star Mexican inn for four nights in La Paz for a spontaneous solo getaway that starts this week. Tomorrow to be exact. Because we kept in touch, she knew I was wintering in Cabo, only couple of hours away by car. She texted me and asked me if I could meet her for lunch tomorrow in La Paz. I said yes, hung up, and, without her knowledge, I called the place where she was staying. I was hopeful that I could get a room for tomorrow night so we could have a long lunch and I wouldn't have to put in a full four hours of driving the round trip on Mexican highways.

When I called the inn, the proprietor said a minimum of two nights are required. I called Jennifer back and impulsively asked her if she could put up with me for two lunches instead of one and then boldly added maybe a couple of dinners, too. I was worried that I was intruding on her sabbatical but she surprised me and said it'd be great to spend that time together. I promised her I'd give her space, but I was not sure how much since there was so much we could catch up on. Within a minute of hanging up, I called the proprietor back and booked not two, but four nights in the last available room. A last-minute cancellation on a four-night reservation got me a room. I texted her with the news and said I'd pick her up at the airport and together we could drive to La Paz.

She wouldn't need to rent a car. I'd get a rental, pick her up at the airport and drop her off when it was time. How much time she wanted to spend with me was up to her. I was perfectly willing to explore the town on my own.

Four nights for me? Might seem a little excessive to come out of a lunch invitation. I obviously didn't give it much thought. I guess I needed a getaway too because I unhesitatingly signed up for four days for myself, the full length of Jennifer's stay. We would be guesting at Hacienda Paraiso, which is a quaint but classy six room, old world B&B designed in the concept of a traditional Mexican hacienda. Its spacious courtyard, which encircled a beautiful blue tiled swimming pool, was more of a compound in size and scope. Loaded with palm trees and manicured gardens of native flora, the lush setting within its network of stone walkways created a perfect oasis in the heart of hot and dry La Paz. All six rooms, advertised as unique in their interiors, were artfully tucked away among the foliage and sectioned off into various semi-private patio areas. Each room had a semi-secluded porch with two chairs and a glimpse of the pool. The *hacienda cocina* and dining areas were at one end of the pool, attached to the proprietor's living quarters. This layout comprised an enchanting setting for in-house breakfasts and a common area where the guests gathered for meals or simply to socialize with other guests.

The getaway gave us both a chance to do some serious catch up as well as some private relaxation apart from each other. We would have lots of fun when we were together but we both appreciated our own space and some private down time that came with time apart. Besides lunching, I was happy to play the role of dinner partner and hang with her to see some of the sites. That's a good thing for her because petite, blonde, good looking women probably shouldn't be walking around Mexico alone. With Jennifer at my side, I anticipated everyone's first question and prepared my answer, which would almost always be, *Soy su tio,* which means, I am her uncle. Why not? Saying "friend" leaves room for misinterpretation, so uncle is an acceptable lie, as I see it. Her dad and I are the same age, uncle is believable.

In the weeks before booking the Hacienda Paraiso, I had heard many nice things about La Paz before I even knew I was going there. It was most often described as an authentic Mexican town. Charming was another word. It was also described as arty and cultural and very low key when compared to the American tourist mecca of Cabo San Lucas to the south. And a lot cheaper than Cabo. As it turned out, it was all of these things.

Airport pick up and our first day in La Paz - Friday, March 3

At noon, I picked Jennifer up at the airport in my rental car, a car that cost me about fifty dollars a day with full insurance. Not bad a deal. It was an easy drive on mostly a recently paved highway. Time on the road flew in our excitement to see each other again. There was a lot of territory to cover, literally and figuratively, but we had four days to do it. An hour out of the airport, we stopped in Todos Santos, a famous old, artsy village on the Pacific Coast halfway to La Paz. The Hotel California sits in the middle of the town. It is the town's number one tourist attraction. It is the same hotel featured in the title track of the Eagles' album of the same name and released as a single in February 1977. Since then, the locals made the Hotel California a tacky, crass tourist trap that played an endless loop of that well-known song. We passed on it. I told Jennifer that it was a trap, which I learned when I visited it six years ago. Wasn't worth it.

Todos Santos was the mid-point to La Paz and our destination for lunch. We got lucky when we pulled up to an open-air taco stand called Barajas Tacos and Carnitas. It was a perfectly relaxing setting for eating perfectly delicious tacos that we washed down with a couple of perfectly made margaritas-salt-rocks. How perfect! Check-in time in La Paz was at four so we were in no hurry. Jennifer and I spent our first two hours at our table laughing over our memories of the good ol' days, which we decided were in fact pretty good. Her memory was better than mine as we dissed the full roster of employees, several of whom I had forgotten for good reason. The stand out was a young woman neither of us could forget, early twenties young, ditsy, and way-too-good-looking. It was easy for us to remember her name, the same name of the hurricane that devastated New Orleans in 2005. She was a temp, provided by some Napa service, that cost me a lot, not to mention that she ran up huge unnecessary expenses from her countless mistakes. For example, when I told her we pay our suppliers promptly, she sent our checks to them via FedEx. It took a month to see what was happening. My FedEx bill her first month was over eight hundred dollars, compared the usual fifty. I fired her after five weeks of total destruction of everything she touched. Same year, 2005. Katrina caused a lot of pain and suffering. Both.

<u>Check-in at Hacienda Paraiso - Friday, March 3</u>

Check-in at Hacienda Paraiso was quick and easy. The inn was busy with some turnover of guests so the proprietor didn't mind giving us the short version of the inn's history while he walked us to our rooms, which happened to be on opposite sides of the pool. With luggage unpacked we showed off our rooms to each other. Pretty similar but, yes, different enough to support the claim of unique, and very nice. I liked the big walk-in shower in my room, an important feature for me everywhere I stay. Jennifer didn't get that.

The Hacienda was a perfect place for keeping the world out. Neither of us felt compelled to leave the grounds, except for our shared interest in eating out and getting some sense of the town. We got that just by driving to and from a different restaurant every night of our stay. Three of the four were on the Malecón, which is a major paved serpentine promenade that runs for five miles along the shoreline, winding through the heart of the city and into the beyond. La Paz's social life revolves along it and, of course, restaurants looking out over the water lined it on very coveted real estate.

As it turned out, we picked a different restaurant every night for some excellent Mexican food on three nights and Mexican style sushi on the fourth. Meals in all four restaurants in La Paz were fabulous. They all deserved a heavy up on stars when we googled them. Jennifer and I spent much of our time doing our own thing in the day at poolside or in our rooms. She couldn't completely escape work. I saw her often under one of the umbrellas by the pool, on her phone and laptop, while I relaxed on my little porch reading and writing. But no arithmetic. I busied myself with studying *Spanish for Gringos* and assembling my long-term plans and material for my book.

Dining the first night in La Paz - Friday, March 3

The first restaurant Jennifer and I dined in was The Tailhunter restaurant with its FUBAR cantina. It was a happening place and full of energy, which was the atmosphere we both needed after a day of traveling. Located on the Malecón, the restaurant offers three floors of great views of the gulf. We got the best view, a bird's-eye view, on the third floor. Besides the sea vista, we were perched at a table on the railing which was great for people-watching right below us and across the street on the Malecón.

The food was highly recommended by the proprietor at the inn. We were not disappointed. The food is homemade with a commitment to local ingredients, which was the inspiration for their famously diverse menu. Really diverse, including their special La Paz hot dog, Mexican style. That's right. Here's what the menu says: *Two bacon-wrapped hot dogs grilled and layered with minced chiles, onions, tomatoes, mustard, mayo, and catsup. Piled up high on lightly toasted grilled buns. Ahhh, a La Paz street delicacy!* I thought of the stray dogs on the streets all over town. Jennifer and I both had a good laugh with the last line, *a La Paz street delicacy.* Maybe the stray dogs were a part of the promise of Mexican-style hot dogs. Sick, I know. Not at all funny. It's funny how my mind works sometimes, or doesn't.

We limited our intake at The Tailhunter after our big lunch in Todos Santos by sharing an appetizer of grilled shrimp brochettes, which was grilled shrimp and vegetables on a skewer. Also, we split the fresh grilled sea bass, again Mexican-style, for the main.

All authentic, every bite delicious. And two margaritas each. The place gets a five-star rating, deservedly so. Oh, so do the margaritas. Top shelf too. I think we each had two. Probably not exactly.

The best beach in La Paz - Saturday, March 4

We knew that all work and dinners out was not enough for Jennifer and me to feel the relief of a getaway adventure, so we did the number one thing tourists love doing most in La Paz: going to the beach, specifically Balandra Beach. It is not only the best beach in La Paz, there are many beach lovers who say it's the best beach in Mexico. Jennifer and I had to see it. At noon, we drove twenty-one miles north of La Paz on the serpentine coastal road up the western side of Pichilingue Peninsula. The beach was easy to find. Signage was good. We could see parked cars up ahead and a half mile to our left, down a dirt road, which we took. That was the way to Balandra.

When we arrived at a dead end off of the coastal road we counted fifteen other cars in the dusty, sandy parking lot, all of them and our car in a barren, brown, arid setting right up to the beach. I found an open space in the front row overlooking the bay and turned off the ignition as both of us stared over the sandy strip of beach dumbfounded by seeing a picturesque pristine bay without water. The small horseshoe bay in front of us was nothing but a vast expanse of smooth, wet sand. The only thing we could surmise was that water had completely drained by the pull of the low tide, something we did not expect. However, five hundred yards toward the sea, just outside of this drained horseshoe bay, we could see people wading knee high in the beautiful cerulean blue water at the entrance to the bay. Jennifer and I decided to hike there to see what we could see. We got out of the car and removed our shoes determined to join the distant beachcombers in our investigation of what was supposed to be the best beach in Mexico.

I must say that Balandra Beach is a gorgeously stark place, even when the tide is out. Even then, there is a beach, a temporary one, several hundred yards outside of the horseshoe inlet. Once one gets out there, a couple of football fields of shallow knee-deep water fronting the deeper sea sits atop beautiful soft, white, rippled sand. The sea waits at the threshold of the bay for a change in the tide that will push the water back into the drained inlet. A fellow beachcomber told us that peak tide was not due for another four hours. Good to know. Jennifer and I, shoes in hand, barefooted it back to the car wanting to find a tiki hut restaurant on the road back to La Paz. And a bathroom. We decided to return to Balandra later, when the water was in.

With no restrooms or restaurants in sight at Balandra, I pulled out of the parking, put the pedal to the metal, something my rental car did not respond to, but wasted no time going to a tiki bar five miles down the road. We both remembered it as being nice enough for our needs. Food, drinks, bathrooms, on the water, all that, just what we wanted. Quenching our thirst was our second priority. What we saw at Balandra was unique in its beauty and configuration, but we were both slightly disappointed in a way. Our enthusiasm drained out of us just as thoroughly as the water drained out of the bay on the falling tide. On an upbeat note, if and when we returned at high tide, we were sure it would be vastly different. We could easily imagine how that was possible.

Lunch just south of Balandra Beach - Saturday, March 4

Four miles south of Balandra Beach, on the same serpentine road we drove on an hour earlier on our way to Balandra, we were coming through a blind curve when, very suddenly, as we came out of it, dozens of roadside flares sparked in the bright sunlight. I came to a quick stop, requiring a heavy foot to the brakes. Had to. The rooftop lights on two cop cars were strobing red, white and blue just fifty yards ahead of me as a dozen men were scurrying around like ants surrounding a toppled grasshopper. A very big double-load truck was on its side, just off the road, wheels hovering over the shoulder of the road. It was a very big, toppled grasshopper. I guess, it must have happened only ten or fifteen minutes earlier. We guessed it came around the curve a little faster than we did an hour ago. I flicked a wave of my hand to first responders a couple of times while steering carefully through the conglomeration of vehicles. I was relieved that we weren't caught up in that mess in any way. I was also quickly reminded of the dangers of country roads in Mexico. People drive here Mexican style. Everything is Mexican style, not just the food. I hope the driver wasn't hurt. How could he not be?

A mile later we pulled into the hardpan parking lot of an open-air tiki restaurant and a full bar that was right on the water's edge. We liked it when we saw it on our drive to Balandra Beach. Now we liked it even more. Its only two exterior walls were bright lemony yellow. On the wall facing the road, it was easy to see big hand-painted purple lettering announcing the name La Luna Bruja. I'm not sure if I got the translation right but I think it means the The Witch Moon, or some kind of moon. We speed-walked in on the side of one of the missing walls, both of us making a beeline for the bathrooms. I finished first, a male thing, and got a table for us under thatch at the edge of the tile floor that was closest to the water. Our table overlooked a fifteen-foot sandy slope that ran down to the gently lapping ripples of the Sea of Cortez. It was perfect for us. It was the perfect getaway for lunch. Mexican-style.

Jennifer arrived at the table a minute later and then chips and salsa showed up a minute after that. We ordered three grilled shrimp tacos and three grilled fish tacos. The top shelf margaritas we asked for were served a few minutes later and then the tequila shots followed as we worked our way through the tacos. The most-delicious-tacos-ever probably saved us from alcohol poisoning. I think we were close to bringing real meaning to that stupid t-shirt imprint that goes like this: one tequila, two tequila, three tequila, floor.

Jennifer and I stopped after the third shot and who knows how many margaritas. Of course, by that time I was convinced there wasn't any alcohol in the tequila shots. A stop sign, if ever.

After we quit shooting each other, we spent the next two hours at our table downing bottles of *agua* throughout our conversation, laughing and luxuriating while transfixed by the beauty of the wonderfully blue and infinite sea in front of us. It's a shame the afternoon wasn't infinite as well. We could see the tide was coming in. Our beach was shrinking. We laughed over so many stupid stories and shared many truly brilliant opinions of timely topics that it would not be right to only summarize all the things we talked about, even if I could remember them.

It was time to get back to Hacienda Paraiso. I drove with great care, perfectly aware of the possibility that my blood alcohol level exceeded my blood level and would probably not meet USA standards even though my last shot was over three hours ago. I was pretty sure I was under the blood alcohol level for tourist standards, but extra care behind the wheel was a good thing, and necessary. All we had to do was find the car. I knew I left it somewhere in the middle of the very small parking lot, next to one other car. We got back to the B&B without incident. I did not turn into a grasshopper. And we agreed to try Balandra Beach *mañana*, with the tidewater in. I needed a nap before dinner. Jennifer went off to her room, probably with the same thing in mind.

Dining the second night in La Paz - Saturday, March 4

On our second night, Jennifer and I returned to the Malecón because of the reputation of the restaurants and for the seductive view of the water. We tried El Bismarkcito, the little version of the highly rated and somewhat fancy parent restaurant called the Bismark. Its high thatched roof gives it the feel of a tiki bar, but it looks like a distant relative of the tiki bars in Cabo, being not nearly as commercial as the Cabo scene. The variety on the menu is excellent and diverse but Jennifer and I stuck with our common interests in simple cuisine. We both responded to our addiction for fish tacos, which you could get with smoked marlin, if you wanted. We didn't; we're purists. Besides, neither of us were into smoked anything. You could say that neither of us are smokers and leave it at that. But wait! There's more! The guacamole was excellent with crispy salty chips that worked just fine as our appetizer. We both agreed that because we overdid it a bit on margaritas on our first day, we avoided them tonight. Jennifer opted for a glass of a buttery chardonnay and I fell back on my tried and true bottle of Pacifico. Preferably sweating, the bottle, not me.

A return to Balandra Beach - Sunday, March 5

Jennifer and I returned to Balandra Beach to see it again with tide sensitive timing. It was another perfectly sunny day on the eastern shore of the Baja overlooking the sparkling waters of the Sea of Cortez. This time we arrived late in the day, around five-thirty, the afternoon time of high tide. When we pulled into the parking lot, the scenery was dramatically different in addition to sporting three times as many cars. We could easily see past the dozen or so vendors hawking blankets, trinkets and driftwood carvings; they weren't there yesterday, but neither was the water. Today, that moment, the water was in. The bay's entire basin was now full of water. People could be seen throughout the inlet all the way to the far side, wading in water that was never higher than their waists. Mostly knee high. Walking, kayaking, paddle boarding, and floating on air rafts were the main activities. The water was breathtakingly beautiful in its color, even jaw-dropping. It was that perfect postcard of crystal clear, aqua *agua* in the inlet eventually merging with the deep blue sea. An exquisite beach of white soft sand was now clearly defined as a perfect white ring around the bay, one that almost completely encloses the gentle, far-reaching shallow waters of Balandra Beach. I could see how it just might be the best beach in Mexico. Entirely believable. Jennifer agreed. We hung out for about two hours under one of ten thatched umbrellas ten feet off the water's edge. There for the public, the only one not in use, we took advantage of it before someone else did and chilled. No charge. Worth every penny. And more. A lot more.

Dining the third night in La Paz - Sunday, March 5

Our third night together over dinner was not at a table on the Malecón, nor was it in the commercial part of the town. It was in a backyard garden tucked into a nondescript building behind a nondescript wall in our nondescript residential neighborhood around the corner from us. An easy walk. It was another one of the restaurants recommended by the innkeeper upon our arrival. We considered it for lunch until we decided to skip lunch and spend the middle of the day poolside, fasting from two days of excessive indulgence. We put it on the docket for dinner.

At dinner time, after dusk, after a day at the beach, we hoofed it five blocks with a right, left, and then a right to the under-the-sky, totally outdoor restaurant *El Jardin Secreto*, which in Spanish is The Secret Garden. It was that. It was such a well-kept secret we walked past it twice before locating the entrance. A small hand-painted sign, with only the restaurant's name, was affixed head high on a worn stucco wall inches from a rusty gate that led down an alley, presumptively to the restaurant. Easy to miss. We navigated the alley, alert to the possibility that it might not be the entrance, but seventy feet into it, the open-air restaurant appeared. It looked like someone's well-groomed backyard, but with a dozen of those white plastic tables. It certainly must be a well-kept secret because there were no customers. I guess it was the best kept secret in town, that night anyway. Just us. Two Americans, one, a tall bald, elderly man and the other his blonde bombshell niece. Nonetheless, regardless of the absence of any other customers, it was magical. Or maybe that was part of the magic, only us. All the other customers were invisible as we are to them. Fortunately, the service staff wasn't invisible, nor the furnishings. Ten white plastic tables were neatly organized on a concrete slab, each with four white plastic chairs. A very small open bar was set up on one side of the slab, not the side that was adjacent to the garden. We took a table on the garden side. With a little stretch of my legs, I could eat while barefoot with my toes curled in the lawn. The entire backyard was carpeted in manicured grass, then rimmed with trimmed flower beds, then surrounded by ten-foot-high shaped hedges. The hedges were implanted with small white lights, what I call Italian Christmas tree lights, which under the evening's full moon created a very memorable setting. The secret garden became the enchanted garden to us.

Jennifer and I liked The Secret Garden right away. We sat across from each other at a table for four at the edge of the lawn where we were surprised by the presence of half a dozen big bunnies on the loose. That's right, big tame bunnies, all grazing on the grass, all within twenty feet of us. They had fur in different colors of black, white and brown. And, they were terribly cute. I told Jennifer not to order rabbit stew. A good laugh however quirky. Jennifer and I thought it would be good to take a couple back to the States, then laughed over sharing that same thought at the same time. The bunnies were clearly pets, just not ours.

The last time I was in a restaurant with so many darling bunnies was in Chicago thirty years ago at a place called The Playboy Club. Two of the bunnies even came up to the leg of Jennifer's chair, so tame and, maybe, begging for a salad. Jennifer stood up and approached the nearest one, wanting to fondle it. I remembered that exact feeling myself long ago. They weren't interested in human contact so the effort, I told her, was futile, something I also learned in Chicago. The bunny apparently didn't want to be fondled. Futile for the both of us, then and now.

We left The Secret Garden ninety minutes later, having happily enjoyed a delectable margherita pizza with a self-imposed two drink limit of excellent margaritas. I also had a Pacifico, from the habit of having beer with pizza. Jennifer and I ambled back to the Hacienda under a jet-black sky pinpricked with millions of stars. We were satiated and carefree from a full day of lounging. And maybe a little light-headed, mostly from the pleasure of a perfectly enjoyable day. Relaxation and the release of stress were in play. First poolside, then at Balandra, and then in someone's garden. I said goodnight to her with an air kiss on her cheek. We were both ready to retire in our rooms for the evening. When I climbed into bed, I couldn't think of any problems in the world so I went right to sleep.

Dining the fourth night in La Paz - Monday, March 6

Jennifer and I hardly saw each other on our fourth day after meeting over the B&B's authentic, Mexican-style breakfast of fruit, egg burritos, chorizo, and too many choices of beans. After breakfast, we were both busy with whatever stuff we had to do. Once I saw her at the pool on the phone but opted out of interrupting her. The day went quickly for me, which was a good thing because I was looking forward to our fourth evening out. When we met up at the end of the day, Jennifer and I opted for sushi at Jiro Sushi restaurant on the Malecón. We agreed that it was our first choice. It has some great reviews, which inspired that choice.

Jiro was a hit for us. We shared dishes, as usual, and split a crab and avocado Mexican-style sushi roll and a curry roll. We also split a mango avocado salad that was to die for. We also split our sides a couple of times recalling dumb things that happened to us when we worked together years ago. And if I ate and drank anymore on this trip, I'd split my pants too.

The restaurant setting was nice, not Mexican-style, kind of hip, bright and airy, and certainly different from the usual close quarters of tiki huts. The interior colors were subdued in contrast the usual whacky colors you see all over Mexico. Of course, we had a view overlooking a massive body of water that was as flat as a mirror in its ethereal beauty, which greatly added to the culinary experience. This was not a restaurant for margaritas. Saki was of no interest to us, so we opted for the subtle taste of a soft, buttery chardonnay, this one from Chile. Jennifer's favorite choice in varietals was chardonnay, which worked that night for me too. We toasted each other on our last night in La Paz and agreed it was a great idea to spend so much time together.

Four days is a lot of time with anyone, especially when you're not married to each other or in a relationship. I wondered if she wondered if I wondered about wanting our getaway to last a lot longer than four days. Of course, she didn't. But it made me wonder why I wondered that. It's all silly thinking on my part, but just remember that sometimes if you go beyond wonder you get to wonderful. Whatever that's supposed to mean. Sounds like something sappy printed on a Hallmark card. I made that up. Ugh.

Farewell La Paz - Tuesday, March 7

La Paz was a great getaway, for both of us. And one we both wanted. We had lots of fun time together and plenty of time apart to refresh our spirits and focus on our individual needs. Laughter is the best medicine, whether you need it or not. We had a lot of that. It was good for me to get out of Cabo for a change of scenery and a chance to think outside of my routine. Jennifer told me she was impressed with my Spanish, this coming from someone who doesn't speak Spanish, but I loved the compliment. She also said to me that her time off was exactly the change of pace she needed, but I wondered about that given all the time she spent on her electronics. On the bright side, much of her time working over the phone and on her laptop was spent poolside under a big, pink, sun umbrella, which was a good thing for her.

We checked out of Hacienda Paraiso at eight in the morning, thus allowing us plenty of time to get to San Jose International for Jennifer's one o'clock flight back to San Antonio. It was a very pleasant drive that included a breakfast stop en route at some tiny roadside taco stand. We ate and relaxed in the tranquility of that mid-morning moment, comfortably seated on the only two chairs available for customers. We were content in not having to say anything to each other. We sat in plastic white chairs, of course, and on a slab of red tile just big enough for the two of us and our white plastic table. It felt like private dining. Perfect, actually. We just took it all in, under the shade of the thick fronds twenty feet up from a few palm trees with their trunks just feet away. They also provided protection from a sun that was already hot and getting hotter by the minute. Our *huevos burritos* were delicious, best choice on the menu. And the only choice. Jennifer got her coffee fix. Me, I don't touch the stuff, never have. Waking up to the smell of coffee is not something that appeals to me. It is almost a scary thought.

It was hard to drive away from that taco stand. It symbolized the end of our time together. The end of our shared getaway was about to get away from us. Her departure was inevitable, and soon. Too soon, I thought. It made me contemplative, having to face the end of this surprisingly pleasant and colossally enjoyable time together. I kept my feelings to myself but I was sorry to see our sabbatical end. Our vacation. Our escape. Our fun.

Our time together came to an end when I pulled up to the curb in front of American Airlines departures. Our goodbye was quick. I watched Jennifer, with her roller bag in tow, disappear through the sliding doors, bound for home. Bound for her crazy busy life in San Antonio. It was easy to see she is special. Besides having that look that gets every man's attention, she is a very together and amazing person in all she does. I've always known it and easily remember seeing it when she worked for me. I shouldn't be surprised that I could see her work ethic translate into success in her personal life, her mom life, and her management of all the things she does in twenty-seven hours a day. She makes me wish I were twenty-four years younger. I had no idea what she was thinking, but I confess, I have some feelings for her and always will. Uncles are like that.

I love Mexican food but I'm not eating much of it - Tuesday, March 7

As I have stated many times, I love Mexican food even though I don't eat it every day. La Paz was an exception; I indulged in it for four days in a row. Ordinarily, I'll have Mexican every other day or once in every three days. I must have tremendous self-control because I can resist a daily temptation to eat grilled shrimp tacos at Gardenias for every meal. My typical daily diet couldn't possibly appeal to many people, but it works for me and I don't get tired of it even though it's pretty much the same thing day after day.

In mid-morning of each day I steam two cups of frozen mixed vegetables from Walmart. When ready, I dump them onto a plate, add two table spoons of chopped jalapeños and two pre-cut slices of Mexican cheese. With that colorful mound begging to be eaten, I top it with a tablespoon of extra virgin olive oil. a squirt of mustard, and a couple of shakes from my bottle of Valentina Salsa Picante. When I remember, I add a teaspoon of turmeric powder. Sometimes I turn the heat up with a few added drops of *El Yucatec chili habanero*, an XXXtra *picante* sauce, not for the faint-hearted. With that orchestration completed, I mix it up, almost by tossing it, and then dive in with a soup spoon. I do the same thing for my mid-afternoon meal, if I am not having Gardenias tacos, which usually completes my food intake for the day. Along with my spinach-mango smoothie, of course. I alternate kale with the spinach. I'm not Popeye.

If I cheat a bit by eating more than my double dosage of steamed vegetables, it happens late at night with two eggs, over easy, covered in chopped jalapeños. Love those jalapeños!

Long time not seen at CC - Tuesday, March 7

In the afternoon, I dropped in on my friends at CC. I hadn't seen them for a week but it seemed like ages. I wanted to tell them about my trip to La Paz. The trip gave me a fresh topic to talk about. It was a chance to practice using the Spanish words that I knew rather than sweating through some I didn't know when I let Andres and the boys pick a topic. When I showed up, smiles everywhere and embraces all around. A Pacifico was already on the table and it made me wonder how it got there so fast given the unknown timing or my return. I missed these guys, hearts of gold, all of them.

We all agreed that La Paz is authentic Mexican and Cabo isn't. My pals know Cabo is not a real Mexican town, not in their eyes anyway. Cabo is an American tourist's idea of a place to party

Mexican-style in Mexico. La Paz is more a Mexican's idea of a place to party in Mexico. Alas, this left no doubt in my mind that there was very little that is authentic about Cabo except, of course, my friendship with the guys at CC. And all the Mexicans that live in Cabo, whether I knew them or not.

It's not happening with Lourdes - Tuesday, March 7

When I was on my way into the night life in *el centro*, I passed the open doors of the G Spot and was coming up on Esteban's, about fifty yards in front of me. I could see the delicious Lourdes standing at the front door, ready to pounce on tourists looking for a place for dinner. She saw my white flasher approaching. I would have to stop and say hello. I did, but I didn't get off my bike, which would have implied a real conversation, something that I am not capable of with her. We swapped *holas* and a few other words in Spanish. I asked her if she was working hard, *trabajando duro*? It was a stupid question because only one table was occupied on the patio. Obviously, she wasn't. I stumbled over a few more words and managed to say yet one more stupid thing as I rode away. I said, *Buena suerte*, which means good luck. She smiled. Lulu knows she needed it. By the way, I'd never call her Lulu, even though I maul the name Lo-Uuur-Dez.

Paul and Julie from Minneapolis - Tuesday, March 7

I like Esquina. It's a good place on any night. Mixed crowd, often packed. It's a casual but sophisticated restaurant. The women are always dressed well and coifed up and wearing nice jewelry. The men looked like they have been dining at Burger King, but not entirely in t-shirts either. Sometimes I'd see a Tommy Bahamas shirt. Most people look like they have money, honey, in this joint. This time I dropped in at dusk and left two hours later, well into post-dusk darkness, after an earlier visit to The Baja Brewery for the cocktail hour. Even if I am not looking for a conversation, there's a good chance I might get one at Esquina. Tourists are a yacky, often tacky, group of people so as soon as I occupied a barstool with two empty seats next to mine, which happened to be on my right, I was betting something interesting might come up. Not always the case, but usually. Esquina is almost always good for a conversation with a stranger at the bar. In English, of course, because everyone here is American or Canadian except for the bartenders and the waitstaff. It gives me a break from my full day of Spanish routine. The two empty stools next to me didn't stay empty for more than a minute.

A good-looking couple, obviously in the money, both tall and blond, probably from Minnesota, took over the two empty barstools next to me. I heard their drink order. He, a martini up and dirty, with two olives. She, took the bartender's recommendation for a glass of chardonnay. Sometimes couples like this, in my age group, turn out to be yik-yacky. I got one of those tonight and, as usual, I did most of the listening. I usually get in a little bit of my own chatter in too, so there's no suffering in silence on my part in my solo endeavors on barstools, usually.

The conversation tonight was with Paul and Julie. Scandinavians through and through. Easy for me to guess that at least one of them has the surname Johnson in their family tree. Minnesotans all the way. Paul looked like a regular customer at a Tommy Bahama store. He could have been Joe Montana's older brother, that kind of look. Julie was dressed nicely enough for any cocktail party in New York City, but not in an overbearing way, rather tasteful actually, and understated except for her jewelry. Nothing understated about the rock on her wedding finger. It's that look of casual sophistication that I like to see in uppity bars like Esquina. Especially down here, because it's a pleasant contrast in this Mexican outpost of shorts and t-shirts.

I listened to a lot about this couple's history in Cabo, mostly from Paul, who is the chatty one of the two. They have a condo here, had it for almost thirty years. They might have said two condos, something about a second one still under construction. Lots of renovation stories, blah blah blah but a nice blah blah blah, easy to listen to. They like Cabo this time of year and stay for a month or two. Who wouldn't like coming to Cabo after four months of a Minnesota winter? But I didn't say that. They look like sturdy stock so maybe they love months and months of freezing temperatures and perpetual slush on the streets with a little Cabo tossed in to break up the monotony.

We three are contemporaries. I discovered that Paul and I are five months apart in age. Julie, a very pretty blonde, is probably a few years younger. I didn't ask. In addition to personal background, I got thirty years of Cabo history from Paul, mostly about the Bisbee fishing tournament, which I liked hearing about. If it's interesting, I don't mind chatty. The Bisbee is in October, when I'll be long gone. I knew about it, of course, because I like fishing and it is the biggest fishing event of the year in Cabo. It's actually a world-famous event. Millions of dollars of prize money draw some competition from all four corners of the world. A million goes to the winner, not a bad haul for a good day of fishing in the Sea of Cortez. Julie was very attentive as Paul dominated the air time. Fine by me, of course. I'm a good listener. Clearly Paul and Julie got along well together, which is safe to say since they were into their thirty-third year of marriage. Like me, she's probably a good listener too.

After the Bisbee news, Paul and I returned to our conversation about our more youthful days, our college days to be precise. We discovered that we were skiing about the same time in Colorado in our freshman year, me for the first time. He was an excellent skier from his childhood in Minnesota, like all Minnesota kids. Julie nodded in confirmation. Me, never very good. But I did have a good story for him about my first time, first time skiing that is, which took place in Colorado. Julie was all ears too as I promised them both that it was, indeed, a good story, but in fewer words than what's presented below.

Once upon a time, along with six of my Indiana University fraternity brothers, I committed to a week of Colorado Rocky Mountain skiing. In early January, we seven piled into two cars for the semester break. The drive from Bloomington to Aspen was twenty-two hours, with one very important stop, scheduled in both directions, the Coors Brewing Company in Golden, Colorado. Our ultimate destination was Snowmass-at-Aspen, a new ski resort twenty minutes past Aspen's Ajax mountain. I think the at-Aspen was dropped a couple of years after Snowmass opened. Anyway, it was touted as a great place for all skiers, but best for moderate and beginner skiers, unlike Aspen. A lot of easy slopes, the brochures said, which is good thing because four of us had never skied before. The three who had, were advanced and, somehow, they talked all four of us beginners into starting at the very top with them. College kids do that sort of thing. Rational adults don't. I was still in college.

For me skiing down from the top of the mountain made for a long day, a lot of snow-plowing combined with occasional bursts of speed that come with being completely insane and then a good out-of-control tumble followed by a face plant. After many hours of skiing, downhill rolling in the snow, and sitting on my ass with skis akimbo, I made my way to the middle of the last slope that funneled everyone to lodge-world, the end of the line. I think that last run was called Fanny Hill, or maybe that's what we called it, because that's where the beginners are supposed to get started, unless they're crazy college kids. Halfway down that hill, about fifty yards out from my ski-in ski-out condo rental, I stopped to gather my thoughts, take in the scenery, give thanks to the gods above for not breaking any of my bones, and rejoice over being so close to a raging fire in a fireplace and a cold six-pack of Coors. That is what was waiting for me in the condo.

I probably shouldn't have stopped on Fanny Hill, but I did. It was all so beautiful. The slope was very wide at that point. I was well off to one side, so I wasn't in anyone's way. Which turned out to be not true because I got blindsided by another skier. Seriously whacked. Me, totally decked out, spread eagle on the snow, face plant. It was probably the biggest wipe-out of the day for me, which is saying more than you can imagine. I was face down so I didn't see the whacker. I was also afraid to move, fearful I'd discover that I was paralyzed with a broken neck.

Fortunately, I wasn't injured. And, very relieved to be able to discern my state of health right away was still one hundred per cent. The whacker, a woman, who had run into me wasn't as lucky. I could see that, when I rolled over about a half minute later, about the same time that the bells in my head stopped ringing. I sat up, a little nonplused. From about fifteen feet from her, I watched three of her male friends suddenly materialize out of nowhere, huddle over her, thus, effectively blocking me from seeing her in pain. Which was a good thing because it couldn't have been good. I could see enough through the scrum to see the downed woman was wearing a bright red, one-piece ski suit. As bright as red gets. Curiously, it matched the color of her hair. I might have been a little dopey because, at that moment, I wasn't really sure where I was other than sitting in the snow, dazed, watching the commotion and in awkward reach of my skis. About three minutes after the collision, she was shuttled downhill on a rescue sled guided by her three friends and a latecomer to the party. As I was coming to my senses, the three men who were helping her were with Ski Patrol, according to their parka insignias. My eyes were beginning to focus. All I could say about the latecomer, was that she was a woman who was squawking an awful lot. All this time, from some unknown reason, I was invisible. Probably because I was wearing a long corduroy jacket, not exactly looking like a skier, maybe more like a bystander. No one asked me how I was doing. Chopped liver in Snowmass! Eventually I got up, got my skis back on and glided in one piece for the final fifty yards to the condo's slope-side door. Relief, in the form of a frosty cold libation, was waiting for me in the kitchen, along with a couple of my friends who already downed uncountable cans of Coors. Thirty minutes later, we three, secure in our natural state as beer drinking couch potatoes, watched the local news on TV report that Lucille Ball had broken a leg an hour ago on Fanny Hill at Snowmass. Yep, the lady in red who nailed me was Lucille Ball. That Lucy, the one I love. Of course, I love Lucy.

Two weeks later on some live TV show with a name I can't recall, Lucille Ball hobbled onto the stage on crutches masterfully maneuvering with a full hip-to-toe, white plaster cast on her right leg. I knew the full story, but the audience didn't, so she told them part of it. She had a bad spill at Snowmass, she said, but was recovering nicely. She was thanking the Ski Patrol in her rescue. She said they were at her side every minute. So was I, briefly anyway, but she skipped that part. When the credits rolled at the end of the TV show, I didn't get mentioned, which is a good thing. I didn't deserve any credit for that accident because it wasn't my fault. Besides, I was invisible at the time. That's my story. Paul and Julie liked it. A lot.

I finished my Pacifico moments after I finished my story, paid my tiny tab, and then thanked Paul and Julie for a perfectly enjoyable conversation in which we took turns talking about whatever we felt like talking about. I expressed my hope that I'd bump into them sometime in the next few days, before they returned to the land of ice and slush. Nice couple. I walked out with a memory that I had forgotten a long time ago. Yep, I love Lucy.

Martina unzipped - Wednesday, March 8

Martina is always nice and always on the run. The only thing faster than her pace is her speech. Just listening to her makes me want to accelerate out of Mexican time. This afternoon she knocked on my door. We exchanged a few words faster than a speeding bullet, a real shoot out. One hundred words and fifteen seconds later, she turned her back on me for assistance with another zip up of her dress. It wasn't the first time, so I know the drill. I can do this sort of thing with confidence despite what little practice I've had zipping up dresses over the years. None. I was happy to oblige and silently noted once again that she has a nice back.

She's was on her way out, she said, to meet a girlfriend for drinks. Politely, with no innuendos, I invited her to stop by after her evening out. I even said I'll help her again with the zipper, but in the other direction. I said that with a friendly smile, not a lascivious smile. She must be getting tired of my saying that. I am getting tired of me saying that. Anyway, we laughed, which is a good thing. I am just being flirty with her and am not looking for anything more than a chuckle over attending to her wardrobe needs.

Frankly, I can't see us spending any time together other than over a five o'clock cocktail. She is very pleasant but, alas, she is not my type in a romantic sense. And, I am sure I am not her type either. Either case, it's all irrelevant because she told me she is married and faithful to her absent husband. For some reason, too personal for me to explore, he never visits her while she is wintering in Cabo. I'll take a wild guess anyhow; here it is. He runs a year-round business in Holland and she hates the winter in Holland. Winters in Holland are long, longer than five months. Logical enough. Not that logic has anything to do with romance.

Esquina two nights in a row - Wednesday, March 8

I rode the cruiser to Esquina at six o'clock, locked her to the usual lamppost. Surprisingly, at that hour Esquina was pretty empty. Four at the bar. Four in the dining room. Fine. I wasn't looking to run into any one in particular. And I didn't see anyone I wanted to run into. I made the most of my visit. I introduced myself to the bear of a bartender behind the bar. Ramon. He is pretty good with English so it's easy to learn a few things from him in Spanish. He was my silver lining for the cloud of vacancies on the barstools. I had one Pacifico, finished it off after ten minutes of conversation with Ramon, then left. I tipped big, which isn't much in the States, but big enough here to be memorable. He called out my name as I walked out. *Adios, Tomas!* Score one for immersion!

I think the beer boosted my appetite because I made a beeline to Gardenias for an as yet unknown amount of food. I've done as many as five tacos in a sitting. I pulled up to the front having made the decision to have just two as I parked the cruiser right in front of the place, unlocked, and in my sight line. Gabriel, not on the fly this time, greeted me as usual. Sometimes when the place is not super busy he spends a minute with me to test my Spanish and improve his English where he can. This was one of those nights. As I learned many weeks ago, Mexicans, servers in particular, are so appreciative when gringos attempt Spanish and help them with their English. I think I am more relaxed here so the Spanish seems to flow out of me faster.

I left after one Pacifico and two grilled shrimp tacos and, more importantly, chit chat with Gabriel, all of that accomplished in thirty minutes. I hang a lot longer at CC so maybe that's why it is a different, a more relaxed experience at Gardenias. I think maybe that CC is more like a classroom at times, which is fine, but a little stressful too. I left Gabriel a relatively big tip too. I like to throw in a little extra for any server willing to help me with my Spanish. It's a win-win arrangement.

Ocho MIA - Wednesday, March 8

Ocho has been MIA more days than I can count. Why? I hope nothing has happened to him. It's too much time for hide and seek or sunning poolside. His absence worries me. It makes me review in my head possible predators for geckos. Snakes for sure. Birds too. Maybe really big spiders, a thought that gives me the willies. Oh, cats too, probably the most feared predator of all because they torture their captives first before pointlessly killing them. Cats are no threat to me. Rattlesnakes are worrisome, especially since the bottom of my front door is one inch off the floor. I've heard that there are plenty of rattlesnakes in the Baja terrain, though I haven't seen any, yet. I think my condo is too sterile for snakes, but that might be a dumb assumption. I just don't know.

There are cats around here, feral ones, no doubt about that. Nocturnal screaming is all the proof I need. When they catch a gecko, I'm thinking the torture begins with biting off a leg, then a second leg. I've seen geckos with stubbed tails. They must be the ones that got away. All that torture for the fun of it. Cats are really sadistic creatures. A study in Australia several years ago concluded that feral cats kill five animals a day. The mix includes birds, of course, moles, mice, frogs, and geckos. There are a lot of animals that have much to fear from cats, and they all die at the pleasure of the cat, rarely for food. In one year, the numbers of animals tortured and then murdered by a single cat adds up to just over eighteen hundred. Per cat! Ocho is my buddy. I hope he's okay and just sagely enjoying his time away, surely to be back soon, I want to see him again, all of him, all four legs and a tail. He's probably sunning on the other side of the pool and sleeping around. His idea of a Gecko getaway.

Cats are non-stop screamers this week - Wednesday, March 8

I can't make sense out of the high frequency of screaming cats. Is it one, or is it several cats working on separate shifts? Or is it three cats at once? It could be. I hear them at night as I doze off. They rarely wake me in the middle of the night, but sometimes they do. But only when I have a bad conscience. I also hear them in the middle of the day once in a while. What's that all about? Some cool cat getting a nooner? Will the screaming ever stop? No. The best I can hope for is that I fall asleep with a clear conscience every night.

CHAPTER TEN

Week 10

<u>First day of Spring Break - Thursday, March 9</u>

My only comment on this first day of Spring Break is about the girls on the beach, specifically about what I did not see. I did not see an ounce of fat on any of them and I did not see any bikinis with more material than three eyepatches. Maybe it was just a massive commercial shoot for a beer commercial. If it wasn't, it should have been. I remember telling myself long, long ago that women's bathing suits couldn't get any skimpier. Boy, was I wrong.

<u>Third night in a row in Esquina - Thursday, March 9</u>

Early into the evening. Thursday night. I called it quits on the town and decided to spend the evening in my condo. And then I didn't. Just before nine, I jumped on the cruiser, tore out of Coromuel, waved to the guard in the security gate, and went to Esquina, clearly now my favorite evening hangout. I needed the noise of people, which is often the case after spending most of my hours of the day in studying and writing. Those are two endeavors that create a solitary existence. Solitary confinement, whether self-imposed or not is not a good thing for humans, or any social animal. Tonight was a beautiful night. Another beautiful, crystal clear evening for shorts and t-shirts, under a half moon. I put the front and back flashers on while I was riding, trickier than you think, and then picked up the pace still on the sidewalk. I was across the street from the G Spot, which was closed at the time of this impulsive venture into the unknown. Of course, I knew exactly where I was going.

It wasn't a super busy night in Esquina, but busy enough to create a buzz in the air. And shortly, I'd have a buzz in my head. When I walked in, there were several open seats at the bar. I took one that put a beautiful woman and her scruffy boyfriend on my right, she next to me. Two seats to my left were vacated by a couple that paid their bill and left as I made myself comfortable at the bar. Ramon was working the other end of the bar. He's the friendly bear of a bartender I met last night. He's bigger than Jorge. Live music was pouring out of an acoustic guitar coming from the low stage set up in the dining room, back behind the bar. Before I could say *buenos noches* to anyone, Ramon was pouring out a bottle of Pacifico into the glass in front of me. Good bartenders always remember a customer's drink of choice. And hey, what are friends for! After that one quickly disappeared down my parched gullet, I ordered another Pacifico from another bartender who I recognized from another night but who's name I didn't know. Or didn't remember. Maybe Rodrigo. That sounds right. I'll have to ask him later when he's not in such great demand. Surfing highlights were running on the big screen at the end of the bar to my left. There is no TV at the end of the bar to my right. That's where the restaurant is. The surfing was mesmerizing but too much of a stretch for my neck. Directly in front of me, higher than the heads of the bar crew, was another big screen, this one featuring a pro basketball game which held no interest for me. Fine. I'm comfortable just looking around or looking at nothing but taking it all in.

That scruffy young guy to my right, one seat beyond the pretty girl next to me, was having trouble dealing with the peso conversion on his bill, clearly causing some confusion with the bartender. I intervened with an offer to help in my beginner's Spanish, directing my offer to the bartender. Rodrigo? Unlike Ramon, his English wasn't very good. I also offered my help to Mr. Scruffy. He accepted and promptly handed me the bill. I did the conversion for him from dollars into pesos, simple math, added a nice tip, handed it back to him and told him to sign it. His date smiled at me. Me, Mr. Helpful. Mr. Scruffy, who is a lot younger than me, maybe mid-thirties, got up and walked away. After ten minutes, it looked to me like he left, but if he did, he left his girl behind. She and I chatted to satisfy my curiosity on them, with way more curiosity in her. She was way too young for me, but that didn't stop me from chatting her up.

We did the introduction thing. Her name is Lindsey, a Canadian. She said she dropped in tonight, by herself, for a drink. She confessed that she just met the fellow who was on her right an hour ago. He bought her dinner at the bar, one for himself too. He paid the bill, which is where I came in, and then excused himself from the bar to go up to his hotel room to shower. Lindsey said he said he'd return. He'd be a fool not to return. If he didn't return, then I had a shot at being a fool. She was happy to wait for him and the fulfillment of his promise to take her out on the town tonight.

Lindsey told me her story, the abridged version; it's all we had time for. She and her boyfriend had been dating for the past ten years and, for the last three, they have been living a good life in his condo in Cabo. He was supposed to be her forever boyfriend. She told me that the relationship ended last week. Forever is never forever, but never say never. It was his call, but she didn't give me the reason. And I didn't ask. I just listened, something I'm getting better at. It hurt me to hear her say that she has been crying her eyes out all week. She's returning to Canada in two days. Tonight, she decided to take a break from tears and go out and have some fun on her own. When she finished confessing to that, her eyes started tearing up. We shared a minute of silence for her to regain her composure. She continued by telling me that she was on "a date tonight with herself." That's how her night out started, but now she was actually on a date, with someone else, Mr. Scruffy.

With only two more nights in Cabo, Lindsey wanted to get out and get on with being single again. She wanted to have fun, to bust out from a week of hurt. Her boyfriend, make that her ex-boyfriend, left town last week, leaving her by herself to figure out how to leave his condo in Cabo and get back to Canada. She surprised me when, out of the blue, she said she saw me on my bike this afternoon, describing the cruiser as a cool bike. Not the rider. It was me alright. She remembered my front wheel basket. A chick magnet? She was on her bike and asked if I saw her. I should have said yes.

Twice in the middle of our conversation she was interrupted by a man seated to my left, but who was actually behind me because I had my back to him while I was facing Lindsey. I was totally unaware that he was making faces at her and being obnoxious enough for her to call him on it, twice. She asked me if I knew him. I turned to look at him and immediately said No! I cringed upon seeing him, some seedy old man, three days of a beard on his face, wearing a grungy wife beater shirt and a pork pie hat. Ick. A loser. Maybe a sicko. I had never seen him before, but it only took me a minute to conclude he is a drunk. And a potential problem.

Did I say how pretty Lindsay is? She is a brunette with shiny chestnut hair flowing down to her shoulders. Her face is dominated by big brown eyes. It is a sweet face of innocence contrary to a curvaceous body that looked tantalizing in an airy white summer dress that fully exposed her porcelain shoulders and the kind of cleavage a man finds hard not to stare at. Believe me, it was hard. That, too. I could tell she was a little shy and unsure of her decision to take herself out on a date. After a couple of drinks, she must have gotten over her sorrow and loneliness because now she was no longer on her own.

Mr. Scruffy returned to her far side, not looking any fresher to me than when he left. But that's me talking. He took her by the hand and they walked away after she and I said goodnight to each other. As I watched her leave the restaurant, I reminded myself that getting back into the dating world is a real challenge, full of sadness and joy, but what's the alternative? Stay at home? Write a book? Study Spanish? Not bad choices, actually.

I spun in my seat and went back to facing forward in the bar when the sicko drunk on my left started saying stupid stuff to me about Lindsey. I ignored him until he turned on his iPhone flashlight and shined it in my face. I slid one seat to my right, the seat that Lindsey vacated. The drunk continued to harass me with inane comments, most of which I didn't understand because of he was slurring his speech. A minute was all I could take. I got up and discreetly went to the manager and complained.

The manager's name was Julio, a top-notch guy whose English was top notch as well. He said he'd toss the drunk, not exactly in those words, informing me at the same time that others had complained. Julio offered me a drink and a table in the dining room close to the music. For some reason, I didn't hesitate. He led me to a nice table for two, waved a server over who took my request for a Cuba Libre. Julio then thanked me, yes that's right, and excused himself to personally handle the situation. A real pro. First class guy.

When I finished my Cuba Libre, I ordered a second one along with a margherita pizza. One Cuba Libre was one more than I should have had, but two, that's mind-numbing for me. Literally and figuratively. Dinner and cocktails weren't part of the evening's plan, but I was enjoying myself and the ambience of the evening. I could see the moon through the panels of white fabric above me that floated on a wooden trellis. It was all very romantic, which is why the tables were occupied by couples.

The tranquility of the *al fresco* setting was suddenly interrupted by the crash and clatter of a champagne bucket and its empty bottle and spent ice tumbling to the floor. A customer caused the mishap. He stepped too closely to the empty table in front of me and accidentally kicked the bucket, literally, not figuratively. It created a mess, of course, spilling quite a bit of water onto the floor around me. Less than a minute later, a robust Mexican woman on staff mopped the mess up. As she finished, I tapped her arm, got her attention, and discreetly stuffed a fifty peso note into her hand and smiled. She was very surprised and very grateful, however small my gesture. Fifty pesos? That's two and half bucks. It's doesn't cost much in Mexico to play Mr. Big Tipper. After an hour at my exclusive party of one at a table for two at the very hip

Esquina's restaurant and bar, I left. I shouldn't have had the two Cuba Libres, but I had no regrets in devouring the margherita pizza with gustatory pleasure. Interesting night. I felt happy. I'm glad I didn't kick the bucket, literally and figuratively.

Esquina four nights in a row - Friday, March 10

I rode all over town in the hour after dusk, watching Cabo retailers ramp up for tonight's onslaught of college kids. It was still a little too early for the kids to be out but the town's eagerness to see the nightlife begin was palpable. I dropped in at CC to say hi to my crew, especially chat with Guillermo and Gabriel, and ordered a Pacifico. Nothing much was happening so I left after a half hour. I am almost always too tired to keep the Spanish going with my friends in the evenings. Tonight was no exception. I rarely stay more than an hour at CC in the evening, so my departure was par for the course. I said *buenas noches* to everyone I knew, which was everyone, and rode away.

I decided I'd have one more beer for the evening before calling it quits. Either The Cock or Esquina. Tonight, I wasn't feeling like The Cock. I just couldn't do another word in Spanish, however much I like José. Esquina it was. When I walked in, I was hopeful that I'd see Lindsey, but she wasn't there. It's her last night in Cabo. I wondered what she was doing. Besides being pretty, she was in a party mood, which to me, meant a couple of drinks together at the bar and nothing more than that. Which was fine, that's about as wild as I get in Cabo. In a funny way, I'll miss her. She was a good conversationalist, with great cleavage. Really, I would like to have continued our conversation. I was the only one with that fantasy. Comes with age. She leaves on Saturday so forget seeing her again.

Cabo Cantina lost Oliver - Saturday, March 11

I walked into CC just before the lunch hour crowd would show up. Said hi to Andres right off the bat and looked for his sidekick,

Oliver. No Oliver. I never see Andres without Oliver. For some reason, I think of Oliver and Andres as Laurel and Hardy, which will mean nothing to you if you're under sixty. Oliver is Andres' trainee. I asked Andres right away about the absence of Oliver before I filed a missing person's report. Oliver, Andres informed me, had his last day at CC yesterday. He quit for a trainee job at the Westin Resort, one of the fanciest resorts, about twenty minutes north of town. I enquired about details and learned he didn't quit for more money. In fact, Andres said they didn't offer him more. He didn't quit because its location is more convenient, it's not. It's a thirty-minute bus ride up the coast. He didn't quit because he wasn't happy. He loves the gang at CC. But he did quit for a good reason. He quit because the Westin offers an excellent training program that includes rigorous courses in English.

Being able to speak English is critical for any Mexican wanting to climb up the economic ladder. I get it. Oliver's English wasn't good and his progress was dependent on learning as you go, which can be a long, slow road. The Westin runs intensive classes and tests its trainees every day in English. Oliver could see the value in that, so he took the job. I'm sorry I didn't get to say goodbye to him, but I understand. I think it was the right call. I will miss my young friend. And teacher. And student.

Andres introduced me to Oliver's replacement, Fabian. Fabian is a very nice young man, very polite, and very young. Maybe nineteen. His English was very thin but Andres would help him with that. Fabian was thin too. String bean thin. He is as tall as me and half my weight. I guess that means you can think of me as a cucumber. But, please, not a gourd, which is interesting because the Spanish word for fat when describing a person is *gordo*. Close enough.

Getting hotter - Saturday, March 11

As the days go by faster and faster toward my departure day, I can tell that the mid-day temperatures are increasing with the passage of every few days. Week to week is definitely noticeable. I'm not sure I feel the difference in the night time temperatures, but definitely can feel the change in the afternoon temperatures. Of course, not a cloud in the sky, seems like it's been that way forever. Except for that freaky downpour, it's been like that every day here. Like, whatever, you know, like, you know whatever. Or something like that, but even more profound. Whatever.

The Chef's Special at Captain Tony's - Saturday, March 11

Today I tried something different for lunch or, more accurately, dunch. I just couldn't get myself to stay for lunch at CC. That stress induced weird feeling of pressure was still with me when I walked into CC. Instead of lunch at CC, I returned to the restaurant where I lunched with Stew and Londa a few weeks ago, where we had the kitchen clean and prepare the fish Stew and Londa caught that morning. That's right, Captain Tony's.

Like all the tiki restaurants on the marina Captain Tony's draws a lot of tourists, this one more than most. It's a lively place and it does have a reputation for good food. Not all marina places do. But food isn't the reason I walked in. Captain Tony's is located on an inside corner of the marina walk, right at the junction of two of the marina segments and a major pass-thru to the parking lots and shops in the center of town. It is a great place for people watching, none better in the marina, because no place has as many people walking by. I needed that kind of entertainment as weird as that sounds. It is creatively stimulating because of the constant shock value of the eclectic appearances of tourists. I took a front row seat, three feet above the fray.

I ordered a Pacifico and followed it up with an order of what the couple next to me was having. I said, I'll have what she's having, but no one got my humor. I bet her name is not Sally. She had the Chef's Special of the Day, a feast of seafood for two. It looked great, I don't see how I could have said no to it. So I didn't. I was hungry and the combination of sushi and sashimi on a massive serving plate for four looked delectable in all six of its forms. But wait, there's more! It was a huge serving dish, not just of sushi and sashimi, but King crab legs too, some grilled shrimp, and two cutlets of grilled snapper. Forty minutes later, I ate it all and washed it down with a second Pacifico. It cost me only thirty-five bucks, which was a big splurge for me but I rationalized it as a steal compared to what I'd pay in the States. Three times as much, at least. I concluded a binge was worth it, once in a while. And, of course, I was captivated every second by the non-stop parade of tourists that almost killed my appetite. Tourists seem to compete with each other on who can be a bigger slob. I guess it's that way these days, not like when I was a kid. I probably won't do Captain Tony's again, unless it's with Stew and Londa. The food was very appetizing. The people watching was very unappetizing. I won't do that again, not by myself.

Expectations are too high - Sunday, March 12

Today, I dropped by Cabo Cantina around noon. The place was busy and the guys were double timing it back and forth between the kitchen and tables. Ray was playing manager by being invisible in the corner with a watchful eye over the entire staff. He strolled over to my table and started up a conversation. A moment later Andres stepped out of the fray and up to my table too, asking what's up. I blurted out to both of them that my self-imposed expectations for speaking Spanish have been too great. It was my way of addressing my growing reluctance to show up at CC. I need to release some pressure, take some of the heat off myself. Ray and Andres are very sympathetic and take the time to remind me over and over, *poco a poco,* which I keep forgetting. Andres said the best way to learn Spanish is to just do it, don't go academic and start planning next stages. Just do it!

I hadn't forgotten that he ribbed me yesterday because I said I hadn't studied future tense conjugations so he wasn't allowed to quiz me on them. I told him that I'll start studying future tense verb forms tomorrow, in the future. I said that because sometimes I have to think so hard what to say that I wear myself out. Future tense wears me out. So does past tense. All tenses other than the present tense wear me out. I live in the now. Andres said a schedule for learning was not a good idea. He said it's best just to speak it as it happens. Yes, I said to him, I get it. That makes total sense, but in my head, I was thinking that might be easier said than done. Everything is that way.

By now I think of Andres as a true friend. He's always helping me and rooting me on to get past my frustrations. I believe he has my best interests in mind. I wish I could do something specific for him. I want to make some kind of gesture so he feels that I am his true friend. Can we be true friends to each given my three-month existence in Cabo? Of course, but whether or not that happens is hard to say. I can't help thinking about an old definition stuck in my head from years ago about a true friend. I think it's funny. Here goes. A friend will help you move; a true friend will help you move a body. That might be asking too much.

Another day at the beach - Sunday, March 12

Yes, Spring Break is well underway. You can't miss it. You see kids everywhere, mostly in bathing suits, during the day of course. It's been launched with a different and fresh rotation of students every week. To the moon. There could be no doubt about that as I walked down the beach, by Mango, through the throngs of thongs. The Mexicans do not call it Spring Break. They have a different name for it. They call it *Estudiantes*, which means "Students," but it is so dominated by college students that calling March's Spring Break simply "Students" is enough. Every Mexican worker in Cabo is familiar with that term at this time of the year and they know it's not referring to the neighbor's grade school children. These college students have an enormous impact on the local economy, even the ones with only a little money to spend. Of course, they're noticeable.

Some businesses need to make a lot of money during *Estudiantes* to reach their annual profit goals off the Break. Strike while the iron is hot motivates them to go all out to appeal to the kids. For some, it can even be a do or die situation depending on the crowds they get, or don't. Of course, not every business in the marina depends on the Break money. Ray told me that some restaurant managers say the destruction of their establishments in this crazy period isn't worth the business. It doesn't even have to be a horde of troublemakers; a few destructive students can wreck a place as much as a few dozen. Also, some managers don't like the intrusion of students because it can erode the loyalty of the regular, year-round customers. Of course, many establishments do whatever they can to appeal to the students, drunk or not. Ray and Guillermo told me on separate occasions that CC doesn't cater to students as customers, but they won't turn them down. Their preferred clientele is mostly middle aged, moneyed tourists. These are people that generally have a lot more money to spend than the students. They come for the drinks and, importantly, the food. Students come to drink, not eat.

I'm sure good behavior is a boundary that's easily crossed for many of these students. After all, the whole point of Spring Break is to misbehave. And if you ask the students directly, both genders, they'll tell you that the whole point is to have as much sex as possible. That's what I've been told. I kid you not. It's not shocking to me because I thought the was the whole point of life.

It is very difficult to see a connection between students here on Spring Break and the image in our minds of America's fine, young adults diligently studying on campuses everywhere and aspiring to success on their way to becoming future leaders of their communities or, maybe even the world. Since it is easy to state the obvious, I will. Two different worlds on and off campus, but the same folks.

I generally don't go to the beach, Break or not, but I can say Break time is a lot more interesting. The college girls on Medano Beach are not wearing much. I'd say less than I ever imagined possible. Most are wearing floss in the back of the bikinis to connect the three small triangles of material in the front. Eyepatch size triangles. Their parents couldn't possibly know. Regarding the bottom back half, picture a piece of floss worn around the waist, then picture another piece of floss going down from the middle back of that belt through the center of their buttocks, also known as their butt crack. This means that from the back, the girls look pretty much naked.

Curiously, powered by nature's DNA coding for the college species of humans, starting around one o'clock in the afternoon and for the next three hours, most of the students begin to wake up from the night before to begin the daily migration from their hotels to the beach. Once at the beach, the students begin serious mating rituals with heavy reliance on alcohol. They consume massive amounts of it. The subsequent behavior will require massive usage of various means of birth control, hoping, of course, that students today are more responsible than ever with this endeavor.

I'm in the middle of an interesting migration, as I see it through my own eyes as an amateur anthropologist. From hotels all around the downtown area, small groups of almost completely naked girls walk out of the hotel lobbies for the trek to Medano beach, specifically, to the restaurant Mango. None of them are wearing a wrap or shirt or cover up of any kind. Most are barefoot. This lack of accessories demonstrates a modicum of rational behavior because there is no place to stash that stuff upon arrival at Medano. And in many cases, hours later and after countless margaritas, no one would have a memory of where personal stuff was stashed anyhow. That means right after noon, beach-bound college girls are walking down every sidewalk, converging in greater and greater numbers after each block with other parades of beach-bound girls until you have a human river of hundreds of scantily clad college girls jamming the sidewalks. From about three blocks out from Mango, they merge into a single mass of flesh moving steadily to the beach like a pyroclastic flow. College males are intermingled into this women's march to the sea, of course, but they get very little attention, probably because they are wearing clothes.

In a semi-circle radius of six blocks from Mango, you have never seen so many doorsteps packed with Mexican men seated on each step in your life. I am sure the locals have a name for this annual mind-boggling ogling that occurs daily in March, other than *Estudiantes*. I just don't know what it is. Maybe the Mexican wives call it their version of March Madness. The men might call it the March of Heavenly Dreams, however that translates, or simply *loco hombres*. The only thing the wives privately say to each other is: I will kill him if I catch him sitting on a doorstep near Medano beach. As for me, I can't begin to say that in Spanish. I still have a lot to learn.

Yes, nearly naked young women. But what about the guys? Have we reached parity in our society in presentation of the male and female form to the public? Not by a long shot. The guys are wearing the same stuff they have always worn. For decades. Long shorts and scrubby t-shirts in two styles, sleeveless or tattered sleeves. This seems like some kind of gender inequality but I don't know what else to call it. You tell me. If equality was in play, the girls should be wearing cargo shorts and dirty t-shirts to the beach or the boys should be wearing nut bags only. Nut bags? You know what I mean. Other terms include marble sack, banana hammock, sausage sling, and the most outrageous in my humble opinion, boner suit. That last one may sound completely off the wall until you know that I heard about a college girl with a tattoo of two words on her stomach, just below her navel, with a tattooed arrow pointing downward. The two words? Boner Garage. Who says tattoos can't be classy!

Hey, it's *Estudiantes* month here in Cabo, which means no rules, anything and everything ludicrous and lascivious applies, so back off. Kids are just letting off a little steam after working really hard for months to get that 4.0 grade average for a future in medical school. What is regarded as proper attire for the beach, which is virtually no attire, is also what I have seen on women short-cutting through the bar area at Esquina to get to the Bahia hotel lobby entrance on the other end from the front door. The parade of young ladies makes a beer at the bar worth every *peso*. Shirtless guys in shorts cut through the bar too, but I don't notice them.

These cats are not cool - Sunday, March 12

The nocturnal screaming cats are back. There is nothing I can do about this audio irritation. It has been going on every night for a week. The screaming occurs late enough to wake me from a deep slumber, which puts it somewhere near four in the morning. Martina would say I have a bad conscience, but I really don't think it's that. More likely, it's a bad cat. Even so, it is not a call to action. There's nothing I can do about this cat-astrophe. I don't know exactly where those cats are but my best guess is right outside each of my windows. After some time, maybe ten minutes, I fell back to sleep, helpless about doing anything about it. Martina mentioned the screaming cats bothered her, too, a few days ago in passing. Now I know I am not the only one sitting up in bed at three in the morning. That wouldn't happen if she didn't have a bad conscience, which is what I say to her. Sometimes the cats wake me up at three but only for twenty minutes. At four that insane barking dog across the parking lot takes over, but only for twenty minutes. At five the screaming cats are back at it. And, yes, around six the dog jumps in again. Instead of jumping in, I wish the dog would jump out, out the window. Sorry, I know, that's not nice. I only wish the best for him. And for me. Peace and love, too.

Two grilled fish tacos at Gardenias - Monday, March 13

I cruise past Gardenias just about every day and my drop-in frequency for lunch is about every other day. It has become my go-to place for lunch, which, for me, isn't really the lunch hour, per se. Lunch hour at Gardenias starts about noon and the place is quickly packed by tourists who love really good food at a really good price. My lunch hour at Gardenias is about three in the afternoon, well after the noon lunch craziness has subsided. Well after Gabriel has stopped sprinting from table to table to kitchen and back.

When I eat at Gardenias I almost always have two grilled shrimp tacos. I get to sit just about anywhere I want because usually only four or five tables are occupied at three o'clock. At this post-lunch hour, most of the customers are locals. Americans have moved on. Tourists have a schedule, I guess. Or Americans do. They like to eat at noon so they can be hungry for dinner at five. When I eat at three o'clock I often make that my last meal of the day, which is a good thing. I can't imagine how any gringo eating Mexican food three times a day doesn't go back to the States packing a lot of extra pounds. Just two meals a day could do that, pretty sure about that.

I only eat one Mexican meal a day, if I eat Mexican food at all in a typical day. Far more often than restaurant meals, I fix my meals at home.

I have simple tastes in food with a commitment to a healthy diet as much as possible. At least a relatively healthy diet compared to what the vast majority of Americans eat here and in the States. I know, I know, there's some argument against consuming eggs every day but I think of them as a valuable and simple source of protein. The shrimp and fish I order are always grilled, never fried. More protein. And no worries with double helpings of steamed vegetables every day. But, you got me on the alcohol, guilty!

I believe alcohol should be excluded from every diet if a person is truly in pursuit of a healthy diet. In the bigger picture, alcohol never made anyone's life better. But life aside, just with respect to diet, over-consumption of calories from alcohol can quickly make you fat. It's not because alcohol is transformed into sugar in your body, which it is – it's because of the way it is metabolized and stored as fat. Alcohol is more quickly stored as fat than even excess calories from sugar (carbohydrate), or from protein, or even from fat itself. Alcohol's conversion to sugar means a lot of sugar goes into your body whenever you drink alcohol. I drink it every day, not much, but at least a beer. I know sugar is the enemy, regardless of the delivery system. I know, too, cancer feeds on sugar. And sugar is bad in many other ways. My next big move up to a higher level in health is to eliminate alcohol consumption. I can do that, I know I can. That means that in the future, the memory of my last Pacifico, my last Cuba Libra, and my last margarita will be intrinsically tied in with my adventure in Cabo San Lucas. I can do that. I can quit. When I get back to the States.

<u>One beer at Esquina - Monday, March 13</u>

I showed up early at Esquina for cocktail hour. Said hi to Ramon. He knows me now. He knows I drink Pacifico. And Rodrigo. I know him by now. Two old ladies are seated at one end of the bar, the end closest to the front door. All the other barstools are empty. I took a seat at mid-bar, directly in front of the TV. It was broadcasting in untranslatable Spanish. Usually it's English. I ordered a Pacifico, my brand of choice for no reason that I can identify other than I like consistency in my life. That doesn't explain why I choose Pacifico over other brands. And, for the only reason of wanting to speak a little more Spanish with Ramon, I asked for a lime and a glass with ice with my beer. That's, *con lima y un vaso con hielo con mi cerveza*. Ramon double checked me and asked back, *con hielo*? Yeah, probably not many people order a glass of ice for their beer, but I was in the mood to say something in Spanish and that's what came into my head and out my mouth. He brought me a tall glass with ice in it. It foamed big time when I poured the beer over the ice. Had to wait for the head to clear. Not mine, the one in the glass. I sipped with a determination to hang for an hour with just one beer. I didn't want two, too much alcohol in the very recent past banished that possibility.

I sat at the bar flanked by empty stools for ten minutes, hardly enthralled with an NBA game on the TV above the bar bottles. I hate professional basketball except for the championship games. However, I like college hoops a lot. Especially this time of year. March Madness is underway in NCAA college basketball. After a few minutes of nursing my beer on the rocks, a nicely dressed, clean cut college kid plunked down on the stool next to me. Like me, he wanted to sit in front of the big screen. Right away he introduced himself as Tommy, a senior at TCU. That's Texas Christian University. He was here for *Estudiantes*. We chatted a couple of minutes before he asked me if I'd rather watch college hoops than an NBA game. "Definitely," was my reply. He said USC was playing Providence and it could be a good game. I was game, so I asked one of the young women assisting Ramon if she could change the TV channel, not exactly in those words. One minute later, the college game was on the tube. Tommy's parents went to USC, which explained his interest. We watched the game and we chatted on and off.

Tommy told me he bought a Spring Break package from a travel agency at his school. This was his last night. He said he paid eighteen hundred bucks for airfare, five nights in the tony Bahia Hotel, which is attached to the bar, and some organized parties with his fellow TCU students. It sounded steep to me, but what do I know. We covered a lot of topics quickly, including how cheap Mexico is right now for U.S. dollars. I asked him what a typical night was for him down here in the way of activities. Of course, there is no such thing as a typical night during Spring Break, so, dumb question. Nonetheless, he gave me some idea of his itinerary after raving about all the cool things to do in Cabo, including the Booze Cruise. I guess I missed that one.

Tommy's answer to his activity in a typical day was very revealing of life as a college kid on Spring Break in Cabo. He woke up every morning just before the morning ends, which probably would be one minute before noon. The afternoon is well spent at the beach, presumably with hundreds of college girls thinking they are in bathing suits instead of a geometry of three triangles connected by floss. But that's me talking. After quality beach time, he and his friends sought out great restaurant food and ordered huge amounts of food, like burrito appetizers with a 16-ounce steak and more drinks. I expected him to say he stuffed face every day at the two-buck taco stands lining the streets. He said great food can be had at an unbelievably low cost in good restaurants. He said the cost was about forty bucks a head with his voracious TCU buddies. This was the prelude to the real partying.

I'm not sure what goes on every hour of the day in the life of a college kid on Spring Break, but here are the broad strokes of activities after dinner. The party gets started around ten with an enormous amount of time committed to drinking in loud, raucous, jam-packed clubs loaded with strobe and neon lights in a large space with a huge variation in music played at the deafening level of decibels maxing out human tolerance. That goes on until about four in the morning with a string of clubs, sometimes as many as five or six in a night. He didn't say how much alcohol is consumed by his friends in that period because no one keeps track, but doctors would tell you that it was enough to interfere with every motor response a kid has. Me talking, with a vibrant imagination. Just before the sky shows any light on the eastern horizon, he and his pals and their newest girlfriends meet at a pre-designated spot on the beach to hang for two hours. Sometime after that, an early breakfast is scarfed up and followed by crashing in bed. Tommy said sleep wasn't a high priority this week, so no one was chasing it. Chasing girls was a high priority however. I asked about that endeavor, of course.

Since the topic was girls, my opening gambit was a stupid attempt to sound like I was cool. It didn't. It made me sound like a parent. I asked if it was true that a lot of sex was happening on the beach? He said, "Of course." He's a polite kid but I could see in his expression that I just asked the lamest question an old fart could ask. I countered with an attempt at sounding like I knew something about that from my own experience, which I really couldn't remember because it was over forty years ago. What exactly did I say? Oh, something like "Sex in the sand isn't always all that fun, you know, with sand getting everywhere, and I mean (pause) everywhere." That's me talking, Mr. Experience, but impressing no one. Tommy nodded, he understood, but he enlightened me by telling me that all the hotels and bars on the water leave their lounge chairs on the beach overnight. Everybody uses them. I thought, lucky everybody for that. And then I almost fell off my stool when he added, "Yeah, a lot of them are in use. It gets to be a busy scene. No sand that way." Wow, I thought, but said nothing. What could I say? Gee, that's clever? How 'bout this: Shucks, I wish I were in college? How 'bout nothing? I certainly could not say my Spring Breaks were pretty much the same. I couldn't say anything. Stunned, I looked back at the game on TV. USC was down by twelve mid-way in the first half. Maybe they'd make a great comeback. I'd say it's likely. Maybe I'll make a great comeback. I'd say not likely.

Thirty seconds later, Tommy's friend Austin joined us. Another polite kid. Tommy did the introduction properly, impressive. A few other guys showed up about that time. My conversation with Tommy was over. More introductions were not necessary; we both knew it. Great kid. I liked him, articulate and very polite. I paid for my beer and his, tossed in a couple bucks extra for a tip, shook Tommy's hand, wished him more fun, and I walked feeling really old. Bed sounded pretty good to me. Any why not? If I was lucky, it would only be eight o'clock by the time I got home. I was ready to climb into bed and when I did, I didn't have to worry about sand getting everywhere. And I mean everywhere.

The Booze Cruise - Tuesday, March 14

In a conversation, I had with some college kid at the bar in The Office, which is a bar next door to Mango, I asked him what was the most fun thing about Spring Break here in Cabo. That's my inquisitive self at work. He answered and I heard about the Booze Cruise for the second time this week. The first time from Tommy at Esquina yesterday. I think the kid thought I just climbed out from under a rock when I told him I hadn't heard of it. I then learned that it's an automatic part of every student's Spring Break experience in Cabo, maybe the highlight, and it's been a tradition in Cabo for years. Apparently, the Booze Cruise had become part of the Cabo lore over the years for every *estudiante* that picks Cabo as a place to go for Spring Break. The kid confessed to doing it yesterday and described it as, "Soooooo awesome, man." I made a mental note to google it. It's probably something I should know about in case I ever return to college and think about going to Cabo for Spring Break.

When I got back to my condo, I googled the Booze Cruise Cabo. Students are promised a lot for paying thirty-five bucks for two hours on a party boat, a price that includes seeing the sunset off El Arco. And maybe an onboard trip back in time to Sodom and Gomorrah. The online site I selected offered a link to a video of the party scene on the boat. The ad copy for the link said this is a must-see link so the viewer can get an idea of content that might be too shocking for them to participate in. In effect, it was a warning to mature adults that their attendance at this college ritual of drinking and debauchery was not a good idea. I clicked on it immediately, of course, to make sure it wasn't something that interested me.

My reaction to the online video of the Booze Cruise? OMG sums it up. I never sucked shots of tequila out of the navel of a nearly naked girl prostrate on a table, at least not with El Arco in the background. A lot of that happens at sea, and it's not sucking down shots just from naval cavities. I can say the footage of the "warning" is not x-rated but clearly it gives the viewer a good clue of what happens in Las Vegas. I mean what happens on the Booze Cruise. Either way, whatever happens stays there, though I doubt it it matters because everyone looks too drunk to remember anything. I think. Maybe that line is true only in Las Vegas. For years and years, I am sure the Booze Cruise is an experience college kids will want to share with their children and grandchildren.

Dinner at Solomon's Landing - Tuesday, March 14

Juan One and Juan Two, the two bartenders at Solomon's Landing. Me, by myself tonight, almost ten o'clock, same seat when I met Bob and Laura, in their honor. I missed them every time I passed the place. I had my usual two Pacificos and was lucky the kitchen was still open so I could have fried calamari and a ceviche crispy taco. Both to die for. After that, I swung by

Esquina but was in and out in less than a minute after seeing only college kids, which made the place feel like it was for kids only. Must have been getting late because not many in the over thirty crowd were hanging. No one in the over sixty crowd. Given that, I opted for some Spanish TV at my place. Or better, as I see it, hitting the hay. Can you tell I grew up on a farm in Wisconsin? And what exactly does it mean "hitting" the hay. I've heard of pitching the hay. Stacking the hay, yes. Harvesting the hay, yes. Bailing the hay, yes. But hitting it? Really? English is so interesting. I wonder if Spanish is the same, but I just can't see it. Yet.

Boat names - Tuesday, March 14

I have always loved looking at boats in marinas, all kinds of boats, not just the yachts and sport-fishing boats, sail too. The harbor slips here are full, so there is much to look at. Mostly yachts here, very few boats with a mast for a mainsail. A couple of catamarans for commercial use have masts but I've never seen them do anything but motor around, as one would expect, while carrying a boatload of tourists for the round trip to El Arco at dusk.

Here are some of the boat names I remember seeing. Sneak Attack, Go Fish, Carpe Diem, E-Z-rollin, Reel Therapy, Salsa, Mi Barco Su Barco, and moored next to each other were two fifty-foot yachts: The Wild Hooker and The Wildcatter. Is that a wild twosome? Is there such a thing having enough money for his and hers yachts? I'm betting the owners of those two boats have a lot of fun. My vivid imagination says she's his third wife. Or, maybe it is just a hook-up for a Cabo getaway? I expected to see a yacht in the next slip named Hanky Panky, but it wasn't there. Nor was Monkey Business. Remember that yacht? Remember Gary Hart? Never mind that, I'm just having fun with words. But I know Hanky Panky is somewhere out there!

In search of the source of my flat tires - Wednesday, March 15

Three weeks of testing my courage by riding in the middle of the frontage road paid off. I have not gotten a flat tire in weeks, not since the creation of my hypothesis that the thorns were on the shoulder of the frontage road. This result was enough to convince me that the challenge of identifying the area was met. I concluded the thorns are present somewhere in the chute. But where? I can't say. I still need to identify the specific source, more specific than just saying chute. Did I want to continue riding in the middle of the frontage road? I can easily say no to that! At that point, some really close-in work requiring scrutiny of the foliage on the shoulder might lead to the identification of the exact source of the thorns. The next few days would be interesting. I had to be mindful of traffic while scrutinizing every shrub on the roadside. Risky business. A thorny situation, if ever.

Return to the G Spot - Wednesday, March 15

Ten days have passed since my last visit to Guadalupana. Ten. The longest run of absenteeism since my inaugural visit. That means I haven't had a Cuba Libra in ten days, not at the G Spot anyway, which is my drink of choice there. I needed to go. I wanted to see my friends Pedro and Facundo so I rode in through the front double door, as usual, and took a quick right turn to my reserved parking space in the corner. As always, customers were scarce. Only one table was occupied, by four middle-aged men, and not one of them noticed a gringo ride a bicycle into the restaurant. It wasn't the kind of action they were used to, but they still didn't notice me. Facundo was tending bar and Pedro stood close to him but on the opposite side of the bar. Both look surprised, like maybe I was just an apparition, some kind of ghost status since my last drop-in. I approached the bar, expressing my happiness in seeing them again, the usual, *Que buena verte otra vez, mis amigos.* And it was true, it is always great to see them. They are truly my friends.

Both Facundo and Pedro gave me a stern look, for the first time ever. I noticed it right away, and knew why. Ten days is a long time for great friends to be out of touch. Then, they both broke into big smiles and welcomed me warmly with some hearty handshaking and some serious but friendly back slapping. True camaraderie. True *compadres*. I was their prodigal son. When I walked up to them, I was surprised over the sudden appearance of my own feelings of appreciation and, yes, joy over our reunion. I have gotten to know both men better than I ever could have imagined when I walked in that first time and sat down for dinner. Both said they had seen me ride past their door several times in the past ten days, as well as seeing my ride by on the sidewalk across the street. Remember, their front door is always open during business hours. Always. Once in a while when I rode past the G Spot just feet from their door, I glanced in and saw a half second of either Pedro or Facundo or both, but I didn't stop. I guess I was on the run, with stuff to do, and then suddenly ten days flew by.

Over the past couple of months, we repeatedly and affectionately referred to our threesome as *tres amigos*. The word *compadres* popped up all the time too. These terms of endearment make me feel good. These two have helped me hugely in my quest to learn Spanish. They are surprised, I think, that I have made so much progress since we met. In a way, I am too. It makes me feel happy. It also makes me feel sad because I know my departure date is looming and inevitable. They too are aware that the end is near. Like any true friends, our sadness will be shared. I know this is true. It occurred to me when I walked out that I would miss going to the G Spot, a lot. It became my neighborhood bar after all.

I feel the heat - Wednesday, March 15

This week, the middle week of March, the sun dialed it up a notch. I definitely feel the heat and it kicks in earlier in the day now. It hangs around a little longer at the end of the day, too. I have no doubt that this is the kind of sun that can really burn. The summer months must be insufferable. I made a mental reminder to not go outside without my broad brimmed sun hat. Any trip outdoors hatless would result in a scorched bald head within minutes. I am sure of that. I need the hat. I look kind of geeky in it, which is okay because I am kinda geeky. At times. I am here for only two more weeks. I bet I'll feel the sun getting hotter with the passage of every day. It hurts me to even think about the pain I've experienced in the past with a sunburned dome. Once it was so bad, blinking was painful.

Ocho is back! - Wednesday, March 15

Ocho is back! I hate it when he goes missing, this time his absence ran a full two weeks, at least. My missing pal has returned. Hooray! That makes me feel good. I don't know why it would. But it does. I love animals, all animals. I think it's cute that he is sneaks stray kernels of corn off the stove top, no worries, though I haven't seen that actually happen. Or eating bugs I cannot see. I'm just glad he's back. There's life in my condo besides me. I like that.

Right now, he's frozen on the white wall above the sink, two feet above the faucet, watching me. I approach him thinking maybe we could be closer than ever. He nixed that idea by suddenly scrambling up to the crease where the wall intersects the ceiling. That's higher than my eight-foot reach, but not by much. He must know my limitations because when I reach out to him, sometimes getting within a foot of his snout, he doesn't move. I won't push it. He clearly needs his space. Besides, I don't want to threaten him with any movement that's closer to him than that. I want him to feel at home. Because, in my mind, he is.

Another afternoon session with Jorge at CC - Wednesday, March 15

After one Pacifico at my regular table chatting away with Andres, I moved to the bar for a margarita chaser and the intent to share some deep thoughts with Jorge. I asked Andres to join us at the bar, though I didn't have to. We hang together wherever I sit. He knows I always like to have him at my side. He and I chatted some more as I dove into my margarita and reminded myself that Andres doesn't drink alcohol. That's okay, lately I've been drinking enough for the two of us. Halfway into the glass, Jorge had a break in a busy day and leaned into us. He wanted to know what's up. I found the words I needed to explain my predicament. I told them both that my expectations were too high at CC but not in play anywhere else. This made being anywhere else easier, less stressful, and, in a funny way, more fun. Without making a play on words, simply said, the bar was higher at CC and I was the one who set it that high, way too high, by the way. Jorge nodded and I knew he understood perfectly what I was saying. Andres got it, too, and told me it's not a good thing to expect so much of myself. I was off the charts on that. Once that was acknowledged, it was easier to deal with. Comments from both of them convinced me that my expectations were not only too high, but entirely foolish. Learning is a process and it takes years to learn a language, any language. There was nothing I could do but lighten up.

Andres and Jorge said all the other guys think it's great that I have been making real progress, truly a commendable effort but they all know that it would take years to be able to speak well enough to be totally at ease. And they're right. This was the conversation that made me believe that I am doing really well for the short time I've been here. Everyone else thought so too. I needed to hear that because my time in Cabo was running out. Only two weeks left! Andres and Jorge yanked my chain plenty of times, all in the name of fun, but on a more serious note they made me realize that I actually had learned a lot. They also reminded me that I didn't know much beyond saying *hola* when I first walked into CC in January. That put it all in perspective for me and with that, the cloud of my hugely unrealistic expectations disappeared altogether. Poof! Next year, we three agreed, will be another year of learning. As will the year after that. That's when I said to myself that I will be coming back to Cabo next winter to brush up on my Spanish, to see my teachers again, who are also my friends.

Eureka! The source of my flat tires! - Wednesday, March 15

Three days of scanning the frontage road's shoulder foliage for a thorn bush turned up nothing. It was on the fourth day that I nailed it, late in the day, just after rush hour. The source was a series of six small rose bushes, curbside, in the elbow of curve coming out of the frontage road. At the big intersection. Each rose bush was about a foot high, planted and irrigated by the city in a small space five feet beyond the end of the crosswalk, precisely where the road curves and becomes the frontage road. This was pre-frontage road territory. Pre-chute, but not by much. Those tiny thorns matched perfectly the same tiny thorns Fernando pulled out of my tires.

City beautification was the culprit. I over looked those tiny rose bushes in the past three days of my methodical search because why? Two reasons occurred to me. One, they are really small. Microscopic is the best way to say it. Two, they were easy to overlook because at that particular point I was looking beyond them for traffic on the frontage road that might take me out. A thin layer of dust and very fine gravel accumulated on the road in the elbow of the curve. In effect, this collection of debris was a sandbox full of thorns. It was a sandbox that I could have easily ridden through many times. And some of those times a thorn was driven into my tire eventually forcing a trip to Fernando's garage. That was a sand box I did not want to play in. Mystery solved. For future trips to Walmart I could ride safely and fearlessly along the shoulder for the entire distance mindful of not riding through that particular sandbox. I'm betting on no more flat tires. Well, maybe one more. Or two. The streets of Cabo have about one million sandboxes. All potentially lethal, I suppose, even the ones without rose bush thorns. Even so, I like to think that the likelihood of another flat tire, like the rose bush thorns, is microscopic. That's what I like to think.

Fernando gets the bad news - Wednesday, March 15

I seemed to have solved the flat tire problem with my discovery of the culprit rose bush thorns. I wanted to share the news with Fernando as soon as possible. I hadn't had a flat in at least a week, so it feels like it's been a long time since I've seen him. Since my last flat tire, I got into the habit of squeezing the cruiser's tires every morning before breakfast to check their air level. I always shared the good news with Ocho. I tell myself that makes him smile though he's so stoic in enduring my constant patter. I know his reaction wasn't any different when I put out a few words of frustration in the days of getting one flat tire after another. Still, we're close now. I know he feels my pain. He feels my joy too.

Besides sharing my triumph in my excellent detective work with Ocho, I wanted to let Fernando know the good news as well, of course. I will have to curb my enthusiasm because flat tires translated into income for him. I think of my flat tires as an American bonus for him. Out of the blue, my flat bicycle tires rained on him for eight weeks. Whenever he saw me ride or push the cruiser up his driveway, ka-ching! in his heart and a smile on his face. The smile was for the pleasure of my company, of course, not just the money, honey.

That's how the afternoon ended, with a bike ride to Fernando's place. When I rode up the driveway he was crouched over an old tire, as usual, making it look like a new tire by painting it with his special black goop. His son Ivan, who never talks to me, was crouched next to him. They both smiled big when I hailed them. I am sure they are amused upon seeing the big mouth, overly friendly, gringo with flat tires every week. Fernando stood up and welcomed me with a firm handshake and a warm smile. Ivan didn't move.

Fernando and I sincerely like each other, despite coming from such different worlds, or maybe because we are from such different worlds. All the creases in his face smiled too. I liked Fernando from the start and at times I wished I could show up on his driveway every day with a flat tire and leave him with a fat tip.

We have fun talking about different things in Spanish, like his family or his business. Our conversations are always short but they are always pleasant as well. I try to engage Ivan every time I see him. I always say the same Spanish words to Ivan, asking him every time if he preferred girls or computers. It made him laugh, but he never answered my question. For that one, his dad always jumped in and said, *Computadoras!* You could count on that. I think Fernando saw a future for his son and it wasn't in his garage shellacking old tires.

I delivered my good news to Fernando about finding the rose bushes that were the source of the thorns. My good news was bad news for him, but I had to let him know. I thanked him over and over for being *mi compadre*. I also told him that I would be returning to the States in two weeks. Maybe back next winter. I tried to give him some hope that I would return with a flat tire before I left. I stated that there are thorns and glass and all kinds of bad things in the streets of Cabo, so maybe I'd see him again. He said he hoped so, which I took in a good way. Fernando had become one of my friends in Mexico and I knew I would miss his congeniality as soon as I pedaled out of his driveway. I won't miss Ivan in any way. He's just a kid and while he rarely says anything to me, he always laughed with me. Or was it at me? Teenagers. Probably at me.

<u>Pizza at the bar at Esquina - Wednesday, March 15</u>

Dropped in on Esquina at the end of the day. I tossed down two very cold Pacificos and a spicy margherita pizza for two for my dinner. Dullsville this time. I was out by seven-thirty. I was pensive and didn't feel like talking to strangers, understandably so. Today I turned sixty-six. Turning sixty-six is no big deal, believe me, other than being thankful I haven't died of old age. Happy Birthday to me. I left in good spirits nonetheless. I thought a stopover at the G Spot would lift my spirits a bit. It was open for another hour. It was a good place to end the evening. I always learned things from Pedro and Facundo.

The usual at the G Spot - Wednesday, March 15

The G Spot closes at nine o'clock. I made it there with time to spare. Of course, with a couple of Pacificos in my very recent past I become fearless in chatting Pedro and Facundo up with some Spanish. They are always so welcoming and supportive of my efforts that walking into their place always gives me a lift to my spirits. I've been in Cabo for over two months and worked hard at learning Spanish but that doesn't mean that finding the courage to create a discourse in Spanish no longer takes courage. It takes lots of courage! My mantra for my drive to speak Spanish is always the same: I can do this. I can do this. I can do this. *Poco a poco!*

The more Spanish I learn, the more Spanish I have to learn because my conversational subjects get elevated into everyday life, well past the basic introductory stuff. My vocabulary has grown a lot though I struggle mightily with anything other than the present tense. I've learned a trick or two to get myself into the future, but conjugation is not part of that maneuver. My trick? I simply say up front "I am going" which is *Voy* immediately before the infinitive of whatever verb I have in mind. That way I don't have to know the future tense of whatever verb I have in mind. For example, I am going to eat. I am going to drink. I am going to buy. And on and on. Smart move. It works for me in French too. In fact, I learned that trick when I was living in France. It's a good trick.

I've said this before, the easiest atmosphere I've found myself in for learning Spanish is with the Lopez brothers. Walking into the G Spot is kind of like coming home, if that makes any sense. Of course, if I show up with any time left before closing time, Facundo puts a Cuba Libre on the bar for me before I park the cruiser in the usual corner. At closing time, which is pretty much nine sharp, Ron Rico's rum on top of my Pacificos always forces me to be extra careful crossing the busy boulevard to get to my condo in Coromuel. The brothers remind me to be extra careful too, always making sure that my bike's night lights front and back are on. I only have a couple of weeks ahead of me. I know I will miss these two men. They have been so kind to me.

Martina, again - Wednesday, March 15

Home at nine-thirty, relaxing after a fun day. My front door is open to the cool night air after a long hot day. I'm typing, my back to the door, and tired. Martina shows up on my threshold announcing she's on an errand, of course, this time to deliver some honey to a sick friend. I could use a little honey, myself. About five-foot-four. Good sense of humor. Bi-lingual. Nice looking. What else? Anyway, I closed our conversation with an offer for a cocktail on her return trip. She said, thanks but no, and disappeared. I couldn't offer wine or anything else. My liquor selection is very limited. Vodka or tequila. Limited mixers, very limited. Maybe we could have opted for shots of tequila. Wild behavior is more likely to come out of a tequila bottle than a vodka bottle. Everyone knows that. I actually don't like tequila, unless it's in a margarita, so shots weren't really a possibility for me, though they went down easy in La Paz! Maybe for Martina, but not me.

Fifteen minutes later, Martina reappeared at my open doorway on her return trip, this time on her way back up four flights of stairs to her place. She stepped into my place, like last time, and asked me if I could come upstairs and help her with her computer. She was having a problem with the software. That's one of those areas that I am totally incompetent in, an absolute nincompoop. I said "Yes, I could help." Then quickly followed it up with the truth and an apology and said, I was sorry but not true. I didn't know squat about computers. We said goodnight. What just transpired? I don't know, haven't a clue if it was something other than a request to help her with her computer. Life is strange sometimes. This was one of those times. However, you have to believe that the simplest answer is the correct answer. She wanted me to help her with her computer.

No such thing as hump day - Wednesday, Wednesday 15

Wednesday is traditionally known as hump day in the States because it is the mid-point, or the hump, of the traditional work week. There is nothing traditional about me. Since my schedule is my own and I report to no one, there is no middle of the week for me. The name of the day makes no difference to me. All the days and nights are the same to me in social value. There is no anticipation of a weekend or of any particular day because of the day. I never look forward to the weekend because I'm living in an endless weekend. Wednesday is no longer hump day, for me, because there is no longer a hump in my week. This also means that I no longer say TGIF because I am thankful for every day, not just Fridays. Today, I suppose I could say TGIW. Tomorrow I could TGIT. But none of those expressions will pass through my lips. Clearly, I lead a different life than most people. I cherish every day and I like them all. I might like my birthdays a little more than the other days. A celebration reaffirms that I am alive, which is a good thing.

CHAPTER ELEVEN

Week 11

Ocho and I surprised each other - Thursday, March 16

I was happy, as usual, to see Ocho, though this time he made me jump. A little jump, not out of my socks, I was already out of my socks. I'd say closer to being startled than airborne. This happened when I stepped into the shower and reached up to adjust the shower head. Ocho surprised me. I think he was sitting on it. I must have surprised him too because he dashed lickety-split up to the corner of the ceiling, well out of my reach, with surprising speed. A regular little green blur, he was. I said a few words to him, my attempt to sooth him and apologize for my sudden intrusion. I could see he was frozen in position, common enough, possibly awaiting my next move, which was to grab the soap, not him. He held his position. So we were both once again at ease.

If you are wondering, yes, I talk to him whenever I see him. Every time. I have no one else to talk to. We are roommates after all. We take showers together, so we should be cordial. At most, it's a short, one-way conversation, like an old married couple I suppose. I talk, he listens, without judgement. The staccato of my comments must be riveting because he never moves when I'm talking to him. However, he does move around quite a bit, just not when I'm around. I had never seen him in the bathroom before this morning. I suppose from now on, I should knock before entering.

La Playa - Thursday, March 16

I walked the beach behind Mango, again, something I haven't done much of lately. It's lunch time and the sun's high and its rays feel good at right angles with my shoulders. I feel out of place among the *estudiantes* and, almost, something akin to a dirty old man in that youthful crowd, packed like sardines on the beach, half scantily clad to a point that swim suits could not possibly get smaller. The other half with thigh length bathing suits and crappy wife beater t-shirts. The guys. Those poor girls, with options in men who are so poorly attired, they must have other criteria for selection. I walked fast to get through the crowd of insanity, suddenly not wanting to be there. With each step moving past the thongs of people and never more than a foot or two from an *estudiante*, I felt older and older. That wasn't my crowd, and it hasn't been for forty-five years. I wanted to get through it, to a part of the beach that was less populated, where I couldn't be mistaken for a grandfather looking for his misguided granddaughter. Hmmm. It would probably not be a good thing if a grandfather bumped into his granddaughter on this beach. True for parents, too.

Crowds aside, and once beyond them, my primary mission was to enjoy the beach. To connect with it through the soles of my feet. Medano is a nice sandy beach with soft, white sand. The lapping water is refreshing, which is to say it is a tad on the cool side, but it feels good once you get in. I did, once. Had to pee and was thankful I was not in the water close to the section of the beach where hundreds and hundreds of students had to pee at some point. Beyond the crowd, when I stepped into the surf, the waters of the Sea of Cortez felt truly refreshing.

All in all, I feel great. I lead a nice life in Cabo, no stress, no demands, no appointments, no meetings. Okay, maybe a little stress from my expectations to learn Spanish, but that stress was short-lived and now behind me. There's nothing else to stress about. However old I feel in the Spring Break crowd, I wouldn't want to be in that age group in this day and age. It is so different from when I was in my twenties that I can't begin to comprehend the demands and pressures those kids have. They deal with stuff that I didn't have to, at a much higher level, much more intense for what it is and the world it is in. A very high-tech world, way beyond anything I experienced in college. I can't describe it, but I just know that I am happy to be where I am in life, not doing much of anything while walking along a very nice beach and wondering about nothing in particular. After about an hour and the start of a bad sunburn on my shoulders I had enough of the great outdoors. It was time to go indoors and get something to eat. And a cold Pacifico.

The usual dilemma. I had to make up my mind on whether to order the grilled shrimp or the grilled fish at Gardenias for lunch. Grilled fish would be a nice change, but grilled shrimp was consistently delectable. Hmmmm. Shrimp or fish? That's a tough call. I'll have to think about that. Maybe I should consider the pros and cons of each, you know, do some kind of benefit-reward analysis. Maybe Gabriel will have some insight for me when I walk in. It would be good to have his opinion. This is going to be a tough decision, the toughest of the day for me. At least I'm getting it behind me relatively early in the day. My hunger couldn't wait until the afternoon. It was the tail end of another busy lunch hour at Gardenias but an open table was waiting for me in the back of the room, where I usually sit. When I sat down, the answer made itself clear. I ordered the grilled shrimp and the grilled fish.

Learning street talk at CC - Thursday, March 16

Mid-afternoon, the usual time I show up at Cabo Cantina. I feel a lot better about hanging out at CC again. That wave of self-imposed stress I was feeling for a couple of weeks seems to have passed after that heart to heart with Andres and Jorge. Pedro and Facundo helped, too. It's a huge burden off my shoulders. I'm having fun again. I am sure this condition happens to others, too. Learning a foreign language is tough, especially if you're older than ten. Especially if you're a lot older than ten. Working through the challenges is helpful. You know what they say, if it doesn't kill you, it makes you stronger.

Today, I learned how to swear in Spanish. I picked up four particularly nasty phrases, which I cannot of course repeat here. It all started when I had the CC guys write all the nasty stuff down in the back of *Spanish for Gringos*. This was a good idea because I could memorize it later. Immediacy isn't critical. Jorge was the ring leader on this. Several of the expressions have the word *madre* in them, the Spanish word for mother. That means if someone is yelling at you and you hear them say something about your mother, they're not complimenting her. Or you. Quite the opposite. I asked Guillermo why the word mother appeared so frequently when Mexicans swear. He said something like all Mexican boys have problems with their mothers. I laughed but thought maybe some of his explanation was lost on me in translation. In a wild guess, I'll say it might even have something to do with Mother Mary, you know, the virgin mother. The little boys probably swear over that possibility with frustration because there's no logic to a mother who is a virgin. Even little boys know that.

Of course, there are all kinds of Spanish swear words that I could not find in my tiny dictionary in *Spanish for Gringos*. And there are some fun things to say as well, which are a little off color. As is often the case with the colorful phraseology of Spanish, sentences can be made nastier or less nasty by the substitution of only one word. Jorge, who is always vigilant about educating me with the language of the streets, taught me a fun way to ask for a beer at a bar. I learned to say, *Quiero una buena cerveza fría, fría como nalga de penguino.* That translates into this: I would like a good, cold beer, cold as a penguin's butt. That's the tepid version of two other versions he taught me. The third version he warned me not to say in the company of women.

As I said, Jorge is the real instigator in my education with swearing. His vivaciousness never settles after he gets me to say stuff he taught me. Now, every time I order a Pacifico from him, I say, *Quiero una cerveza más fría, fría como nalga de un pingüino.* Or even what I think is a nastier version that goes like this, *Quiero una cerveza más fría que el culo de un pingüino*. We both smile over that. It's all about making progress with Spanish. Real Spanish. I tried that expression at Esquina on the bartender Rodrigo and it didn't go over so well. He shook his head and waved his finger at me indicating that the word *culo* was a little harsh for the clientele there. Rodrigo suggested I substitute *nalga* for *culo*. I think he was saying it's better for me to use the Spanish word for "butt" instead of the one for "ass." I'm not sure, but I think *culo* might even mean a-hole. If that, then I'll use *culo* only when ordering from Jorge. That would make Jorge laugh. Only at CC, never anywhere else. I don't want to get my ass kicked out of some fancy place for using an overtly offensive word. Context is everything, like in any language. Since I don't have a clue about context in Spanish or any idea of the nuances of Spanish, I probably shouldn't take many chances with iffy words. If *culo* isn't iffy, I don't know what is.

Clearly, I am learning all kinds of useful words in Spanish. Upon taking a closer look at *nalga* in *Spanish for Gringos*, I learned that the Spanish verb "to spank" is *nalgar;* some kind of connection, wouldn't you say? Nalgar el nalga which literally means to spank the butt. Interesting to know, maybe, but I'm not sure when I'd ever use that phrase. Maybe this learning could become more useful if I work those words into a sentence like *Quiero nalgar tu nalga,* which means, "I want to spank your butt." I still can't see how I'd ever use that.

<u>Lourdes was gone - Thursday, March 16</u>

I stopped at Esteban's after my Spanish lesson at CC to say hi to Hector. It turned out that he wasn't working then, but Saul was. Saul, who pronounces his name Sah-ool, was working really hard, putting in his twelve-hour days, he said, six days a week, like he always does. It doesn't take much to remind me that Mexicans are very hard workers. I am sorry they work so hard. I looked over Saul's shoulder, hoping to see Hector. Saul told me that it was Hector's day off. It was just Saul serving the customers, from eight in the morning till eight at night. The place wasn't crazy busy just then, nor is it ever. I could only see a few customers at that moment, on the patio. I saw no one at the tables inside. No sign of Lourdes either. I inquired about her hours, knowing that she was a night shifter. He said Lourdes wasn't there either. I asked if she was going to be in tonight. I wanted to know so I could avoid her by taking the long way home, the route around the back, past the soccer fields, through the busy intersection, the one that takes me to Walmart.

Saul told me that Lourdes quit Esteban's. He said she left for a better job, to work full time selling timeshares. I think that was a good move for her. I bet she could sell anything to just about any man. She was a babe, but all she did for me was to make me nervous over my ineptitude with Spanish. Why was that? I don't know, maybe my tongue stumbled over her beauty and that's the explanation. It's possible. Beauty can have a funny effect on men. I need to talk to a shrink for some insight why I get nervous around really beautiful women. I must be shallow.

This morning's ride - Friday, March 17

This morning I skipped my ride to Walmart. I had plenty of food in the refrigerator and with my time running out, I needed to reduce my freezer inventory to zero. Not wanting to lessen my usual workout on the cruiser, I did the circuit out to the entrance of the harbor and then back again through the center of town and past CC then up to Esteban's. Then I repeated the route. *El Centro* was very quiet with very little traffic this morning. Most tourists were still in bed even though it is already the ninth hour of this gorgeous day. Most tourists this month are students on Spring Break, so I expect they'll be in bed until about noon. The store owners were organizing their merchandise and, as always, acutely aware of wandering tourists as opportunities for a sale. Some called out to me. I yelled back, no thanks, not interested. *No gracias! No me interesa!*

There weren't many shoppers out and about this morning but there were some, mostly older couples, ambling or limping or suffering in a walk around town. Lack of exercise and a bad diet take a toll on older Americans. Eventually, many of them will pay a price for eating all the crappy, sugar-laden packaged food that fills the shelves of our supermarkets. As in Europe, the Americans on the streets are easy to identify; they are the overweight pedestrians, often overweight by more than a few pounds. Obese is more like it. This fact is the sad outcome of big food corporations spending billions of dollars in advertising their sugar boosted products in boxes and bottles and every other container. Fresh produce is often an incidental purchase in the States or, at best, a relatively small one. My guideline is simple: if it can be found in a package in a supermarket, you probably shouldn't eat it.

The downtown circuit is my usual exercise route. I do it daily. It presents several options once I looped through the marina. This time, coming out of *el centro* I bear right and head for a run past the best trio of beach bars: Mango, The Office, and Billygan's. I find that part of my ride stimulating because it's the only uphill workout I get, though it's only a gum drop hill. These are the three bars that comprise the epicenter of the drunk student population during the day. I don't know where the epicenter is at night because I'm not up at two in the morning. It's probably the club scene close to the marina. I learned from some conversations weeks ago that just before dawn, the epicenter shifts back to the beach, where indescribable behavior occurs on countless beachfront lounge chairs, one after the other, until the crack of dawn. I am not expecting to see any students on the beach at this hour of the day. Minutes later my expectation is verified. It is easy to see that there are very few tourists on the beach. Mostly, at that hour, beach life is comprised of restaurant and hotel workers scrambling everywhere to organize the layout of chairs and tables and line up the lounge chairs for the lunch crowd. I hope they wipe down every lounge chair. Could they possibly know what happens on those lounge chairs from four to five-thirty in the morning? Probably.

Oliver wants back in - Friday, March 17

When I walked into CC today I was pleasantly surprised when I bumped into Oliver. Of course, I was very happy to see him again. It had been two weeks since he left CC for the job at The Westin and I didn't get a chance to wish him luck before he left. We embraced as he too remembered that he didn't get a chance to say goodbye to me. I invited him to join me when I took a seat at my table. I wanted to hear about his new job.

Oliver said he wasn't happy at the Westin, and I wasn't happy to hear that. From what he said it was easy for me to discern that The Westin was a whole different *enchilada* than CC. It is a huge operation with hundreds of staffers and Oliver was just one in a million, but not in the good way. He felt a little lost in the crowd. I also learned that a lot of his time, something like three hours a day was spent in class learning to speak restaurant English. This part of the job was the reason he took it. He said the classes were difficult and every night after twelve hours of work for six days of the week at the resort he was given two hours of homework. Sounded pretty grueling to me, but I'm guessing the intense curriculum worked for those who applied themselves. Oliver didn't mind the classwork nor the homework. There was some other reason he didn't like his new job.

Oliver's problem with The Westin Resort was the absence of anything like the camaraderie he experienced at CC. He missed the guys and especially his mentor, Andres. I get it. I told him that I understood perfectly what he meant. And, I confirmed that CC is a special place. Hard work doesn't seem so hard when it feels like everyone you work with is family and the job is fun. With that structure, work becomes fun in the job despite its many challenges. I don't even work there and I'm family.

Oliver said he missed Andres most of all. I get that too. I've seen Andres give Oliver some tough love during on-the-job training, but it was delivered by Andres acting like an older, wiser brother. I understood Oliver's description. Andres is a hugely likable bear of a guy who really knows how to work with customers. Andres was like a big brother and now Oliver wanted back in the family. He told Andres as much and Andres told him to stick it out at The Westin. Work hard and learn and make the most of it, that's what Andres said. Maybe come back to Cabo Cantina someday. It was tough for Oliver to hear that because he so badly wanted back in. I think in his heart he knew it was good advice. I've never known Andres' advice to be off the mark. I don't know about being a big brother to me, my age trumps that possibility, but I am happy to think that Andres and I feel like brothers in our friendship. As the clocks ticks down to my departure from Cabo, I know I will miss him. It will be tough to say goodbye, especially for an old sentimental fool like me.

The marina cops don't bother me anymore - Saturday, March 18

I've been riding the sidewalk again, all around the harbor periphery. Not a single cop stops me. It's been several weeks, maybe more, so long ago that I can't remember. Maybe they've given up due to my persistence. Maybe they see me as a local now since they've seen me so many times that it's okay for me to be there. Maybe they are showing mercy because I am really slow and careful around pedestrians. For whatever reason, I'm glad I can once again cruise the marina sidewalk. The harbor is so much more enjoyable that way.

Weather - Saturday, March 18

Blustery this week, which means not much except for a little rattling of the palm fronds overhead. The daily temperatures continue their slow ascent. The forecasts say the week ahead will have daily highs in the mid-eighties. That's up fifteen degrees since January. Other than the heat, the forecast tells me to expect an unbroken and seemingly endless string of perfectly sunny days in the week ahead. And the week after that. Again, not a cloud in the forecast, or in the sky. I barely remember what a cloud looks like.

Okay, I'm clowning around a bit but here are some of my favorite lyrics made famous by Judy Collins, with a minor modification.

> Isn't it rich?
> Are we a pair?
> Me here at last on the ground,
> You in mid-air,
> Where are the clouds?
>
> Isn't it bliss?
> Don't you approve?
> One who keeps tearing around,
> One who can't move,
> Where are the clouds?
> There ought to be clouds.

Sunday lunch at CC - Saturday, March 18

I was comfortable again in my shoes, sitting at my usual table in CC, and exchanging a few words with Andres every time he had a little time between waiting on tables. It was a busy lunch hour so he and I didn't chat much, but like the old friends we've become, we didn't need to talk in order to enjoy each other's presence. He continues to be helpful in teaching me new words and working with me on syntax. Since we met, I bet he's scribbled on a hundred napkins for my enlightenment.

I hung out for a couple of hours, engrossed in basketball on TV, like many of the other patrons. The NCAA college basketball tournament was well underway and appropriately known as March Madness, just like Spring Break. At CC you would hardly know Spring Break is happening in Cabo. Very few students walk by CC, most are on the marina or the beach. I watched Wisconsin upset Villanova, last year's NCAA basketball champion. Having grown up in Wisconsin it was easy for me to root for the Badgers, so this time, my team won.

During the timeouts, I turned to the inside of the back cover of *Spanish for Gringos* and reviewed all the swear words I have been learning in the last two days. There are a lot. In the last two days, each waiter wrote down two or three of his favorites, which created quite a list. Everyone stopped by to review the latest list because it was so funny to see all that stuff that was being entered into my workbook. Everyone laughed. I did too, though of course I didn't understand what the entries really meant or how they fit into the culture. Andres and Jorge spent a little time, on and off, trying to explain the real meaning and background on these terms. I didn't understand everything they said, but I did understand that I needed to be careful which ones I used. Some could get me into real trouble if I said them to the wrong person. That would surely be worth a big laugh, especially if I got in a big fight, but I wouldn't be the person laughing.

Since I couldn't understand the precise meaning in all the phrases or the connotations I substituted the Spanish word *postre* for the nasty words. *Postre* means dessert and every time I substituted *postre* for a word I didn't know I got a good laugh from the guys, especially when I reacted to a nasty expression and then said I love dessert and sometimes I have a double order, things like that. Guy humor. I quickly discovered that I could get an even bigger laugh when I added *con crema*, which means "with cream." More laughter. Boys being boys. I am sure that much of what I was saying was totally nonsensical, but who cares. That I was making the effort and all of us were getting a laugh out of my words just added to our camaraderie and the fun of just being guys with a special friendship, our common denominator.

Saturday night at Esquina with Janelle and Susan - Saturday, March 18

I strolled into Esquina around eight, after locking the cruiser to my favorite lamppost. This time I entered the bar through the Bahia lobby entrance. I've been using that entrance lately because it gives me an easier blend into the crowd than the front door entrance. It also gives me a better vantage point on the seating at the bar because the hotel lobby is two steps higher than Esquina's bar. Tonight, I could see that there were no open seats at the bar but it was easy to identify the best prospect for a seat.

I walked up to the center of the bar and stood behind my best prospect for the next open seat. It was occupied by a very young woman, very young. She was slouching on her bar stool with both elbows on the bar and with nothing in front of her, not even a glass of water. I was hoping she was on her way out. Upon getting her attention, I asked her if she was coming or going, hoping for a "going" answer so I could sit there. I got neither. With what struck me as a great effort she replied, "Waiting, for a take-out pizza." I stepped back and hovered, wanting to see a waiter hand her a pizza box that very moment. No such luck. Too bad because her seat was centered on the TV over the bar, a seat I coveted as a solo person. Besides looking very pale, she was looking pretty lifeless, like a lump of a human torso resting on two very long, bare legs. Her short shorts made her legs look freakishly long and that's why I guessed they were longer than mine. She didn't move. Didn't even stir. Waiting. Waiting. Waiting. A real mannequin. I waited, impatiently while I was trying to project my impatience on to her, but she missed the vibe, or didn't care. She couldn't have been more than eighteen, probably a college kid on break, but maybe even younger, someone's teenage daughter dragged to Cabo with the parents. I was hoping in the name of politeness that she'd turn her seat over to a senior citizen, me. She didn't. I guess I'm not ready to play that card so I hovered some more in silence. Waiting. Waiting. Waiting. She was still the frontrunner for the first vacancy at the bar. I know because I was constantly scanning. Sometimes I have walked into Esquina and waited so long that I gave up and walked out. I was getting close to that point again.

Ramon, my new bartender friend, recognized my plight and the fact that she was depriving him of a paying customer's seat at the bar. Me. He asked her if she needed anything; in other words, implying that she order something at the bar or give the seat up. She glumly told him she was waiting for a pizza to go, impervious to his innuendo to vacate the seat. On the spot, he yelled to the kitchen for that pizza. I like sympathetic bartenders.

A very long two minutes later, a boxed pizza was delivered to the blonde still life. She stood up, quickly confirming that she was my height, and walked out expressionless. I couldn't get myself to say thanks. I sat down and Ramon immediately placed a Pacifico in front of me. I like responsive bartenders, especially if they are sympathetic. They get the biggest tips. The woman on my right, a basketball fan with her fellow fan husband on her other side were mesmerized by the TV action. Nonetheless, she broke her concentration to volunteer a comment about the recently departed tall blonde. "She's drunk and not feeling well. Couldn't talk." Sounded entirely plausible. I think it's called Spring Break Syndrome, but before I could come up with a witty retort, the woman was back into her game on the TV. It was a good game but Nevada, her team, just couldn't turn the corner to get a comeback victory. I ordered a second beer and fought off the temptation to order a margherita pizza. By the way, I caved to that very temptation last night, almost the same seat. I wasn't about to do it again; it went against my interests in eating well. A little voice in me said, eat your vegetables. My mom's voice?

Thirty-five minutes later, the deal was sealed: The Nevada team lost and the crestfallen couple on my left, vacated their seats. In less than ten seconds, a cute, snappy blonde who was a bit younger than me plunked down in the open seat next to me and said, "Hi, remember me?" Those are words out of a woman's lips that always terrify me. I drew a blank. She saw that the answer was no. My face was absent anything that could resemble recognition. My fear was that I was in danger of some kind of embarrassment, but don't ask me why. I guess it's in my history. I knew I hadn't slept with her, that's for sure. Having conveyed that I had no memory of her, she quickly added, "You're the guy on the bike, right?" Another question that gave me pause. More clarification from her followed. "We talked about skimpy bikinis in front of Mango this afternoon. I was with my sister." Yes! It all came back to me, though I don't know if the trigger was skimpy bikinis or

Mango or something else. No matter, I did remember chatting with two women on bikes, both wearing disguises aided by sunglasses and sun hats and neither had any resemblance to the good-looking woman in front of me. But I perked up and exclaimed to her that I remembered her, which had become the truth.

Anyway, our conversation took off like an old barn on fire. We clicked. Ten minutes later her sister, who was hanging at the end of the bar, reluctantly joined us, saying she was fine standing between and behind us. Janelle, the snappy blonde, who had become my best friend in ten minutes was an extrovert. In sharp contrast, her sister, Susan was an introvert. I can be both, so we all got along fine.

We three actually had a lively conversation all around, mostly because Janelle did everything she could to suck sister Susan into our whirlpool of conversation. I learned that Janelle has been happily married for twenty years. Susan, about ten years younger than me, had never married. Well good, I thought to myself, we got that out of the way, though I was hoping for the reverse. I said I was single, which made Janelle very happy because right away she figured Susan and I would get along just fine. I didn't see that as a possibility but said nothing and showed no inclination of interest beyond the conversation we were having. It was a relationship she was promoting with unabashed enthusiasm, like one could expect from a wing man, which she obviously wasn't. Susan and I got along just fine after hard work on Janelle's part, but not like a barn on fire. No sign of smoldering either. No smoke, so no fire.

For thirty minutes the conversation, facilitated by Janelle, focused on how perfect Susan and I were for each other. However untrue that was, it gave us some great fodder for mirth and merriment and harmless fringe flirting. Janelle was really working it. Our trio's second hour was just as lively but now beyond anyone's imagination that Susan and I would become an item. We got past that, thankfully. Two hours was fine. Janelle and I continued with our rapport but I didn't need another beer and conversation was getting thin, from fatigue. Also, Susan was sucking the air out of the room. I wanted to go home. We three had fun so our goodbyes were really chummy. That's Janelle doing that, taking one more shot at fixing us up. Maybe we three will see each other at the bar tomorrow night. I told them I'd be there. I knew that the possibility of my attendance was very likely because I've been going to Esquina almost every night for the past ten days. I'd enjoy continuing the conversation with Janelle. Not so much Susan.

The gecko gets intimate - Sunday, March 19

I don't see Ocho every day but maybe every other day of this week, so I know he's around. I saw him this morning when I woke up. He was not missing a leg or the tip of his tail, a good sign. He was above the bedroom door, exactly where I first saw him two months ago. As usual, he's motionless on the wall and looking at me. By now, he knows I won't approach him. He has known that for quite a while, which is good. I want him to feel safe around me. Whenever I see him I send him good vibes as I am happy to share the bedroom or any other room in the condo. Maybe he roams the bedroom when I'm asleep. I'm not sure how he feels about me so I can't be sure what he does. Maybe he isn't a he. Maybe he's a she. Ocho could be Ocha. Yes? How would I know the truth? In this case, the truth doesn't matter. We're tight regardless of which way my roommate leans.

The weather is changing - Sunday, March 19

When I stepped out of my condo this morning for the first time, which was around ten, I noticed the total absence of a blue sky. That was strange indeed. With virtually no departure from clear blue skies for two months, the dim on the day was noticeable. And a surprise because it was not in the forecast. The bright gray ceiling was heavily back lit so I knew the sun would be back within an hour or two. I also noticed in the past week that the afternoon temperatures were getting a wee bit warmer. I also noticed that more of the pool area was washed by sunshine, quite a bit more than when I arrived eleven weeks ago. This was good. To me this meant that the pool might actually be warming up, maybe enough for me to jump in. It would be the first time. I should do that before I leave Cabo. It seems funny to me that I haven't. The cruiser went in the pool once, to get a bath. No one caught me.

Sunday night at Esquina - Sunday, March 19

I'm a little surprised at my consistency with Esquina at night. It has become my go-to place for night life. The G Spot is my go-to place as the last stop of the day, if it's before nine. I always enjoyed seeing Pedro and Facundo. But Esquina is a very different kind of place. For one thing, I don't have the bond with the bartenders that I do with the Lopez brothers, the latter is very special time with my compadres. It is a full-blown hour or, sometimes two hours of Spanish only. I love those two. We could not have become friends unless they decided to put up with the gringo who rode his bike through the front doorway, right into their restaurant. It's on the opposite end of the spectrum from the Esquina experience.

Esquina may be the coolest bar in Cabo, cool because of its draw on sophisticated Americans. Like me. Kidding. For me, it's not really a leap into a Spanish speaking opportunity. I don't have any real connections with the staff. When people ask me about it I describe it as the closest thing in Cabo to a Los Angeles bar. I'm not sure what exactly that means, but they get it. I never get push-back on the concept. It is also a lively place for great conversations with people, but not, as I said, bartenders or waiters. The customers are often interesting, well-educated, and well-traveled. In other words, the money crowd. I don't know where else to find that profile in Cabo.

Tonight, I bumped into Janelle and Susan who I met the night before. They dropped in for a drink a half hour before my arrival and they said were close to leaving, but a glance at their drinks told me not that close. Makes me say the glass is half full when talking to Janelle and half empty when talking to Susan. They said they still had a lot of packing for their early morning departure back to the States. I wondered in my head how that could take more than a few minutes, but it was pointless to ask as they were determined to leave. I wished them well and moved down the bar a bit to grab an open stool. Halfway into my Pacifico I watched them get up, leave the bar, and disappear into the hotel lobby. I guess they were staying at The Bahia, of course. Maybe next time I'll stay there just because it's so close to Esquina. Maybe. And why not, I practically live in Esquina now.

When one door closes another one opens, so it is said. Janelle and Susan walked out just as Cindy walked in and up to me. She probably wanted to help me close my mouth. It was agape from the moment I laid eyes on her. She was with a well-heeled couple who followed her into the melee. I was in the center of the melee which is the only reason I could think of for why she'd say hi to me. Maybe she got have me confused with someone else but didn't realize her mistake until after we said hi to each other.

I've been confused with a lot of people over the years, for a while it was pro golfer Tom Weiskopf, though he's ten years older. His best years were in the seventies. Maybe mine, too. Also, the actor Bruce Dern, but that was really long ago; he's eighty now. Even the musician James Taylor who is only a few years older than me. The personality that gets me a mistaken identity most often is California's governor Jerry Brown. Five years ago, when I visited San Francisco, dozens of people said things to me like "Hi Governor" as I walked down the sidewalk. In those days, I had a crown of short salt and pepper hair. Now I am sporting the shaved head look. I think it's my bald head and my dark eyes, mostly my bald head, that drives the perceptions of mistaken identity.

Oh, also, forty years ago I was arrested by the FBI because my twin sister identified me in a photo showing an armed man robbing a bank teller. He was my physical double. How they found me and finger printed me is a long story, too long. It's a story I don't have time to tell. Basically, as I see it, in my age group, a lot of bald guys resemble each other. The tennis player Andy Murray could have been my twin if I pulled out a photo of me when I was his age now, on my way to losing my hair, like Andy now.

But I digress. It only took another few seconds to solve my personal mystery with Cindy's choice of me as a person to say hello to. A glance at the bar scene underway gave me the answer. The place was crammed with people, too many for her and her two friends to move any further into the bar room. Their three-person party got stuck in traffic right next to me, when I was facing more or less out and surveying the bar room. By the way, bar room is actually one word, barroom, but I think it looks so stupid as one word that I use two.

I'm glad I solved the "Why me?" mystery because Cindy is striking in looks. She is very tall, very thin, and very busty. Some could simply say she is a beautiful blue-eyed blonde with looks made to order for every modeling catalogue in the world. She could have any man she wanted and she surely wouldn't have picked me, thus the mystery why she did. Now, it's no longer a mystery. I was standing at her dead-end in the bar, which is an interesting metaphor. Putting aside the prejudices and stereotypes that come with looks, in fifteen minutes of conversation with her I learned she is a sweet, interesting mother of four children who works hard for disadvantaged people in Los Angeles. She was in Cabo as a houseguest of a big, handsome, strapping guy named Craig, who was standing behind her talking to the woman that he walked in with on his arm. They were busy in their own conversation. Cindy was his friend. She said she was tagging along with Craig and his very low key, but very pretty girlfriend named Jennifer. Craig and Jennifer finally interrupted us. They wanted drinks. Cindy did the introductions and I got Ramon's attention for them. We all chit-chatted but I could tell it was just superficial stuff and nothing more would come of it that could come of it in fifteen minutes of a superficial conversation. They moved on the only way they could. They took a U-turn which is the only way to escape a dead-end.

The revolving door of bar characters turned once more and my next conversation was with a very attractive brunette, in her mid-thirties, wearing a very big rock on her wedding finger. She gave me a great smile just before she walked up to me. I read it as I am Mr. Right, but of course I read it wrong. I couldn't miss the sparkle of her very big diamond wedding ring. Or her eyes. Out of habit, I guess I looked at her ring finger right away to determine her status. The ring certainly caught my eye. I wasn't sure what to make of this move but I'm sure I'd find out shortly. I never fool around with married women, so her ring was the green light for some harmless flirting if we got past introductions, but nothing beyond that. Her name is Kristina. We exchanged basics in a matter of minutes. She is from Atlanta, a serious believer in God, here for a long wives' getaway weekend. We both knew nothing beyond a conversation could come of this so we got on famously right from the start. Compliments were traded and bonding was easy. God was the great divider, though Kristina tried to convert me.

Kristina sells anti-aging products. When she told me she thought I was fifty years old she had me eating out of the palm of her hand, so of course I liked her, not just because of the babe she was. I would have said that about her regardless of her compliment or the number of Pacificos I already downed in the past hour and a half. I was on number four, topping out, when she and I met. We spent the next thirty minutes talking about the importance of nutrition in skin care. She knew a lot about nutrition. I like to talk about nutrition, so we had a good connection. It's one of my favorite topics, ever since my mom explained to me, when I was very young, that we are what we eat. I wonder if that also means we are what we drink. That would make me a brewery. Probably, but I didn't want to think about that because of my investment in The Pacifico Brewing Company. I was little buzzed. It doesn't take much. Kristina and I had a lot of fun and some fantasies too, I'm sure but we didn't share them. It was time for me to make my move. I did. I told her it was a pleasure talking to her but it was time for me to go home. That was my move. What other move was there?

I unhitched the cruiser from the lamp post, mounted her, the cruiser, not Kristina, and then shot down the gum drop hill that Esquina sits atop. As I rocketed through the intersection at the bottom of the hill I yelled José! I could see him behind the bar at The Cock Cantina. I am sure I looked like a comet whizzing past. Well, that's how I felt. He saw me and waved. So did his two barfly friends, Sergio and Arturo, both hanging at the inside end as usual. They know my yell, too. I was moving fast with the momentum of a steep hill behind me. The cruiser was smooth and programmed to avoid the potholes, which it did with ease as it cut through the cool night air, fully streamlined for virtually no resistance. I got up to max warp speed two before laying in the reverse thrusters for modest de-acceleration as I re-entered civilization in anti-collision mode. When I re-entered, people everywhere were overflowing from packed bars onto the sidewalks. Music reverberated out of every open door. Moonlight lit everything up. Life was good and I was bombed. It was too late for a night cap at The G Spot, thank god, so I put the cruiser on auto-pilot and told her to take me home.

On the marina walkway - Monday, March 20

Mid-afternoon. Monday. My eleventh week in Cabo, second to last, makes me marvel at how fast time flies. I was riding my cruiser slowly around the uncrowded marina sidewalk. I passed two security cops on the same leg where the cops booted me and my cruiser from the marina seven weeks ago. I said, *buenas tardes* to both and they responded with the same to me with a smile. They showed no inclination to stop me from riding. No frowns, no nothing, *nada*. These days I am prone to push the cruiser on the walkway because it is usually crowded with students, but, lately, a couple of times I tested the waters by mounting up in a low density stretch and didn't get busted. Maybe different rules with Spring Break are in play. Maybe different cops. Maybe they are so busy watching the bikinis walk up and down the marina sidewalk they don't see me.

I turned the corner to go down the barren segment of the marina that hosts the Gray Ghost, always the least populated leg of the seven legs. It's kind of the divider between two busy halves of the yacht basin. Just out of my turn onto the run past the Gray Ghost, a bikini was sitting in the middle of the sidewalk twenty feet in front me, with a college coed in it. A very cute coed was in it demonstrating what you could call almost total exposure. She was sitting Indian style with a cop standing a few feet away, hovering over her. She was gently rocking a bit, but only a little, tiny bit. Hardly discernible. My first thought? I was thinking she was going to get the bottom half of her white string ensemble dirty from sitting there, but then I realized there was no material touching the ground. She wore an itsy bitsy, teeny weeny bikini, that is what she wore. Sitting in the middle of the sidewalk, couldn't be good. My second thought? Why was she sitting there? A few seconds later, I realized, too, she was sitting on the sidewalk by herself, with no friends in sight. Why this situation? Her long straight, chestnut hair was flowing in tangles over her shoulders. With her head upturned, she was looking a little disheveled while she was talking to the security cop standing four feet from her. He was close but not too close, as if she were a snake. My third thought? OMG she's too drunk to stand up. And then the scenario became clear. I surmised the cop was too nervous to lift her to her feet. It was a touchy situation, literally and figuratively. Too touchy for him to put his hands in position to pick up a nearly naked girl and hold her in his arms, which is probably why he was just standing there, doing nothing but fantasizing. I don't know. More likely, he was waiting for reinforcements, which I knew were nearby because I passed them moments ago, right around the bend and they were heading this way. I guess it's easier for three or four cops to support a nearly naked coed than one cop. Maybe a stretcher would be the most appropriate way to do it, and a blanket to give her a little cover, a thought that emanated from my quirky brain.

The cop standing over her was clearly uncomfortable, but not at a loss for words as he spoke into his lapel-mounted walkie-talkie. I slowly glided by and turned in a few circles within hearing range. I don't know what he said into it, but it was probably telling the cavalry to hurry up. I heard in his voice a tone of urgency. Or was it fear? Because maybe this scene would jeopardize his standing with the force. The girl, however, was in no hurry, apparently quite comfortable sitting on concrete and did not appear to be in distress. There wasn't anything I could do, of course. I kept my glide on, not wanting to be accused of rubbernecking, which sounds bad enough.

<u>Monday night at Esquina- Monday, March 20</u>

Spent twenty minutes in Esquina tonight. Didn't want to make a night of it. I was slipping a bit on my nighttime studies with Spanish and wanted to re-commit to an hour every night. I wasn't there long, but long enough for one Pacifico and one very interesting conversation with two women, Felice and Rebecca. Friends, probably in their late forties. Both are good-looking blondes, one well connected socially in Los Angeles and the other out of the East Coast. They are also very interesting and funny. Which makes them very attractive in my eyes. They are here for a long weekend of fun, a reunion of sorts, an annual thing that goes back to the days when they met in college.

In the course of our conversation, the La Paz beaches came up. Felice and Rebecca drove up there yesterday on a day trip. They didn't like Balandra. Felice described it as stark and boring. I can see how that is true when the tide has sucked the water out to sea.

Rebecca said that Felice ribbed her the whole way for excessive speeding on the Mexican highway. They joked about the perils of speeding on those roads, and in particular the risk of getting a speeding ticket because, Rebecca said, neither one of them wanted to give a blow job to a *Federale*. I had to laugh at that, too. Coarse, of course, but I wondered if there was any truth in that scenario. It was funny. I've heard of things like that happening in Mexico. In the States, too.

I finished my Pacifico and treated Felice and Rebecca to a drink. They ordered their second Gray Goose martinis, with a twist. When I got the bill, I was shaken and stirred. Since I only drink beer whenever I'm there I forget how expensive cocktails are in Esquina. The atmosphere matches up with Los Angles nicely, so do the prices.

We three agreed to keep in touch when we returned to the States. It's the thing to say, you know, the usual when a connection is made, but rarely does anyone follow up on it. But I confess, I wouldn't mind being in touch with these two women. They were very funny and great conversationalists. And I liked their style. I rode home on the cruiser into a warm breeze, under a beautiful sky that was black and full of shining stars. I was good for about another hour, which I would dedicate to *Spanish for Gringos* in my condo. I wondered if Ocho was missing me. Maybe he was still out on the town. I never know. He is so unpredictable. Like life.

Olivia - Tuesday, March 21

I have been so good about developing friendships with the locals in Cabo. It doesn't really take any effort because the inhabitants of this tourist haven are generally very friendly in every way imaginable. I can easily recall the fine lunch I had somewhere off the edge of the commercial district under a shaded tree in a quiet neighborhood at a table on the side of a trailer kitchen run by an old lady. That old lady was Olivia, the ancient who gave me a heaping plate of great traditional Mexican home cooked food, what the Mexicans call *comida corrida*. She gave me the gift of two hours of a terrifically delightful conversation in which neither of us were intimidated by a language barrier. I left her that afternoon with a great experience, satiated and content, thinking I'd see her again, probably on a regular basis. I liked her.

I am surprised I haven't seen Olivia since our first meeting. I rode my bike past her property last week and there was no sign of her. Her outdoor *cocina* was locked up and the yard was unkempt, noticeably worse than before. Two white plastic tables were overturned on the ground by a stack of matching chairs. I moved on. I hope she's okay. She was very old. Very. And I feel bad that I didn't spend more time with her.

The G Spot for the last stop of the week - Tuesday, March 21

Once again almost for the last time, I rode the cruiser right through The G Spot's open double doors, the usual mode of entry. I parked the cruiser in the usual corner, dismounted and turned off my flashing lights, front and back. Two tables were busy, the usual. Pedro was sitting at a table, watching a soccer game on TV, sometimes the usual. I called out a loud greeting to Pedro and Fecundo, the usual, which is, *Que bueno verte otra vez!* Good to see you again! What was unusual was that a customer was talking to Fecundo at the bar. By the time I got to the bar, Pedro was up and made it a foursome. We three are always happy to see each other, it's almost mayhem and certainly laughter, like the laughter that comes when old friends reunite after a long time. For us, this is the way it is every time I ride into the G Spot.

The fourth man was Umberto, an old friend of my two friends, which makes him a friend of mine. That makes sense to me. We four immediately launched into a fun yakkity-yak-yak conversation, all in Spanish, of course. Me mostly laughing my way past my ineptitude with Spanish. Actually, Fecundo said I was doing really well, but what are friends for! I like Umberto right off the bat. Casual, refined, intellectual, and out-going gave me the impression right away that he was an educated person. Umberto was very inquisitive from the start and willing to put up with my Spanish. And, me being anxious to try my Spanish out in front of my two old friends. I learned he is a veterinarian, which was great because I know the names of all kinds of animals. I asked what he does for his most frequent patients, which are dogs, cats, and horses. *Perros, gatos, y caballos.* I told Umberto that I like to come to The G Spot for dinner because the elephant burgers are really good. So are the giraffe burgers. That got all of us laughing. I knew it would. Pedro, Facundo, and I never tire of that. I asked

Umberto if had any elephants or giraffes come into the office lately. We all laughed over my silliness but he demonstrated obvious skills in talking about elephants and giraffes. I know the words for big, tall, heavy, all kinds of adjectives that fit those creatures. Pedro and Facundo always get a good laugh over those big animals. I kidded them about that one night and we three have never forgotten to laugh every time one of us brings it up, which is just about every visit.

I don't know how it happened, but suddenly an hour passed and I had to go home. I didn't even have my usual Cuba Libre. I think I was a bit tired from some restless sleep the previous night. Or, it is possible that such intense concentration in my effort to understand and speak Spanish wore me out. Probably the latter. We had a lot to talk about. Remember, the first time I met them I didn't know more than thirty words, if that. I told Umberto it was a pleasure meeting him and thanked him for the encouragement with my Spanish. It sure was a fun evening. As I rode out the front doors, Pedro yelled at me to turn on my flashing lights. I stopped outside the door and turned them on and then proceeded.

My condo was only two blocks up the street. It was also across the street, a street that is a major boulevard going in and out of Cabo. I always had to be careful getting across it, especially at night. It'd be a rotten deal if I got hit by a car so close to my departure date. That stupid thought aside, I was happy and feeling good. My friendship with Pedro and Facundo means a lot to me. Spending time with them at the end of any evening is a great way to close out a night! It was nice meeting their friend too. I could see how new friendships could be made over time. Unfortunately, time was running out for me.

My last week here begins tomorrow - Wednesday, March 22

My departure from Cabo is approaching. Well, it has been approaching since I got here, but now the end is near. I can feel it. I have an awareness for it knowing that whatever I am doing this week might be the last time I do it. Tomorrow is the first day of the last week here. I woke up today acutely aware of the fact that I would be on an airplane returning to the States in exactly a week. In effect, this was my last Wednesday here. In a few days my last weekend begins, and a few days after that, my last day. I wonder if I'll treat this coming week any differently than the others, you know, like become a wild and crazy Cabo guy. Will I go Cabo Crazy? I doubt it. I don't want to miss chances to be with my friends knowing that I will be saying goodbye to them soon. I don't want to nor need to change my routine. I like it as it as and I've had nearly three months to perfect it.

Today, like every day behind me, I have three major rides on my itinerary: morning, noon, and night and, as always, I'll be enjoying every minute of it. Riding my bike has been a great way to see the sights and get some exercise. It has also given me a wonderful chance to feel close-in with Cabo's community, the one dedicated to the tourist trade. I am familiar to a lot of locals, and many know me by name. And, they know I am here to learn Spanish because I have been telling everyone that since I got her. My quest has given me a fab opportunity to interact with the locals. For some locals, I have become a daily sighting in their world and, possibly even a character to them. I am that gringo on the cruiser, *el gringo con la bici*. *Bici* is short for Bicycle. Buying that bike at Walmart was a really good move on my part. I never regretted it, even when faced with a succession of flat tires which, by the way, created a nifty friendship with Fernando.

My morning rides almost always include a run to Walmart, but that won't happen today. That might not ever happen again. I probably won't be needing any more food because I have a freezer full of frozen vegetables. I need to draw that inventory down. My mid-day rides take me all over town and sometimes to the outer limits of town. Of course, they almost always include a stopover at CC to see the boys and get that chance to improve my Spanish. My night rides give me a whole different view of Cabo from the day because I cruise aimlessly through *el centro* with my bald head reflecting the neon lights overhead, my ears tuned into the music pouring out of doorways, and my eyes wide open for a myriad of things, things like holes in the sidewalk and weaving pedestrians, and more things to be seen, like things that could not be seen anywhere else along with anything that interests me. It's all eye candy. Every night the marina is lit up for the tourist-driven revelry that will continue for many hours after I've gone to bed. Lately, I've added visits to Esquina into the nighttime itinerary, which while not an opportunity to enhance my Spanish, it has enriched my experience down here. When I ride around the next week I will begin to get a feeling for how many things I will miss, though what I will miss most will be my friends. Of course.

CHAPTER TWELVE

Week 12

What about parasailing? - Thursday, March 23

I wonder if I should try it. Parasailing. I didn't really want to. Truth. A lot of rationalizing going on. A lot of cons for me, some pros. I've never done it before, for numerous reasons. I'm running out of time to decide if it's something I should try in Cabo. After all, it's really popular here, so what better place to do it? That's rationalizing, because I have never succumbed to that argument before, for anything. Especially cliff diving in Acapulco and bungee cord jumping off canyon bridges. I suppose it means it's likely that I have to go out on big, bumpy water, which translates into barf. That's an argument not to go parasailing. Frankly, I admit, it scares me a little bit, being up there like a kite, maybe throwing up on myself like I do in small airplanes. I wrecked a lot of kites as a kid. I know what can happen to a kite that dives into the ground. From way up, the surface of the water can feel like the ground, hard, really hard. Hard as cement. Anyone who has done a belly flop off the high dive knows there is some truth in this. And I don't particularly like the idea of a harness running through my crotch area while I'm at the mercy of fickle and unseeable air currents. That said, as I see it, I was shamed into parasailing. That's the only explanation.

Last week, I met some old, fat lady from Minnesota at Gardenias, about my age, who told me she went parasailing that morning for the first time in her life and had a blast. Maybe I'm being insensitive describing her as fat, but no one would disagree. One look at her, and I couldn't have possibly guessed that she was the person to do something like that. No one, and I mean no one, would have guessed that. I know, bad and unkind stereotyping on my part, clearly. This is an important moment to remind myself not to judge people on their looks. On an upbeat note, she was upbeat. But, she wasn't jolly. Ooops, I slipped. She was also friendly, out-going, and had a lot of energy. With all those positive qualities, I should not have been surprised that she was also adventurous and courageous. But I was surprised, really surprised that she did it. When we switched the topic to something else, I remember saying to myself that I was truly impressed by her, but I'd never do that. I'd never try parasailing. It wasn't my thing and I never had the slightest interest in it.

Chicken! Chicken! Chicken! Those words repeated in my head over and over the rest of the day, and for twenty-four hours after I met Minnesota Fats. Ooops, again, dammit. Clearly, I need some work. Clearly, I need to become a more accepting and loving person. I recognize this and I know I have to deal with it. I am sorry for being judgmental. And shallow. I should turn this moment into a learning experience. That's right. I'm dead serious. Becoming less judgmental would be a really good thing to get out of my Cabo experience. With this self-rebuke behind me, I caved to my inner voice. The hell with it, don't be a chicken! I'm here in Cabo on an adventure and what could be more adventurous than parasailing?

Another question I asked myself is what could be the stupidest thing I could do in Cabo? Lots of things come to mind. Parasailing is one of those things. But, I say, the woman from Minnesota did it! Why can't I! She even said it was totally cool. I swallowed hard on this, okay, and committed myself to trying parasailing before I left town, which means sometime in the next few days. If Ms. Minnesota could do it, so could I. Suddenly I feel a lot of admiration for her. How curious that she inspired me to put aside my fears. More importantly, she opened my heart and mind to be a more loving and accepting person. She did that. I hit a tipping point with her. That's a lot to happen coming out of a ten-minute conversation at Gardenias. Now I had to make these things happen.

First, I had to go the marina to get some information, you know, some brochures from a marina vendor, from one of my casual acquaintances, no doubt. With such short notice, I decided a face-to-face search was better than googling. I knew several vendors that could answer my questions and quickly get me into the wild blue yonder, the one above. Ruben came to mind, so he was my connection. And easy to find. He worked from his booth every day on the same strip of the marina as the dolphin prison. I guess I was giving myself the green light on this caper.

Ruben made it easy, like I am sure he does for tourists every day. He had several brochures for parasailing but pointed me to an outfit called Cabo Expeditions. For fifty-one bucks, I could be high in the sky, under a parachute for ten minutes, which will probably be long enough for me. And for my stomach. Ten minutes might even be an eternity for the faint-hearted. I might be one of those people. Or maybe not. The brochure said the excursion would take about ninety minutes, ten of which would have me tethered on the end of a kite string. Once up, I would be floating quietly above it all, according to the brochure. The "all" part included El Arco, Medano Beach and the whole Cabo San Lucas Bay. I wondered if "floating" was the right word. I also wondered if the word "terrifying" would work its way into my own description of the experience. Of course, I'd have to find out for myself.

There was nothing tricky about making this happen. All I had to do was go to Cabo Expeditions, which has a ticket booth near the marina, not more than one hundred yards from Ruben, then sign up, pay, meet at the appointed time, attach myself to a parachute, fly, land in one piece, and go home. Something like that. It all happened pretty fast, thanks to Ruben who told me to tell them Ruben sent me. That must have greased the skids because I was booked for take-off Saturday morning.

The last ride to Walmart - Friday, March 24

As it turned out, I had to go to Walmart one more time. I didn't mind running out of eggs yesterday but now I wanted some. I love eggs. Why was I thinking I could make it a week without them? I made my last run through the kill chute today, both ways of course, which has to happen every time I make a trip to Walmart. I haven't had a flat tire in six weeks, which tells me that my assessment about the rose bush thorns near the pedestrian crossing was correct. The thorns were a perfect match. The squatty little rose bushes were the source of those microscopic thorns, the ones that gave birth to my friendship with Fernando. Every cloud has a silver lining. Which reminds me, I need to drop in on him before I return to the States. We've had some nice conversations since my last flat tire, when I just dropped in for no reason. I should do it again. I haven't seen him in three weeks. He is always happy to see me but would probably prefer to see me pushing the cruiser with a flat tire up his driveway instead of riding up it with two perfect tires and a smile on my face. Maybe not. I will miss him. His teenage son, Ivan? Not likely.

I have to say it. The Walmart in Mexico is pretty much like every Walmart in the States, but with one remarkable difference. During my time in Cabo, I purchased a carton of eggs every week. And I did again today. In this store, over the course of three months, I opened twelve cartons, which is one a week. I never once saw a broken egg in any of the cartons I opened. Not one. Never ever. What are the odds of that happening with the purchase of twelve egg cartons in the States? Zero is my guess. But here, I cannot definitively explain a perfect track record like that. Tougher cartons? Tougher egg shells? Tougher eggshells must mean tougher chickens? More calcium in their diets? Whatever, don't mess with Mexican chickens! How would you explain it?

Up, up, and away! - Saturday, March 25

Today's the day. I'm doing it. I committed to parasailing two days ago. Cabo Expeditions had me booked for a ten o'clock departure. I was told to meet at their main reservations office located on the main boulevard by the marina, next to Dairy Queen. When I heard of the proximity to DQ, for a half second, I wondered if I could hold a peanut butter shake down. I decided I could, but only if it was after parasailing, not before. I see it as a reward for having done it. I love DQ's shakes, though it's been six months since I had one. They're so bad for one's health. Sugar bombs. Even so, for me, any DQ shake is a major temptation, but it's one that I rarely succumb to. In this case, it would be an appropriate and massive indulgence for my derring-do. When I showed up at the office there were three other apprehensive tourists signed up for the same ride, a couple in their mid-thirties and their teenage son, who was probably fifteen and definitely pimply. Ten minutes after signing the releases, we four boarded the tricked-out boat for the start of the adventure.

As our boat pulled out of the marina, I was able to discern that the couple was pleasant, the mom chatty. From Minnesota! Minnesotans must be into parasailing. Go figure. The son was totally non-communicative, but for conceding a grunt or two and a couple of one-word answers. The level of communication skills at his age is probably in line with a typical teenage boy. Fine by me, just sayin'. I'm glad he was there, which means that I would not allow myself to scream like a girl. Funny, aren't I? I know I'm kidding. I'll be very cool about this, because that's what I keep telling myself. The skipper said thousands of tourists a year go parasailing with no problems. That can't be the complete story. I wanted to ask him what about the thousands that have problems? I restrained myself, which is not like me. I am sure there are some problems but I am also sure I don't want to know what happened to the not so lucky ones. Odds are way in my favor that I'll fly like a bird, and land like one too.

The craft for this endeavor was what I expected, a power boat with twin Mercs, big ones. It was about twenty-five feet long with a big chrome roll bar positioned across the boat at the midpoint of the boat's bow and the stern. A giant winch was bolted to the deck under it. Between the roll bar and the stern there was a platform with an eight-foot diameter. On the platform, painted and centered over its entire surface was a red and white bull's-eye. For what? An ad for Target? I wondered if that was a take off aid or, more likely, a target for the landing. Maybe a target for free fall when the tether broke? Probably the second possibility. Really? A bull's-eye was necessary for something like this? I'd find out in a hurry because things were happening fast on board. The boat was outside of the harbor in minutes. As soon as we entered the open water of the gulf, the deck hand prepped the launch pad and released a parachute from a storage box I didn't see earlier, off the stern railing. Almost instantly the chute popped open, filled up, and held steady in place by a tether about fifteen feet up and twenty feet behind us on a very short line. I surmised it was ready for tourists. That be me and the Minnesota trio.

The chute looked awfully small to me, but what do I know. Secured to the ropes that ran back to the parachute were two harnesses, just like the harnesses used when people parachute out of a plane. Side by side, they hung over the bull's-eye, waiting for two people to slip into them. To me, they looked more like two swings stolen from someone's swing set, but I wasn't going to let myself worry about anything so I pushed the comparison out of my head. I put a new thought into my head. I wonder what it will feel like a hundred feet up when the crotch straps start yanking my crotch. I immediately put another new thought into my head. Something about DQ. I guess my imagination was working overtime. I confess I felt a little jittery about this. I was also hoping that I wouldn't throw up. Thankfully, the surface of the water looked like glass much of the way. After we ran out of glass still while heading for the starting point, wherever that was, the water rippled a bit, but not much, not too much. Thankfully, there were no swells. Swells guarantee barfing.

Since there were four of us daredevils, I knew that I'd be sharing the experience with one of the Minnesotans. If I went up with the kid, I'm sure I'd feel like I was totally on my own, seated next to a mannequin, which might not be a bad thing. However, I thought the kid as my partner was unlikely. One of the parents would want to share the experience with their son, surely with the hope that it would trigger some kind of memorable experience, one that maybe even elicited more than one word from him. I didn't want to go up with the dad. I don't know why, maybe two grown men up there would be awkward, especially if one or both of us started screaming like little girls. I was guessing my partner would be the mom. This way, dad could have that great father-son experience with his mute offspring; maybe actually they could scream together to strengthen the bonding experience. Mom was the chatty one and easiest to be with. I was hoping she would be my partner. Moms are much more sympathetic to people who throw up, because they've seen so much of that as mothers. Even so, I wasn't expecting to throw up. The surface of the water stayed relatively calm even though we were moving farther and farther from the land. As it turned out, the mom was my partner. Her name is Helen. Her husband is Howard. And, I kid you not, the kid is Howie. But he wasn't called junior. Just Howie. Like how we doing? Get it? I almost said that to him, and would have if he had ever made eye contact with me.

Helen and I were first up, figuratively and literally. She was sweet and not the least bit nervous about going into outer space. She had a calming effect on me. We laughed as we got strapped in and stood on the target platform, ready for lift off. This would be a piece of cake. She said that. I said nothing. Oh, did I say that I am afraid of heights? I forgot to mention that. Too late, the deckhand hit the release button and Helen and I went vertical at four times crotch speed. Or something like that. We were afloat and rising faster than the SpaceX Falcon 9 rocket. By the way, that rocket blew up a minute after the launch. We were climbing so fast that I thought that big winch must be broken, but didn't say anything because I couldn't do anything about it. If it were true,

I'd be dead in a minute anyway, so why care? Really. My stomach was rising too, but this time I was rising with it, so no problem. For starters, my crotch was okay too, the straps were fine, even with the force of two G's. We rose quickly.

Helen and I hung in silence for a half minute, smiling like little kids swinging next to each other on a swing set, while our swing seats were lifted higher and higher. We couldn't see the parachute, of course, because it was behind us. Maybe if I looked straight up, but I didn't. I felt like I was floating. The experience was instantly serene and pleasant. After all my worries, I felt secure in my harness and had an amazing, unobstructed view of everything in front of me. I could see El Arco, the harbor, a mammoth Princess cruise ship, another one two miles out heading to Cabo, a mile and a half of Medano beach, a coastline of timeshares, a ring of brown arid mountains surrounding Cabo and, off in the distance, the Pacific Ocean sparkling in all its vastness as far as the eye could see. I would have thought I was a gull floating on a smooth current of air were it not for the fact that I could see my feet, seemingly detached from my winged body, dangling under me. Not far from Helen's. The whole experience was so liberating and out-of-body that I had trouble believing there were human feet in the scenery. Four of them, in fact. My eye followed the chute's tether downward forever. It appeared to be no bigger than a spider's silk thread until it disappeared into a postage stamp of a boat so far below me that I wasn't sure I was still connected to it.

Chatty Helen and I just sat in silence for the ascent far up into the brilliant blue sky above the Sea of Cortez. We just took it all in, moment by moment, as if no one was sitting next to us, me assuming she felt that same way I felt that way. How can I find the words? A gentle breeze caressed us as we bathed in soft, golden light far above all the stress that comes with living on Planet Earth. It was surreal, and that's all I can say about it, except that I was wondering how the hell we were going to get down in the next ten minutes. How could we possibly be brought back to the boat, to that small bull's-eye on the tiny deck, and walk away alive?

Landing, contrary to my expectations, was a snap. Helen and I touched down on our tippy toes by the time the support lines were locked in. The captain brought us in with the ease and grace of a seagull landing softly with its feet extended, in a slow motion vertical landing on a soft, sandy beach. The landing went without a hitch. That's no jolt. It was so direct and quick it did not wipe out the feeling of nirvana that was so easily and unexpectedly attained while soaring like a bird up in the blue sky over Cabo San Lucas. A real wow.

Countdown at Cabo Cantina - Saturday, March 25

A was an exhilarating morning for me, I got really high up in the sky. Back on earth, I still could not see a cloud around. Not a breeze. Summer was coming and couldn't have been far off. My days here are numbered so I allocated a couple of hours in the afternoon for hanging out with the boys at CC. I was trying to avoid melancholy and sappy feelings about my departure and impending farewell to the CC staff, but it was hard. Andres was the first to greet me when I turned the cruiser into the side entrance and parked it. Usually Guillermo is the first because he's hawking customers on the sidewalk, but today he was elsewhere in the restaurant. Andres is quick too, though he's often working the tables when I come in. Jorge, forever alert to customers, is also one of the first to say *hola* to me. One aspect of his excellence as a bartender is a constant awareness of everyone who walks in and walks out of the restaurant. He has a third eye. I have never gotten a greeting from him that was less than sincerely inviting and enthusiastic, from day one. I am also aware, that he has been hugely sympathetic to my pain from my self-afflicted delusional expectations, which I no longer have. In this regard, he and I connected in that way more than Andres and I did because Jorge, unlike Andres, spent several years in the States. Ray and Gabriel also spent a couple of years living there so they understood the challenges of learning the language of a foreign country while residing in it. It makes a difference in experiences but it's a difference that is not worse nor better than learning from someone, like Andres, who has never lived in the States. It's just different. I learned a lot from everyone, regardless of their personal experiences, but I have to say Andres was *número uno* in time spent with me. I embraced the process just as I embraced the people. And, I think, they embraced me because of it. I believe that.

In challenging myself to learning Spanish, I learned that the concept of total immersion doesn't mean a strict commitment to only the language to be learned. With some of my friends, like Pedro and Facundo at the G Spot, Spanish-only conversations were terrific learning and listening experiences. My time with them was total immersion. If we three were to communicate we had only one language to figure it out. There was no default position to English. At times, it was frustrating but with every inch of progress came elation and wonderment that it was even do-able. It was such a wonderful exercise that I never wished that either of them could speak English, nor were they interested in speaking English. Every encounter with them was a marvel on how people without a common language can communicate enough to create a warm and meaningful friendship. In my mission to learn their language we had to go beyond words and work our way through it all with a lot of pantomime and pointing. That's what we did. Conversations in Spanish-only with Pedro and Facundo were made possible over the months because some other native speakers, like the crew at CC, could explain things to me in English whenever I got stymied in Spanish. That way, at CC, I learned things about the language that I never could have picked up in a Spanish-only venue such as the one I had with Pedro and Facundo. At CC, it wasn't true language immersion but I felt truly immersed in the experience. These two different routes were mutually beneficial to me, the student.

Also, having someone help me with Spanish was never a one-way street for them. I reciprocated whenever I could. I enjoyed helping the CC crew with their English, it was the least I could do. And, I was helpful to Pedro and Facundo, too, in broadening their experience by discussing issues and life in the States and in Mexico. In addition, at times I think I was pretty entertaining. Everybody was a winner, either way and I believe we all had fun doing it.

The concept of immersion is terrific, but it's only a concept. Maybe at the Berlitz school of language it's only one language at all times. Not so with my real world methodology. I generally avoided speaking English, except at night. I sought out every opportunity to speak Spanish by day though sometimes at night, too, be it with retail people in stores, pedestrians on sidewalks, the police, vendors in the marina, restaurant wait staff, and every Mexican who gave me an opportunity to say a few words, even if it was only a simple greeting, an expression of gratitude or a request for directions. I was happy with my kind of immersion subversion, however different from the concept I originally intended to use in Mexico. I suppose everyone has to discover what works for them. I couldn't be a purist in immersion, but I did what I could to immerse myself whenever possible.

All this commitment obviously didn't come without the stress I experienced, not only from self-imposed unrealistic expectations but also from the necessary determination to stick to Spanish day after day regardless of how frustrating and exhausting the effort could be. I got my tongue tied up so many times to the point that I couldn't talk at all. Whenever I got stuck it was time to gather my wits, take deep breaths and remind myself that learning a language is a fun and rewarding endeavor. Yes, my motto is *poco a poco* and I hope I never forget it in my continuing pursuit to improve my Spanish speaking skills.

Yes, the stress was real. And I don't think I was able to handle it very well on my own. I owe a lot to the patience and understanding I got from everyone at CC, especially Andres and Jorge. They helped me over a lot of speed bumps and, at one point, pushed me out of the dark side back into the light. No kidding about that. Learning a language is not easy, unless of course you're a kid growing up in a bilingual household. Ha to the truth in that. But in my sixties, I wasn't sure I could do it. Well, now I know I can and I have over a dozen new friends in Cabo that made me believe it's possible.

I left after three hours of studying in CC at just the right time. I arrived in time to catch the last hour or so of the day shift, which means time spent with Andres, Ismael, Jorge, Guillermo, Leo, and Fabian among others. I stayed almost two hours into the afternoon shift for the camaraderie with Gabriel, Totito, Martin, Ray, Roberto, and Edgar, among others. Three hours and four Pacificos later, it was time to go, time to say goodbye after four beers in three hours. Man-o-man, what a light weight I've become, but it was enough for me. I didn't get sappy because we were all happy, happy for the experience and the friendship all around. I waved behind me as I rode away from CC. I knew I would be swerving a little bit on the cruiser all the way back to my condo with only one thing on my mind, a nap.

My only meal at Edith's - Saturday, March 25

Okay, I caved on eating at Edith's. Last time I was there I sat at the bar and had a very expensive Pacifico. I loved the ambience, the looks of the food, and the hustle and bustle of quality service. The only thing in that first visit that I didn't experience was the food, so I'm doing that now. Generally, I don't eat at restaurants by myself if it means I have to sit solo at a table. There's no chance of getting a table at Edith's on a Saturday night if you don't have a reservation. I didn't have one. Also, Edith's does not have a community table, which is too bad because community tables can be a fun experience. It was my understanding that patrons cannot order food when seated at the bar, which is something I assumed and then, apparently, was proven wrong. Lucky me. It's good to be wrong once in a while. I ordered my dinner while seated at the bar.

Ordinarily, meat is not my thing. I don't like to chew it so I often eschew it. Ordinarily. This exception makes me a cheatin' pescatarian. I don't avoid meat because of a taste or health issue. I avoid it because of animal cruelty issues, which no one wants to talk about at a restaurant in the middle of their filet mignon. Yes, I cheat from time to time. For a good reason. I eat a steak about once every two or three months because it's a good single source for the twenty-three essential amino acids a body needs. I want to be sure I am getting them all. Meat is my failsafe to reliance on a very broad mix of veggies and fish for that requirement. That's my understanding anyway. I'll shut up now. I am not a nutritionist. Here's what I ordered, as described in Edith's menu, verbatim:

Tampiqueña with Center Cut Beef Filet: A combination of mesquite grilled cut filet mignon. Organic Chicken enchilada covered with a red guajillo sauce. Cheese quesadilla with zucchini blossom garnished with chipotle and requeson sauce. Pacific rice, pinto beans and guacamole.

In case you are wondering about guajillo sauce, it is created out of a guajillo chili pepper that is dried, seeded, then soaked and pulverized to a thin paste, then cooked with salt and several other ingredients to produce a thick, red, flavorful sauce. By the way, sauce is what Mexicans call salsa. Guajillos are used in traditional Mexican cooking as pastes, butters, or rubs to flavor all kinds of meat, especially chicken and, in my case, Edith's organic chicken. As for the requeson sauce, that's Mexico's answer to ricotta cheese and who doesn't like cheese? Need I say more?

Okay, I'll say more because you are probably wondering if there was more to my meal. I skipped the appetizers because I like to save some room in my stomach for dessert, which I never order. It's a psychological trick I play on myself to avoid ordering too much food. Of course, after the main course, in this case, after the superbly delicious beef and chicken, dessert didn't have a chance. No room at the inn was reason enough. If I had decided to indulge in a dessert I would have ordered the *Torta de piña con helado de vainilla* or pineapple cake with vanilla ice cream. That's probably a serving of heaven on a plate, but I'll never know. Edith's flan was my next choice. The dessert menu is deep if someone wants to dive in. Oh, by the way, I can safely say that a couple of Pacifico beers poured into a chilled glass never tasted better with a meal. I had a terrific dining experience.

Do I regret having eaten only once at Edith's? Not really, but that's just me. I am not a big fan of restaurant food, too much sugar in it, the obvious and the hidden, which is one reason I duck desserts despite my expressed desires. The check came to eight hundred and fifty-five pesos. That was for one entree, two beers and a twenty percent tip. That's Spanish for fifty bucks. I wouldn't call that expensive. I've had meal tickets four times that amount at "expensive" restaurants in the States and other countries. I guess that's why I call Edith's a good value, all things considered. I say eat it at Edith's, at least once, if you're ever in Cabo.

How do you know if you made it in life? - Monday, March 27

Every day here I can sleep as late as I want, and I have, because I rarely have any scheduled plans for a typical day and whatever plans I have are closer to suggestions than commitments. In addition, to this lifestyle, I get a lot of time to think. It's always interesting to me, as a writer, where my mind takes me. Sometimes it has a mind of its own. Which is a very good thing. Sometimes old memories pop up out of nowhere without any identifiable trigger. I had that happen to me today. Like many people long past their college days, there is much I have forgotten about my days at Indiana University. However, I haven't forgotten everything. There was one late night booze-fueled conversation I remember very well, some of it verbatim. And the setting is still crystal clear in my memory as well.

I was a sophomore living in the Fiji house, which is an on-campus fraternity more formally known as Phi Gamma Delta. I have not forgotten one particular conversation with four of my Fiji brothers on that memorable night over forty-five years ago. I don't know why this particular memory survived the onslaught of alcohol. But it did. It is the most vivid memory I have of a college event except for the night I lost my virginity, of course, but that's a different story.

I remember five of us in a conversation on that night, the hour just before dawn: Cleve, Doug, Dan, Mike and myself, all sagging into two old two-seater sofas and an armchair we named, for a reason I don't recall, the red whore. These three pieces of furniture and the five of us were miraculously jammed into an alcove in one of the two four-man rooms in the house that were located at the end of the sophomore hallway. For four of us, myself included, that was the room where we bunked and kept all of our possessions. Mike, who was also known as Foamy (something to do about ever-present beer foam on his upper lip), lived across the hallway in another four-man room. The alcove was often the final stop for us every night. It was our refuge, the place where we congregated for our tell-all sessions every night of that semester and a few philosophical ones as well.

The conversation on that particular night was about what being rich meant and what it would take. None of us were rich, so we wondered about things like that. I think anyone would have found the entire lively slurry of slurred ideas as pretty interesting stuff but I'm not writing about the whole of it. The part I remember most vividly was our conclusion to the question: How will we know if we've made it in life? We rejected answers such as a million-dollar net worth, great family life, a CEO title, owner of a business, fame, recognition, world travels, biggest house in the city, high political office, and a lot of other possibilities, except one. The final answer we agreed upon was not something most people would have come up with. With the assumption that basic needs like food and shelter were met, we five wise men decided that you know you've made it in life if you can wake up every morning naturally, without an alarm clock. You can get whatever sleep you need because there are no demands, no appointments, no meetings, no nothing you have to get out of bed to do. Waking up naturally means waking up without the albatross of stress or deadlines, but rather when your body has determined by itself that it got enough sleep. It means you could lounge in bed in the morning as long as you desired. That sure sounds like my life in Cabo these past few months. I'm not sure I'd use the words "made it" but I can say I'm lucky I can do what I'm doing.

This morning, waking up was pretty much like every morning, it occurred naturally. I'm usually up around seven or eight. I don't wake up with the sun because daylight doesn't get through my black out windows. And even though I have the option of sleeping late, I rarely sleep in past eight. That is because I am almost always asleep no later than midnight the night before. I think somewhere in the answer to that late-night question, the words "naps at any time" need to be worked into the final wording. Or maybe that is the answer by itself, a four-word answer: naps at any time. If that's the litmus test, I can easily say I've made it in life.

The countdown - Thursday, March 30

The days are definitely hotter since my arrival in January. Even the night time temperatures have climbed a bit above the lows when I first showed up. I still think of the weather here as perfect even though the last three days have been pretty windy. And gusty, giving the palm fronds outside my kitchen window a good shaking from time to time. That cheap kitchen window rattles with the wind. I'll have to remember to tell Ale to replace the window with one that offers better security. This is my last night of sleep in Coromuel. I leave in the morning and I am almost ready. My bag is ninety percent packed and my food supply has been rationed perfectly over the past week to disappear completely with my last meal. I'll have two sunny side up eggs in the morning and that last glass of a spinach mango smoothie that is waiting for me in the fridge. That'll do it. Before I walk out, I'll call out to Ocho, tell him he's been a great roommate. Then, I'll lock the door behind me and drop off the keys in the front office, maybe get to say *adios* to the manager babe before I walk out of my building.

Last afternoon at Cabo Cantina - Thursday, March 30

Today is my last full day in Cabo and this afternoon is my last time in Cabo Cantina, yet I was still meeting some of the staff for the first time, this time some kitchen staffers who I had seen a bit of but never more than a second or two of visibility. Guillermo brought a new chef out to my table to meet me. His name is Efrien, a name I had to ask him to repeat several times. I hadn't heard it before. Like all good chefs, Efrien clearly spent a lot of time sampling the food, as he should. I kidded him about the kitchen's reputation for excellent elephant burgers. He knew that joke because I had been ribbing the cooks for many weeks over that one. We could only chat for a second because no one is busier in a restaurant than the chef.

I walked back to the kitchen with Efrien getting a little background out of him. He had an interesting story but I didn't have time to hear all of it. He, too, worked in the States at one time. It was a fifteen second walk but long enough to tell him that I was leaving tomorrow and hoped to see him next year. When he passed through the threshold I took a second to introduce myself to another kitchen worker. His name is Julio. We know each other through the greetings that fly back and forth between me and Ceci. Now I was able to put a name to a face, as I had seen him many times before. I felt bad meeting these people for the first time because I explained my departure in the same breath. It was okay however to say hi and goodbye because we were all family. I can't really explain why that it is, but it feels that way and I'm going with it. It feels good. Everyone is smiling.

I returned to my table and chatted with Andres for an hour off and on depending on the demands of his customers. His shift would end at the end of the hour, at three and the second team would take over. I planned it that way so I could say goodbye to everyone. Andres made sure I had a Pacifico at my table with a backup on deck as soon as I finished the first one. He said the drinks were on him. I appreciated the gesture. It was my last day, of course, and neither of us wanted to acknowledge that fact. It was the elephant in the room, not the elephant between the buns. After the second Pacifico, a margarita showed up at my table, a gift from Jorge. They all knew this was the last day and a cloud hung above the elephant. I knew Jorge well enough to know that the margarita he sent me was at least three shots of the best tequila and sure to put me on my face by the time I saw the bottom of the glass. After the first sip, I made a mental note to myself to walk out with it in a go cup, otherwise I'd never walk out on my own two feet. Sneaky Jorge. If I drank it all, I'd have a last night in Cabo that I couldn't remember. Sneaky me for taking it in a go cup!

At three o'clock Andres, Richard, Fabian, Ismael, and Leo left. We hugged as friends saying goodbye for a long time. I said something personal to each of them, about their lives that they shared with me, and thanked them for being my teachers and, more importantly, my friends. And I said I'd see them next winter. I can get a little maudlin at times and this was one of them. Ray and Jorge would be around for another hour as a transition between the two shifts, so they stood to the side for this round of farewells. It was Guillermo's day off but I said goodbye to him yesterday. He too had been such a good friend to me. Suddenly, my first shift friends were gone. I already made plans to see Andres early the next morning at Coromuel. I wanted to give him the bike then. So saying goodbye to him could be put off till tomorrow.

I sipped that lethal margarita that Jorge sent to me, determined to get most of it into a go cup, but that meant I couldn't stay at CC much longer. And I didn't. Gabriel, Martin, and Edgar showed up to begin the afternoon shift that would take them to closing time. Totito showed up to take over the bar from Jorge. I couldn't stand the sadness I felt over the parting of ways with my friends, I had to leave. So after an hour, I went to each and thanked him from the bottom of my heart, and said goodbye. I stuck my head in the kitchen to say goodbye again to Efrien and Julio, but mainly to say goodbye to Ceci. Her dark eyes sparkled as always when she came around the counter to hug me goodbye. Her forehead pressed against my sternum. Then, I went to Ray and Jorge as my last gesture, thanked them and told them in Spanish that I did not have the words to express my feelings. But thanks to them I could swear like a motherfucker! They too had been my teachers and my friends. We swapped a few swear words, for each other using our mothers in vain, of course. I would never forget these guys but I didn't say that because it sounded so final. I said I'd see them next year. And I hope I will. I grabbed my go cup, put it into the drink holder on the cruiser, mounted my trusty bike, waved behind me and rode off into the sunset. Yes, I had a tear in my eye as I left behind a group of the nicest guys I could ever met. There is an emotional, sappy side to me. I hope someone some days reads this passage to them. They gave me the greatest gift, their friendship. I hope they know how much it meant to me.

Farewell to Hector and Saul - Thursday, March 30

I didn't stop in at Esteban's much during the full three months of my stay. Maybe twice a week, but rarely for more than a few minutes each time. Actually, only twice did I dismount and sit down at a table, both times for the special of the day. However, whenever I stopped on my bike, I pulled up to the front entrance coming or going home long enough to say hi to Hector and Saul and chat a bit. And sometimes, Lourdes, too, when she worked there. I stopped more often after Lourdes left. I still don't know why I got tongue tied with her. Yes, she is a good-looking woman, a real babe to be exact, but that's not the reason. I think the reason for our weak conversation has something to do with her conversation skills, not mine. Maybe she talked too fast. Maybe she was totally in love with me. Kidding on that. Whatever the reason, I always had a hard time understanding what she was saying. No big deal.

What is a bigger deal is my friendship with Hector and Saul. I had one really fun conversation over a meal one day with Hector who was my server at the time. We bonded then. He kept saying I should go after Lourdes, like he was my wingman. That was a pretty personal conversation, all things considered, but it was something we could have fun talking about every time we saw each other. You know, a guy to guy thing about a babe, that being Lourdes. That exception aside, Hector and Saul, who was also in on my thing with Lourdes, were always happy to see me and, when they could, ran outside the front entrance to greet me on my bike as I waited to exchange a few words with them. We always laughed over whatever simple thing we talked about and it usually wasn't much more than business or family. I learned that they each had an infant daughter. They showed me pictures, as proud fathers do. Their faces were lit up with love for their little girls. I was touched by the gesture and it just heightened my opinion of these two friendly, hardworking kids. They both put in twelve hour shifts at the restaurant and did that for six days a week. No kidding. When they saw me from across the street whether I was heading home or into town, they would whistle loudly to get my attention and then wave. If I saw them from across the street, I did the same.

Earlier in the week, I had an idea, an idea about doing something for Hector and Saul. I learned in one of the conversations that they would both be working in the restaurant at the same time on the day before I left for the States. This meant I could meet with them at the same time and say my goodbyes. I wanted to do something for them on that day.

The day before I left I pulled up to the front entrance and Hector and Saul were right there, on the threshold of Esteban's. I reminded them I was leaving in the morning. It would be the last time I'd see them for a while. Maybe ever. I also thanked them for their kindness and their friendship. It was easy to do because they are two of the nicest guys anyone could meet. As with many of my friends, there was a bit of a language barrier but that never got in the way of a friendship and mutual respect. I have to mention too that these guys were fun. They almost always made me laugh, especially with their comments about Lourdes. Anyway, I thanked them and pulled out a five hundred peso note from my wallet for each of them and told them to buy a present for their little girls. A small gift from me. They were surprised, of course and so was I when I got a big strong-armed hug from each of them. They were very grateful, very. I was sad to say goodbye. The feeling was mutual. I hope I brought as much love and light into their lives as they did mine.

Goodbye to Pedro and Facundo at the G Spot - Thursday, March 30

My last evening in Cabo was launched with a visit to The G Spot at dusk. I had to say goodbye to Pedro and Facundo. I felt sad about my farewell and impending departure before I got there. When I did get there, I rode right into the restaurant, made a run between the tables the full length of the room, and stopped in front of the kitchen window to say goodbye to the cook, who was Pedro's wife. She is always sweet and never has a clue what I am saying even with my best attempts at Spanish. But she knows it's all good. She had to think of me as a regular, though I didn't partake in her cooking except for a couple of times. But she knew I was pals with her husband, good enough for a few visits every week, which is probably more visits per week than any other customer. I pedaled a U-turn and crossed the room again, careful not to sideswipe the empty tables and chairs, and they were all empty, to get to my usual parking space in the corner just off the front door. I dismounted and slowly approached the bar but stopped short to take a photo of my two amigos standing close to each other with the bar running between them, as usual. They stood silently, patient, and posed for a few smart phone pics. Both were smiling, waiting for me. In one pic, Facundo posed with a bottle of Ron Rico raised in his hand, the key ingredient in a Cuba Libre, my usual. The distance between us disappeared as I hugged Pedro and double pumped Facundo's outstretched hand with both of my hands in an expression of as much warmth as I could muster across a bar.

For an hour, we three chatted and laughed and laughed and laughed some more. We laughed about elephant burgers. The G Spot was the original establishment for elephant burgers. Giraffe burgers, too. We laughed about my first visit when I hardly knew ten words of Spanish. We laughed about Ron Rico. We laughed about the recurring joke that I was riding the cruiser back to the States, a trip that would take at least six weeks. Pedro and Facundo, my compadres, two terrific and warm guys who embraced me upon my arrival that first week in January, me, a gringo who could speak no Spanish, a stranger they met for the first time at a dinner table on first of many quiet nights in their restaurant Guadalupana. These are two guys I'd never forget. I'll miss riding my cruiser into Guadalupana, which I will always think of as the G Spot, with great affection.

With every sentence I uttered, I had the thought in the back of my mind that it will be a long time before I see these guys again. Today I was reminded that they are brothers, two of eight boys in the family. I told them they were my brothers. We three said simultaneously one word that said it all, *compadres*. Maybe they told me they had brothers when we met; if so, it was lost in the language barrier, a barrier that was now a lot lower than it was when I first met them twelve weeks ago. Our friendship was solid and it was a fun one, with a lot of laughing and more communication than imaginable among people who don't have a language in common. In that way, it was very special. Tonight, the drinks were on them, which was their going away gift to me. I rode out on the cruiser, one hand on the handle bars, the other waving behind me like a drunken rodeo bronco rider, yelling the phrase they taught me many weeks ago and which became the first thing I said every time I rode into the G Spot: *Que bueno verte, mis amigos.* It's great to see you, my friends! This last time I added a word, *siempre,* which means always.

Last stop, at Esquina - Thursday, March 30

I left The G Spot close to closing time, but this last night was far from over. I planned on making one more stop. Yes, another visit to Esquina. Why not? My last night in Cabo. Says something, I guess, about how much I like the evening entertainment at Esquina. Every night it's a different event, though some nights I am not sure there is an event at all. Tonight, I sat at the bar having found the scintillating Felice with another one of her old friends, Wendy, equally engaging, who also lives in Los Angeles, not far from Felice. They were seated on the corner of the bar. I plunked down on empty barstool next to Felice, the opposite side from Wendy, which was perfect because it created a triangle that allowed us to talk directly to each other. I happily took it and made it a threesome in the conversation. They didn't seem to mind. I was happy to be there and felt welcomed enough. Good all around. I skipped CC tonight because I said goodbye to everyone in the afternoon and, as much as I loved CC, I rarely made it my evening hangout.

Felice and Wendy are two very attractive women, both living in Santa Monica. Felice is fifteen years younger than me. She is the beautiful blonde with gorgeous green eyes who I met ten days ago at Esquina when she was with her friend, Rebecca. That was the first time I met Felice. She has the most beautiful green eyes I have ever gazed into. Totally captivating, but I resisted captivation. It was easy to resist because she didn't try and I'm way too old for her. Wendy, who I met for the first time tonight, was very charming and engaging as well. She was closer to my age, very close, and had a good vibe about her. Both women had a lot of class, and I confess to liking that. It usually means an interesting conversation and, maybe even friends, in common. Tonight, I was not disappointed. We three had a lot of fun chatting. I know this to be true because sometimes all three of us were talking at the same time while listening to the other two talk at the same time as well. The end of the evening came fast, too fast of course, but that's the way things usually work when you're having a good time. I didn't feel like making it a late night. I rarely do. Tonight would be no exception even though it was my last one in Cabo. Wendy and I swapped contact cards and agreed to keep in touch. Felice already had mine. They too were leaving Cabo tomorrow. Alas, Cabo would never be the same without us; we all agreed on that. Or, for that matter, it wouldn't be the same without me, that gringo on the cruiser who shed tears over the friends he had to say goodbye to. I said goodnight to Ramon and Rodrigo, and thanked them. All in Spanish, of course. I didn't want everyone to know that I got bleary eyed every time I said farewell and rode away. That's not very *macho*.

<u>My departure day - Friday, March 31</u>

I'm leaving my condo a few minutes before seven in the morning, my last morning, because I am meeting Andres outside the complex, on the sidewalk, just outside of Coromuel's security gate. After that, I cross the street to catch a bus to the airport for a ten a.m. flight back to Phoenix. It will be a special and sad last goodbye for me. Andres has been a wonderful friend and has enriched my experience in Cabo beyond words. My teacher and my friend, he has been both, through and through. He is here to meet me because I am handing the cruiser to him. When I told him a couple of days ago that I wanted him to have it, a very big smile appeared on his face.

As soon as I got to the security gate, I saw Andres on the sidewalk out front, about twenty yards up the street, on the town side of the gate. I said a few parting words to the security guard and thanked him for his kindness as I pulled my roller bag behind me and pushed the cruiser with my other hand past his booth. Andres had an eye out for me, so he was already walking towards me. I had no idea I would feel so sad in saying goodbye to him, but I kept my sadness under the lid, kind of, because I was happy to give him the gift of my bike. We exchanged way too many sappy words, more than two men should say, and left with the idea that we would see each other again in Cabo next January. I gave him my card and told him that he was always welcome in my home if he ever wanted to come to Durango. The summer, I said, would be a good time for him and his wife to escape the Baja heat. We hugged and said our last goodbye.

I watched Andres climb onto the cruiser and slowly ride away from me, toward town on the sidewalk that I rode on over a hundred times. He's a big guy, bigger and broader than me. As he rode away, toward *el centro*, he looked like a circus bear riding a small bicycle. He'll do just fine on the cruiser. I told him he could do anything he wanted with it, even sell it. I will not ask for it back on my return. I will miss him and my pals at CC and The G Spot. And Esteban's and Esquina. And I will never forget the wonderful people I met along the way and the words Mario, my neighbor, taught me. Those words? *Mexico, no hay dos.* Which roughly means there is no place like Mexico. *Es verdad, mi amigo, es verdad.* Yes, it is true.

E PILOGUE

<u>Looking back</u>

Cabo is all about the entertainment of American tourists in a way that Americans envision Mexico. That vision often hides the real and true Mexico in many ways. I think the American vision includes a lot of tacos and countless margaritas, and mariachi songs like *Guantanamera*, all to be enjoyed and served up to Americans by smiling Mexicans who never appear to be offended by crass and presumptuous tourists, not that every American tourist is like that. The Mexico I saw after three months living in a condo in town is about a friendly and cultured people who work hard with focus on taking care of their family. The motto for most Mexicans might be Family First. There are many things to love about this country, not the least of which is the food. Mexican food qualifies as one of the great cuisines in the world and it is known for its endless nuances in endless variations. A recent nutrition study put it ahead of Chinese, Italian, French, and American in nutritional value based on the twenty-five most popular foods in each nation. Happily, besides great food, fiestas can be found everywhere woven into a culture of very honest and hard-working individuals. That's more evidence that this is a happy culture. I knew many service people in Cabo who work twelve hours a day, six days a week. Yet, the people are by nature happy people and feel it and show it every day, even in the daily grind, and especially when face to face with insensitive tourists (like almost all tourists everywhere). They work hard and are generally not paid well, by our American standards, so when they do receive a good tip, they are some of the most appreciative people in the world.

Perhaps the most profound thing I experienced in Mexico is the indescribable kindness and hospitality I was shown just because I put a little effort into learning their language. It opened many doors for me and got me a lot closer to experiencing this great culture. Mexicans, friends and strangers alike, always responded to me in my attempt to be part of everything that makes Mexico so unique and wonderful. Many, many times a simple exchange of a few words in a greeting, turned into much more and, in some instances, deep friendships. In my travels around the world, there are kind and wonderful people everywhere, but while Mexicans have some equals on this measure, no one is more friendly than the Mexican people of all ages and all walks of life. They are a happier people than Americans and their happiness radiates warmth in every transaction. I cannot say enough about how much I have come to love my Mexican friends in Cabo, but I can also include a feeling of friendship among the restaurant servers and bartenders, the retailers, the sidewalk vendors, even the beggars on the marina sidewalk who I came in contact with along the way.

I am committed to learning Spanish. My friends in Cabo helped me get off to a good start. Learning a language as an adult is difficult. It takes dedication and practice. But it can be done, especially keeping in mind the advice I got over and over again from my Mexican friends, *poco a poco*, little by little. That's how I'll do it. I want to return to Cabo next winter. I already miss my friends and I am looking forward to seeing them all again so I can say to them *que bueno verte otra vez*, it's good to see you again!

The bus to the airport

Three months in Cabo was perfect, not a day too long and not a day too short. Andres picked up the cruiser this morning from my place just before I caught the bus to the airport. We said our goodbyes and re-stated our desire to continue our close friendship next year. It would be the last time I see Andres this year, I was pretty sure of that. Parting was both sad and wonderful, wonderful that I could have such a great friendship in such a short time.

I watched Andres ride off for a minute, until he was hard to see. I crossed the street with my suitcase on wheels and my black nylon backpack, walked past the closed doors of the G Spot and pulled up in front of Esteban's, where I'd flag down the bus for the airport. Hector was at the entrance, staring at me, surprised to see me since I said goodbye to him yesterday. We chatted for fifteen minutes on and off as I waited for the bus and between his dashes to and from breakfast customers. Finally, the bus for the airport showed up. We embraced and said goodbye again.

I wanted the purple express bus but my eagerness to get to the airport, I mistakenly boarded the blue local bus, which I didn't realize until a mile later. I didn't mind adding forty-five minutes to the ride because I wasn't in a hurry. An old man, older than me, played his guitar and sang for the passengers for the next thirty minutes on the bus. A regular entertainer he was, something he does on a regular basis. That's right, he makes his living serenading bus passengers. Live entertainment on a local bus! You gotta love Mexico. He got off the bus thirty minutes later but not before I tipped him lavishly, about a hundred pesos. That's lavish for a local bus full of local workers. As a local bus, there were a lot of stops along the way, about twenty, which is why the forty-five minutes was necessary. I was okay with that. In Mexico, it is best to go with the flow, where the word tranquil comes to mind, along with tequila though the two are in no way related. They are two words that I no longer interchange with each other. I've come a long way since the day of floundering over my words and now, I only had thirty more minutes on this bus and a few hours left in this adventure. I had no choice other than to strike up a conversation with the Mexican man sitting next to me. Why not? Learning Spanish in Mexico means doing it day after day. *Buenos dias, señor. Mi nombre es Tomas.*

The last hour in San Jose Del Cabo airport

In the hour before my departure, I had to blow five hundred pesos, so I went to some airport-rip-off bar and ordered the most expensive thing on the uninspiring menu. I sat between a sturdy guy in his fifties and a babe in her thirties and knocked down a Corona Light waiting for my order. I actually liked the plate of food the guy was eating and I hoped mine would look as good. I asked him what he ordered. I learned it was what I ordered so that was a good thing, not great, but good. It looked okay and it got us into a conversation that lasted for the next hour. I didn't get to look at the babe on the other side of me, but he faced her in talking to me and was constantly checking her out. I didn't blame him. She was hot, kind of a young Cher look, which really isn't my favorite look but she was still appealing. The guy's name was Sam, the VP of Sales for an inventory storage company for medium sized corporations. I didn't get the babe's name. I never saw her again; she left sometime in the middle of my conversation with Sam, my back to her the whole time.

Sam is a very interesting person, so was the conversation. He has a timeshare in the Solomar Resort. He's in GA, Gambler's Anonymous, dealing with his addiction for at least thirty years, he said. He got hooked on "easy money" in college when his first bet paid twenty times as much. He won it on one of those stupid spinning wheels. He didn't even know what he was doing but he won four hundred dollars off a two-dollar bet, which gave him an adrenaline shot to the cortex that he never forgot. He got hooked by the pay off. That was the beginning of consecutive years of losing money in all forms of gambling. Some years were as bad as sixty thousand, which was a lot in those days for him at a time when he was only making sixty thousand a year. He was lucky he had an uncle who bailed him out. I felt sorry for him, for having that addiction. That was his fly in a soup of a life that was otherwise really successful, happy, and going his way. He was still gambling but it was a lot less stressful losing sixty thousand bucks a year because he was making three hundred thousand bucks a year at his job. People often open up when they talk to me.

Sam loved Cabo. He liked everything about it, not just the sports betting in the Casino next to Cabo Cantina. That's right, next to CC. He said he loved that place, without even knowing that it was my hang out. After listening to his review of CC, I confessed it was my watering hole, but it wasn't really that because that implies a lot of boozing, something I did not do there. Or anywhere. For all the time he said he spent there, it's hard to believe we didn't meet. I didn't remember him, which is unusual because I've been open to talking to gringos there, though my conversational preference greatly favored my Mexican friends. Sam raved about the fantastic bartender at CC, a man he described as very affable, fun, and entertaining. He said the bartender was a real performer. I knew that. I knew he was describing Jorge. Small world. It was only yesterday that Jorge and I gave each other the bro hug and said, "Friends forever." Small world indeed. Don't ever forget that.

About the Author

T. D. Lake was born in Milwaukee, Wisconsin. He graduated from Indiana University with a B.A. and an M.B.A. and then enjoyed a thirty-five-year career in advertising, which began in New York City. After living in the South of France, he returned to the U.S. and now has a home in Colorado.

Made in the USA
San Bernardino, CA
19 June 2019